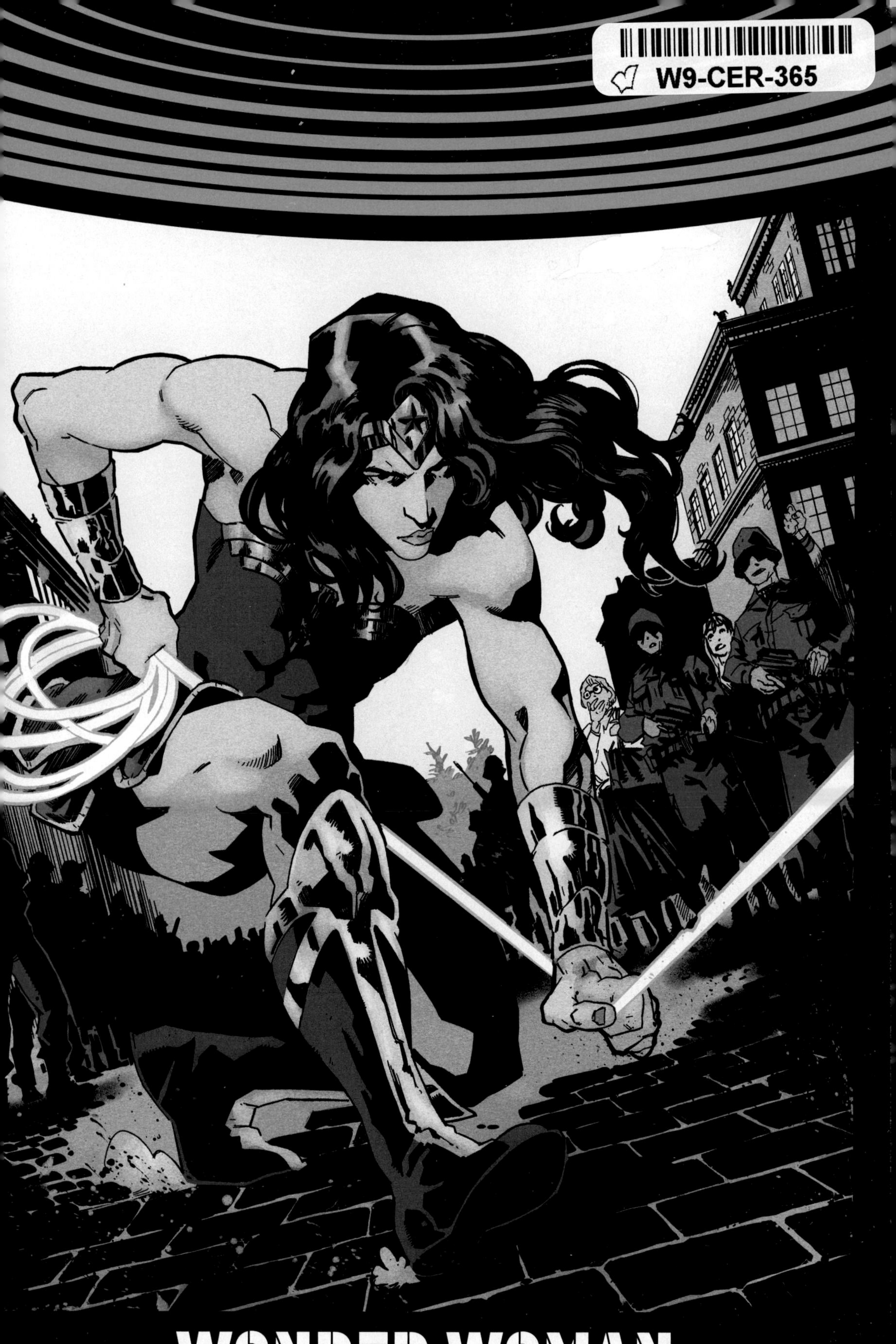

WONDER WOMAN

VOL.5 HEART OF THE AMAZON

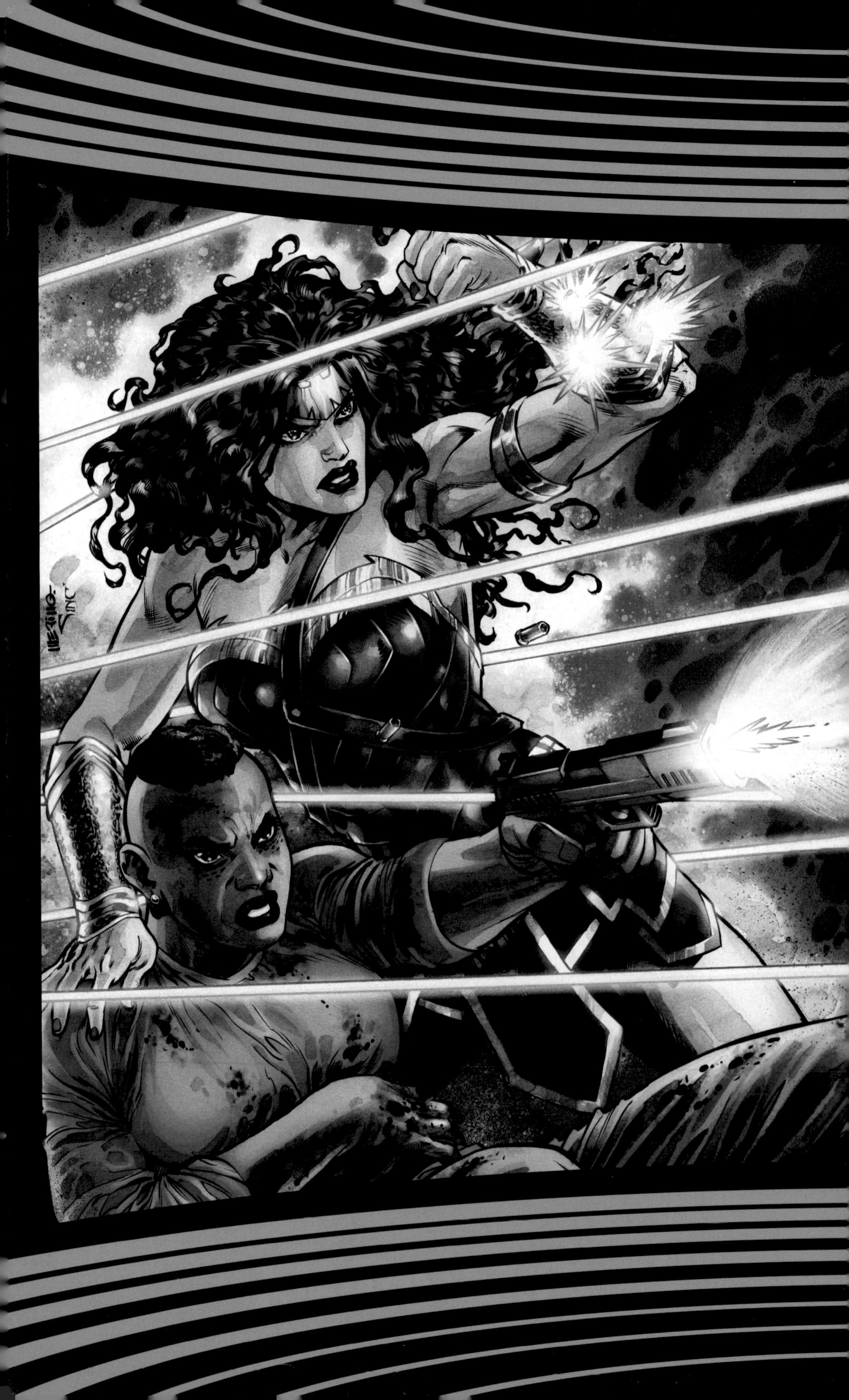

WONDER WOMAN
VOL.5 HEART OF THE AMAZON

SHEA FONTANA
TIM SEELEY * VITA AYALA * MICHAEL MORECI
COLLIN KELLY * JACKSON LANZING
writers

MIRKA ANDOLFO * DAVID MESSINA
INAKI MIRANDA * CHRISTIAN DUCE * CLAIRE ROE
STEPHANIE HANS * DAVID LAFUENTE
artists

ROMULO FAJARDO JR.
ALLEN PASSALAQUA * JORDIE BELLAIRE * JOHN RAUCH * STEPHANIE HANS
colorists

SAIDA TEMOFONTE
JOSH REED * DAVE SHARPE * JODI WYNNE
letterers

JENNY FRISON
collection cover artist

WONDER WOMAN created by WILLIAM MOULTON MARSTON

CHRIS CONROY Editor - Original Series

REBECCA TAYLOR BRITTANY HOLZHERR Associate Editors - Original Series ✳ **DAVE WIELGOSZ** Assistant Editor - Original Series
JEB WOODARD Group Editor - Collected Editions ✳ **ROBIN WILDMAN** Editor - Collected Edition
STEVE COOK Design Director - Books ✳ **MONIQUE NARBONETA** Publication Design

BOB HARRAS Senior VP - Editor-in-Chief, DC Comics

PAT McCALLUM Executive Editor, DC Comics

DIANE NELSON President ✳ **DAN DiDIO** Publisher ✳ **JIM LEE** Publisher ✳ **GEOFF JOHNS** President & Chief Creative Officer
AMIT DESAI Executive VP - Business & Marketing Strategy, Direct to Consumer & Global Franchise Management
SAM ADES Senior VP & General Manager, Digital Services ✳ **BOBBIE CHASE** VP & Executive Editor, Young Reader & Talent Development
MARK CHIARELLO Senior VP - Art, Design & Collected Editions ✳ **JOHN CUNNINGHAM** Senior VP - Sales & Trade Marketing
ANNE DePIES Senior VP - Business Strategy, Finance & Administration ✳ **DON FALLETTI** VP - Manufacturing Operations
LAWRENCE GANEM VP - Editorial Administration & Talent Relations ✳ **ALISON GILL** Senior VP - Manufacturing & Operations
HANK KANALZ Senior VP - Editorial Strategy & Administration ✳ **JAY KOGAN** VP - Legal Affairs ✳ **JACK MAHAN** VP - Business Affairs
NICK J. NAPOLITANO VP - Manufacturing Administration ✳ **EDDIE SCANNELL** VP - Consumer Marketing
COURTNEY SIMMONS Senior VP - Publicity & Communications ✳ **JIM (SKI) SOKOLOWSKI** VP - Comic Book Specialty Sales & Trade Marketing
NANCY SPEARS VP - Mass, Book, Digital Sales & Trade Marketing ✳ **MICHELE R. WELLS** VP - Content Strategy

WONDER WOMAN VOL. 5: HEART OF THE AMAZON

Published by DC Comics. Compilation and all new material Copyright © 2018 DC Comics. All Rights Reserved.
Originally published in single magazine form in WONDER WOMAN 26-30,
WONDER WOMAN: STEVE TREVOR 1, WONDER WOMAN ANNUAL 1. Copyright © 2017 DC Comics.
All Rights Reserved. All characters, their distinctive likenesses and related elements featured in this publication are trademarks of DC Comics.
The stories, characters and incidents featured in this publication are entirely fictional.
DC Comics does not read or accept unsolicited ideas, stories or artwork.

DC Comics, 2900 West Alameda Ave., Burbank, CA 91505
Printed by LSC Communications, Kendallville, IN, USA. 4/6/18. First Printing.
ISBN: 978-1-4012-7734-5

Library of Congress Cataloging-in-Publication Data is available.

PEFC Certified

Printed on paper from
sustainably managed
forests, controlled
sources

PEFC/29-31-337   www.pefc.org

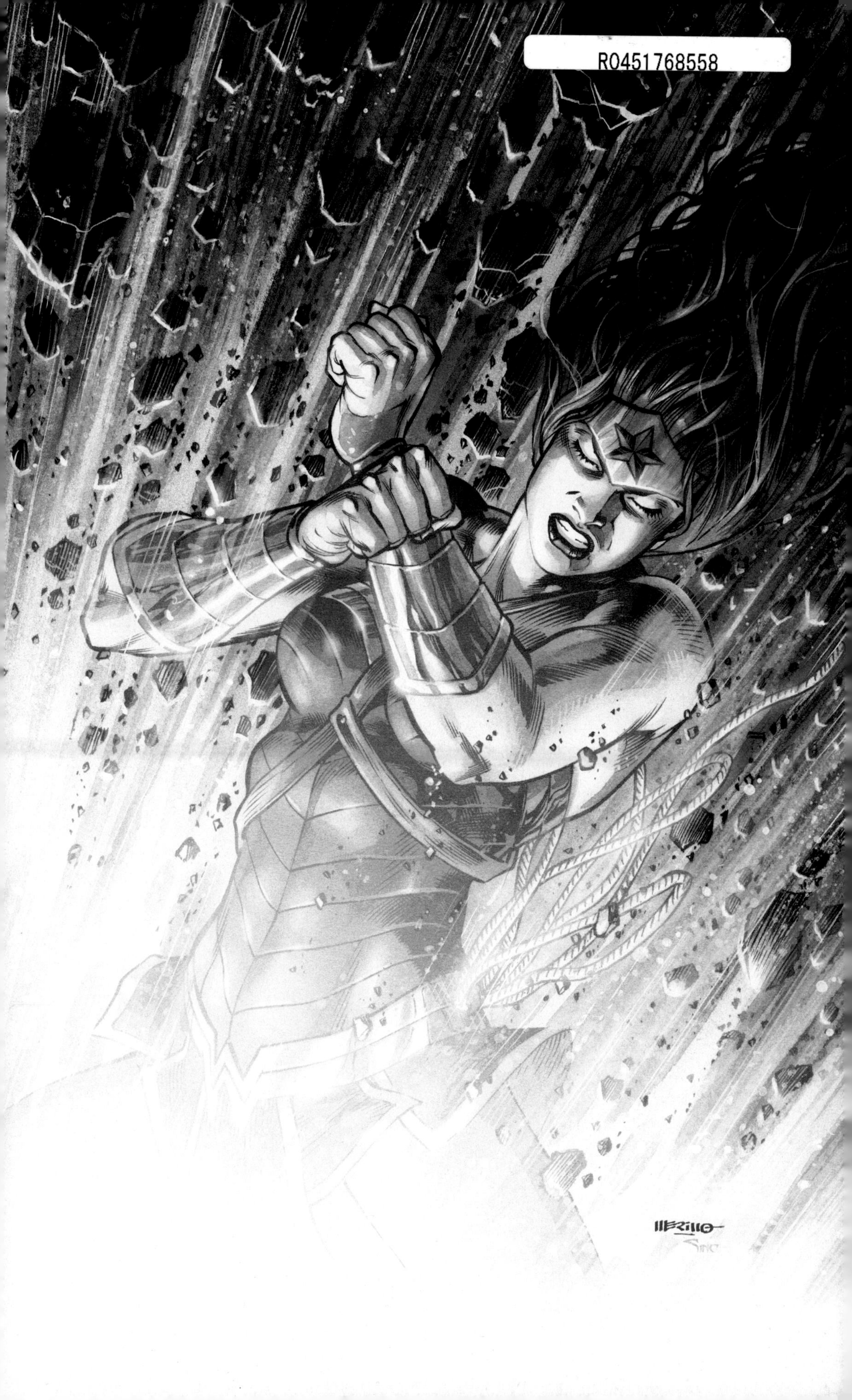

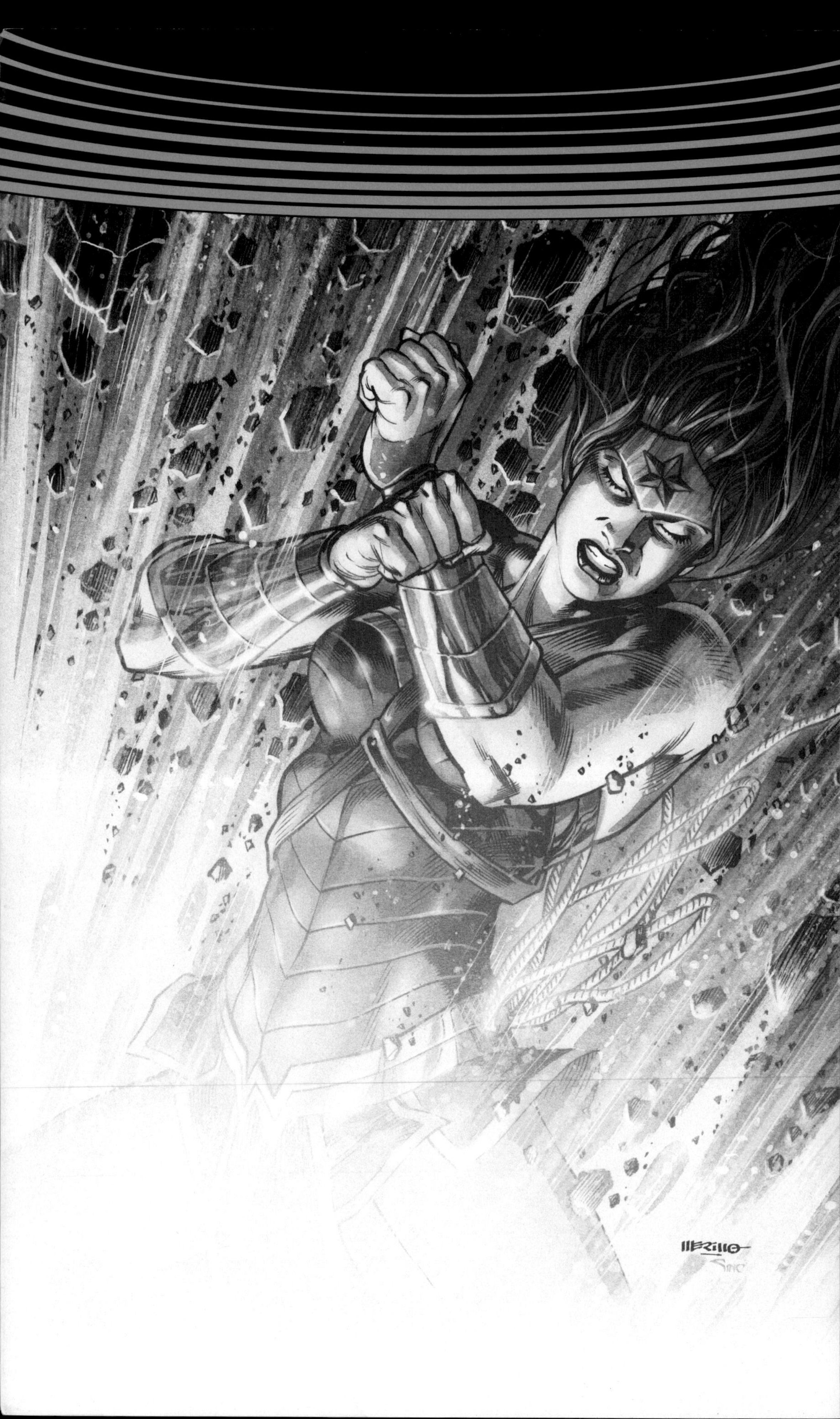

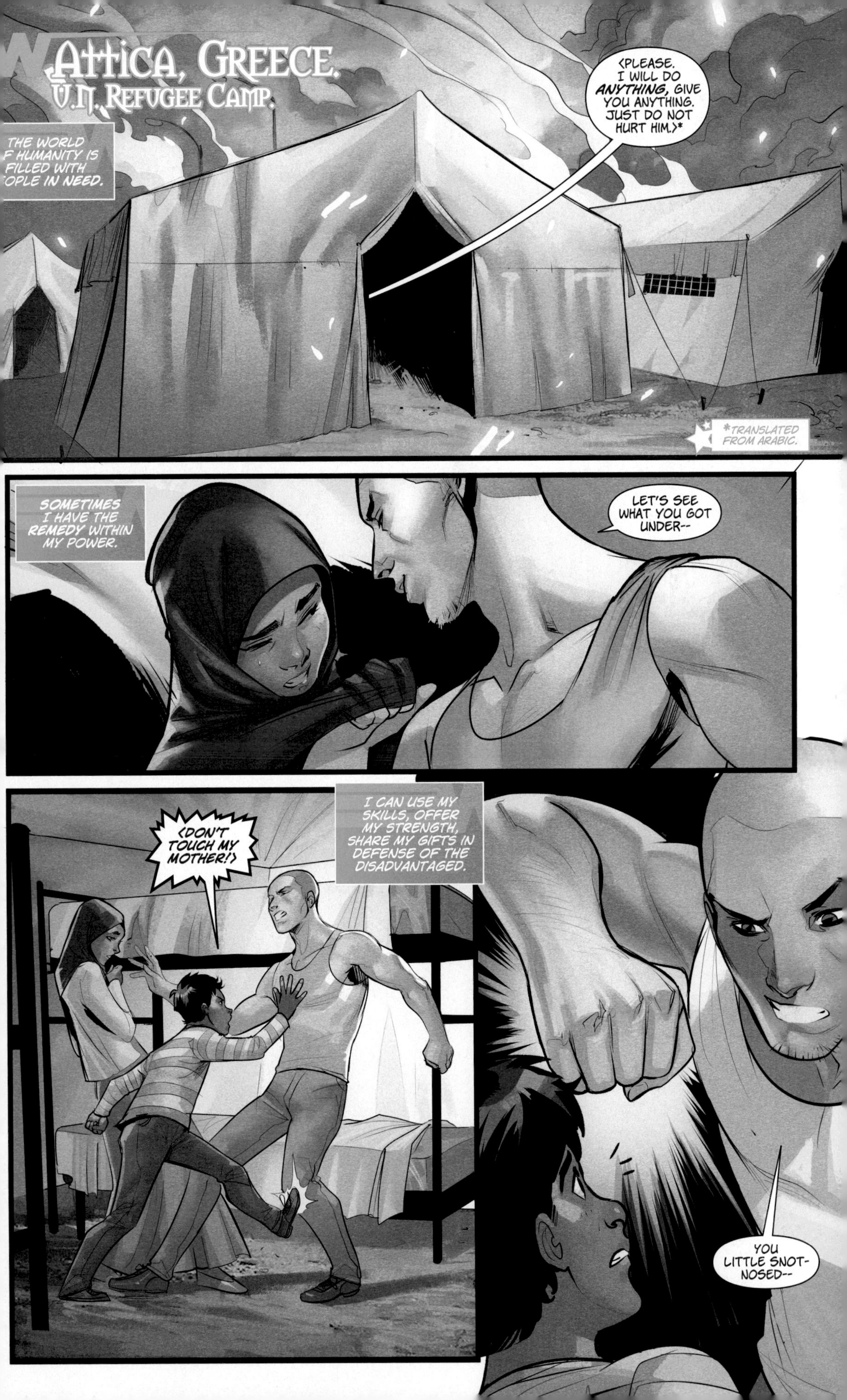

ATTICA, GREECE.
U.N. REFUGEE CAMP.
THE WORLD F HUMANITY IS FILLED WITH OPLE IN NEED.
<PLEASE. I WILL DO ANYTHING, GIVE YOU ANYTHING. JUST DO NOT HURT HIM.>*
*TRANSLATED FROM ARABIC.
SOMETIMES I HAVE THE REMEDY WITHIN MY POWER.
LET'S SEE WHAT YOU GOT UNDER--
<DON'T TOUCH MY MOTHER!>
I CAN USE MY SKILLS, OFFER MY STRENGTH, SHARE MY GIFTS IN DEFENSE OF THE DISADVANTAGED.
YOU LITTLE SNOT-NOSED--

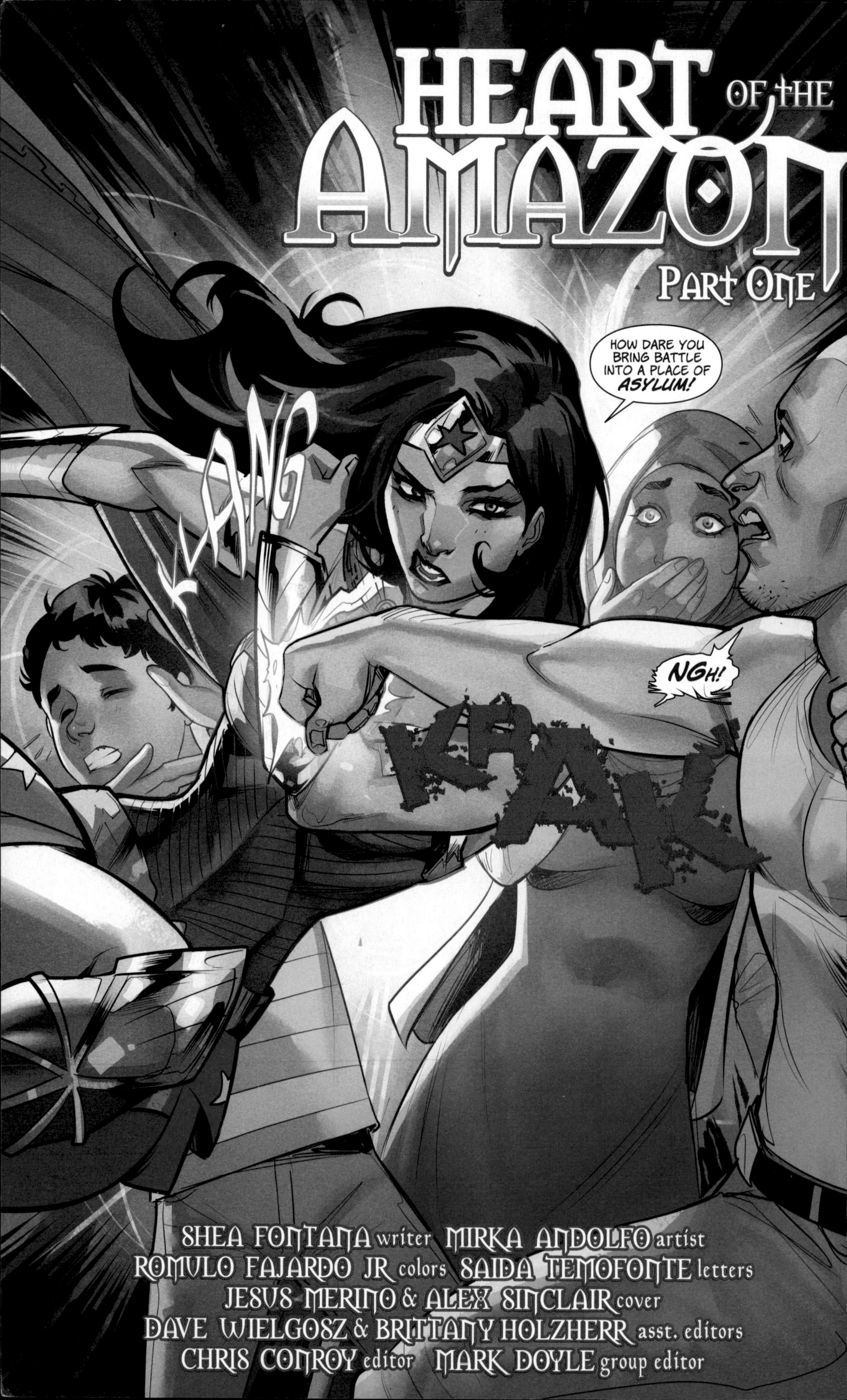
HEART OF THE AMAZON
PART ONE
HOW DARE YOU BRING BATTLE INTO A PLACE OF ASYLUM!
KLANG
NGH!
KRAK
SHEA FONTANA writer MIRKA ANDOLFO artist
ROMULO FAJARDO JR colors SAIDA TEMOFONTE letters
JESUS MERINO & ALEX SINCLAIR cover
DAVE WIELGOSZ & BRITTANY HOLZHERR asst. editors
CHRIS CONROY editor MARK DOYLE group editor

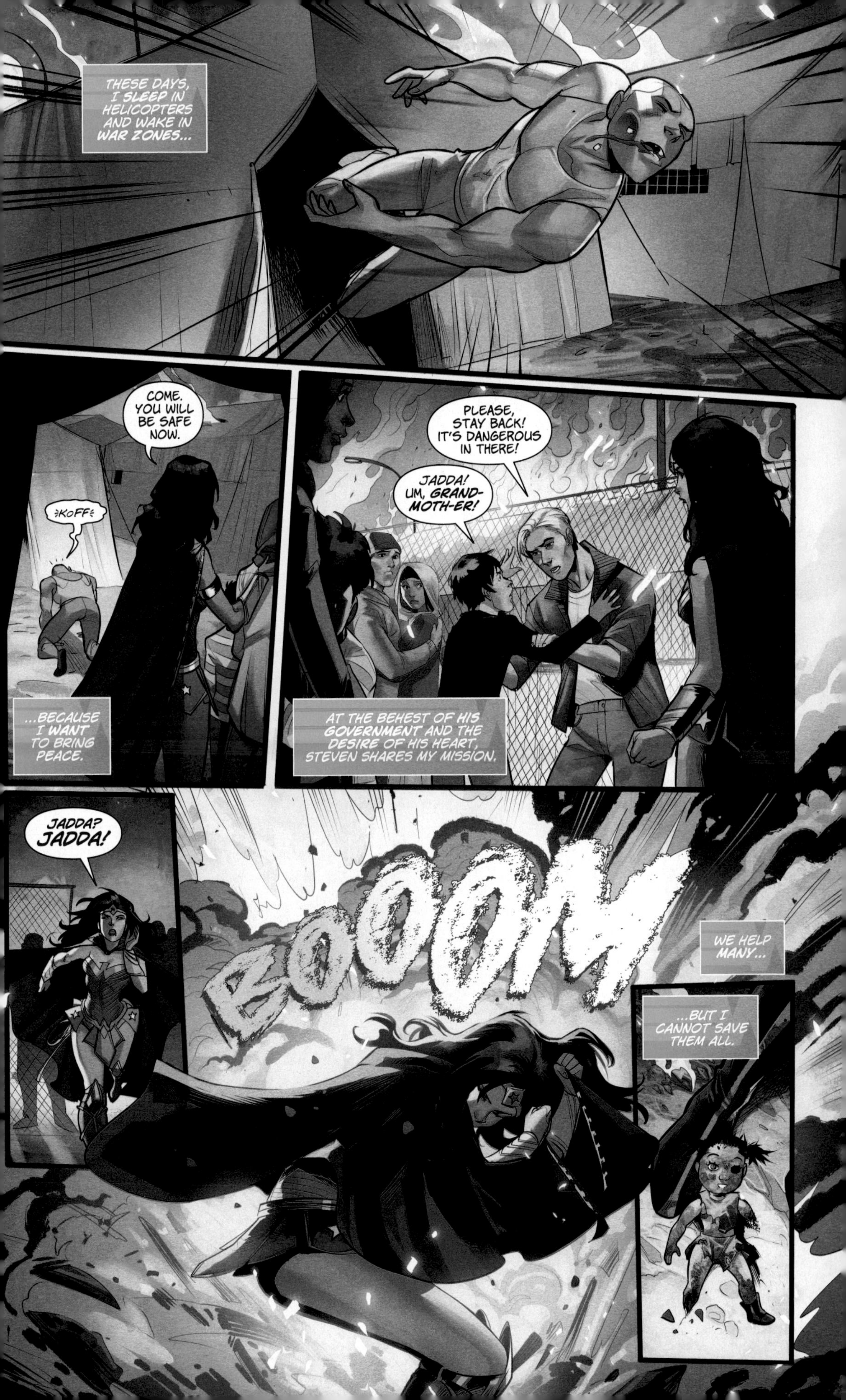
THESE DAYS, I SLEEP IN HELICOPTERS AND WAKE IN WAR ZONES...
COME. YOU WILL BE SAFE NOW.
KOFF
...BECAUSE I WANT TO BRING PEACE.
PLEASE, STAY BACK! IT'S DANGEROUS IN THERE!
JADDA! UM, GRAND-MOTH-ER!
AT THE BEHEST OF HIS GOVERNMENT AND THE DESIRE OF HIS HEART, STEVEN SHARES MY MISSION.
JADDA? JADDA!
BOOOM
WE HELP MANY...
...BUT I CANNOT SAVE THEM ALL.

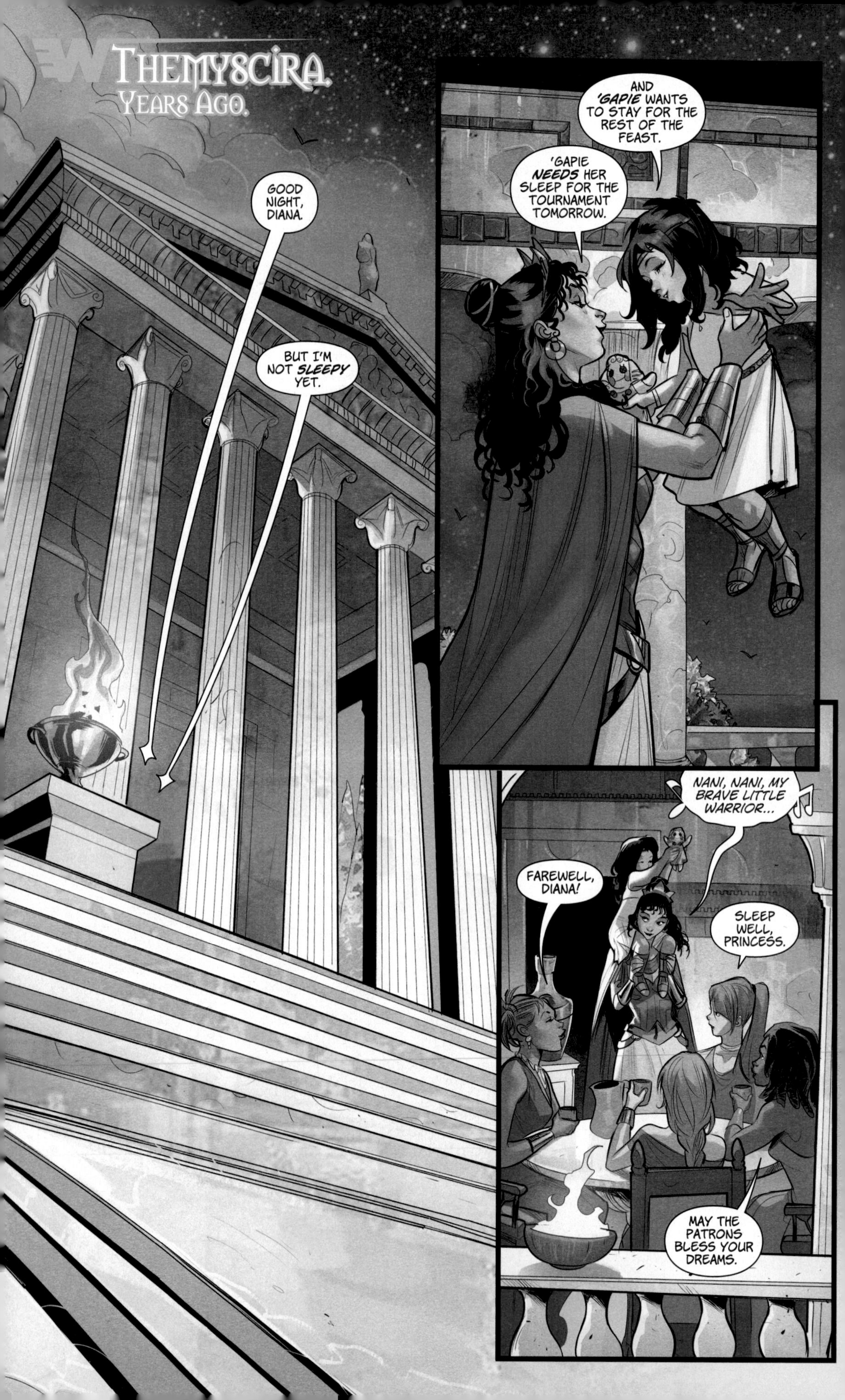

THEMYSCIRA.
YEARS AGO.
GOOD NIGHT, DIANA.
BUT I'M NOT SLEEPY YET.
AND 'GAPIE WANTS TO STAY FOR THE REST OF THE FEAST.
'GAPIE NEEDS HER SLEEP FOR THE TOURNAMENT TOMORROW.
NANI, NANI, MY BRAVE LITTLE WARRIOR...
FAREWELL, DIANA!
SLEEP WELL, PRINCESS.
MAY THE PATRONS BLESS YOUR DREAMS.

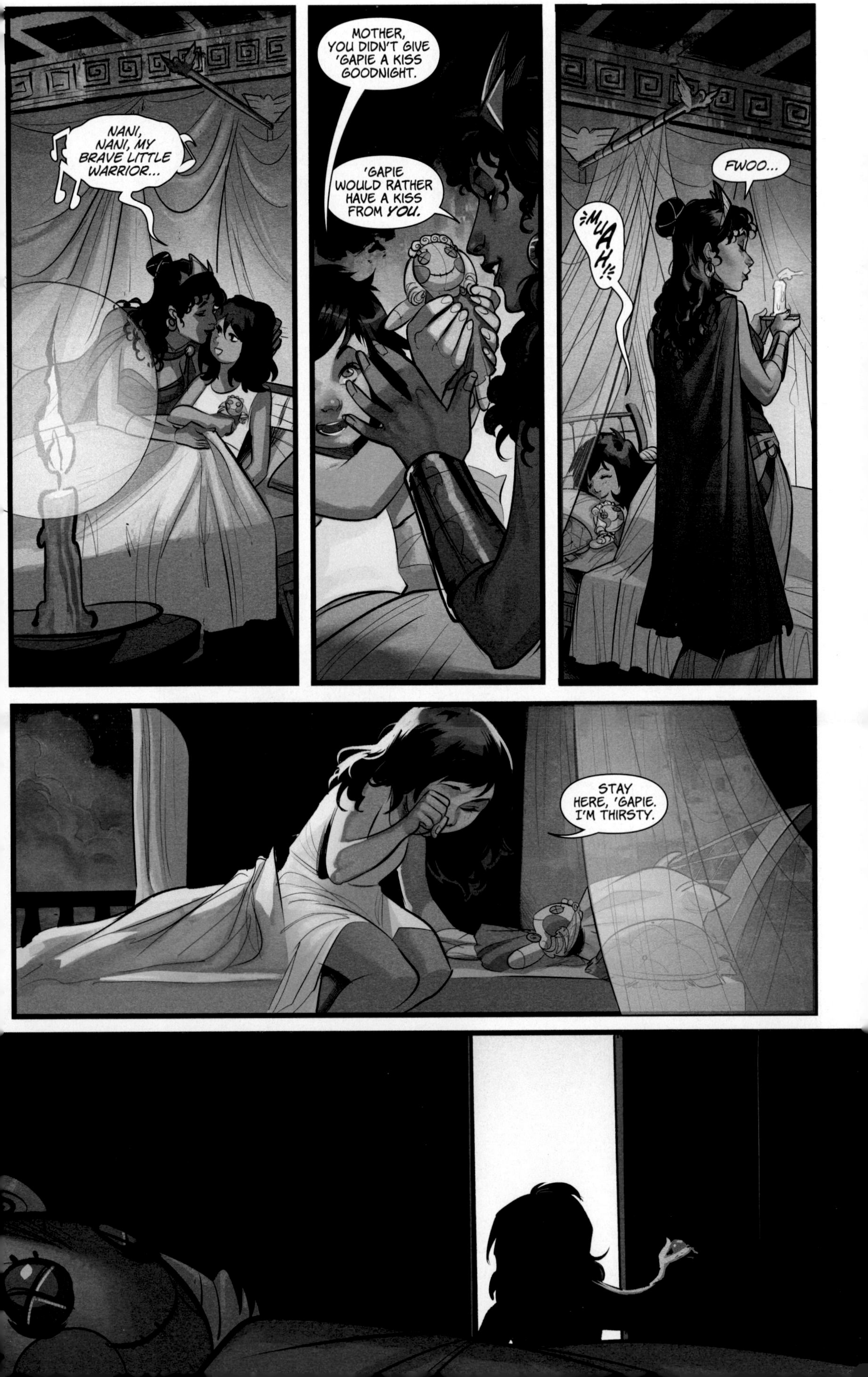
NANI, NANI, MY BRAVE LITTLE WARRIOR...
MOTHER, YOU DIDN'T GIVE 'GAPIE A KISS GOODNIGHT.
'GAPIE WOULD RATHER HAVE A KISS FROM YOU.
FWOO...
MUAH!
STAY HERE, 'GAPIE. I'M THIRSTY.

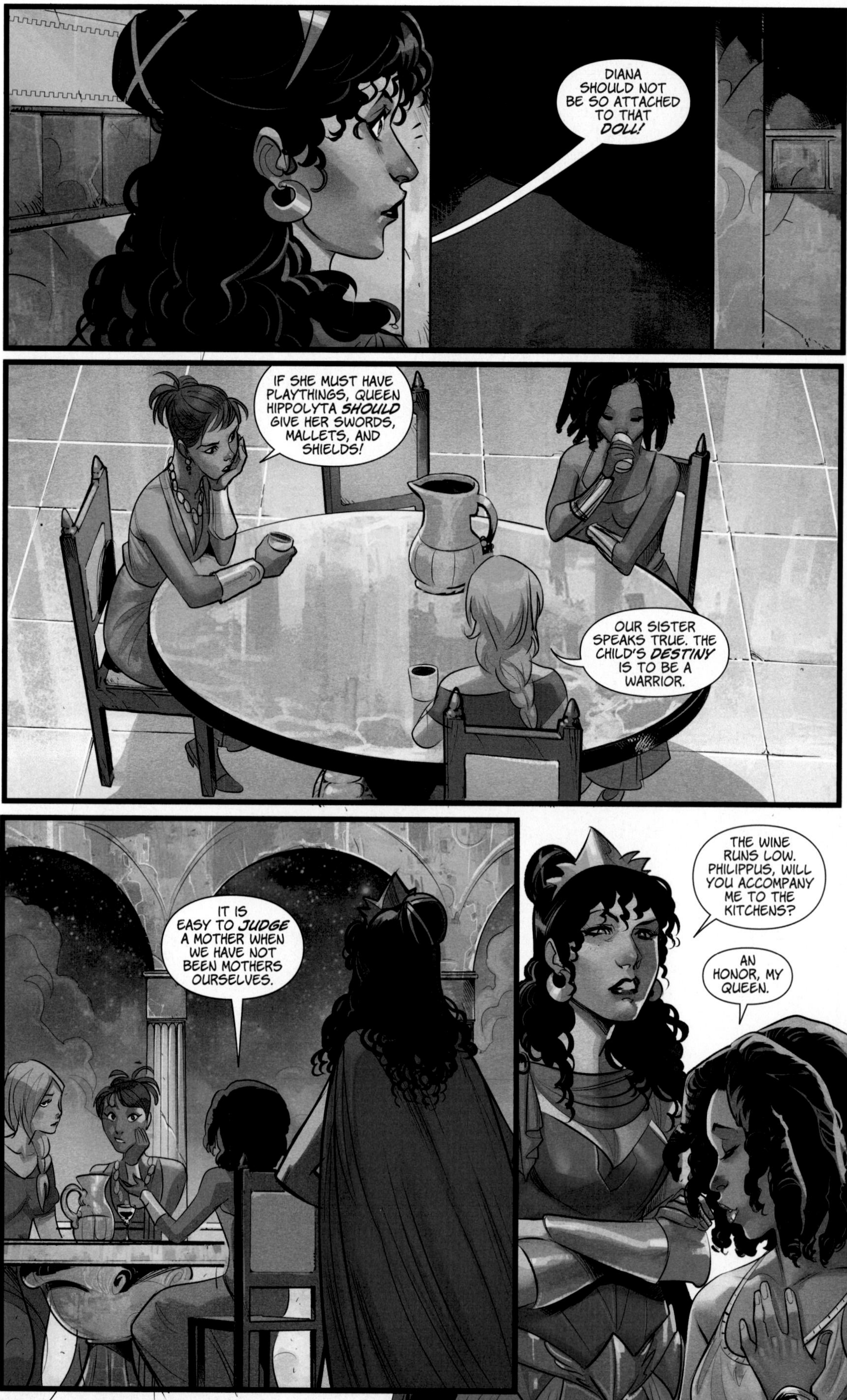
DIANA SHOULD NOT BE SO ATTACHED TO THAT DOLL!
IF SHE MUST HAVE PLAYTHINGS, QUEEN HIPPOLYTA SHOULD GIVE HER SWORDS, MALLETS, AND SHIELDS!
OUR SISTER SPEAKS TRUE. THE CHILD'S DESTINY IS TO BE A WARRIOR.
IT IS EASY TO JUDGE A MOTHER WHEN WE HAVE NOT BEEN MOTHERS OURSELVES.
THE WINE RUNS LOW. PHILIPPUS, WILL YOU ACCOMPANY ME TO THE KITCHENS?
AN HONOR, MY QUEEN.

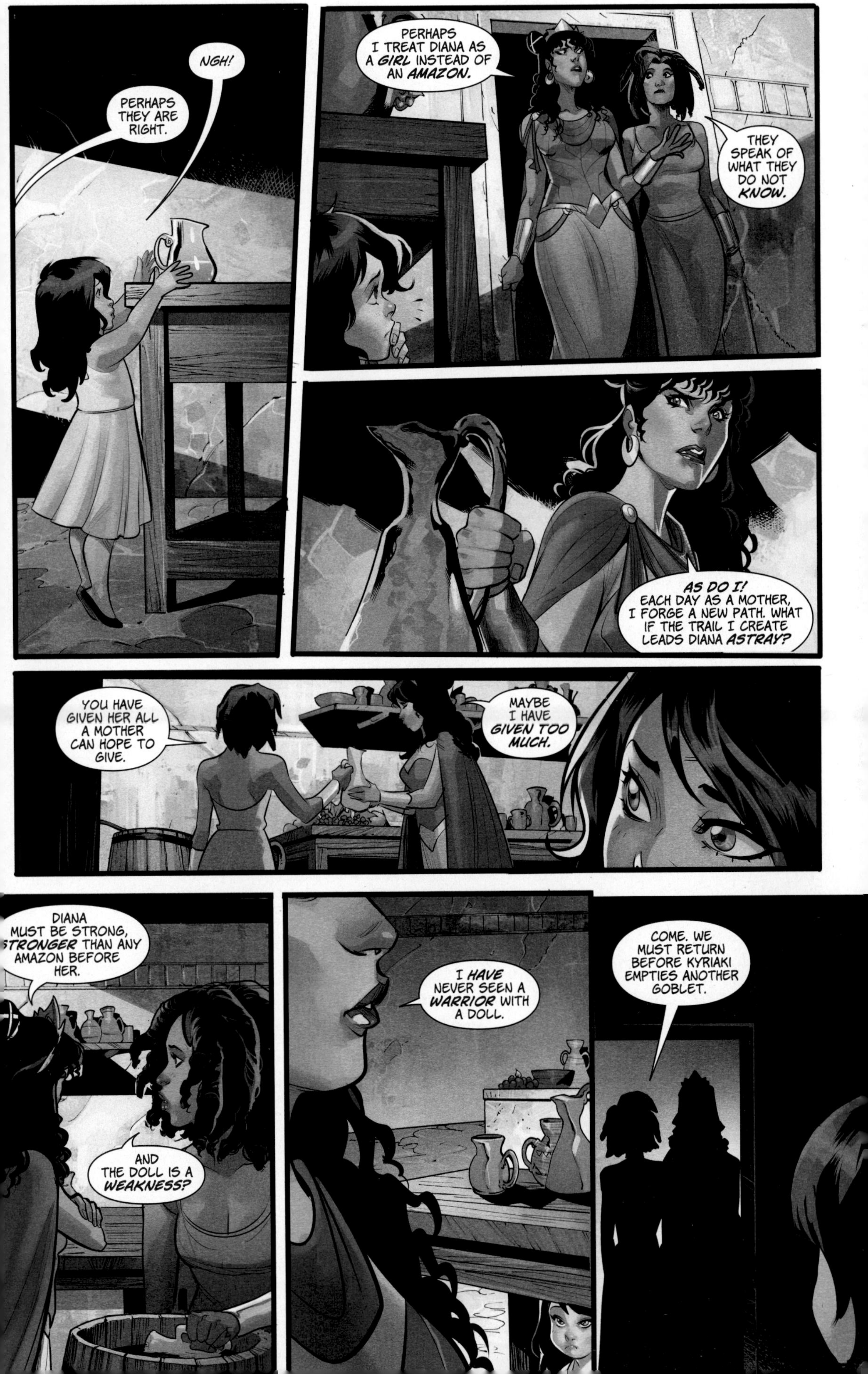
PERHAPS THEY ARE RIGHT.
NGH!
PERHAPS I TREAT DIANA AS A GIRL INSTEAD OF AN AMAZON.
THEY SPEAK OF WHAT THEY DO NOT KNOW.
AS DO I! EACH DAY AS A MOTHER, I FORGE A NEW PATH. WHAT IF THE TRAIL I CREATE LEADS DIANA ASTRAY?
YOU HAVE GIVEN HER ALL A MOTHER CAN HOPE TO GIVE.
MAYBE I HAVE GIVEN TOO MUCH.
DIANA MUST BE STRONG, STRONGER THAN ANY AMAZON BEFORE HER.
AND THE DOLL IS A WEAKNESS?
I HAVE NEVER SEEN A WARRIOR WITH A DOLL.
COME. WE MUST RETURN BEFORE KYRIAKI EMPTIES ANOTHER GOBLET.

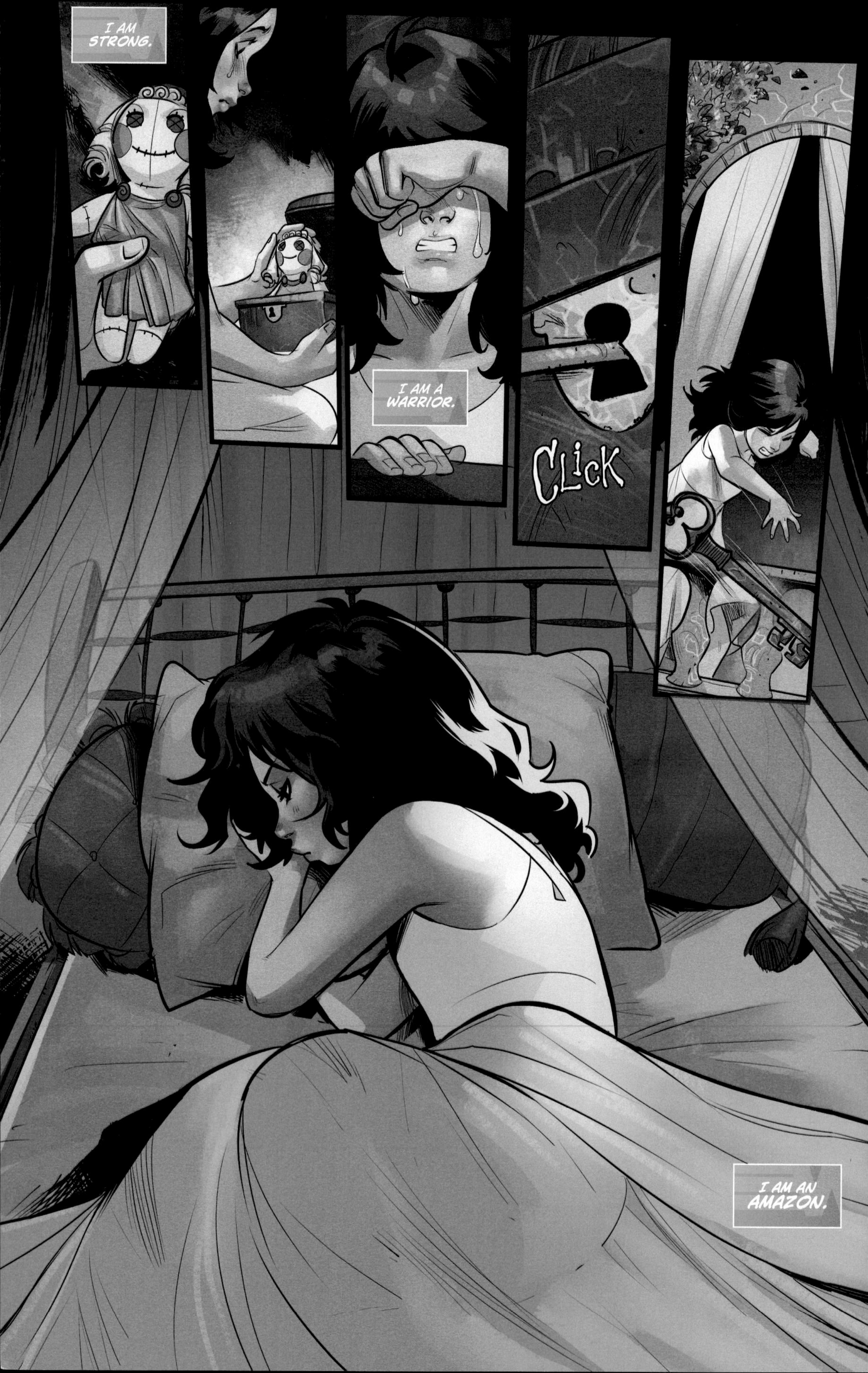
I AM STRONG.
I AM A WARRIOR.
CLICK
I AM AN AMAZON.

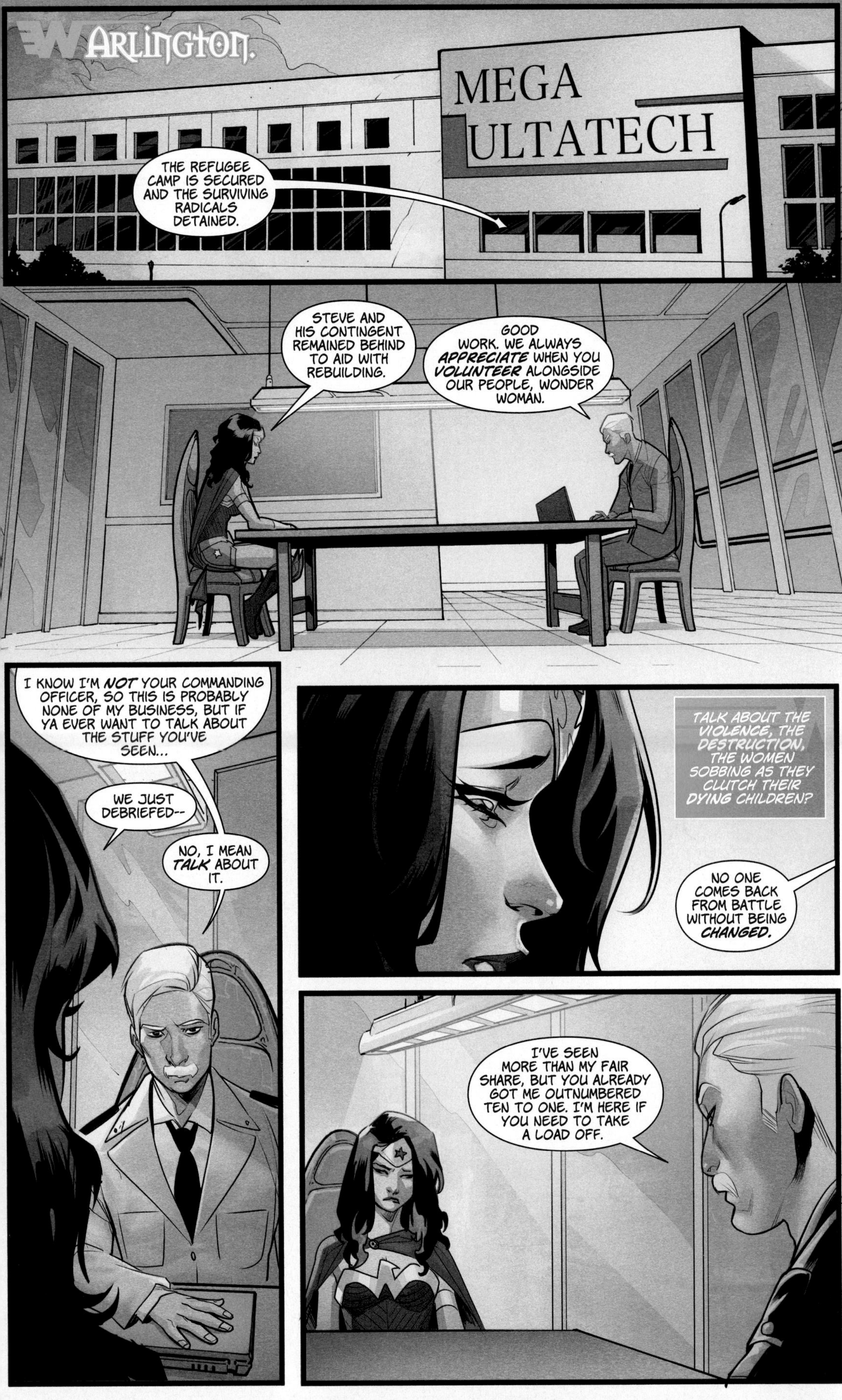
ARLINGTON.
MEGA ULTATECH
THE REFUGEE CAMP IS SECURED AND THE SURVIVING RADICALS DETAINED.
STEVE AND HIS CONTINGENT REMAINED BEHIND TO AID WITH REBUILDING.
GOOD WORK. WE ALWAYS APPRECIATE WHEN YOU VOLUNTEER ALONGSIDE OUR PEOPLE, WONDER WOMAN.
I KNOW I'M NOT YOUR COMMANDING OFFICER, SO THIS IS PROBABLY NONE OF MY BUSINESS, BUT IF YA EVER WANT TO TALK ABOUT THE STUFF YOU'VE SEEN...
WE JUST DEBRIEFED--
NO, I MEAN TALK ABOUT IT.
TALK ABOUT THE VIOLENCE, THE DESTRUCTION, THE WOMEN SOBBING AS THEY CLUTCH THEIR DYING CHILDREN?
NO ONE COMES BACK FROM BATTLE WITHOUT BEING CHANGED.
I'VE SEEN MORE THAN MY FAIR SHARE, BUT YOU ALREADY GOT ME OUTNUMBERED TEN TO ONE. I'M HERE IF YOU NEED TO TAKE A LOAD OFF.

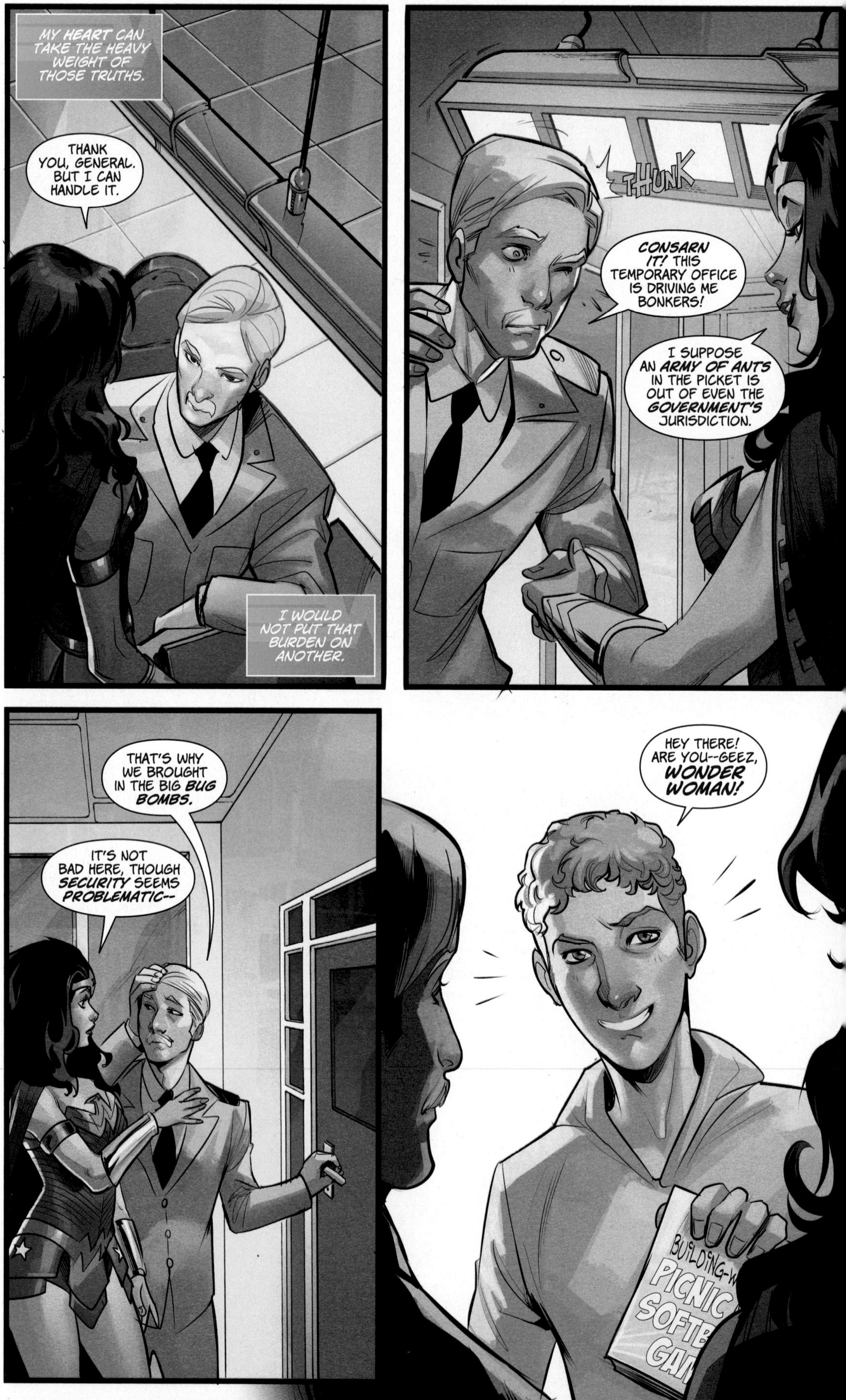
MY HEART CAN TAKE THE HEAVY WEIGHT OF THOSE TRUTHS.
THANK YOU, GENERAL. BUT I CAN HANDLE IT.
I WOULD NOT PUT THAT BURDEN ON ANOTHER.
THUNK
CONSARN IT! THIS TEMPORARY OFFICE IS DRIVING ME BONKERS!
I SUPPOSE AN ARMY OF ANTS IN THE PICKET IS OUT OF EVEN THE GOVERNMENT'S JURISDICTION.
THAT'S WHY WE BROUGHT IN THE BIG BUG BOMBS.
IT'S NOT BAD HERE, THOUGH SECURITY SEEMS PROBLEMATIC--
HEY THERE! ARE YOU--GEEZ, WONDER WOMAN!

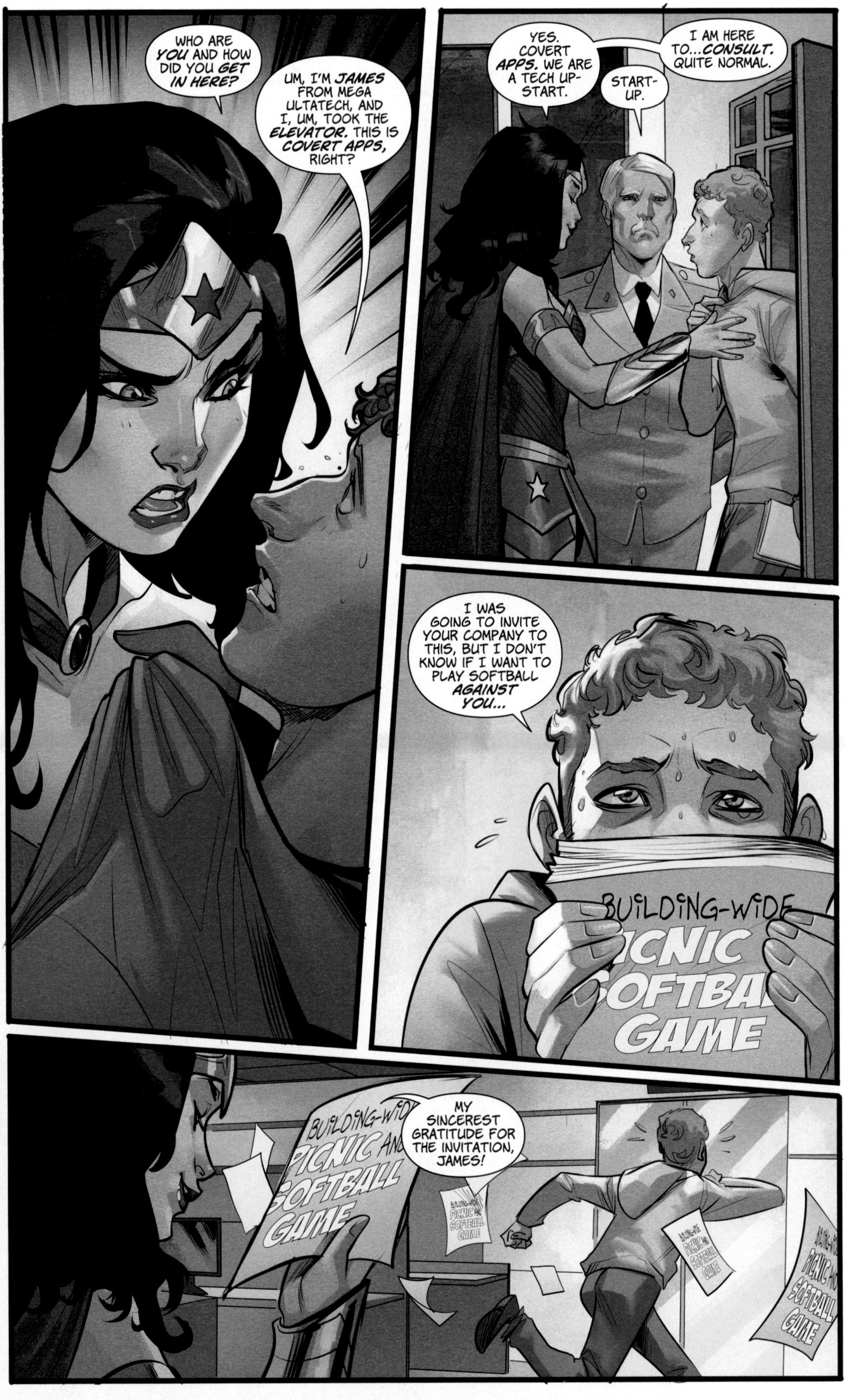
WHO ARE *YOU* AND HOW DID YOU *GET IN HERE?*
UM, I'M *JAMES* FROM MEGA ULTATECH, AND I, UM, TOOK THE *ELEVATOR.* THIS IS *COVERT APPS,* RIGHT?
YES. COVERT *APPS.* WE ARE A TECH UP-START.
START-UP.
I AM HERE TO...*CONSULT.* QUITE NORMAL.
I WAS GOING TO INVITE YOUR COMPANY TO THIS, BUT I DON'T KNOW IF I WANT TO PLAY SOFTBALL *AGAINST YOU...*
BUILDING-WIDE
GAME
MY SINCEREST GRATITUDE FOR THE INVITATION, JAMES!
BUILDING-WIDE PICNIC AND SOFTBALL GAME

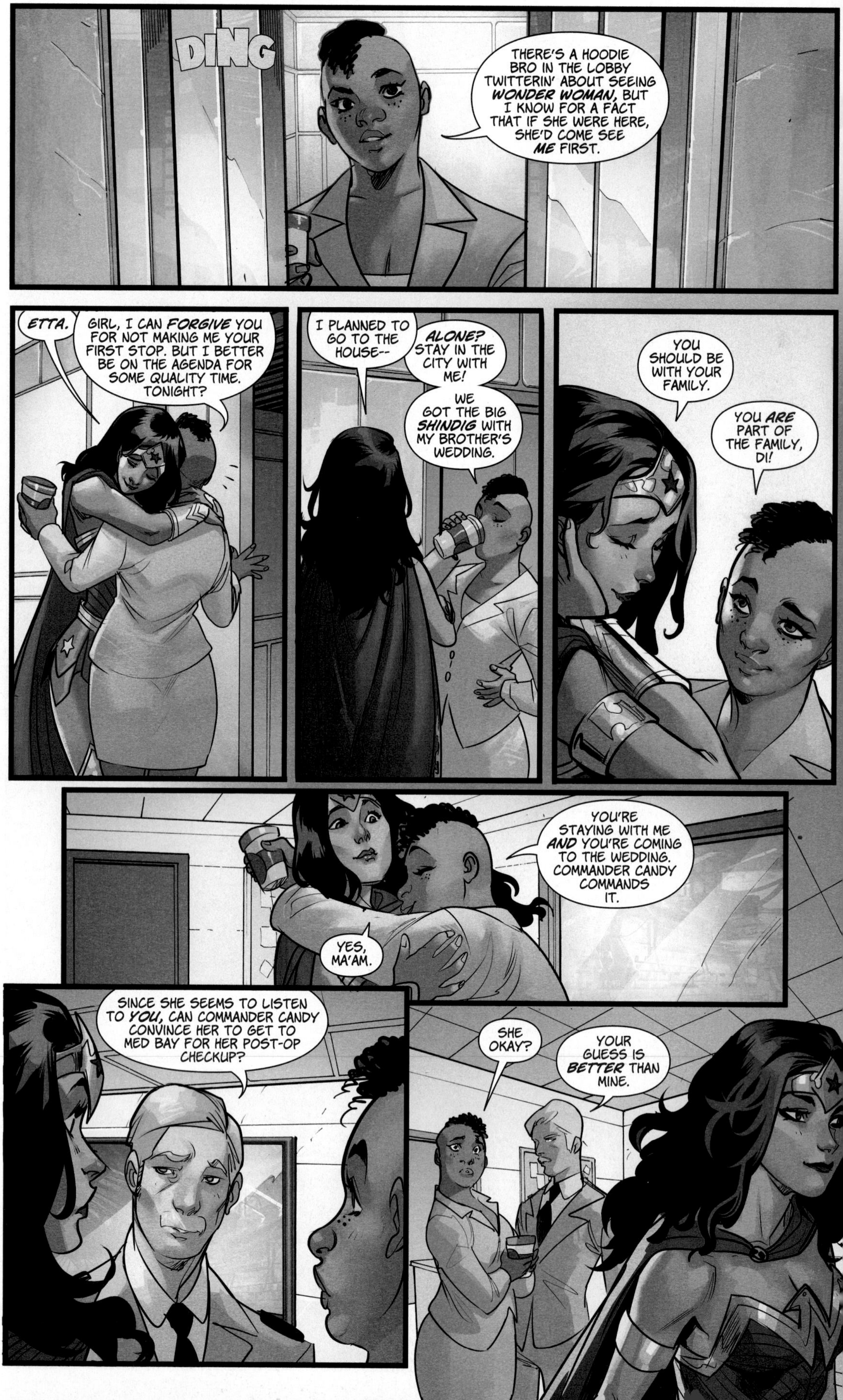
DING
THERE'S A HOODIE BRO IN THE LOBBY TWITTERIN' ABOUT SEEING WONDER WOMAN, BUT I KNOW FOR A FACT THAT IF SHE WERE HERE, SHE'D COME SEE ME FIRST.
ETTA.
GIRL, I CAN FORGIVE YOU FOR NOT MAKING ME YOUR FIRST STOP. BUT I BETTER BE ON THE AGENDA FOR SOME QUALITY TIME. TONIGHT?
I PLANNED TO GO TO THE HOUSE--
ALONE? STAY IN THE CITY WITH ME!
WE GOT THE BIG SHINDIG WITH MY BROTHER'S WEDDING.
YOU SHOULD BE WITH YOUR FAMILY.
YOU ARE PART OF THE FAMILY, DI!
YOU'RE STAYING WITH ME AND YOU'RE COMING TO THE WEDDING. COMMANDER CANDY COMMANDS IT.
YES, MA'AM.
SINCE SHE SEEMS TO LISTEN TO YOU, CAN COMMANDER CANDY CONVINCE HER TO GET TO MED BAY FOR HER POST-OP CHECKUP?
SHE OKAY?
YOUR GUESS IS BETTER THAN MINE.

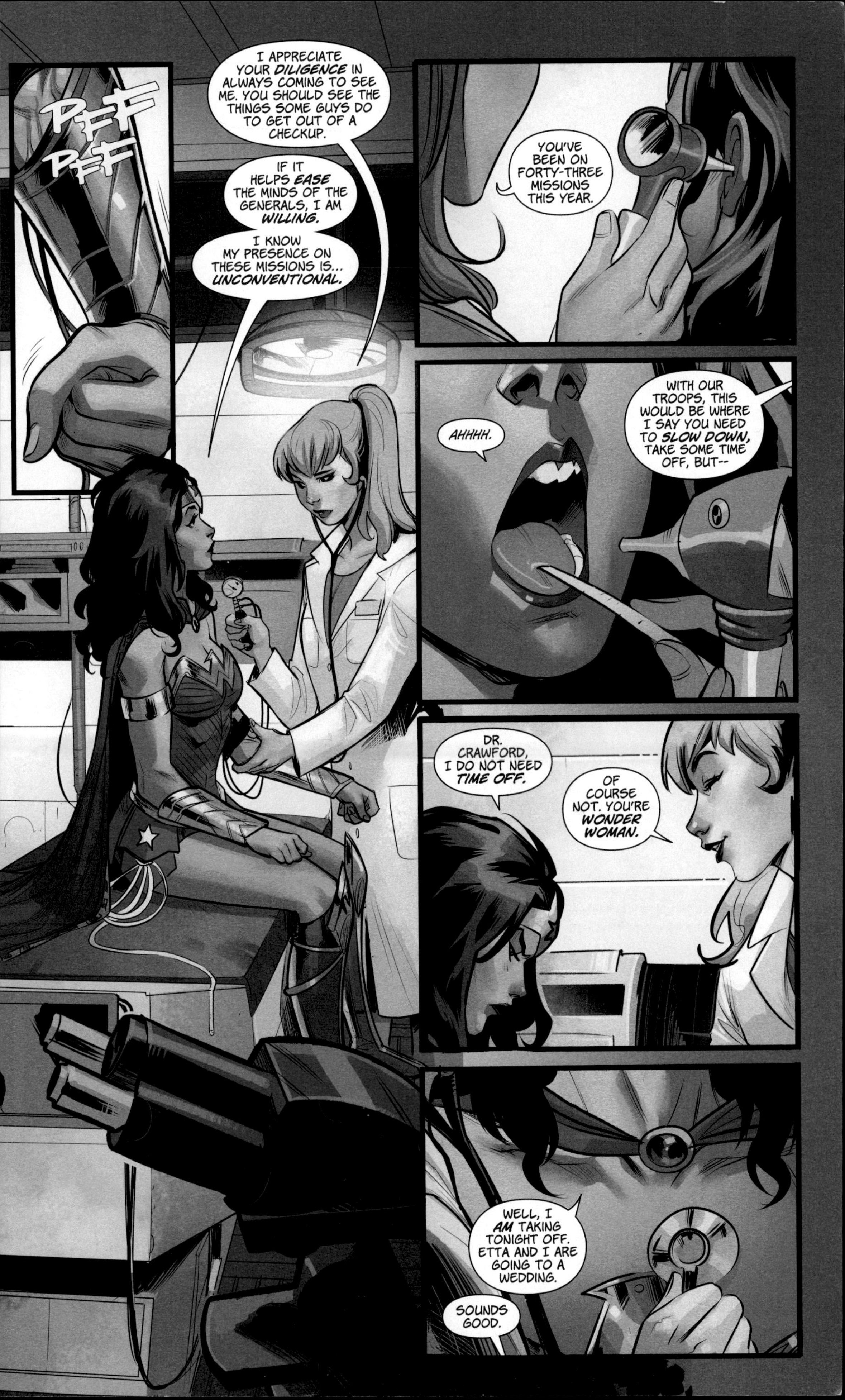
PFF PFF
I APPRECIATE YOUR DILIGENCE IN ALWAYS COMING TO SEE ME. YOU SHOULD SEE THE THINGS SOME GUYS DO TO GET OUT OF A CHECKUP.
IF IT HELPS EASE THE MINDS OF THE GENERALS, I AM WILLING.
I KNOW MY PRESENCE ON THESE MISSIONS IS... UNCONVENTIONAL.
YOU'VE BEEN ON FORTY-THREE MISSIONS THIS YEAR.
AHHHH.
WITH OUR TROOPS, THIS WOULD BE WHERE I SAY YOU NEED TO SLOW DOWN, TAKE SOME TIME OFF, BUT--
DR. CRAWFORD, I DO NOT NEED TIME OFF.
OF COURSE NOT. YOU'RE WONDER WOMAN.
WELL, I AM TAKING TONIGHT OFF. ETTA AND I ARE GOING TO A WEDDING.
SOUNDS GOOD.

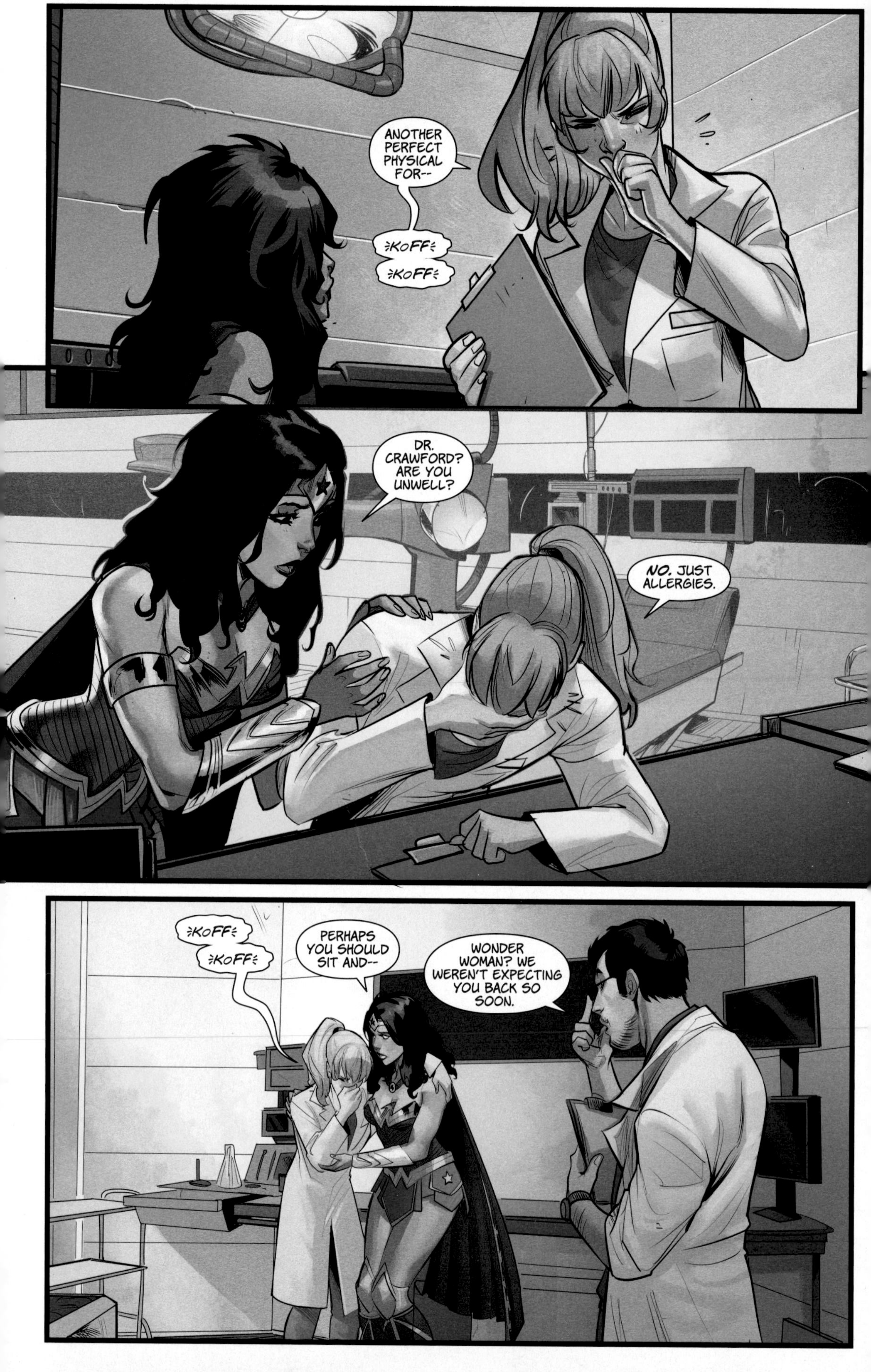

ANOTHER PERFECT PHYSICAL FOR--
KOFF
KOFF
DR. CRAWFORD? ARE YOU UNWELL?
NO. JUST ALLERGIES.
KOFF
KOFF
PERHAPS YOU SHOULD SIT AND--
WONDER WOMAN? WE WEREN'T EXPECTING YOU BACK SO SOON.

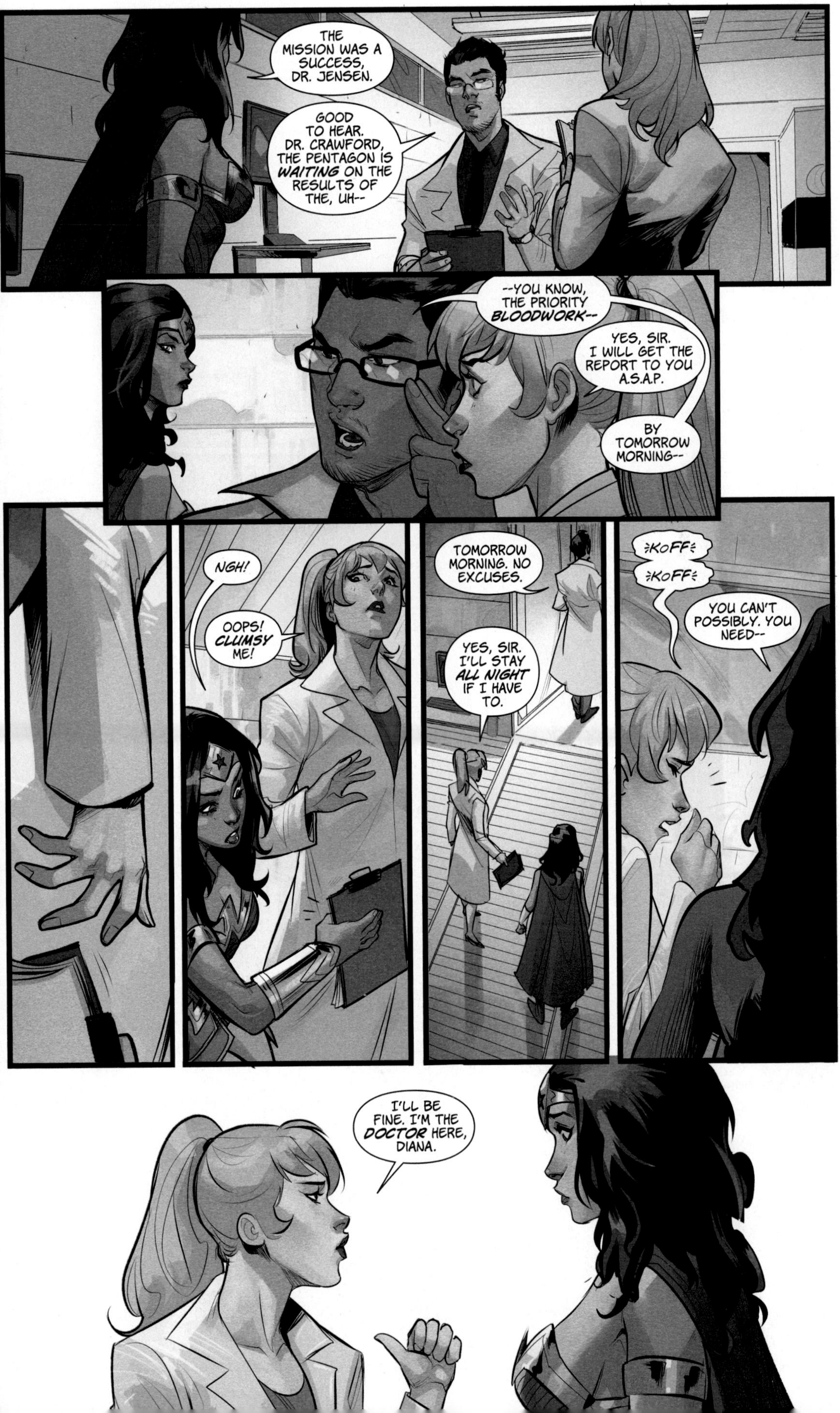
THE MISSION WAS A SUCCESS, DR. JENSEN.
GOOD TO HEAR. DR. CRAWFORD, THE PENTAGON IS WAITING ON THE RESULTS OF THE, UH--
--YOU KNOW, THE PRIORITY BLOODWORK--
YES, SIR. I WILL GET THE REPORT TO YOU A.S.A.P.
BY TOMORROW MORNING--
NGH!
OOPS! CLUMSY ME!
TOMORROW MORNING. NO EXCUSES.
YES, SIR. I'LL STAY ALL NIGHT IF I HAVE TO.
KOFF
KOFF
YOU CAN'T POSSIBLY. YOU NEED--
I'LL BE FINE. I'M THE DOCTOR HERE, DIANA.

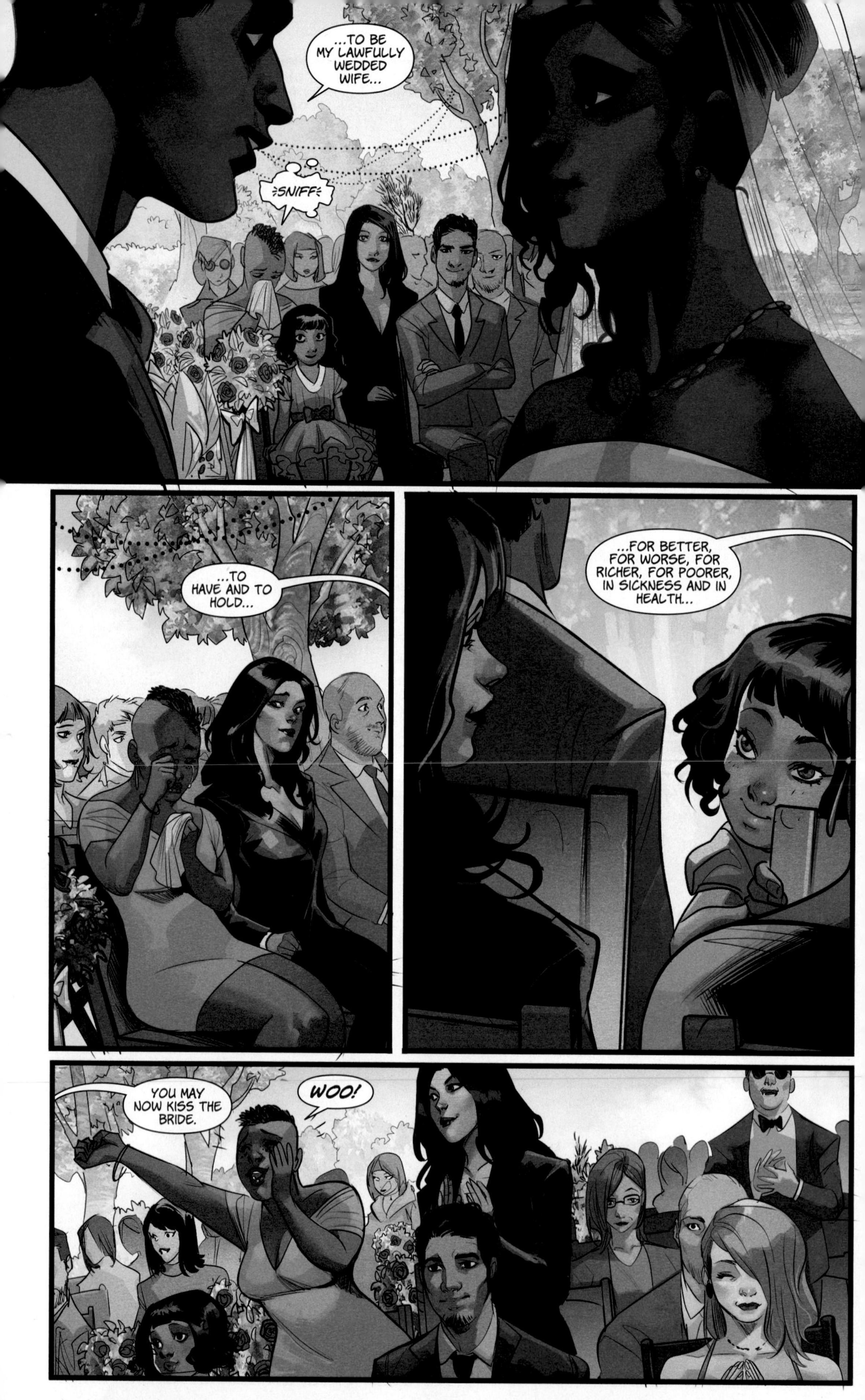
...TO BE MY LAWFULLY WEDDED WIFE...
SNIFF
...TO HAVE AND TO HOLD...
...FOR BETTER, FOR WORSE, FOR RICHER, FOR POORER, IN SICKNESS AND IN HEALTH...
YOU MAY NOW KISS THE BRIDE.
WOO!

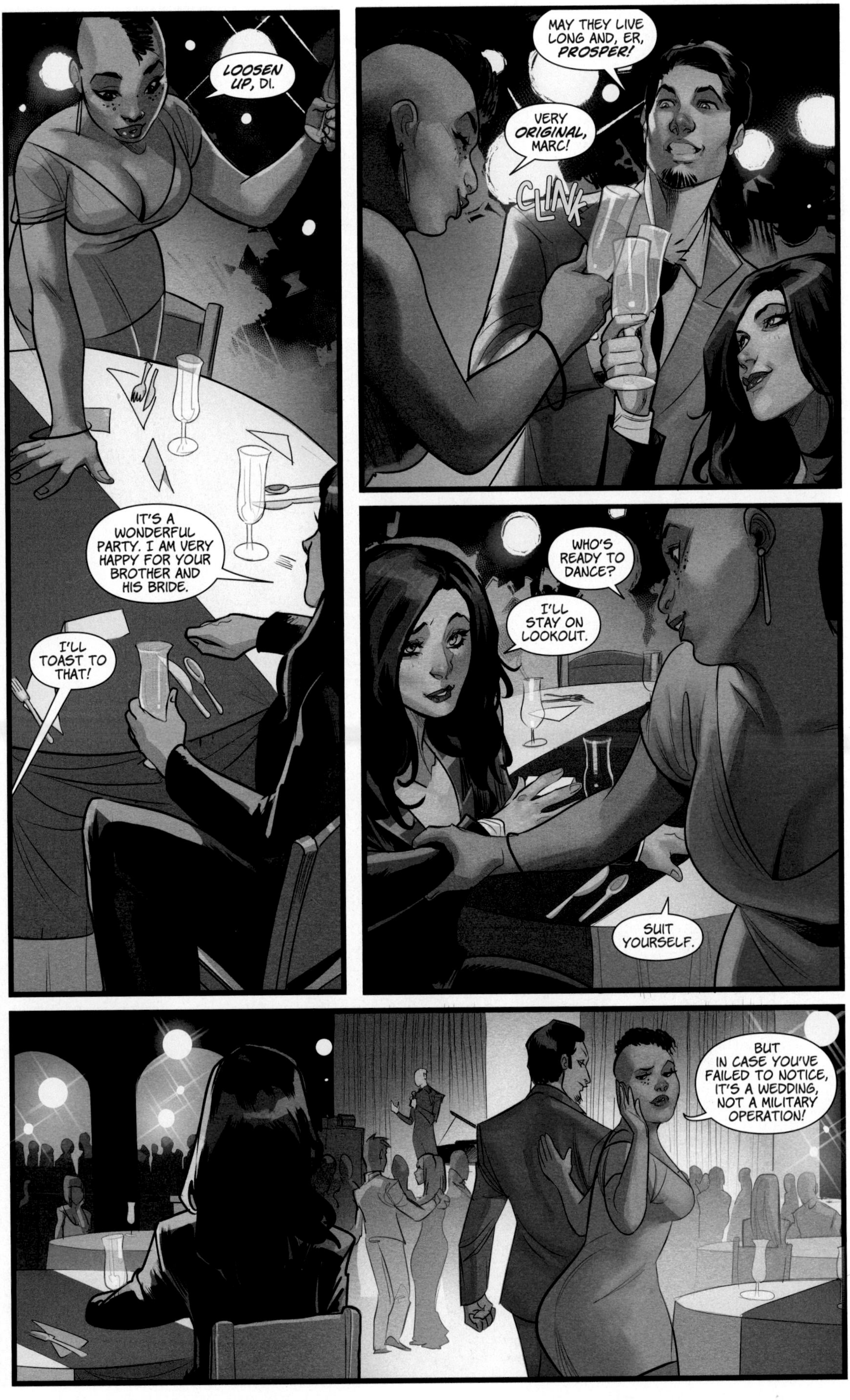
LOOSEN UP, DI.
MAY THEY LIVE LONG AND, ER, PROSPER!
VERY ORIGINAL, MARC!
CLINK
IT'S A WONDERFUL PARTY. I AM VERY HAPPY FOR YOUR BROTHER AND HIS BRIDE.
I'LL TOAST TO THAT!
WHO'S READY TO DANCE?
I'LL STAY ON LOOKOUT.
SUIT YOURSELF.
BUT IN CASE YOU'VE FAILED TO NOTICE, IT'S A WEDDING, NOT A MILITARY OPERATION!

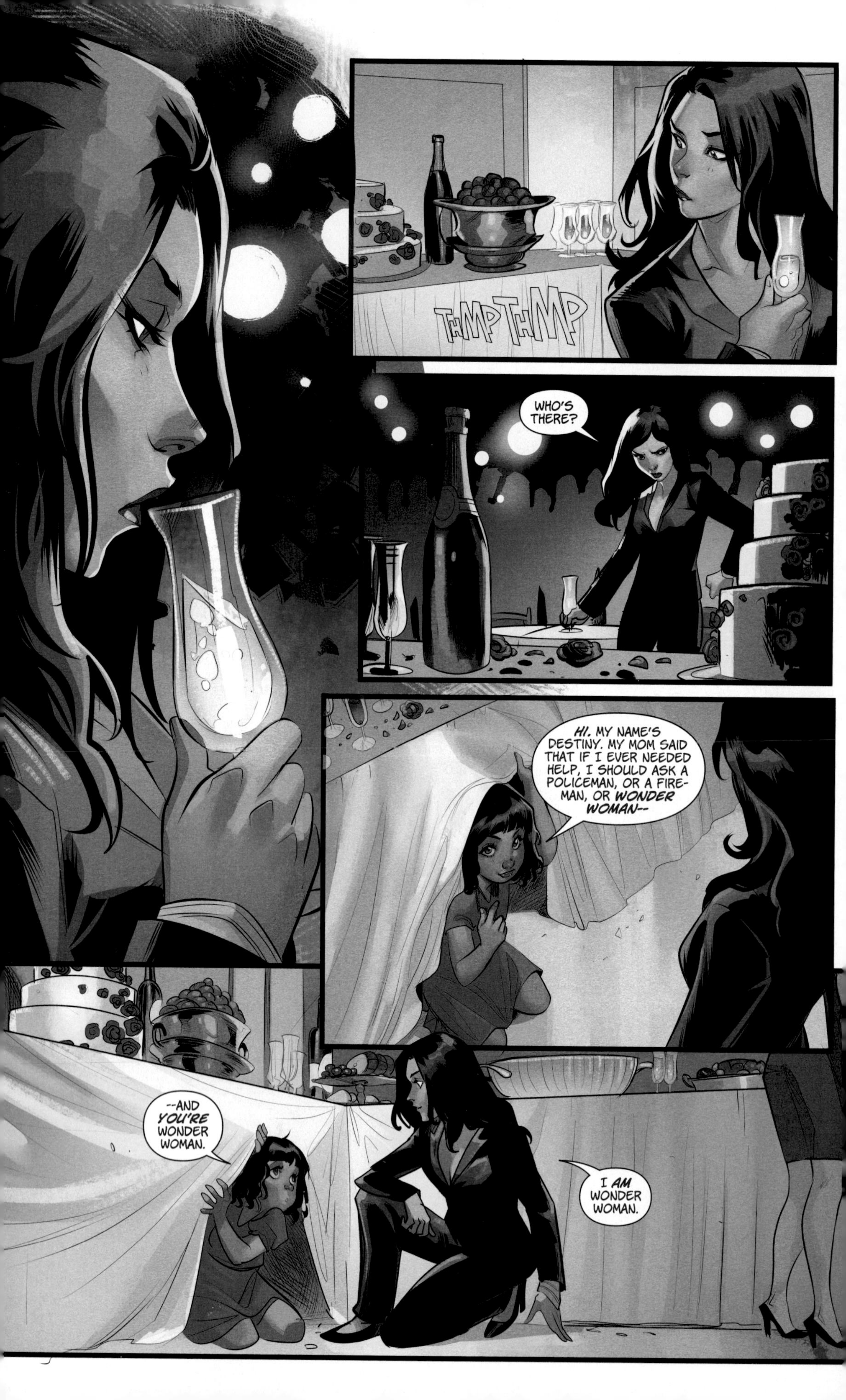
THMP THMP
WHO'S THERE?
HI. MY NAME'S DESTINY. MY MOM SAID THAT IF I EVER NEEDED HELP, I SHOULD ASK A POLICEMAN, OR A FIRE-MAN, OR WONDER WOMAN--
--AND YOU'RE WONDER WOMAN.
I AM WONDER WOMAN.

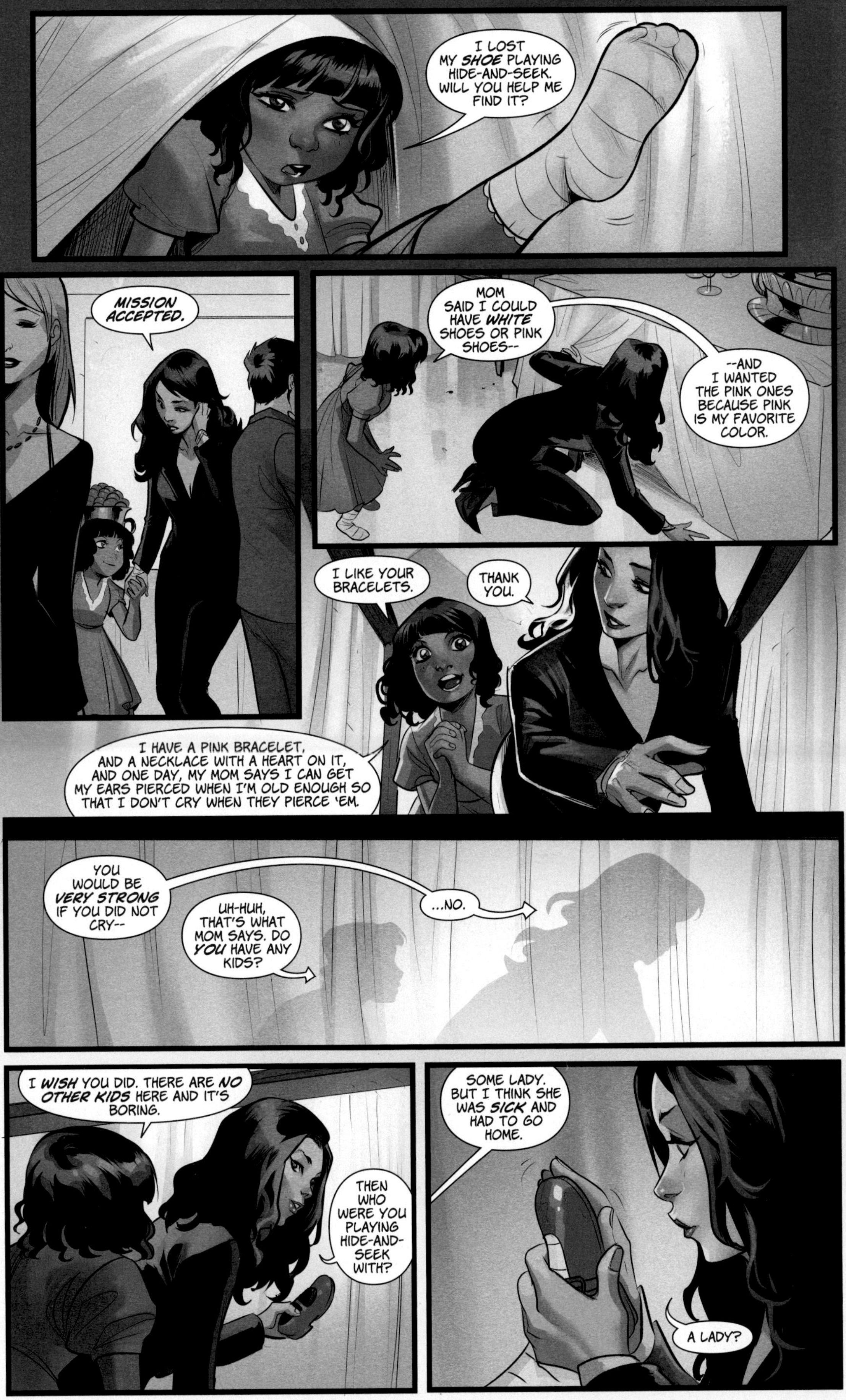
I LOST MY SHOE PLAYING HIDE-AND-SEEK. WILL YOU HELP ME FIND IT?
MISSION ACCEPTED.
MOM SAID I COULD HAVE WHITE SHOES OR PINK SHOES--
--AND I WANTED THE PINK ONES BECAUSE PINK IS MY FAVORITE COLOR.
I LIKE YOUR BRACELETS.
THANK YOU.
I HAVE A PINK BRACELET, AND A NECKLACE WITH A HEART ON IT, AND ONE DAY, MY MOM SAYS I CAN GET MY EARS PIERCED WHEN I'M OLD ENOUGH SO THAT I DON'T CRY WHEN THEY PIERCE 'EM.
YOU WOULD BE VERY STRONG IF YOU DID NOT CRY--
UH-HUH, THAT'S WHAT MOM SAYS. DO YOU HAVE ANY KIDS?
...NO.
I WISH YOU DID. THERE ARE NO OTHER KIDS HERE AND IT'S BORING.
THEN WHO WERE YOU PLAYING HIDE-AND-SEEK WITH?
SOME LADY. BUT I THINK SHE WAS SICK AND HAD TO GO HOME.
A LADY?

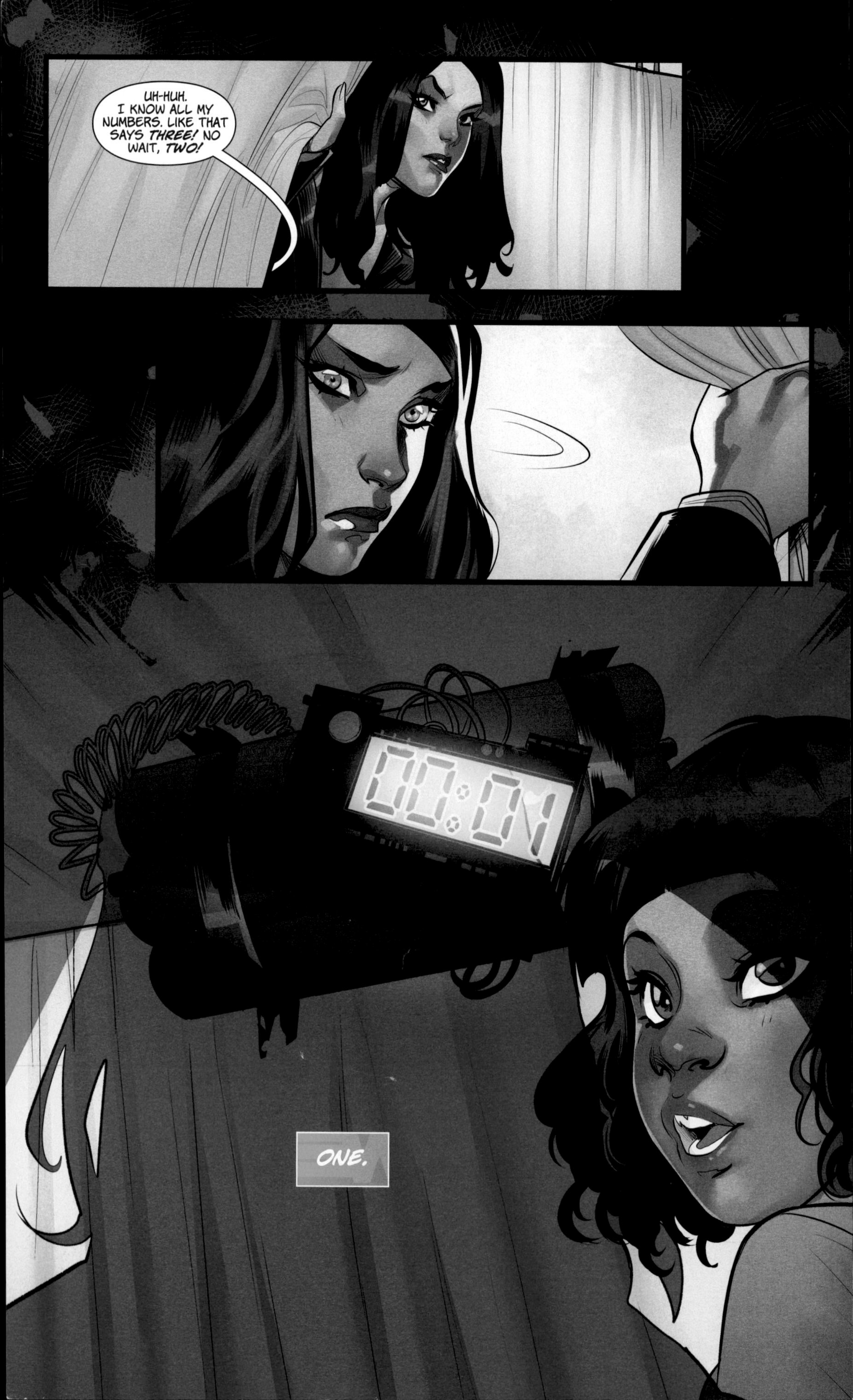
UH-HUH. I KNOW ALL MY NUMBERS. LIKE THAT SAYS *THREE!* NO WAIT, *TWO!*
00:01
ONE.

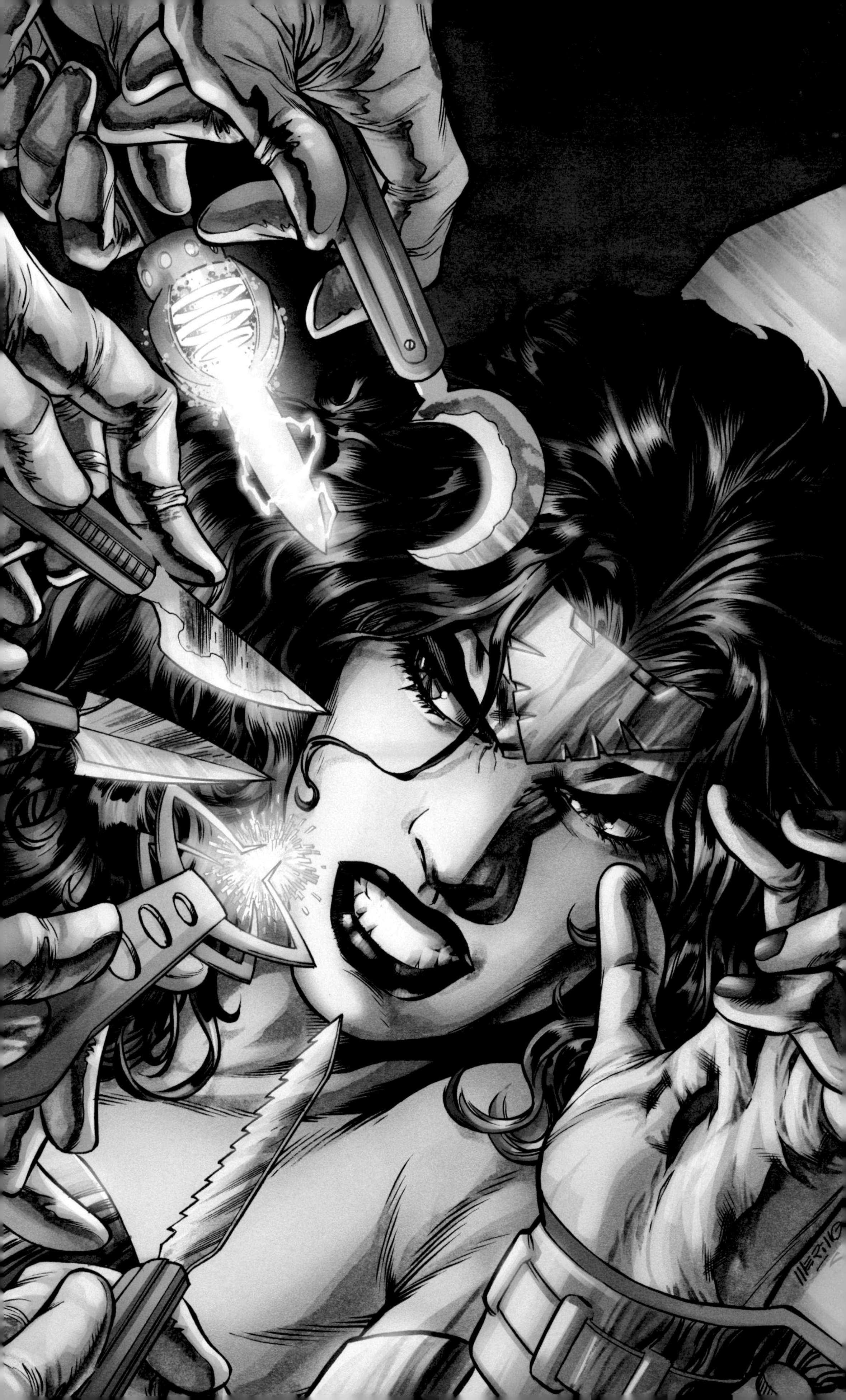

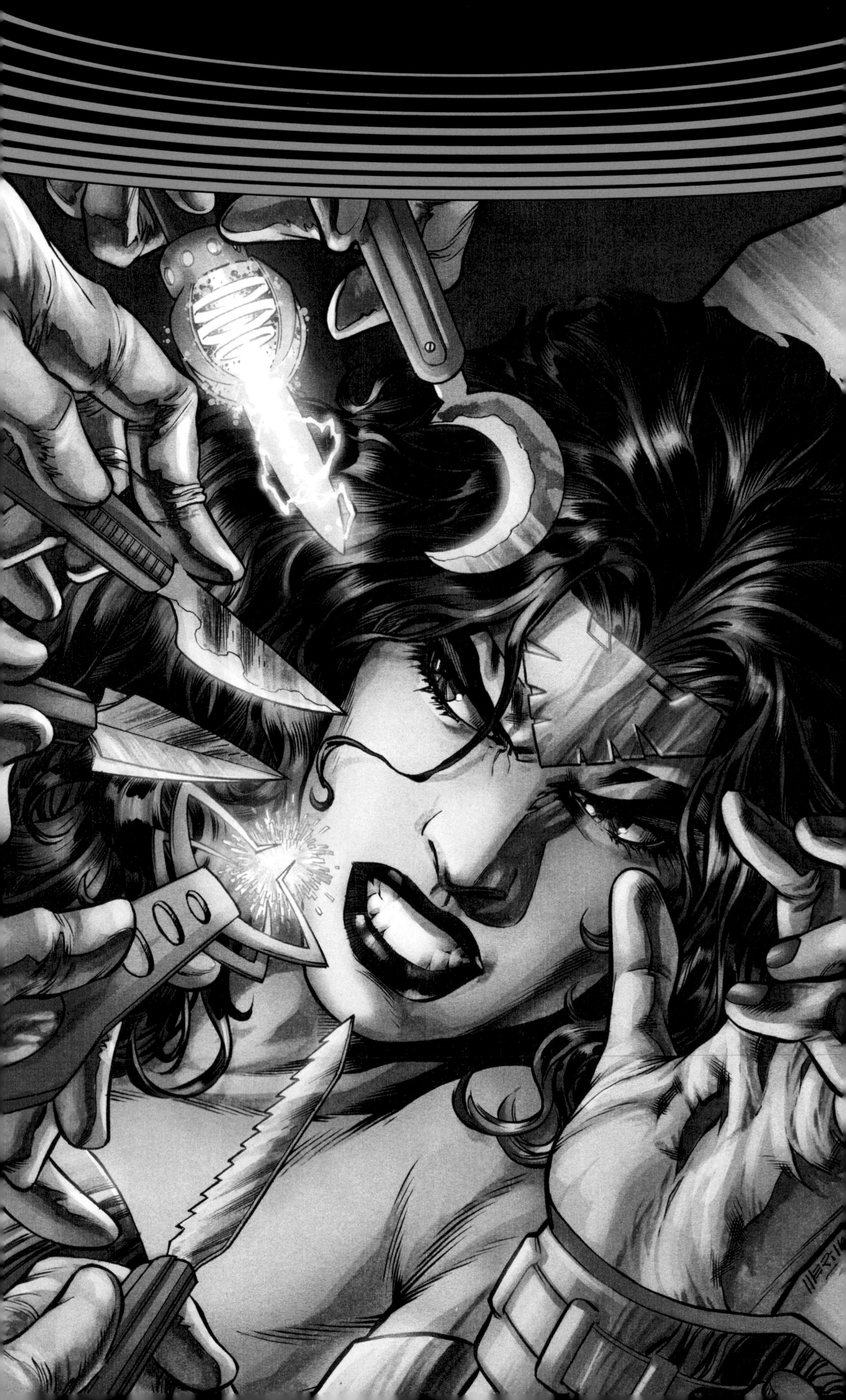

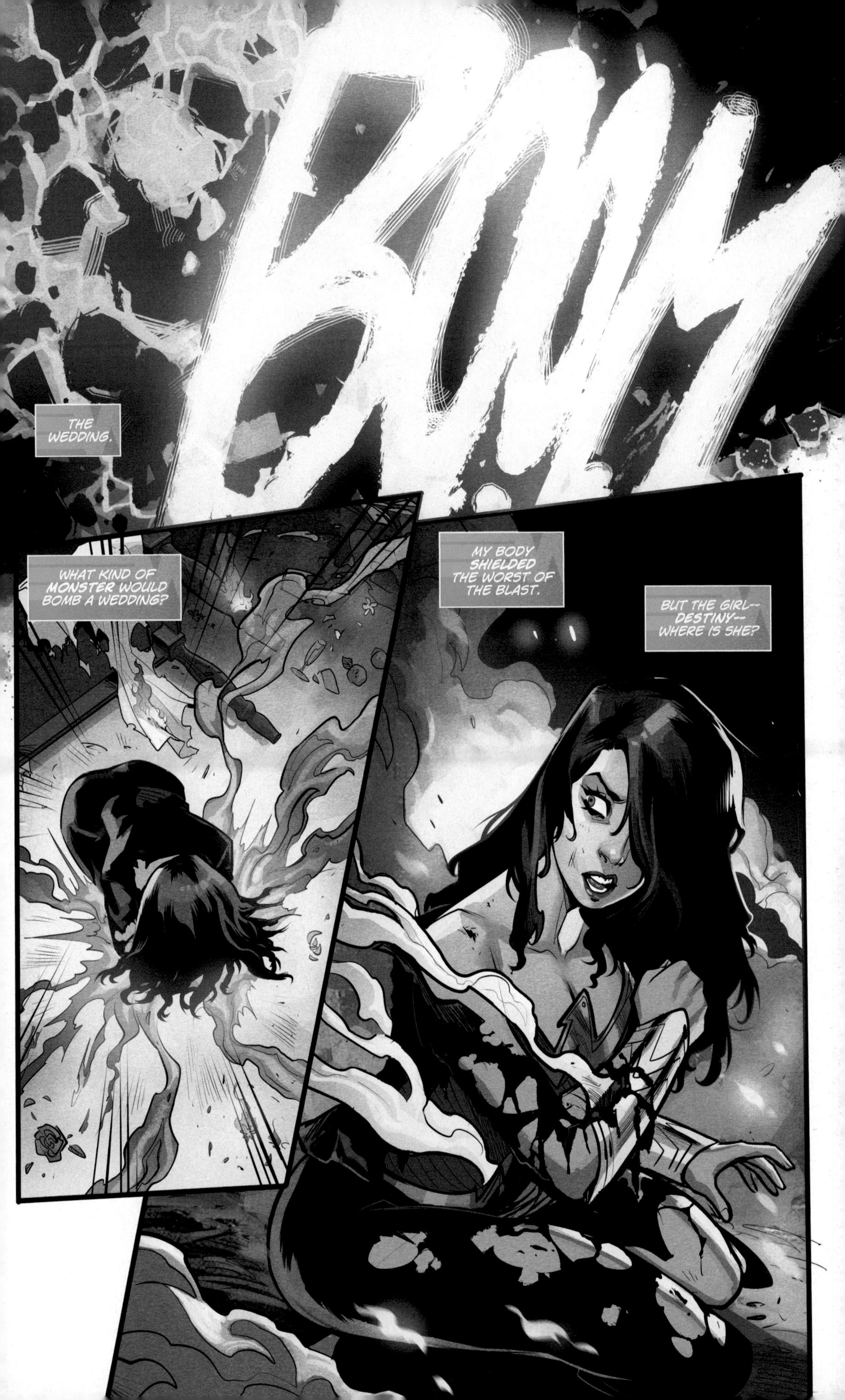
BAM
THE WEDDING.
WHAT KIND OF MONSTER WOULD BOMB A WEDDING?
MY BODY SHIELDED THE WORST OF THE BLAST.
BUT THE GIRL-- DESTINY-- WHERE IS SHE?

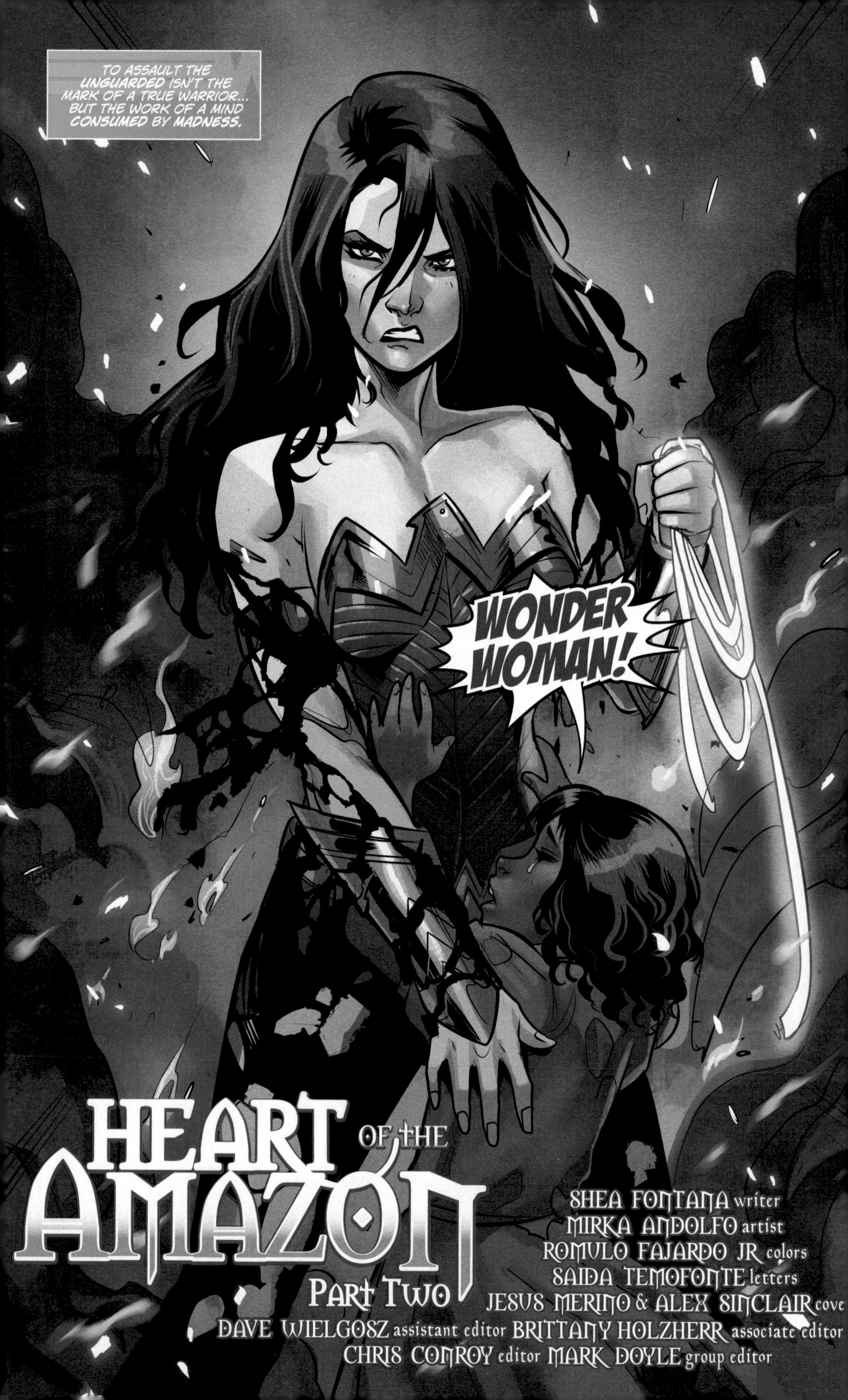
TO ASSAULT THE UNGUARDED ISN'T THE MARK OF A TRUE WARRIOR... BUT THE WORK OF A MIND CONSUMED BY MADNESS.
WONDER WOMAN!
HEART OF THE AMAZON
PART TWO
SHEA FONTANA writer
MIRKA ANDOLFO artist
ROMULO FAJARDO JR colors
SAIDA TEMOFONTE letters
JESUS MERINO & ALEX SINCLAIR cove
DAVE WIELGOSZ assistant editor BRITTANY HOLZHERR associate editor
CHRIS CONROY editor MARK DOYLE group editor

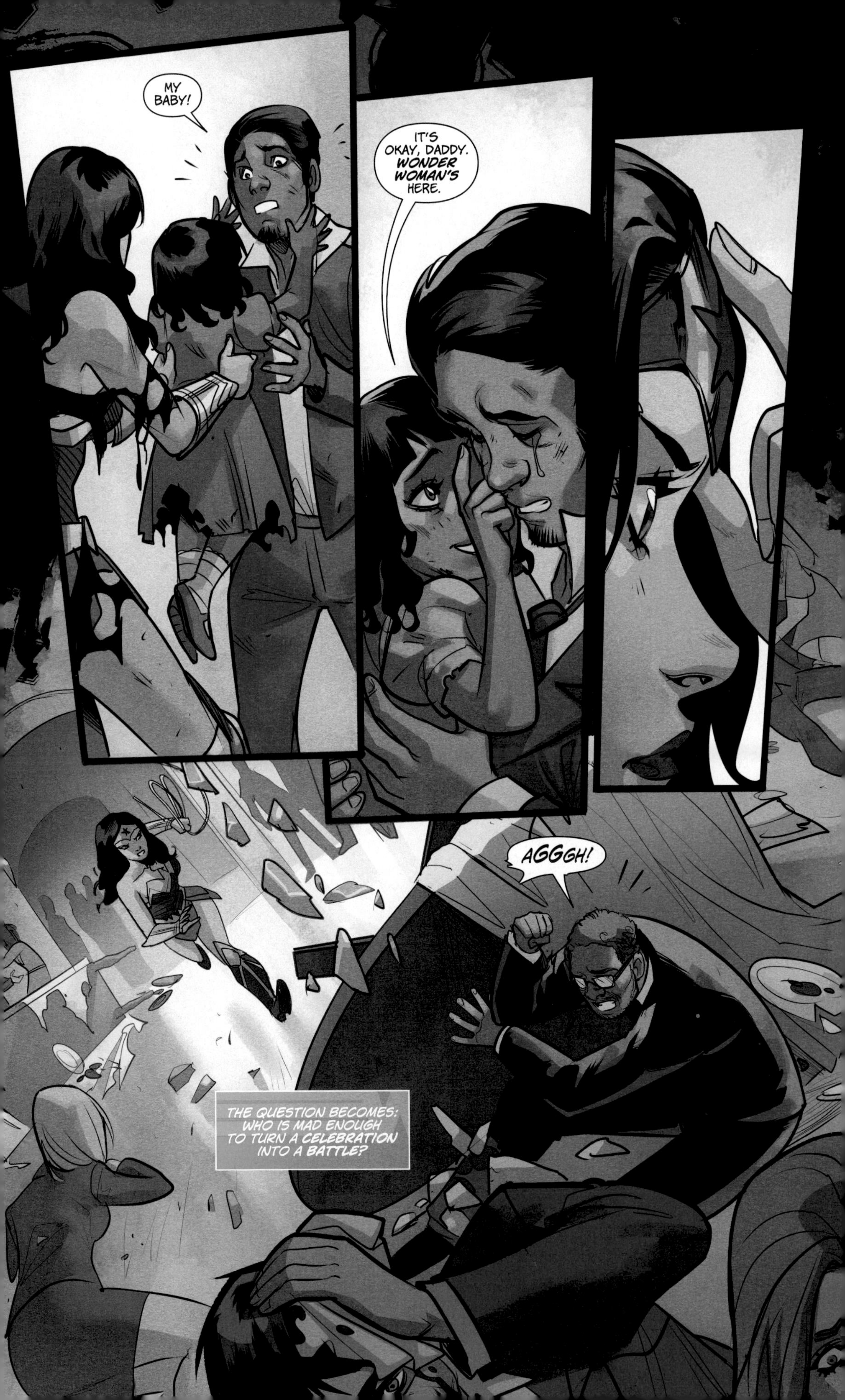
MY BABY!
IT'S OKAY, DADDY. WONDER WOMAN'S HERE.
AGGGH!
THE QUESTION BECOMES: WHO IS MAD ENOUGH TO TURN A CELEBRATION INTO A BATTLE?

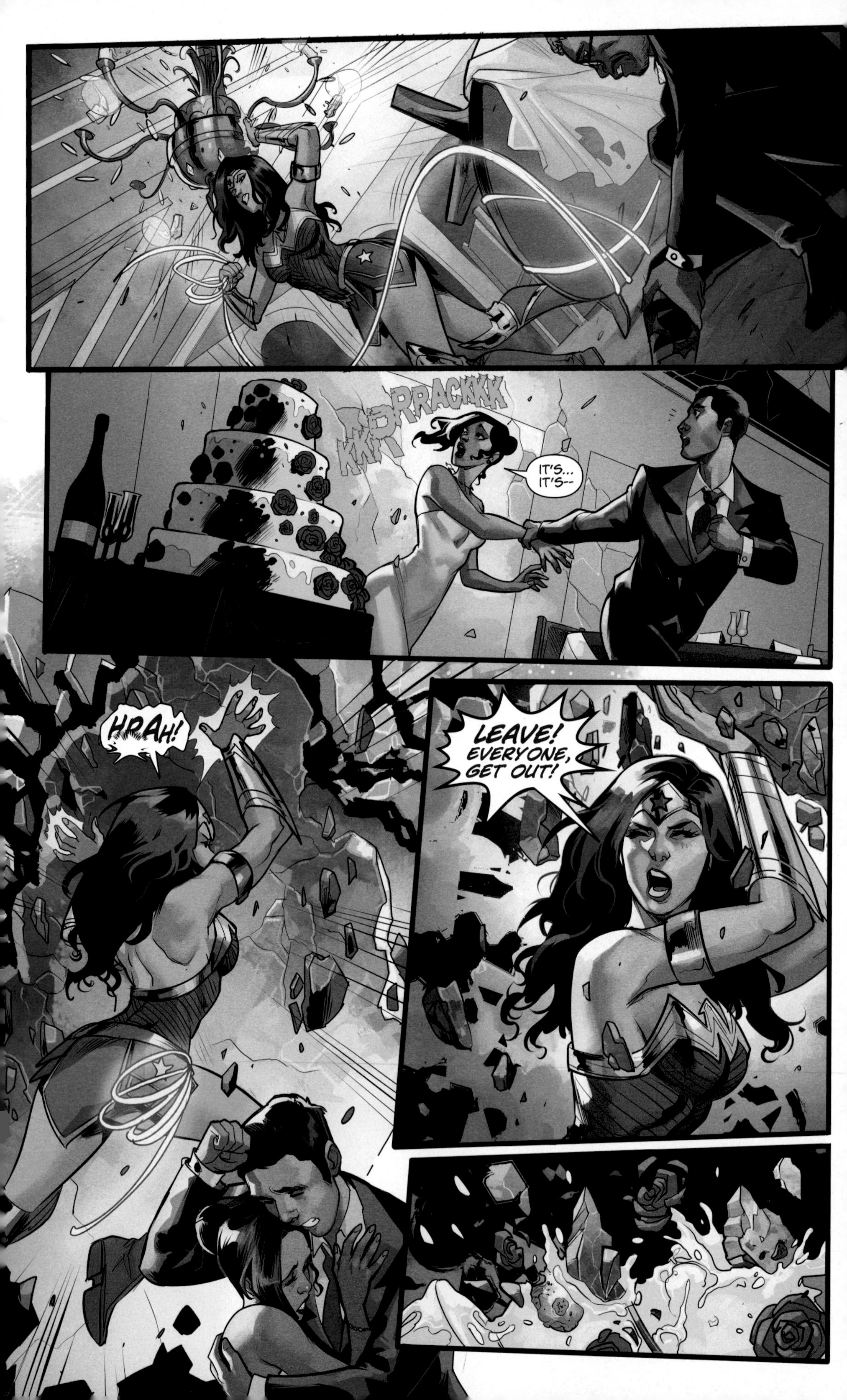
KKRRRACKKK
IT'S... IT'S--
HRAH!
LEAVE! EVERYONE, GET OUT!

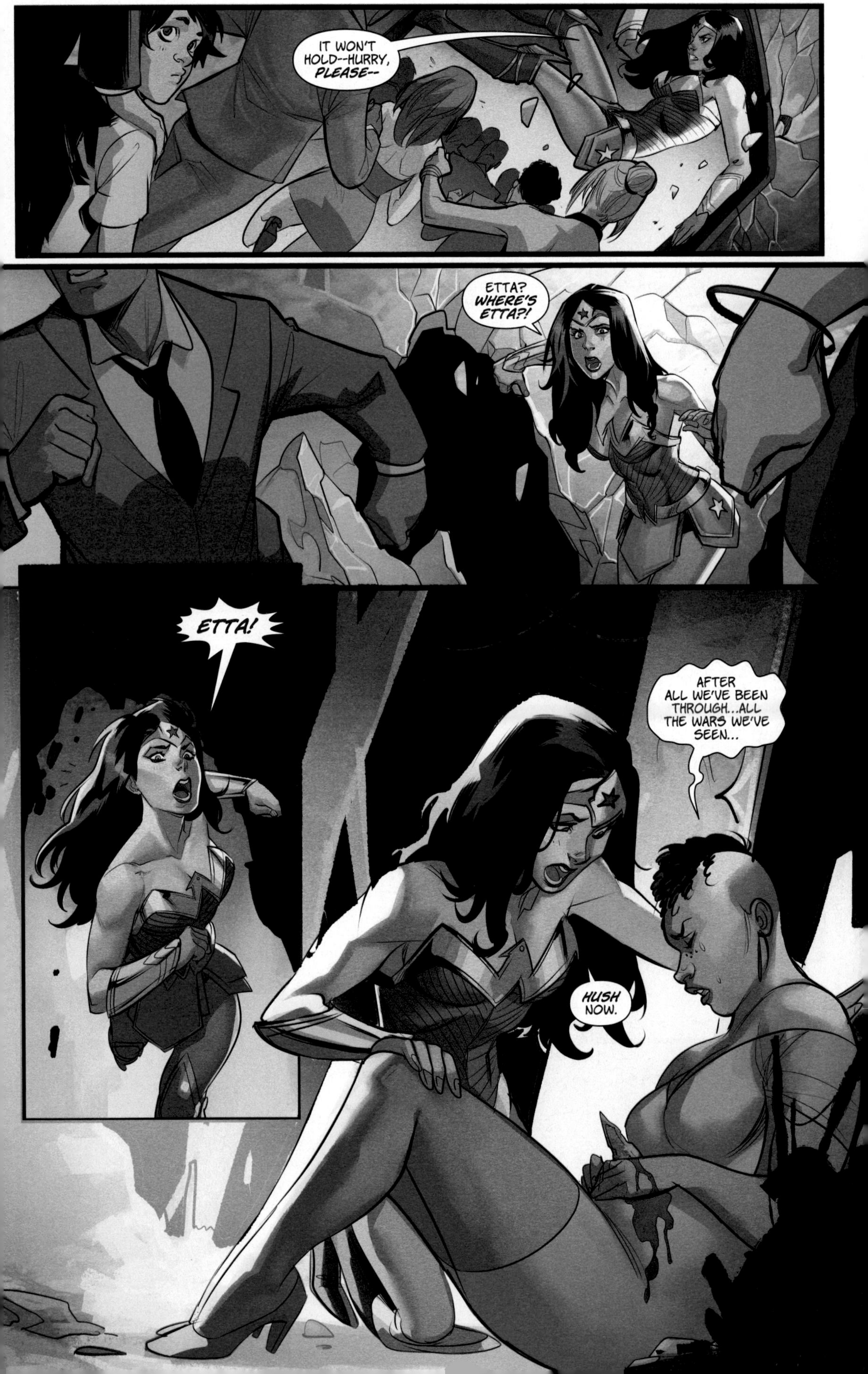
IT WON'T HOLD--HURRY, PLEASE--
ETTA? WHERE'S ETTA?!
ETTA!
AFTER ALL WE'VE BEEN THROUGH...ALL THE WARS WE'VE SEEN...
HUSH NOW.

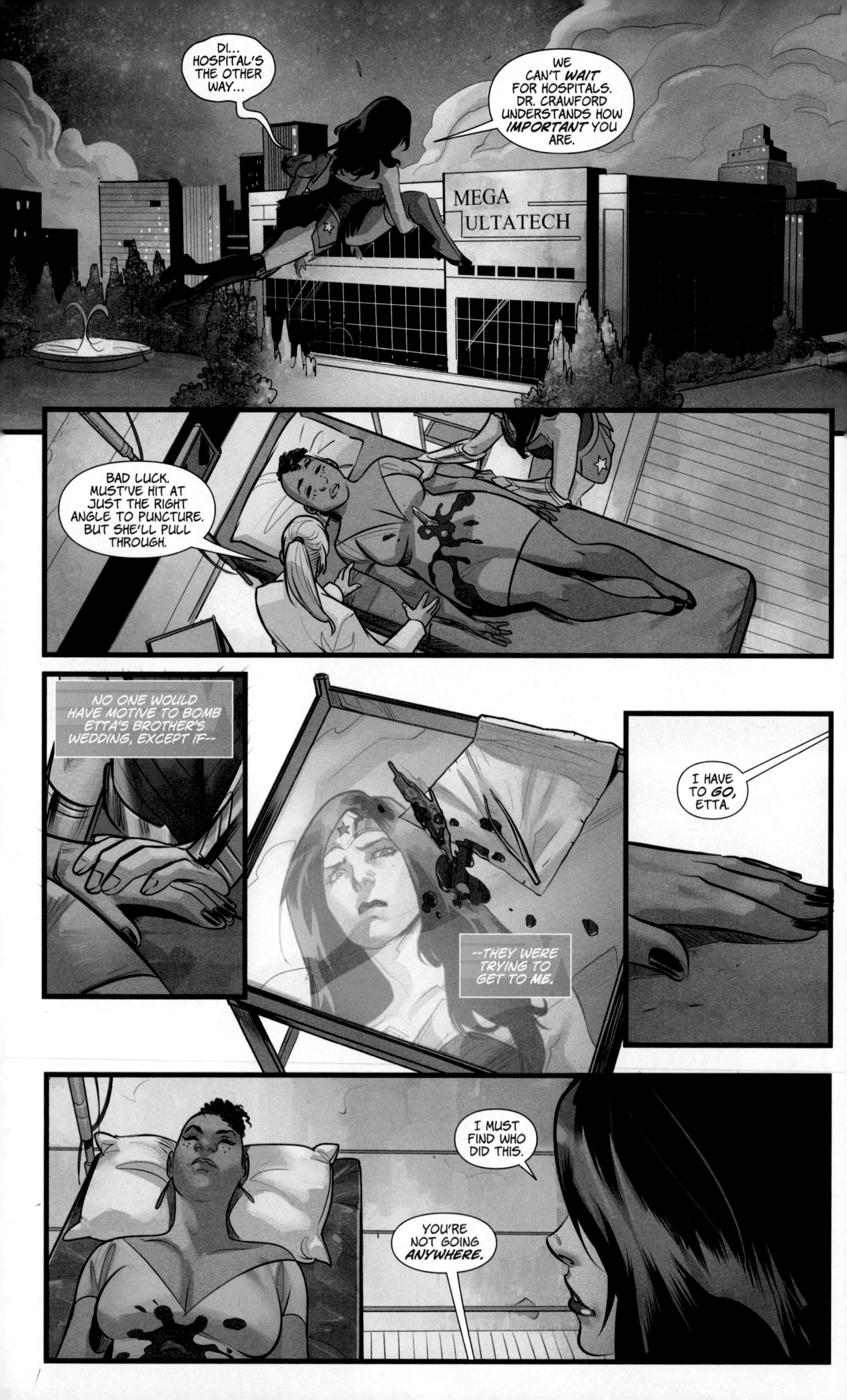
DI... HOSPITAL'S THE OTHER WAY...
WE CAN'T WAIT FOR HOSPITALS. DR. CRAWFORD UNDERSTANDS HOW IMPORTANT YOU ARE.
MEGA ULTATECH
BAD LUCK. MUST'VE HIT AT JUST THE RIGHT ANGLE TO PUNCTURE. BUT SHE'LL PULL THROUGH.
NO ONE WOULD HAVE MOTIVE TO BOMB ETTA'S BROTHER'S WEDDING, EXCEPT IF--
--THEY WERE TRYING TO GET TO ME.
I HAVE TO GO, ETTA.
I MUST FIND WHO DID THIS.
YOU'RE NOT GOING ANYWHERE.

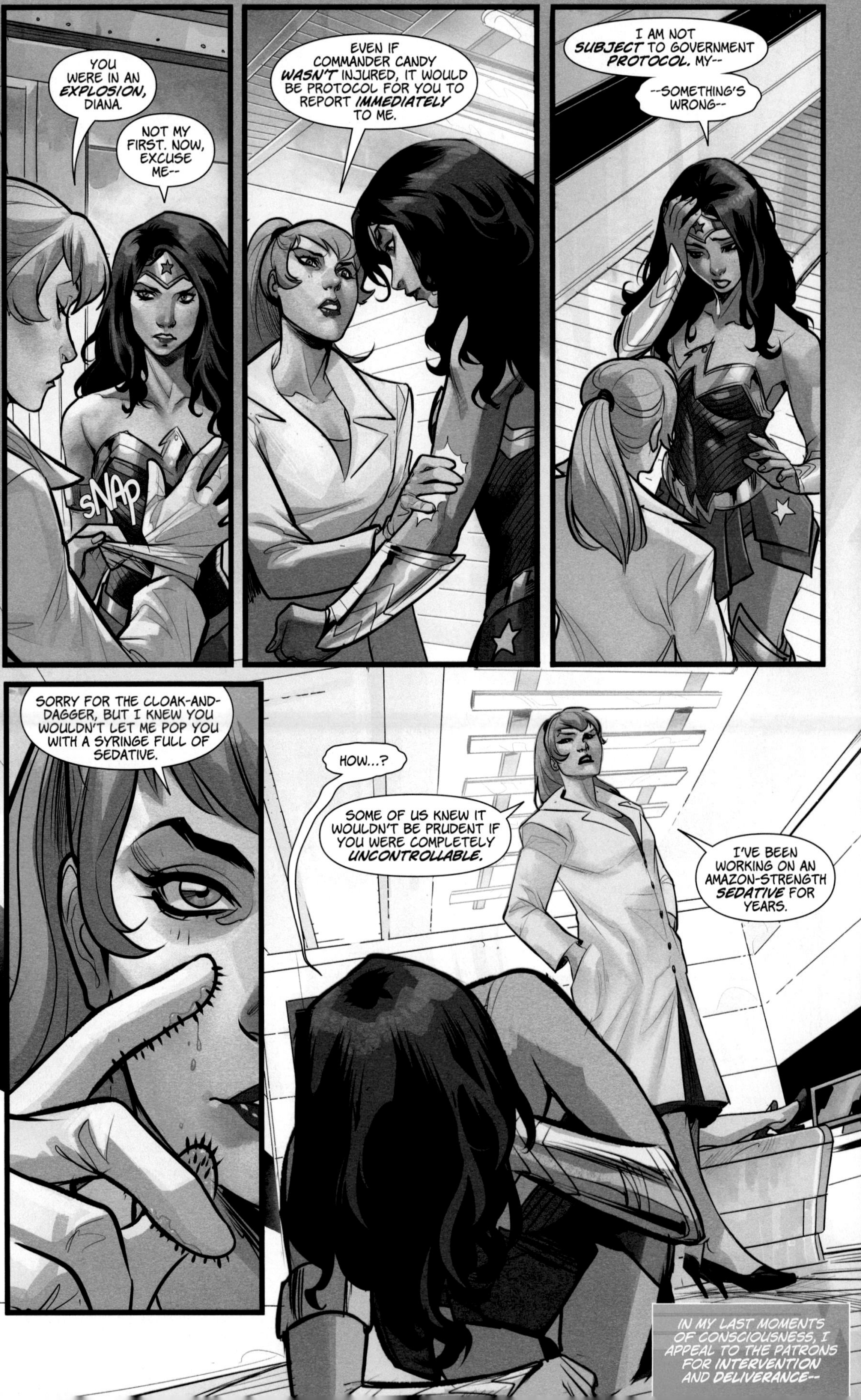
YOU WERE IN AN EXPLOSION, DIANA.
NOT MY FIRST. NOW, EXCUSE ME--
sNAP
EVEN IF COMMANDER CANDY WASN'T INJURED, IT WOULD BE PROTOCOL FOR YOU TO REPORT IMMEDIATELY TO ME.
I AM NOT SUBJECT TO GOVERNMENT PROTOCOL. MY--
--SOMETHING'S WRONG--
SORRY FOR THE CLOAK-AND-DAGGER, BUT I KNEW YOU WOULDN'T LET ME POP YOU WITH A SYRINGE FULL OF SEDATIVE.
HOW...?
SOME OF US KNEW IT WOULDN'T BE PRUDENT IF YOU WERE COMPLETELY UNCONTROLLABLE.
I'VE BEEN WORKING ON AN AMAZON-STRENGTH SEDATIVE FOR YEARS.
IN MY LAST MOMENTS OF CONSCIOUSNESS, I APPEAL TO THE PATRONS FOR INTERVENTION AND DELIVERANCE--

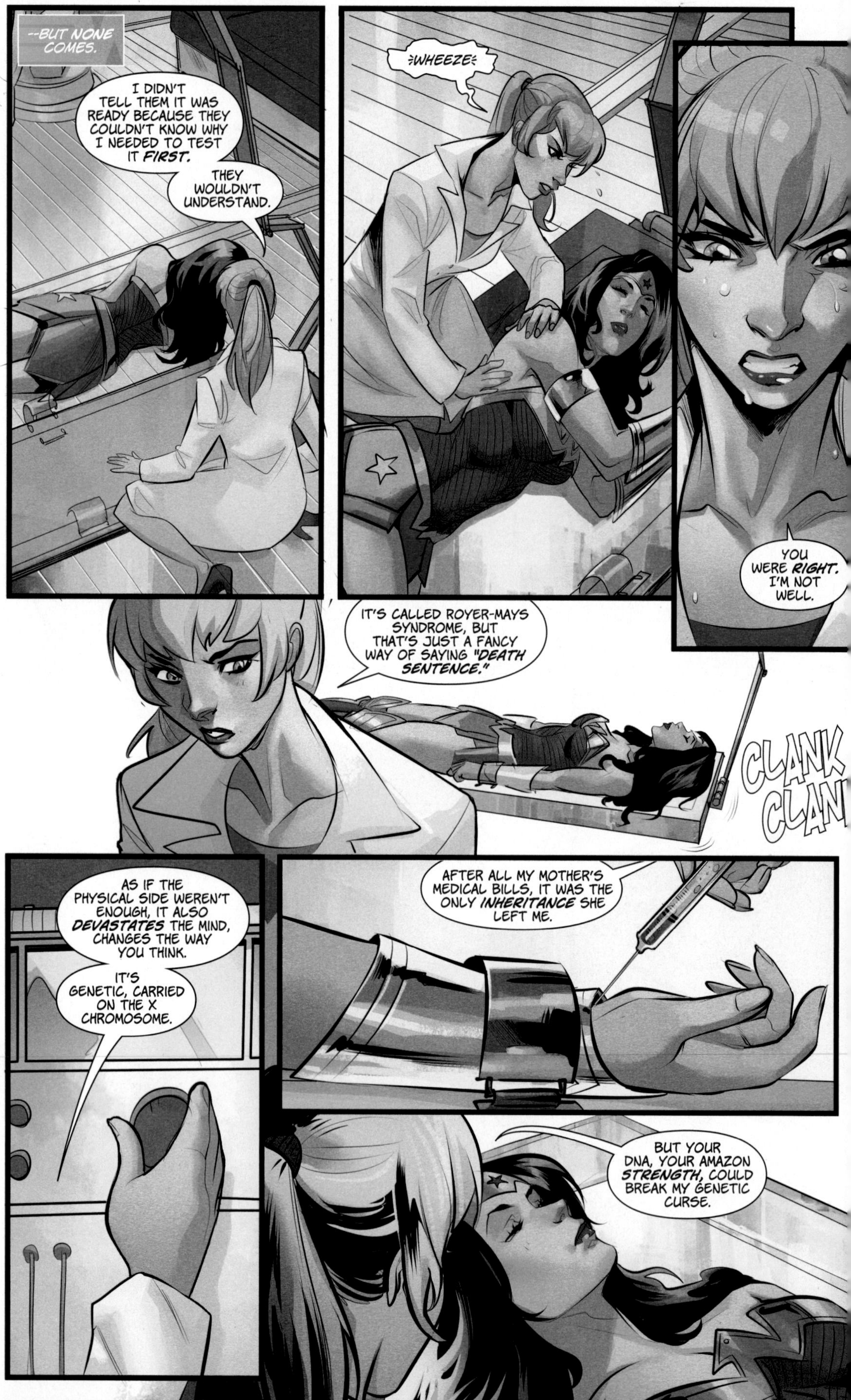
--BUT NONE COMES.
I DIDN'T TELL THEM IT WAS READY BECAUSE THEY COULDN'T KNOW WHY I NEEDED TO TEST IT FIRST.
THEY WOULDN'T UNDERSTAND.
WHEEZE
YOU WERE RIGHT. I'M NOT WELL.
IT'S CALLED ROYER-MAYS SYNDROME, BUT THAT'S JUST A FANCY WAY OF SAYING "DEATH SENTENCE."
CLANK
AS IF THE PHYSICAL SIDE WEREN'T ENOUGH, IT ALSO DEVASTATES THE MIND, CHANGES THE WAY YOU THINK.
IT'S GENETIC, CARRIED ON THE X CHROMOSOME.
AFTER ALL MY MOTHER'S MEDICAL BILLS, IT WAS THE ONLY INHERITANCE SHE LEFT ME.
BUT YOUR DNA, YOUR AMAZON STRENGTH, COULD BREAK MY GENETIC CURSE.

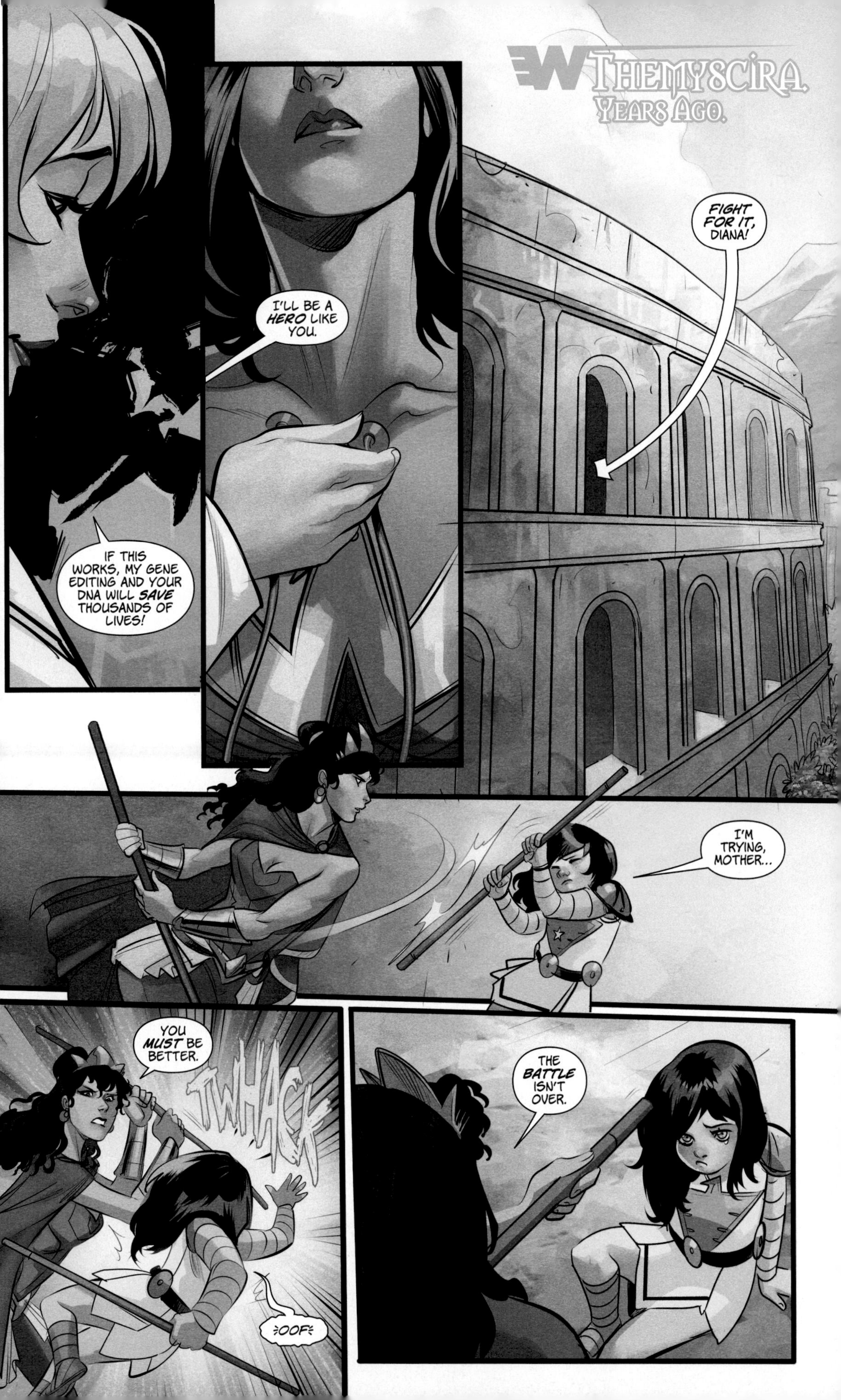

IF THIS WORKS, MY GENE EDITING AND YOUR DNA WILL SAVE THOUSANDS OF LIVES!
I'LL BE A HERO LIKE YOU.
THEMYSCIRA. YEARS AGO.
FIGHT FOR IT, DIANA!
I'M TRYING, MOTHER...
YOU MUST BE BETTER.
TWHACK
OOF
THE BATTLE ISN'T OVER.

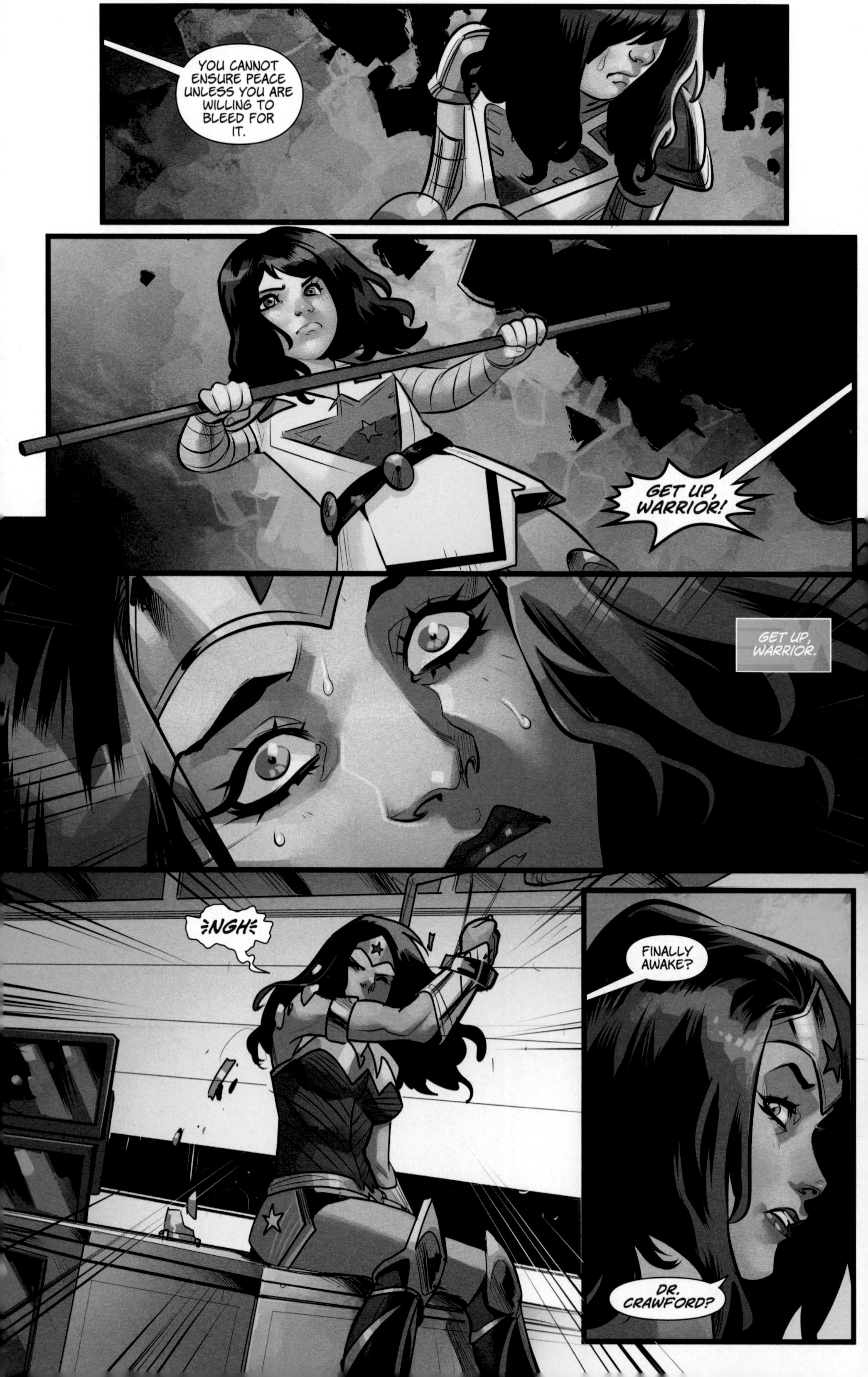
YOU CANNOT ENSURE PEACE UNLESS YOU ARE WILLING TO BLEED FOR IT.
GET UP, WARRIOR!
GET UP, WARRIOR.
NGH
FINALLY AWAKE?
DR. CRAWFORD?

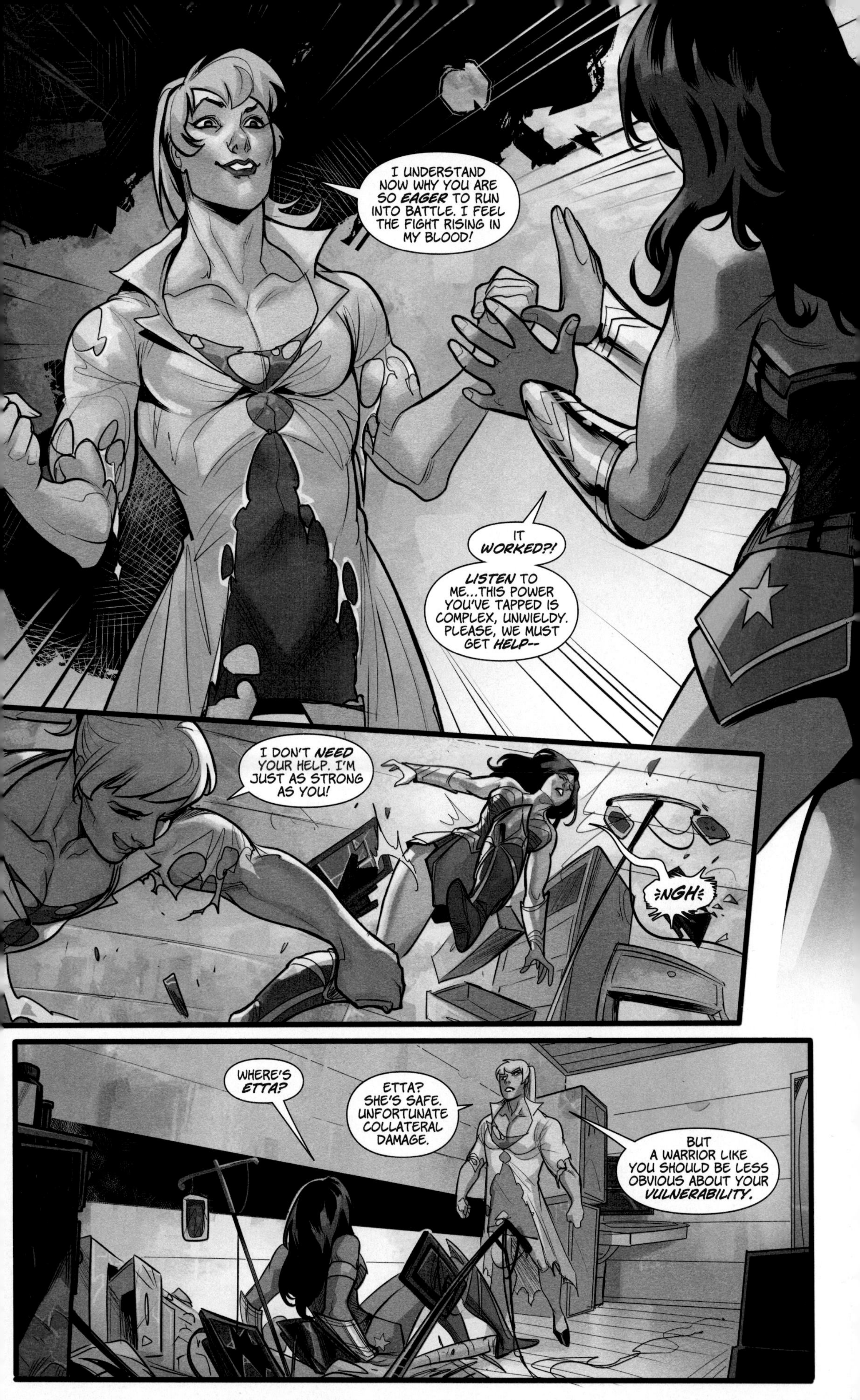
I UNDERSTAND NOW WHY YOU ARE SO EAGER TO RUN INTO BATTLE. I FEEL THE FIGHT RISING IN MY BLOOD!
IT WORKED?!
LISTEN TO ME...THIS POWER YOU'VE TAPPED IS COMPLEX, UNWIELDY. PLEASE, WE MUST GET HELP--
I DON'T NEED YOUR HELP. I'M JUST AS STRONG AS YOU!
NGH
WHERE'S ETTA?
ETTA? SHE'S SAFE. UNFORTUNATE COLLATERAL DAMAGE.
BUT A WARRIOR LIKE YOU SHOULD BE LESS OBVIOUS ABOUT YOUR VULNERABILITY.

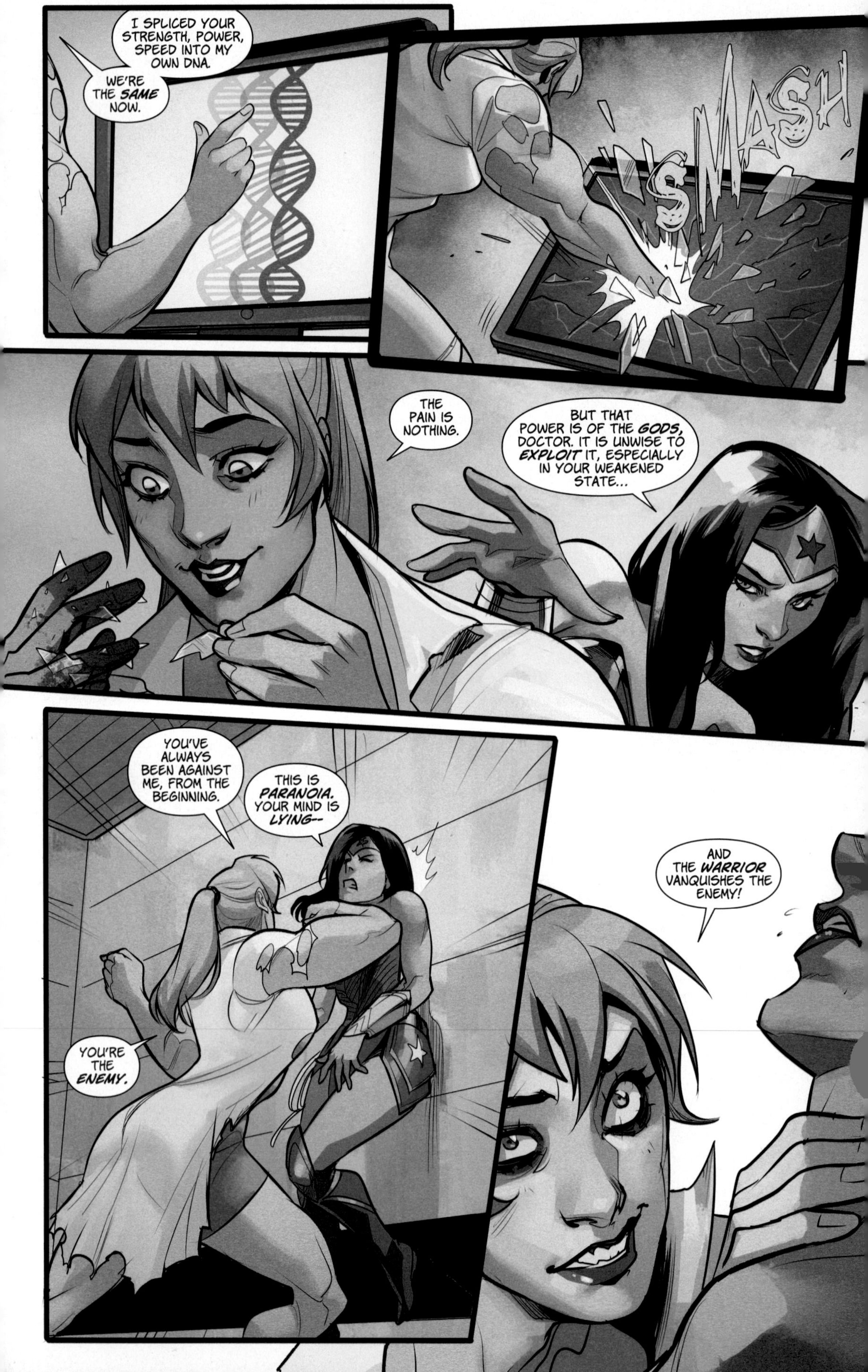
I SPLICED YOUR STRENGTH, POWER, SPEED INTO MY OWN DNA.
WE'RE THE SAME NOW.
SMASH
THE PAIN IS NOTHING.
BUT THAT POWER IS OF THE GODS, DOCTOR. IT IS UNWISE TO EXPLOIT IT, ESPECIALLY IN YOUR WEAKENED STATE...
YOU'VE ALWAYS BEEN AGAINST ME, FROM THE BEGINNING.
THIS IS PARANOIA. YOUR MIND IS LYING--
YOU'RE THE ENEMY.
AND THE WARRIOR VANQUISHES THE ENEMY!

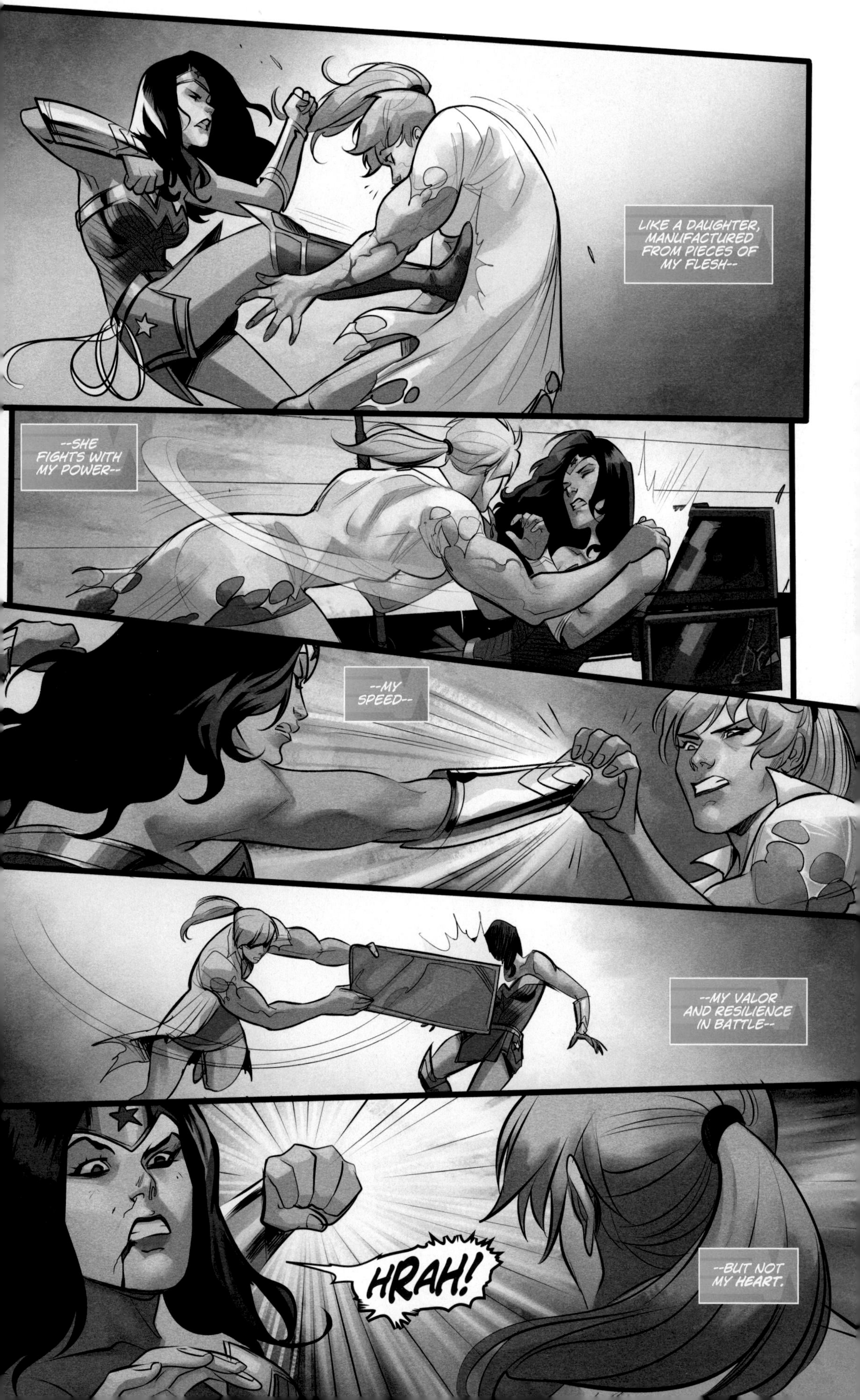
LIKE A DAUGHTER, MANUFACTURED FROM PIECES OF MY FLESH--
--SHE FIGHTS WITH MY POWER--
--MY SPEED--
--MY VALOR AND RESILIENCE IN BATTLE--
HRAH!
--BUT NOT MY HEART.

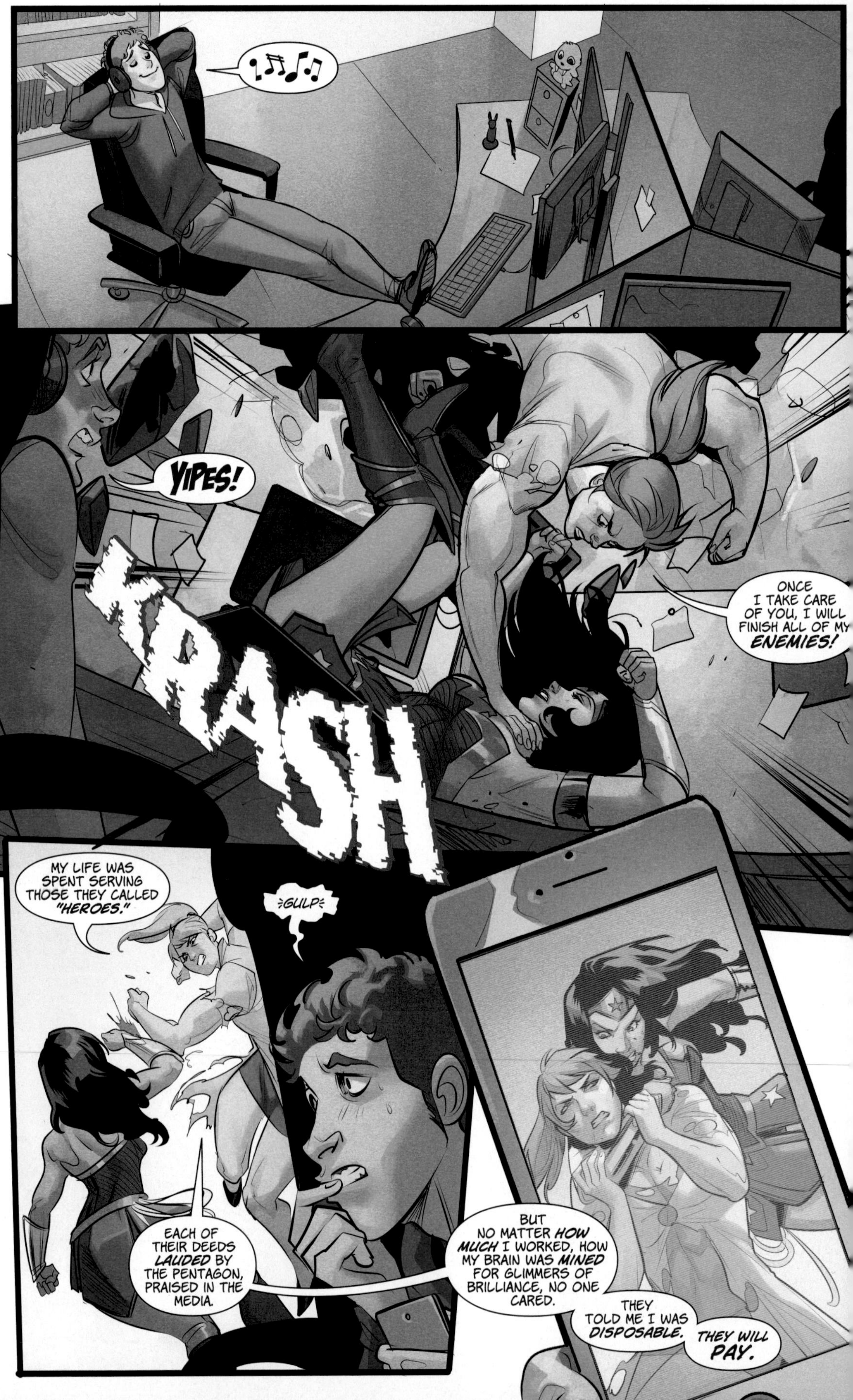
YIPES!
KRASH
ONCE I TAKE CARE OF YOU, I WILL FINISH ALL OF MY ENEMIES!
MY LIFE WAS SPENT SERVING THOSE THEY CALLED "HEROES."
GULP
EACH OF THEIR DEEDS LAUDED BY THE PENTAGON, PRAISED IN THE MEDIA.
BUT NO MATTER HOW MUCH I WORKED, HOW MY BRAIN WAS MINED FOR GLIMMERS OF BRILLIANCE, NO ONE CARED.
THEY TOLD ME I WAS DISPOSABLE.
THEY WILL PAY.

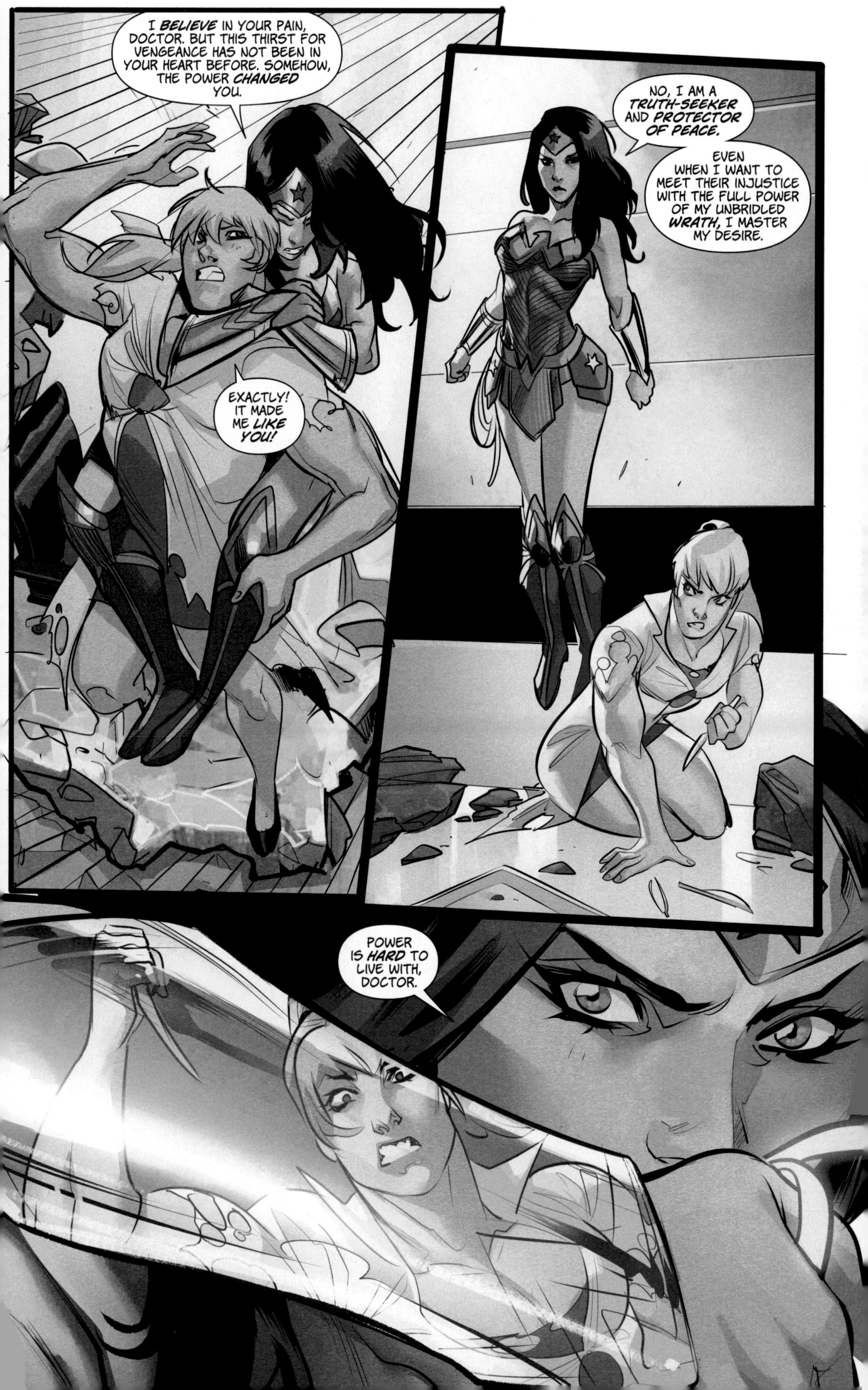
I BELIEVE IN YOUR PAIN, DOCTOR. BUT THIS THIRST FOR VENGEANCE HAS NOT BEEN IN YOUR HEART BEFORE. SOMEHOW, THE POWER CHANGED YOU.
EXACTLY! IT MADE ME LIKE YOU!
NO, I AM A TRUTH-SEEKER AND PROTECTOR OF PEACE.
EVEN WHEN I WANT TO MEET THEIR INJUSTICE WITH THE FULL POWER OF MY UNBRIDLED WRATH, I MASTER MY DESIRE.
POWER IS HARD TO LIVE WITH, DOCTOR.

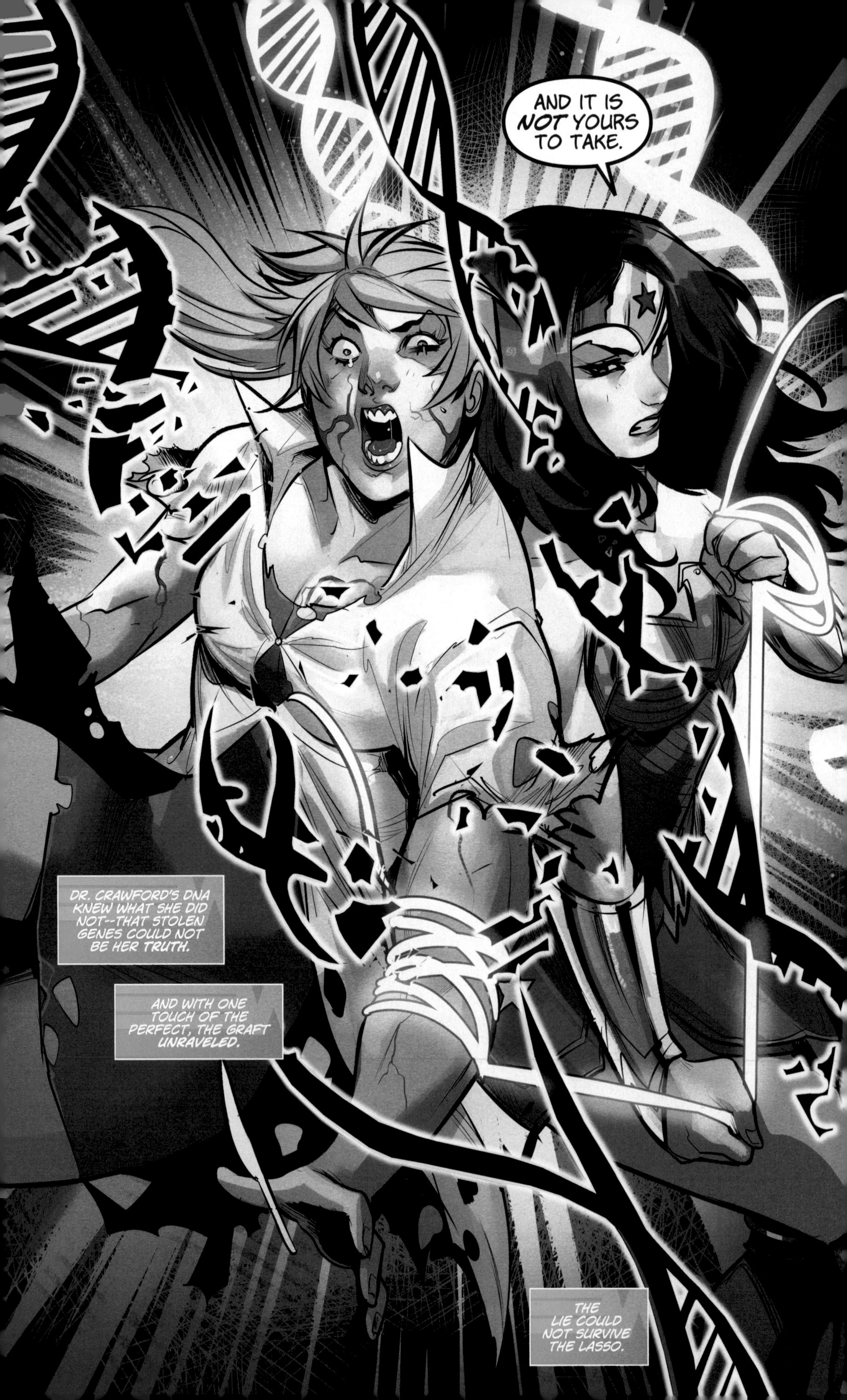
AND IT IS NOT YOURS TO TAKE.
DR. CRAWFORD'S DNA KNEW WHAT SHE DID NOT--THAT STOLEN GENES COULD NOT BE HER TRUTH.
AND WITH ONE TOUCH OF THE PERFECT, THE GRAFT UNRAVELED.
THE LIE COULD NOT SURVIVE THE LASSO.

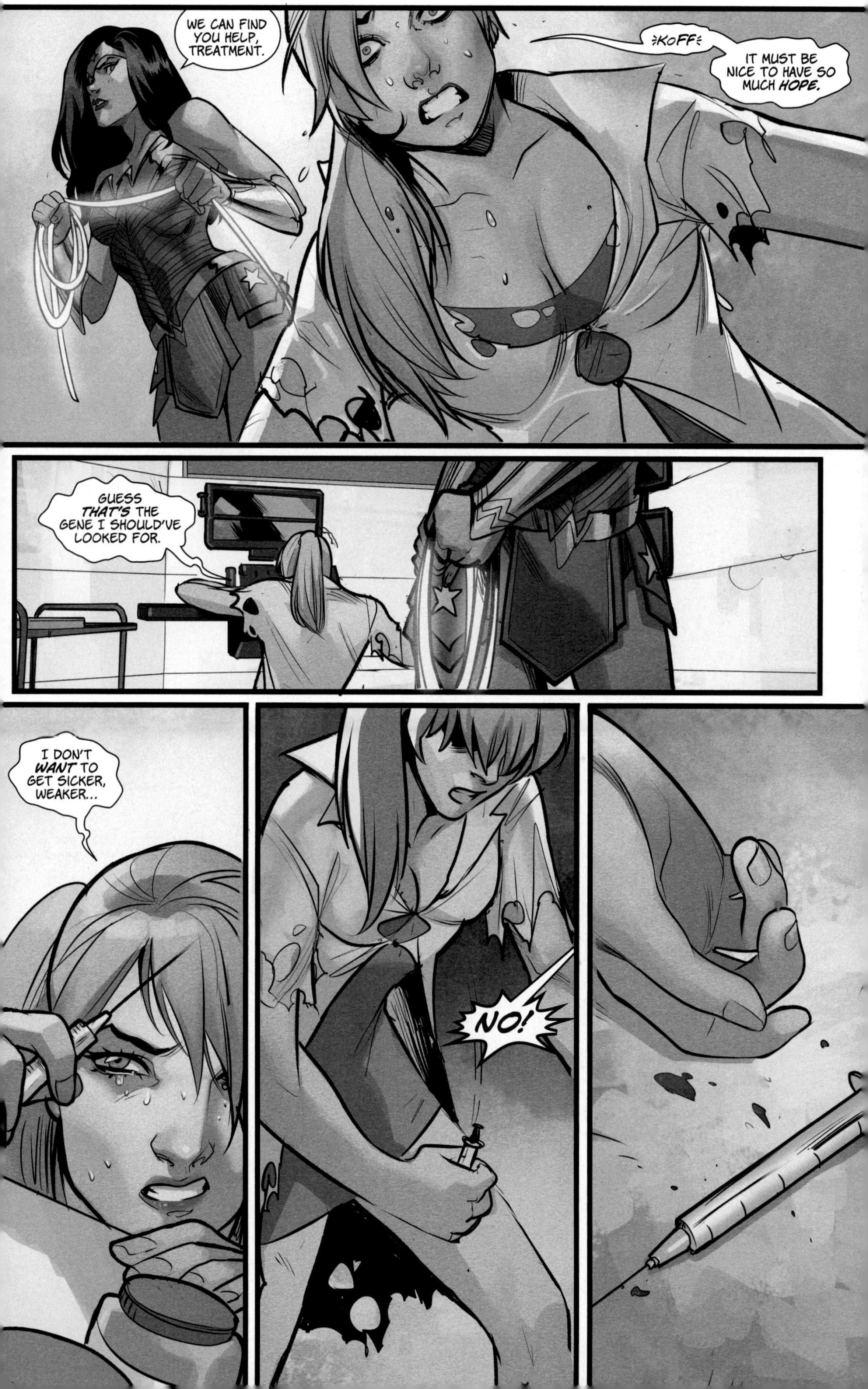
WE CAN FIND YOU HELP, TREATMENT.
KOFF
IT MUST BE NICE TO HAVE SO MUCH *HOPE.*
GUESS *THAT'S* THE GENE I SHOULD'VE LOOKED FOR.
I DON'T *WANT* TO GET SICKER, WEAKER...
NO!

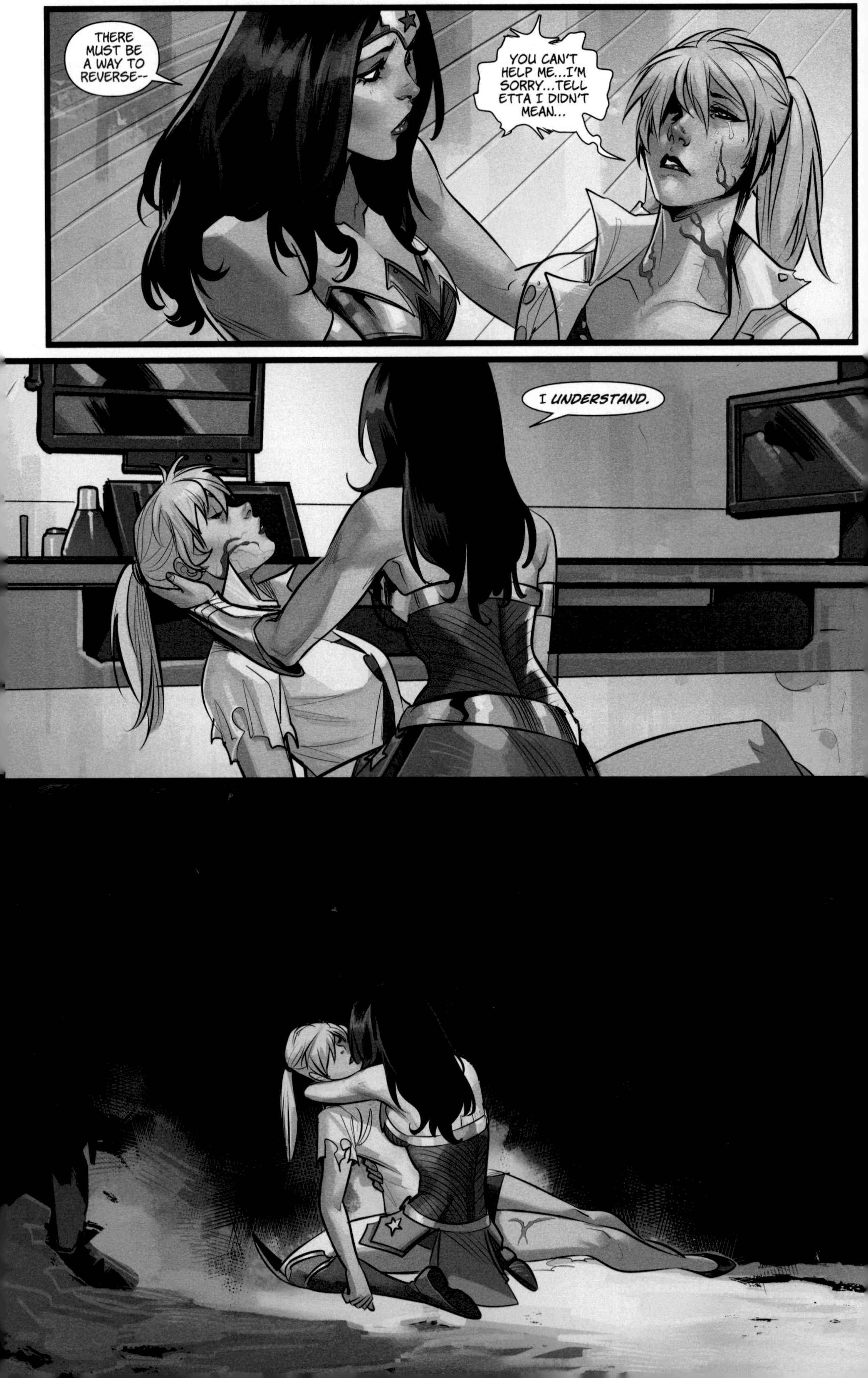
THERE MUST BE A WAY TO REVERSE--
YOU CAN'T HELP ME...I'M SORRY...TELL ETTA I DIDN'T MEAN...
I UNDERSTAND.

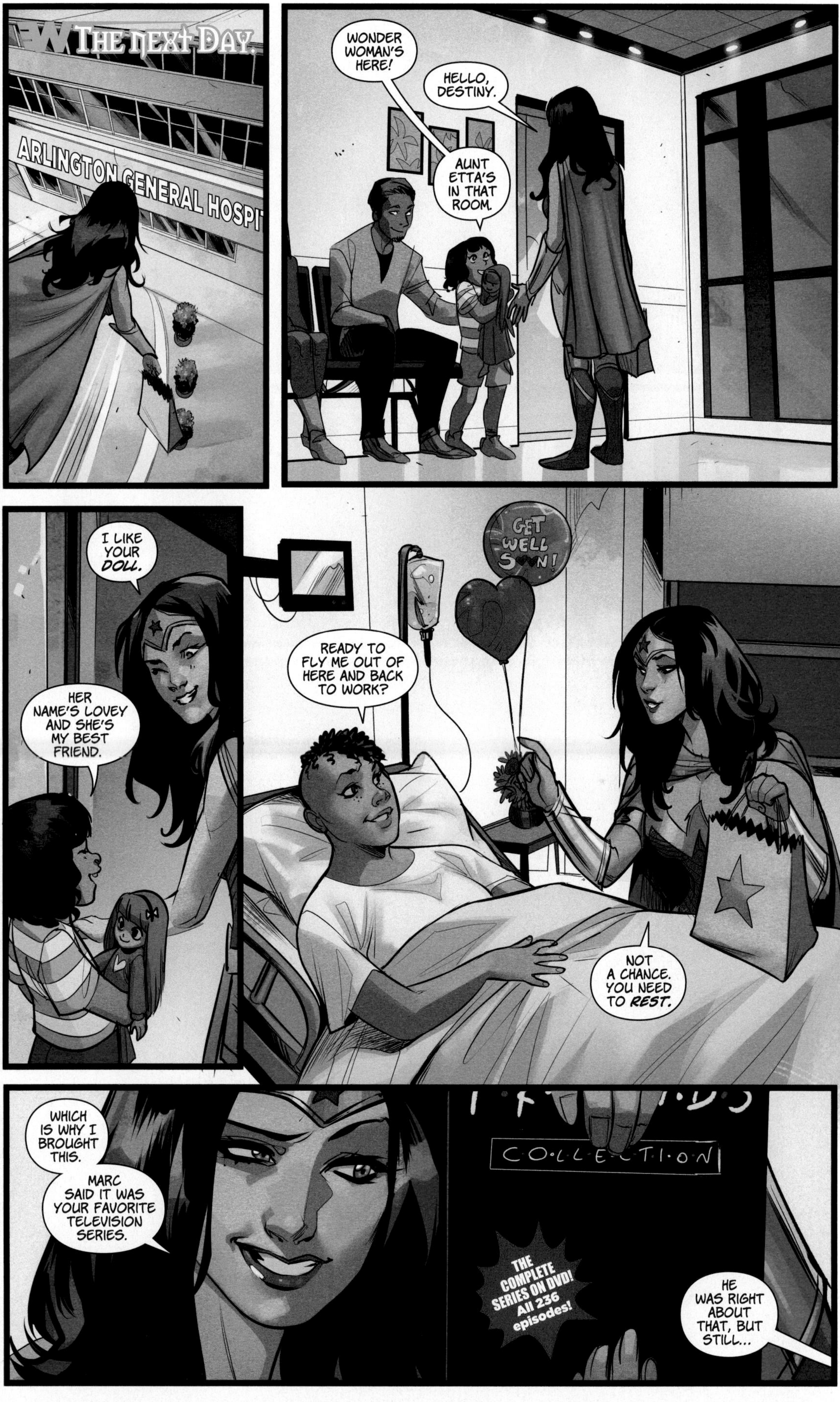
THE NEXT DAY.
ARLINGTON GENERAL HOSPIT
WONDER WOMAN'S HERE!
HELLO, DESTINY.
AUNT ETTA'S IN THAT ROOM.
I LIKE YOUR DOLL.
HER NAME'S LOVEY AND SHE'S MY BEST FRIEND.
GET WELL SOON!
READY TO FLY ME OUT OF HERE AND BACK TO WORK?
NOT A CHANCE. YOU NEED TO REST.
WHICH IS WHY I BROUGHT THIS.
MARC SAID IT WAS YOUR FAVORITE TELEVISION SERIES.
COLLECTION
THE COMPLETE SERIES ON DVD! All 236 episodes!
HE WAS RIGHT ABOUT THAT, BUT STILL...

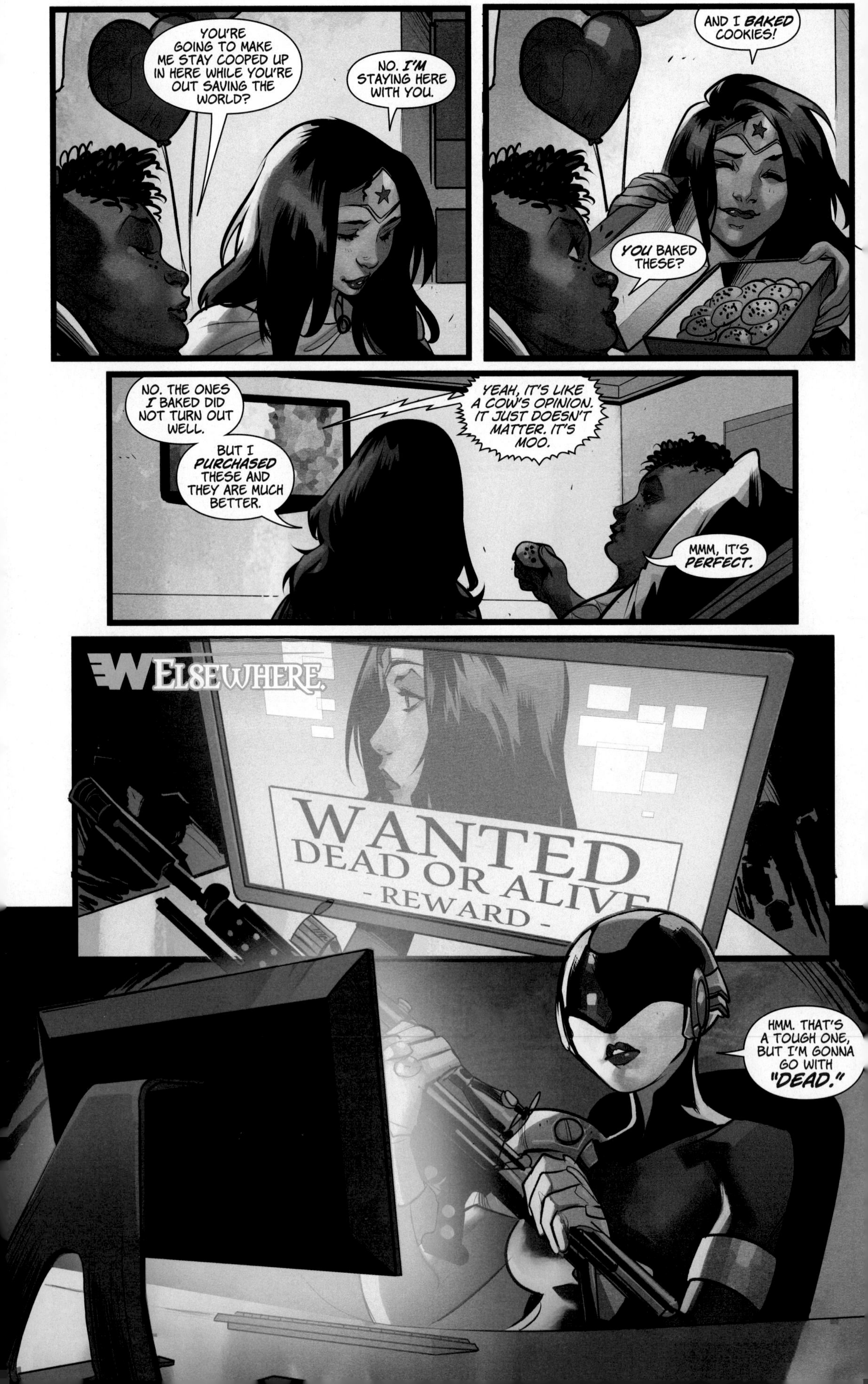
YOU'RE GOING TO MAKE ME STAY COOPED UP IN HERE WHILE YOU'RE OUT SAVING THE WORLD?
NO. I'M STAYING HERE WITH YOU.
AND I BAKED COOKIES!
YOU BAKED THESE?
NO. THE ONES I BAKED DID NOT TURN OUT WELL.
BUT I PURCHASED THESE AND THEY ARE MUCH BETTER.
YEAH, IT'S LIKE A COW'S OPINION. IT JUST DOESN'T MATTER. IT'S MOO.
MMM, IT'S PERFECT.
ELSEWHERE.
WANTED
DEAD OR ALIVE
- REWARD -
HMM. THAT'S A TOUGH ONE, BUT I'M GONNA GO WITH "DEAD."

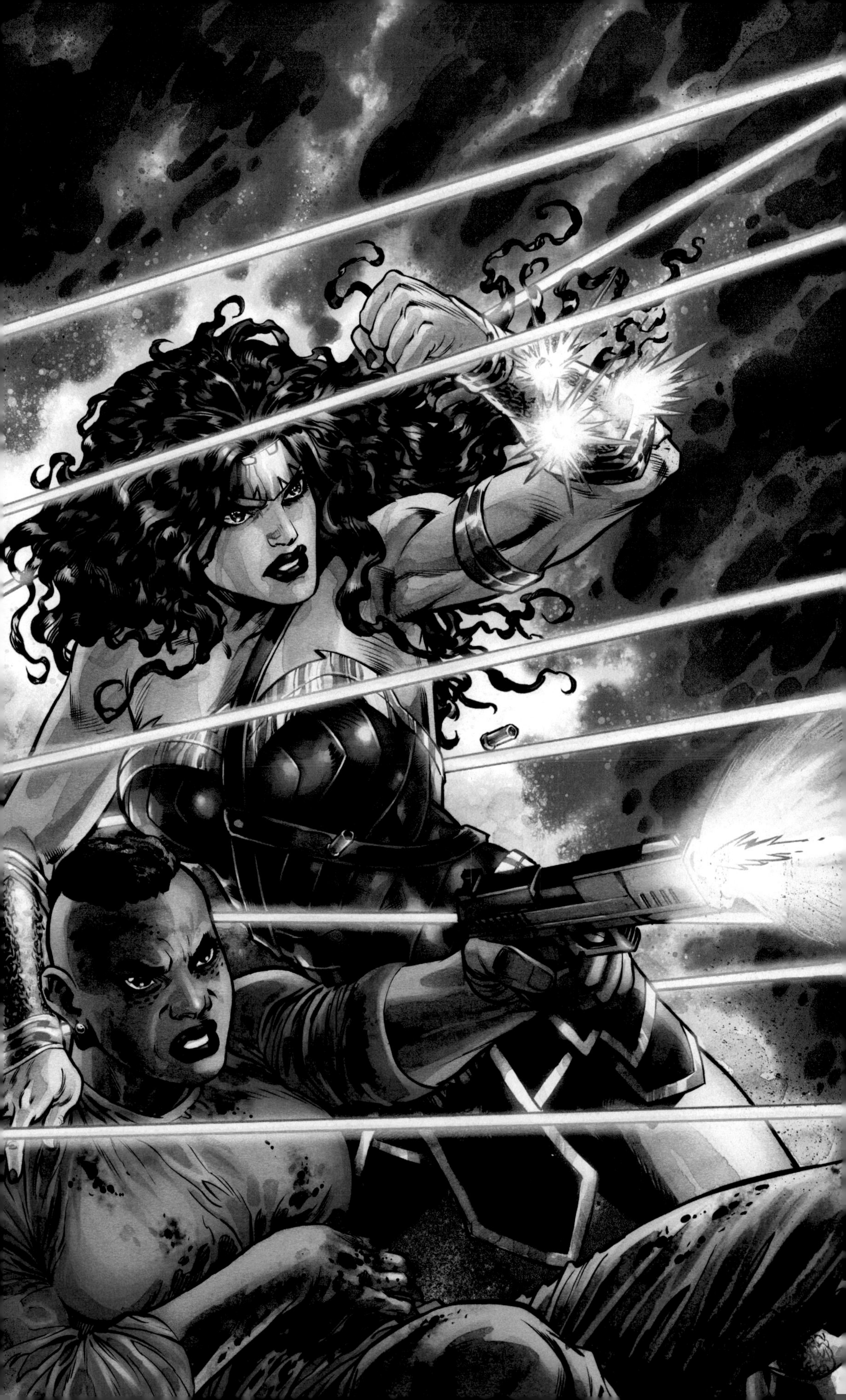

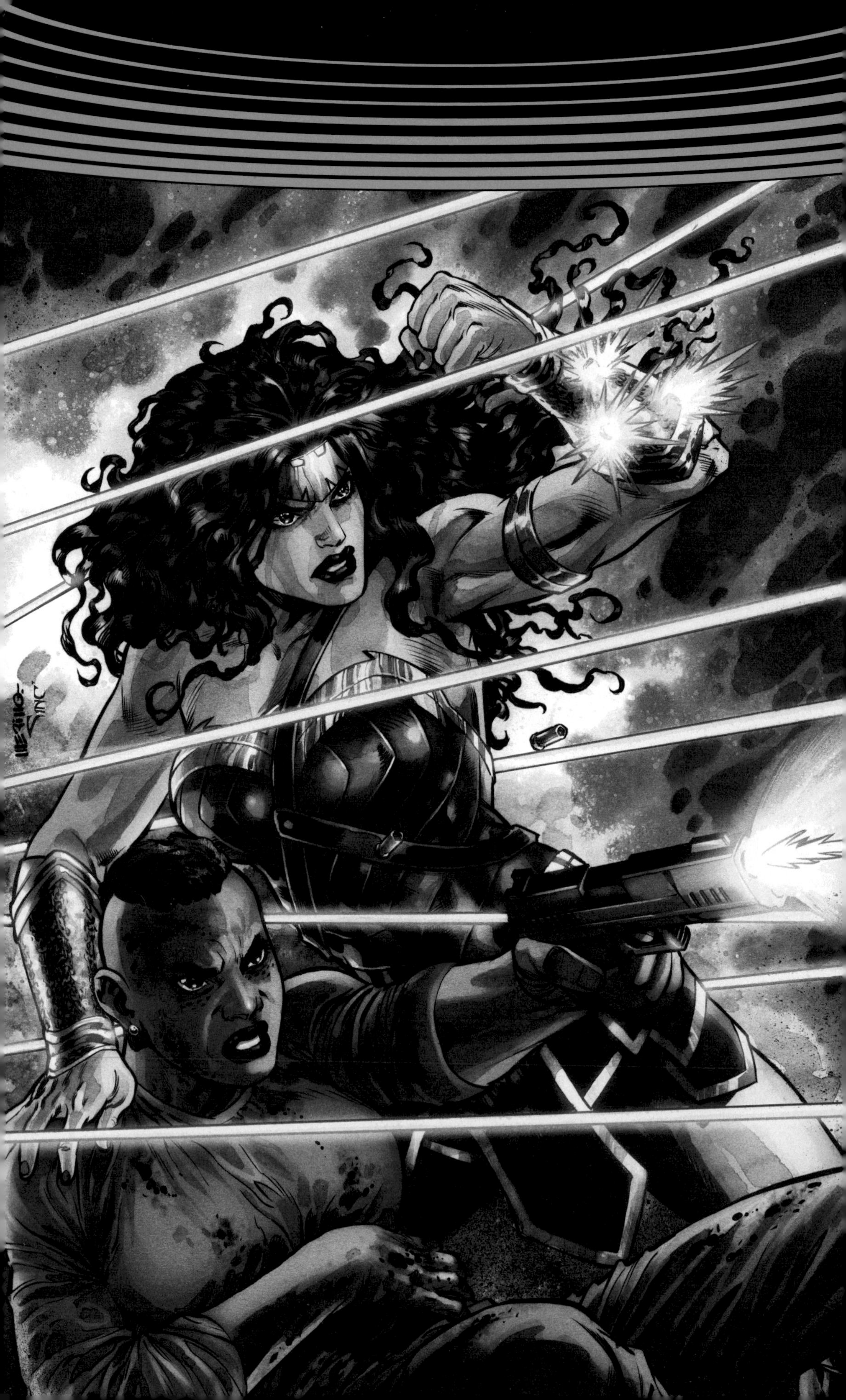

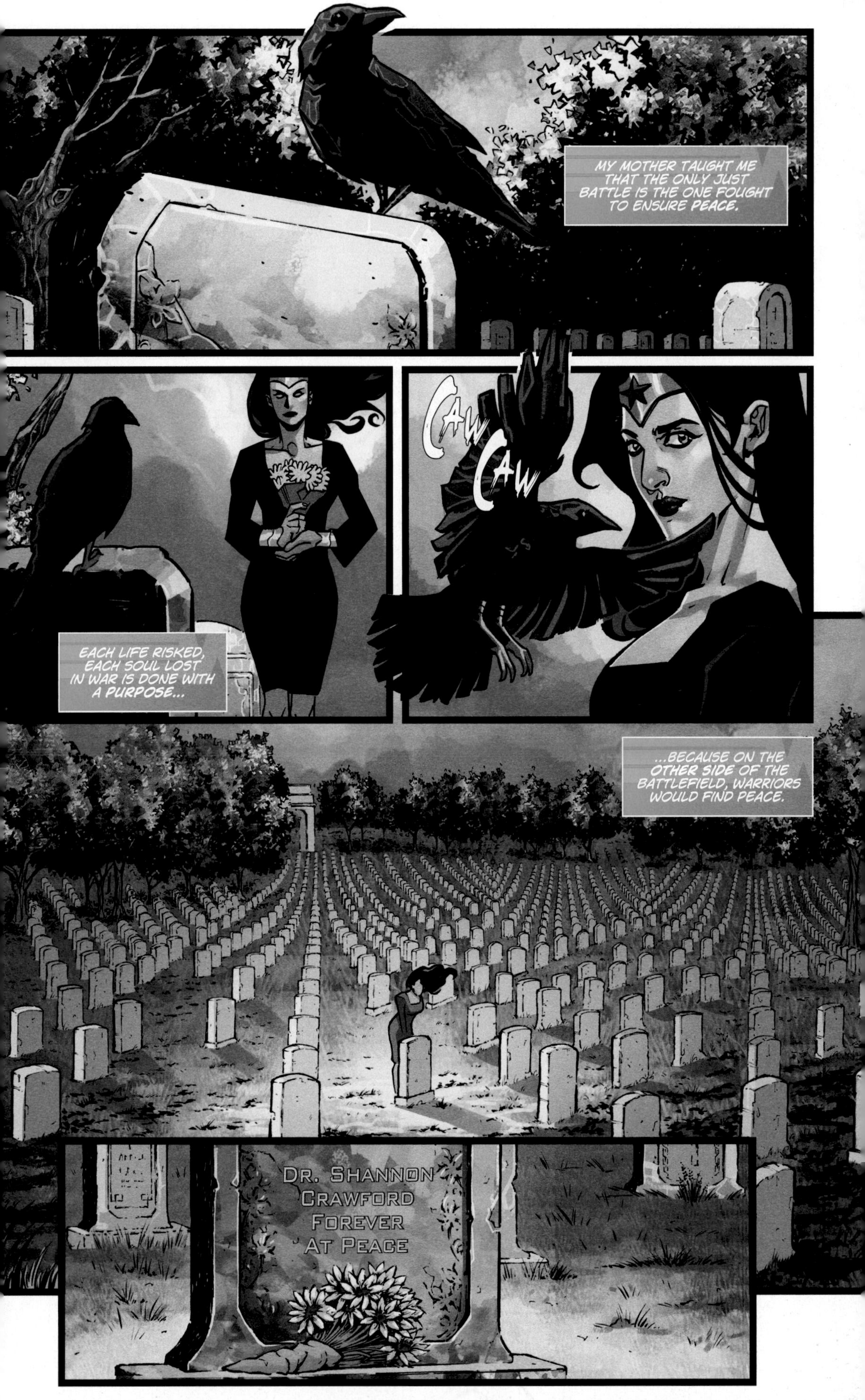
MY MOTHER TAUGHT ME THAT THE ONLY JUST BATTLE IS THE ONE FOUGHT TO ENSURE PEACE.
EACH LIFE RISKED, EACH SOUL LOST IN WAR IS DONE WITH A PURPOSE...
CAW
CAW
...BECAUSE ON THE OTHER SIDE OF THE BATTLEFIELD, WARRIORS WOULD FIND PEACE.
DR. SHANNON CRAWFORD FOREVER AT PEACE

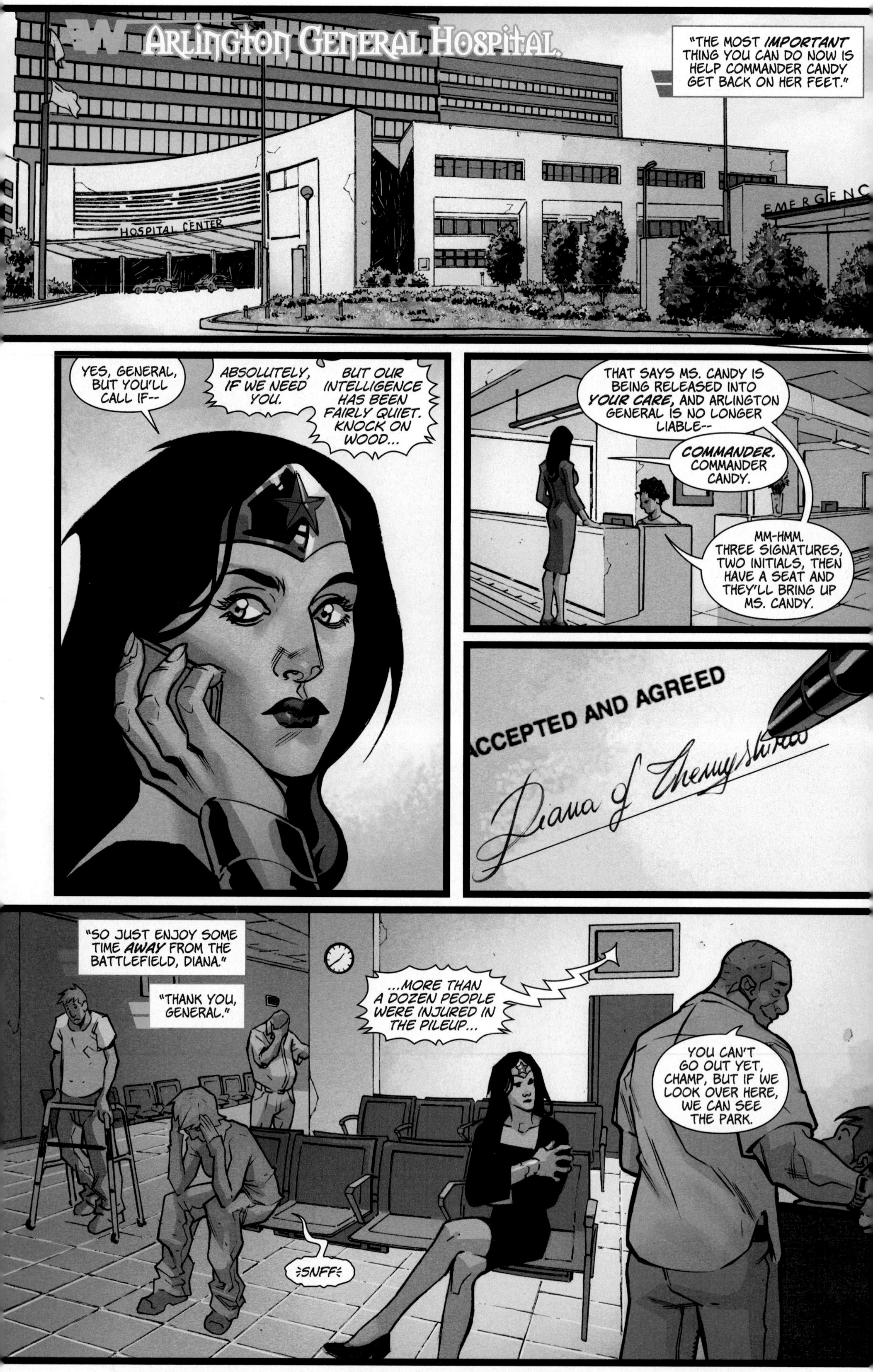

ARLINGTON GENERAL HOSPITAL.
"THE MOST IMPORTANT THING YOU CAN DO NOW IS HELP COMMANDER CANDY GET BACK ON HER FEET."
HOSPITAL CENTER
EMERGENC
YES, GENERAL, BUT YOU'LL CALL IF--
ABSOLUTELY, IF WE NEED YOU.
BUT OUR INTELLIGENCE HAS BEEN FAIRLY QUIET. KNOCK ON WOOD...
THAT SAYS MS. CANDY IS BEING RELEASED INTO YOUR CARE, AND ARLINGTON GENERAL IS NO LONGER LIABLE--
COMMANDER. COMMANDER CANDY.
MM-HMM. THREE SIGNATURES, TWO INITIALS, THEN HAVE A SEAT AND THEY'LL BRING UP MS. CANDY.
ACCEPTED AND AGREED
Diana of Themyscira
"SO JUST ENJOY SOME TIME AWAY FROM THE BATTLEFIELD, DIANA."
"THANK YOU, GENERAL."
...MORE THAN A DOZEN PEOPLE WERE INJURED IN THE PILEUP...
YOU CAN'T GO OUT YET, CHAMP, BUT IF WE LOOK OVER HERE, WE CAN SEE THE PARK.
SNFF

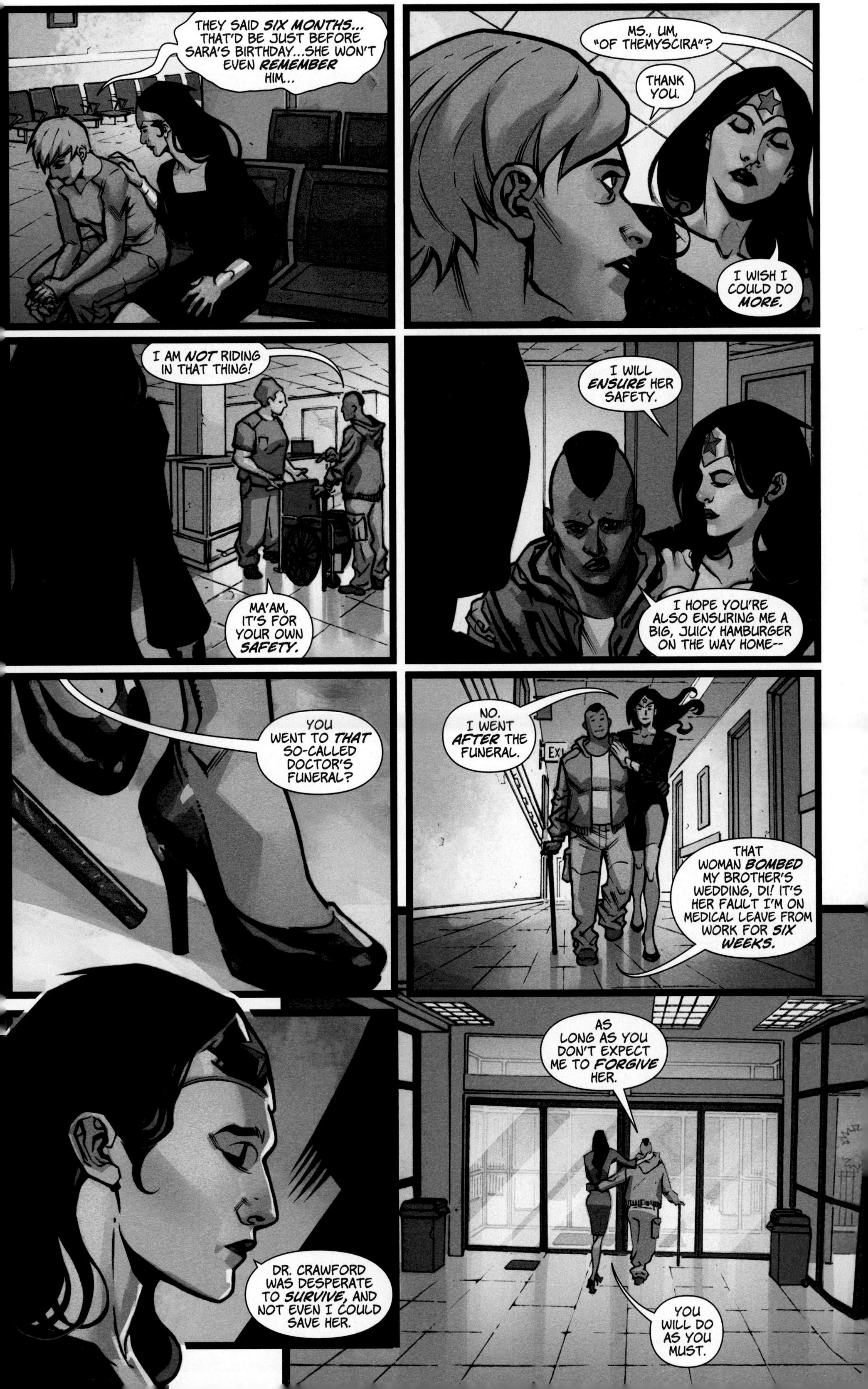
THEY SAID SIX MONTHS... THAT'D BE JUST BEFORE SARA'S BIRTHDAY...SHE WON'T EVEN REMEMBER HIM...
MS., UM, "OF THEMYSCIRA"?
THANK YOU.
I WISH I COULD DO MORE.
I AM NOT RIDING IN THAT THING!
MA'AM, IT'S FOR YOUR OWN SAFETY.
I WILL ENSURE HER SAFETY.
I HOPE YOU'RE ALSO ENSURING ME A BIG, JUICY HAMBURGER ON THE WAY HOME--
YOU WENT TO THAT SO-CALLED DOCTOR'S FUNERAL?
NO. I WENT AFTER THE FUNERAL.
THAT WOMAN BOMBED MY BROTHER'S WEDDING, DI! IT'S HER FAULT I'M ON MEDICAL LEAVE FROM WORK FOR SIX WEEKS.
DR. CRAWFORD WAS DESPERATE TO SURVIVE, AND NOT EVEN I COULD SAVE HER.
AS LONG AS YOU DON'T EXPECT ME TO FORGIVE HER.
YOU WILL DO AS YOU MUST.

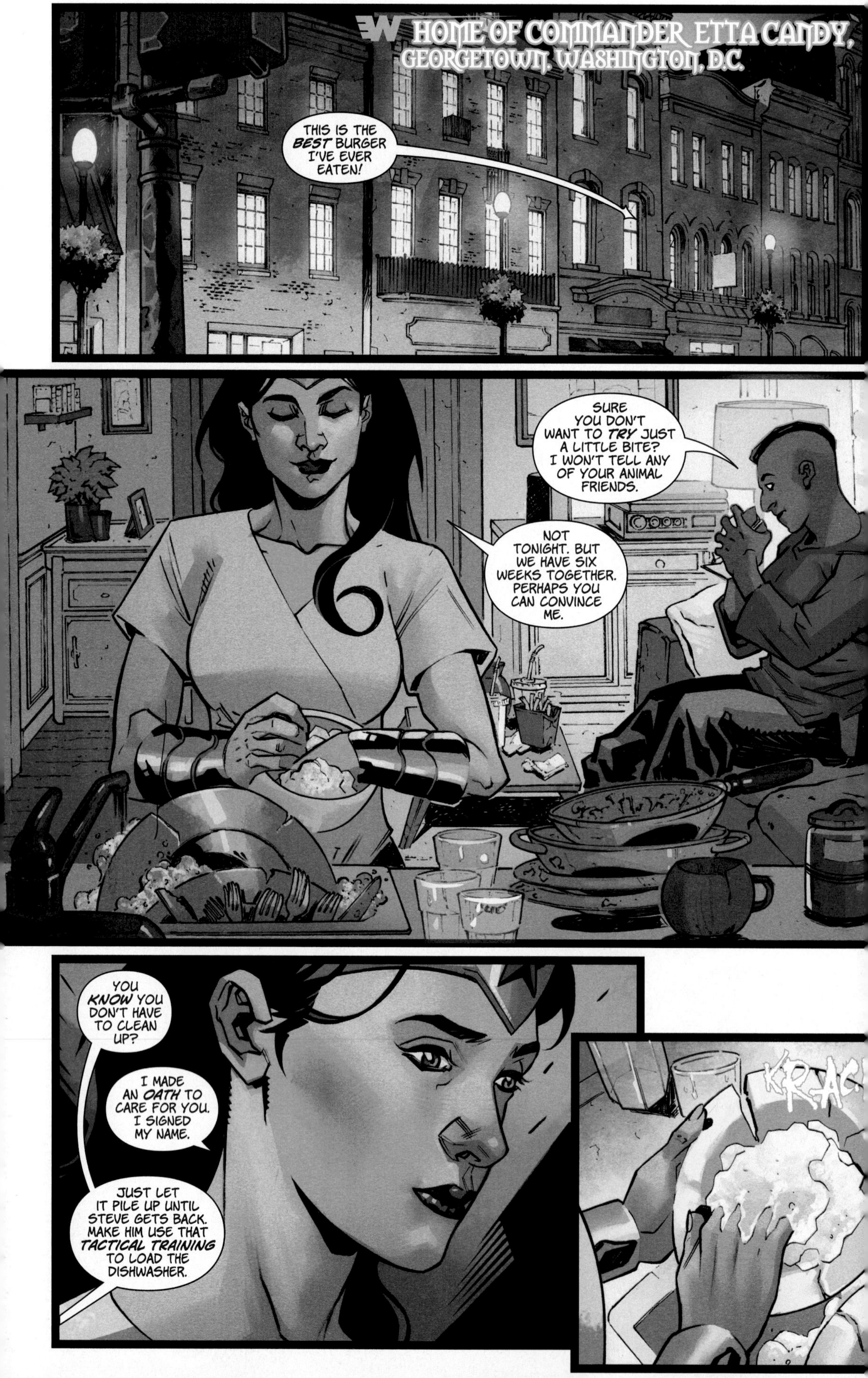
HOME OF COMMANDER ETTA CANDY, GEORGETOWN, WASHINGTON, D.C.
THIS IS THE BEST BURGER I'VE EVER EATEN!
SURE YOU DON'T WANT TO TRY JUST A LITTLE BITE? I WON'T TELL ANY OF YOUR ANIMAL FRIENDS.
NOT TONIGHT. BUT WE HAVE SIX WEEKS TOGETHER. PERHAPS YOU CAN CONVINCE ME.
YOU KNOW YOU DON'T HAVE TO CLEAN UP?
I MADE AN OATH TO CARE FOR YOU. I SIGNED MY NAME.
JUST LET IT PILE UP UNTIL STEVE GETS BACK. MAKE HIM USE THAT TACTICAL TRAINING TO LOAD THE DISHWASHER.

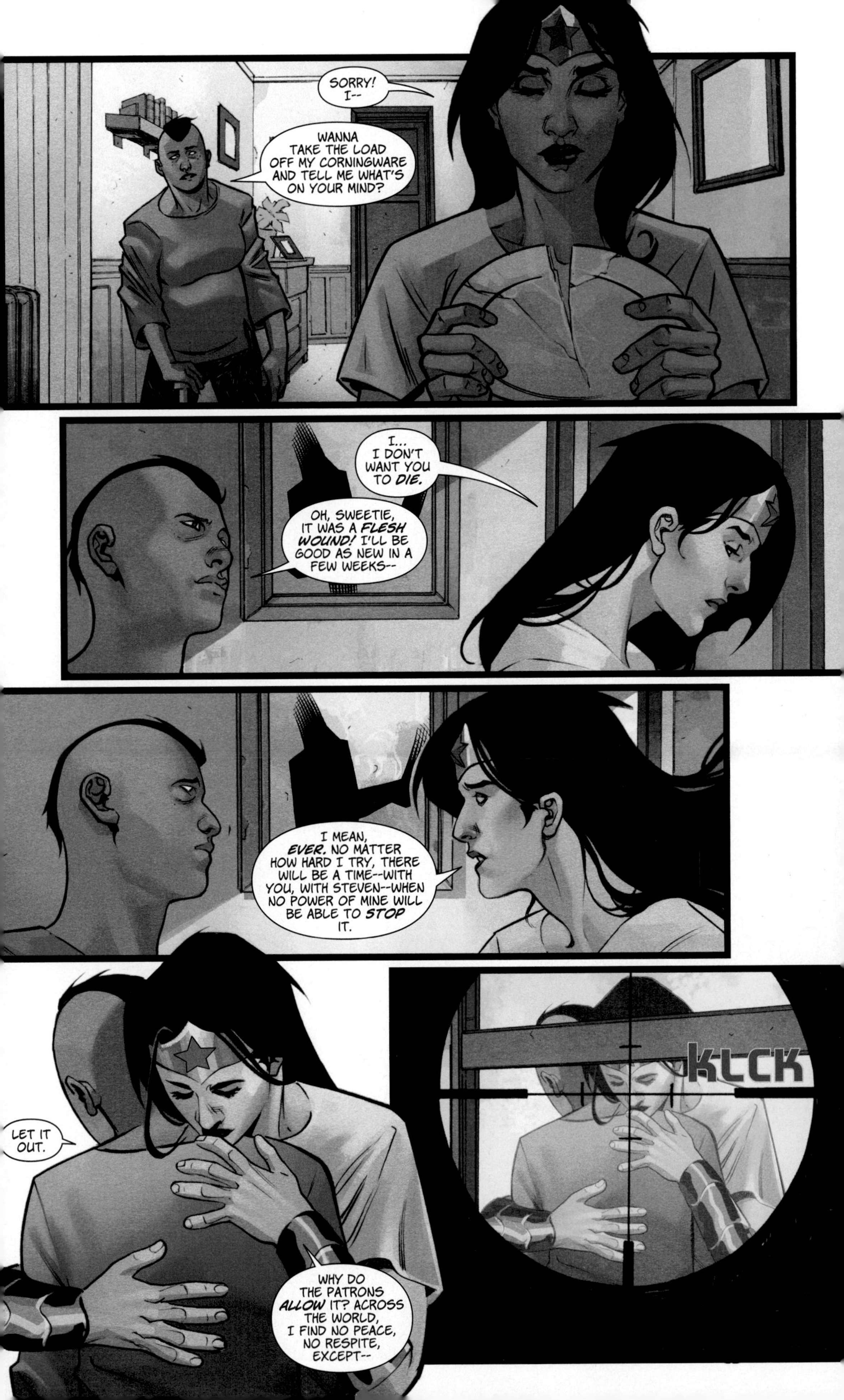
SORRY! I--
WANNA TAKE THE LOAD OFF MY CORNINGWARE AND TELL ME WHAT'S ON YOUR MIND?
I... I DON'T WANT YOU TO DIE.
OH, SWEETIE, IT WAS A FLESH WOUND! I'LL BE GOOD AS NEW IN A FEW WEEKS--
I MEAN, EVER. NO MATTER HOW HARD I TRY, THERE WILL BE A TIME--WITH YOU, WITH STEVEN--WHEN NO POWER OF MINE WILL BE ABLE TO STOP IT.
LET IT OUT.
WHY DO THE PATRONS ALLOW IT? ACROSS THE WORLD, I FIND NO PEACE, NO RESPITE, EXCEPT--
KLCK

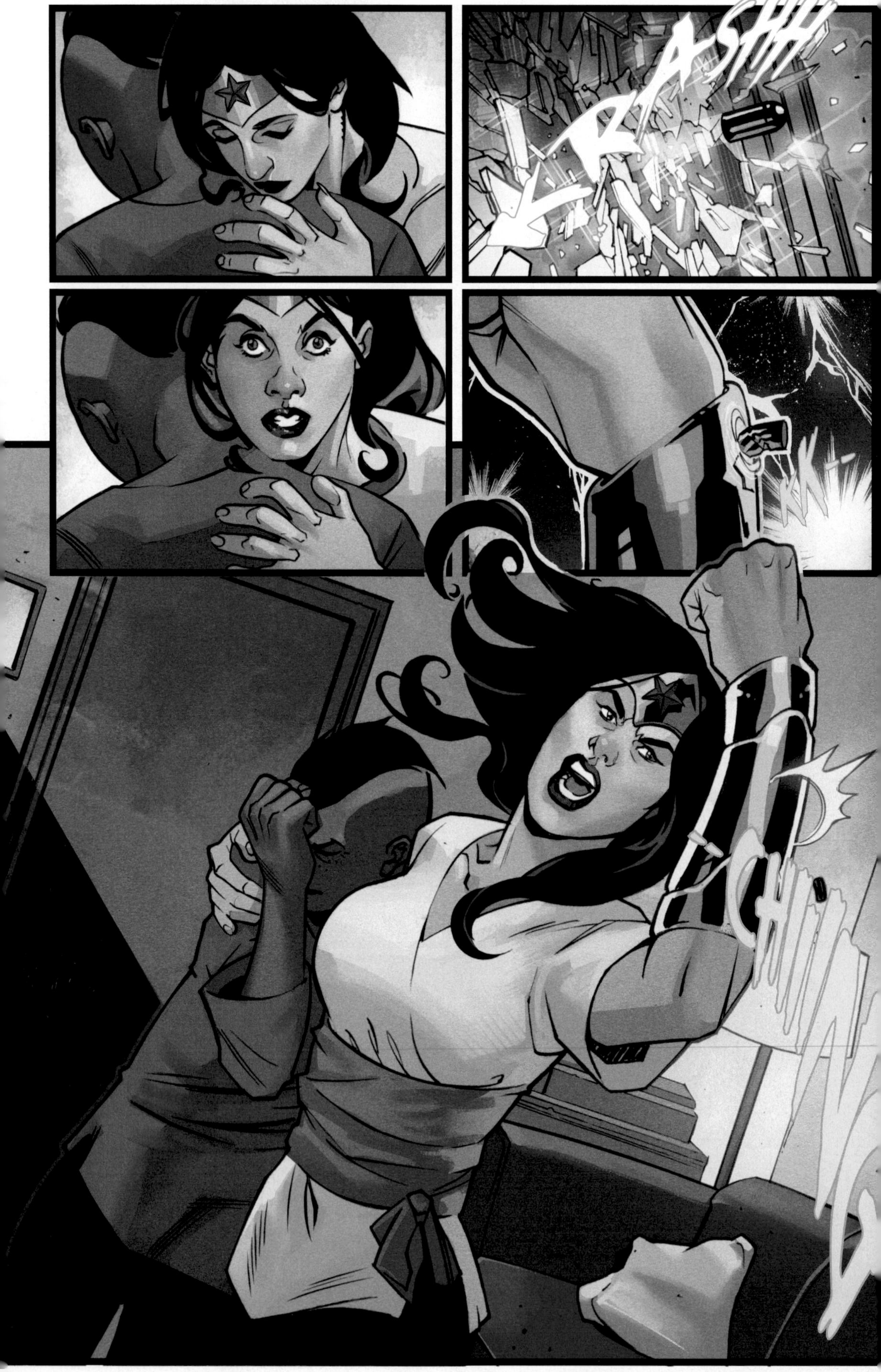
KRASHH
KK--

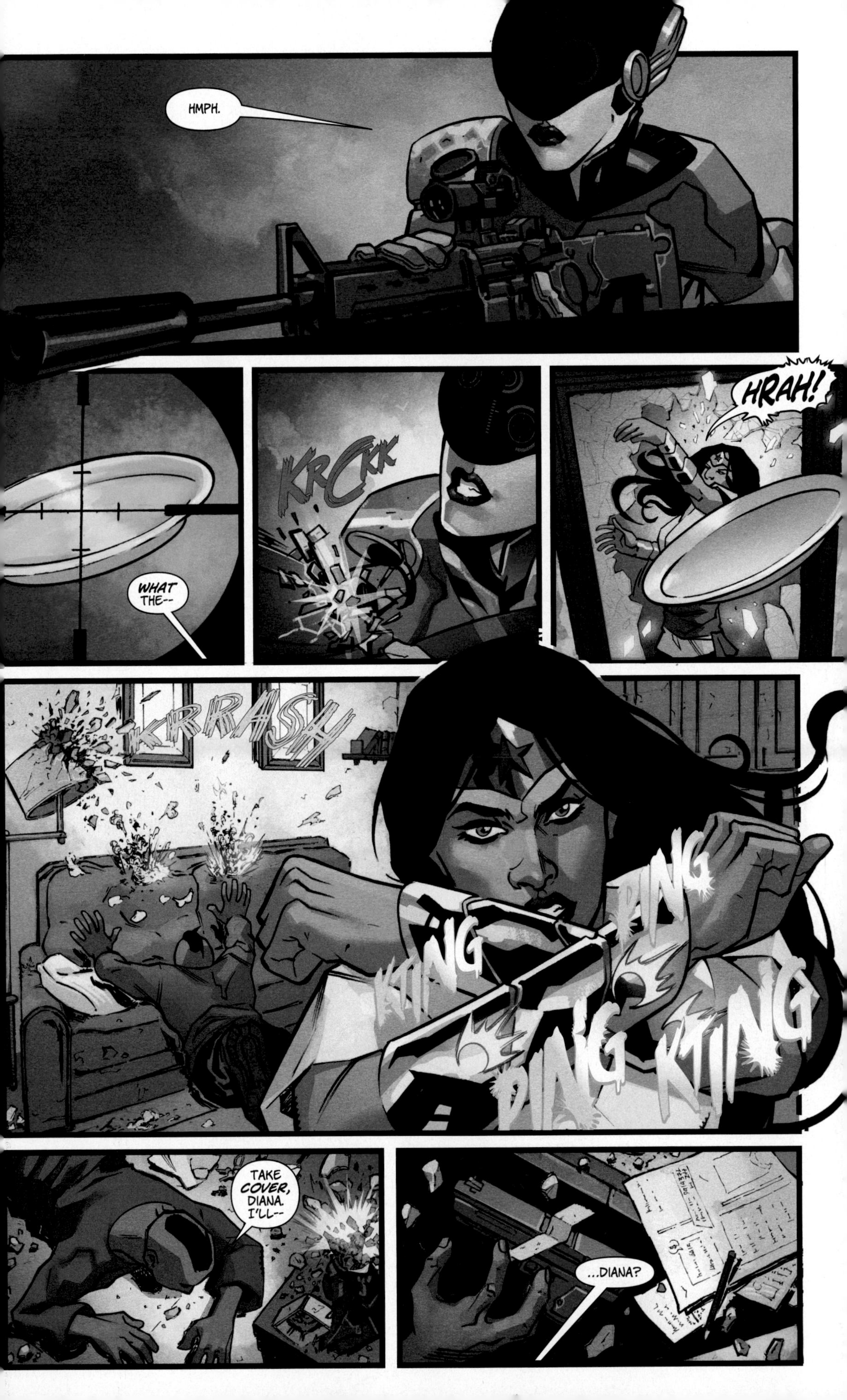
HMPH.
WHAT THE--
KRCKK
HRAH!
KRRASH
KTING
DING
DING KTING
TAKE COVER, DIANA. I'LL--
...DIANA?

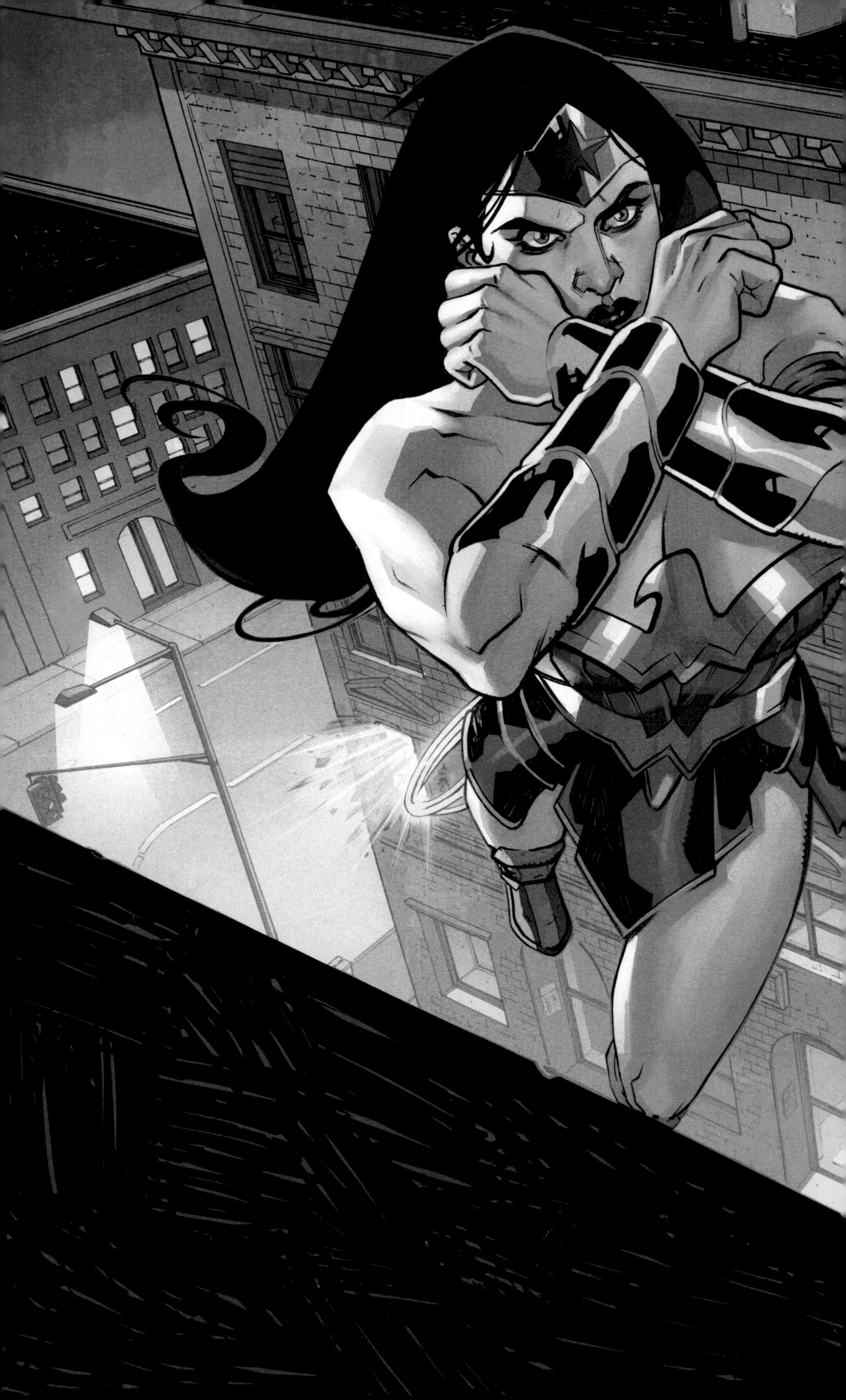

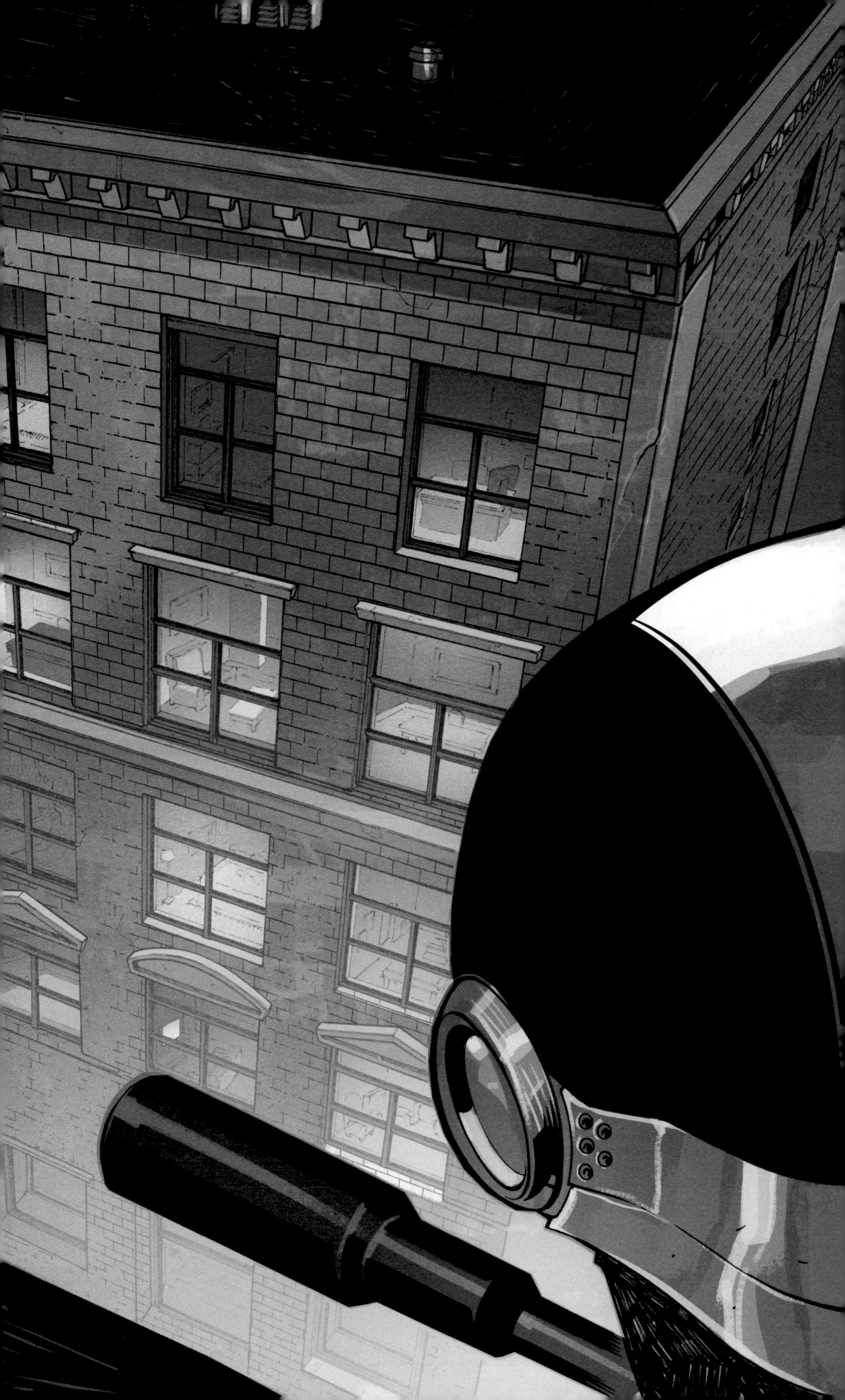

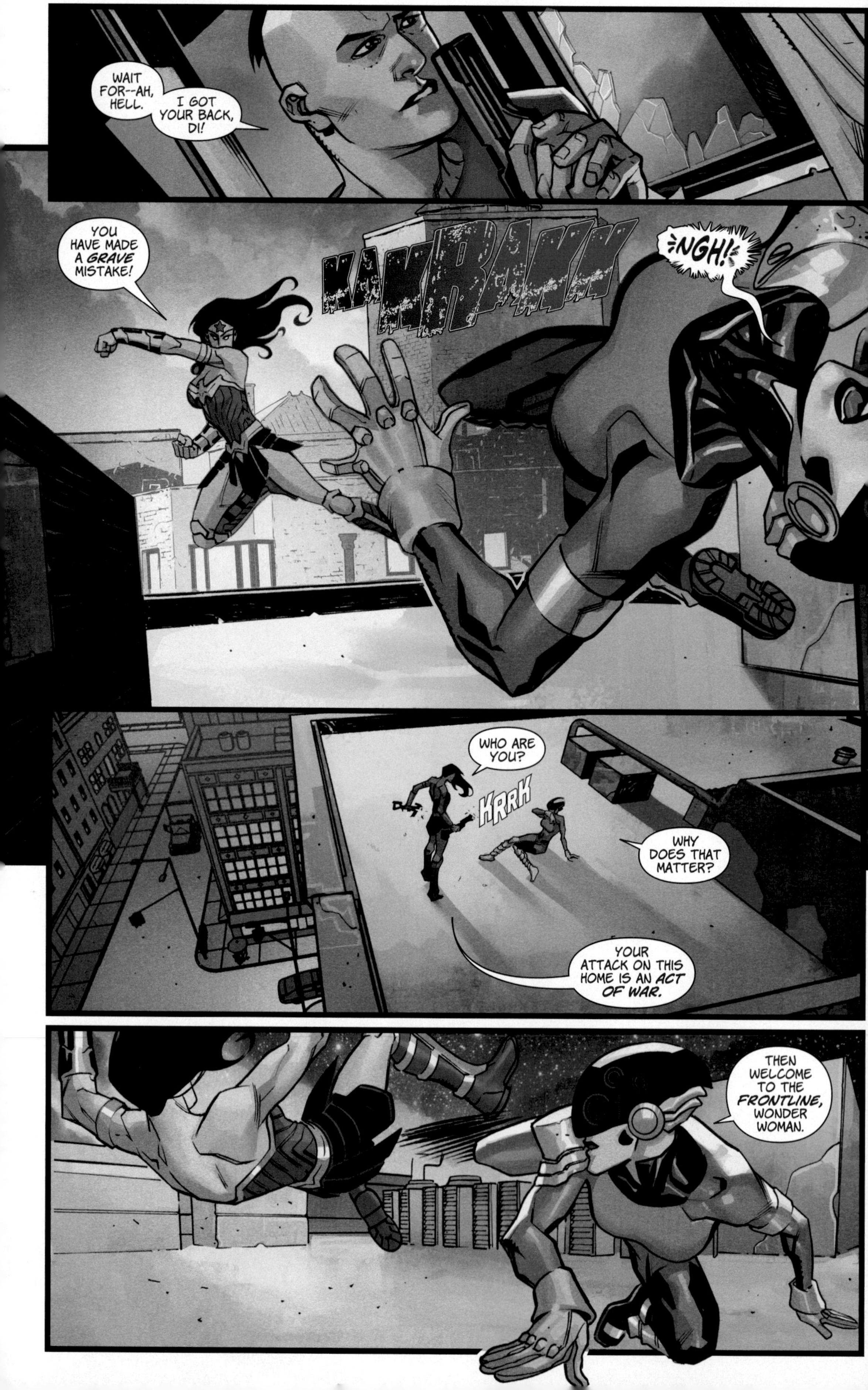

WAIT FOR--AH, HELL.
I GOT YOUR BACK, DI!
YOU HAVE MADE A *GRAVE* MISTAKE!
KAKRAKK
NGH!
WHO ARE YOU?
KRRK
WHY DOES THAT MATTER?
YOUR ATTACK ON THIS HOME IS AN *ACT OF WAR.*
THEN WELCOME TO THE *FRONTLINE,* WONDER WOMAN.

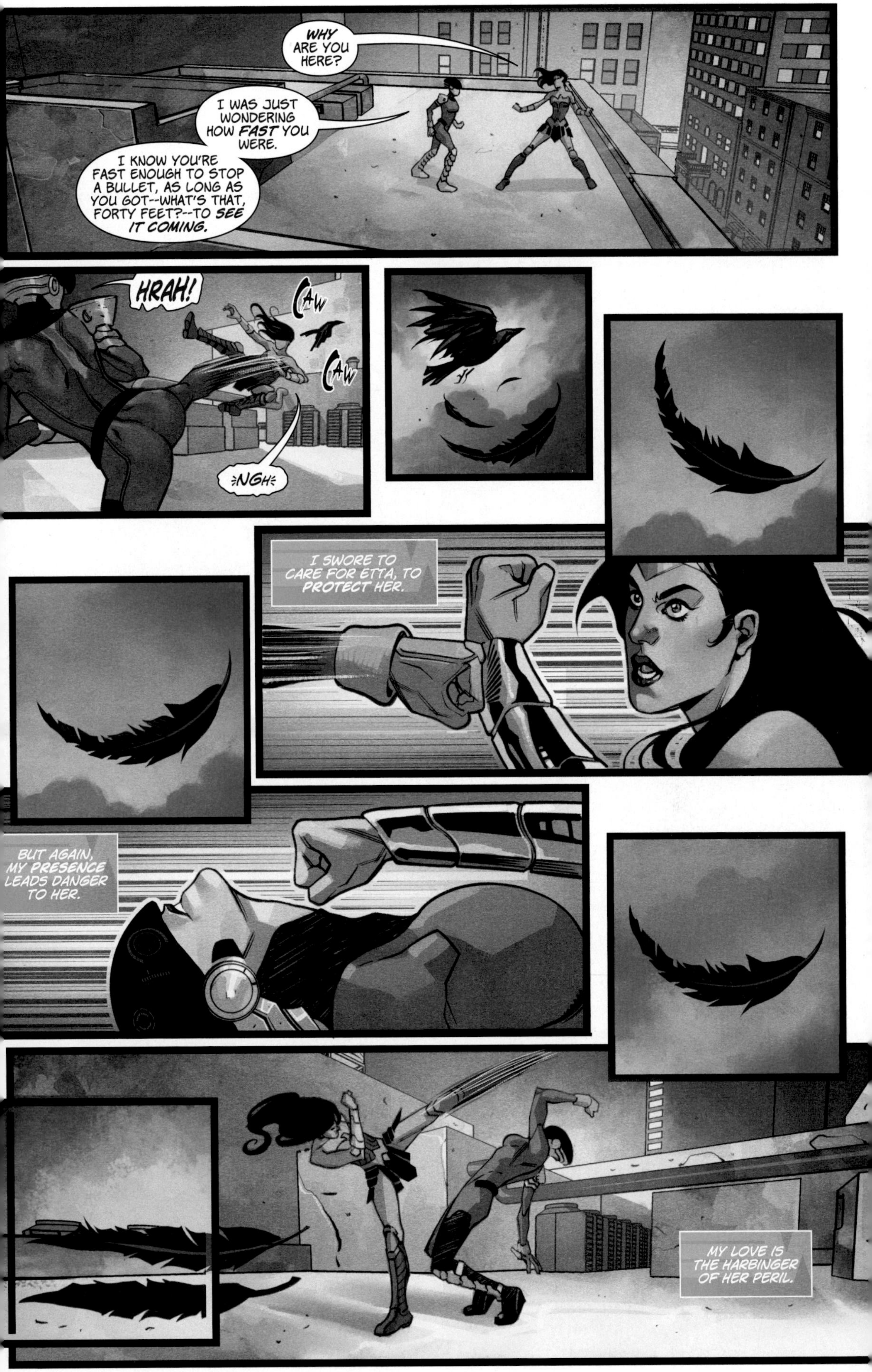

WHY ARE YOU HERE?
I WAS JUST WONDERING HOW FAST YOU WERE.
I KNOW YOU'RE FAST ENOUGH TO STOP A BULLET, AS LONG AS YOU GOT--WHAT'S THAT, FORTY FEET?--TO SEE IT COMING.
HRAH!
CAW
CAW
NGH
I SWORE TO CARE FOR ETTA, TO PROTECT HER.
BUT AGAIN, MY PRESENCE LEADS DANGER TO HER.
MY LOVE IS THE HARBINGER OF HER PERIL.

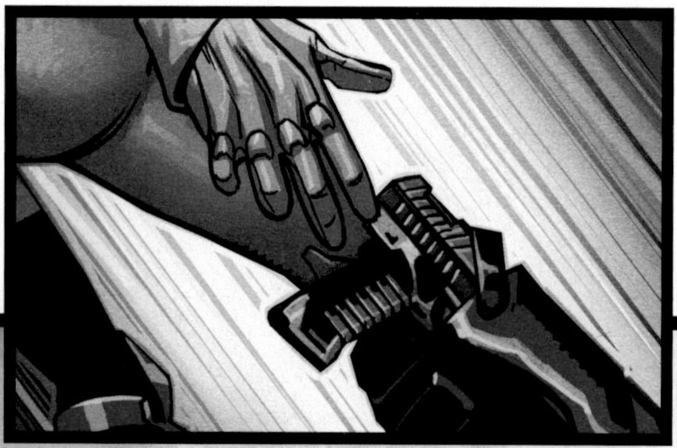

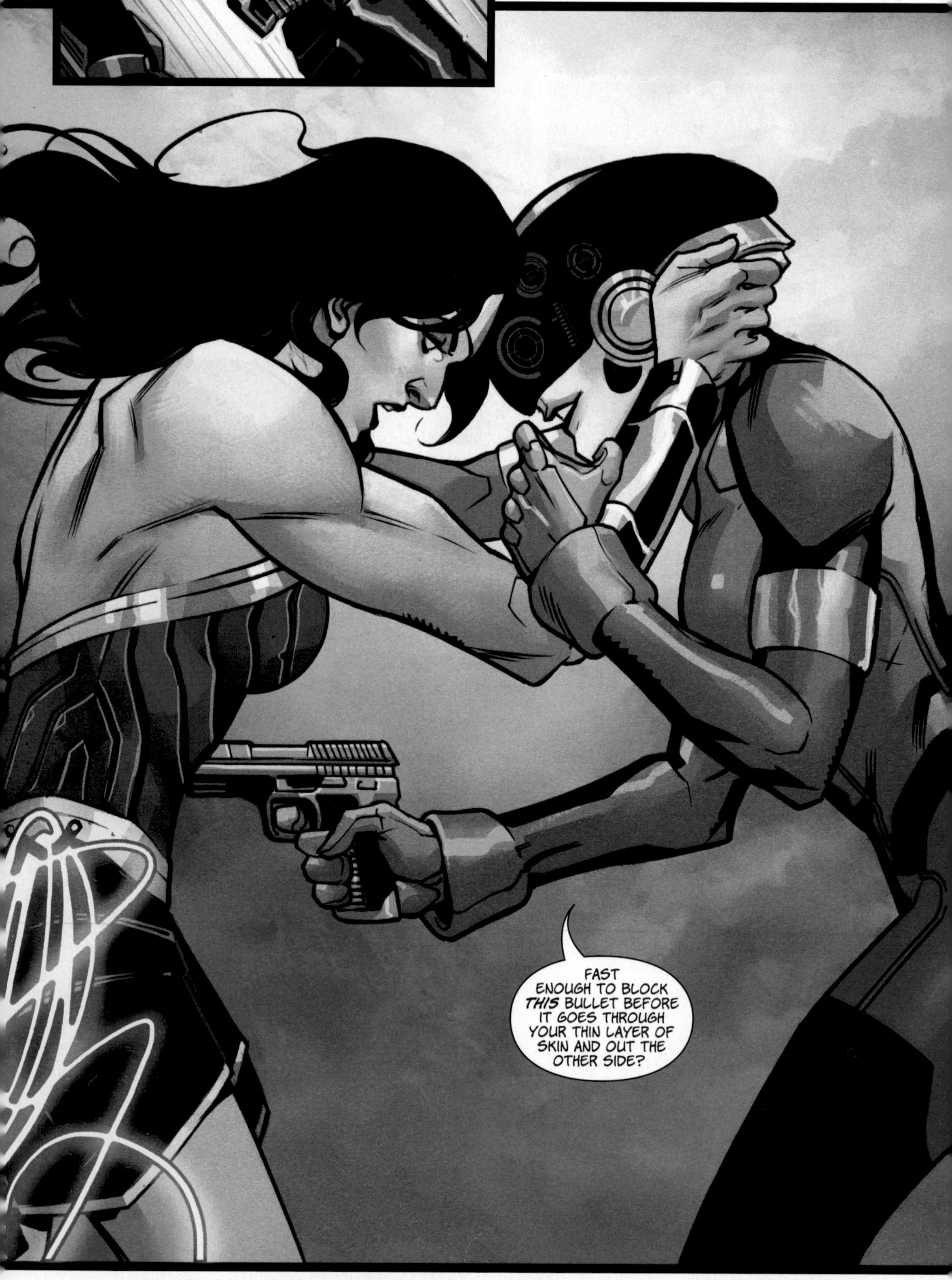
FAST ENOUGH TO BLOCK *THIS* BULLET BEFORE IT GOES THROUGH YOUR THIN LAYER OF SKIN AND OUT THE OTHER SIDE?

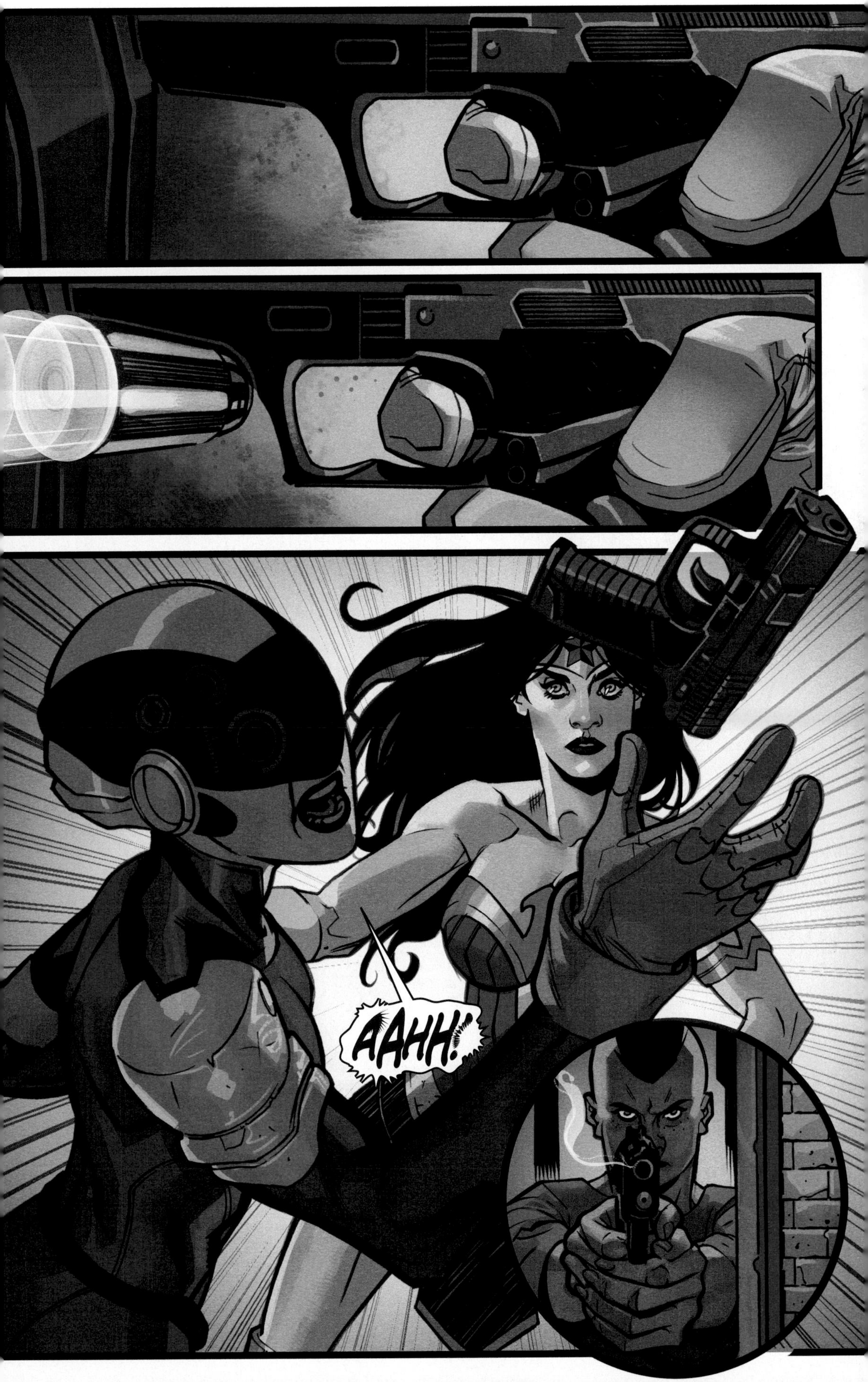
AAHH!

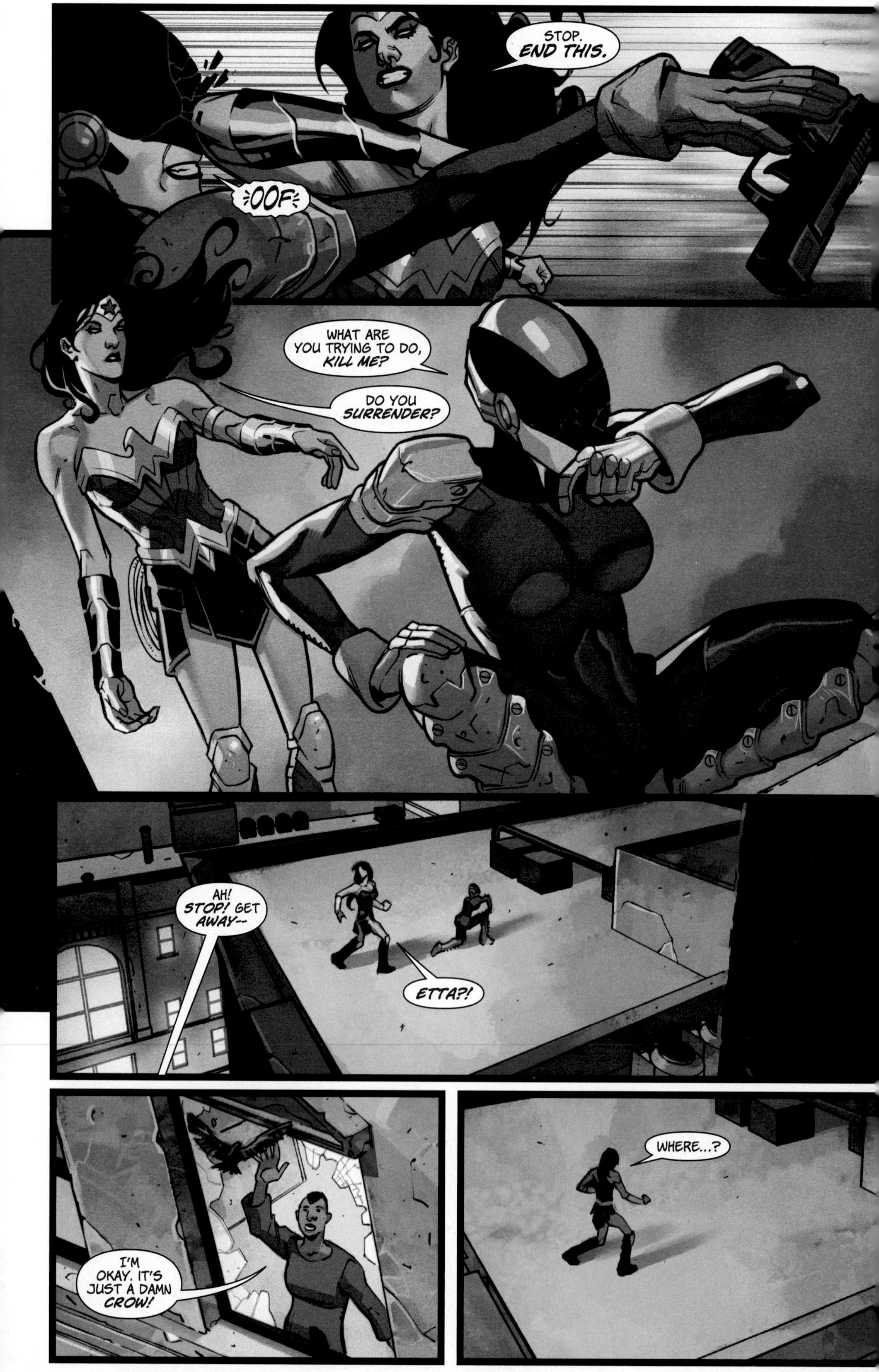
STOP.
END THIS.
OOF
WHAT ARE YOU TRYING TO DO, KILL ME?
DO YOU SURRENDER?
AH! STOP! GET AWAY--
ETTA?!
I'M OKAY. IT'S JUST A DAMN CROW!
WHERE...?

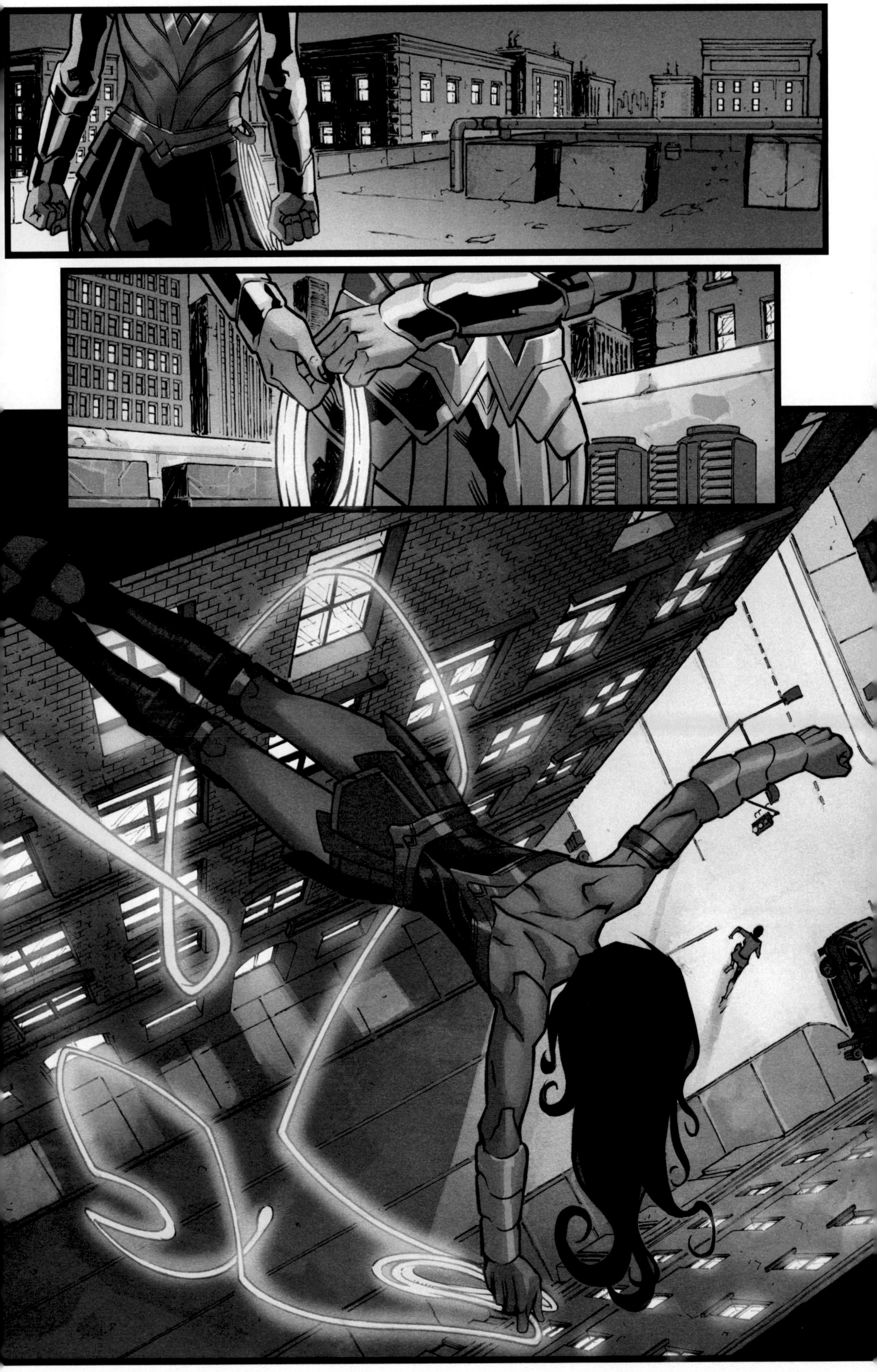

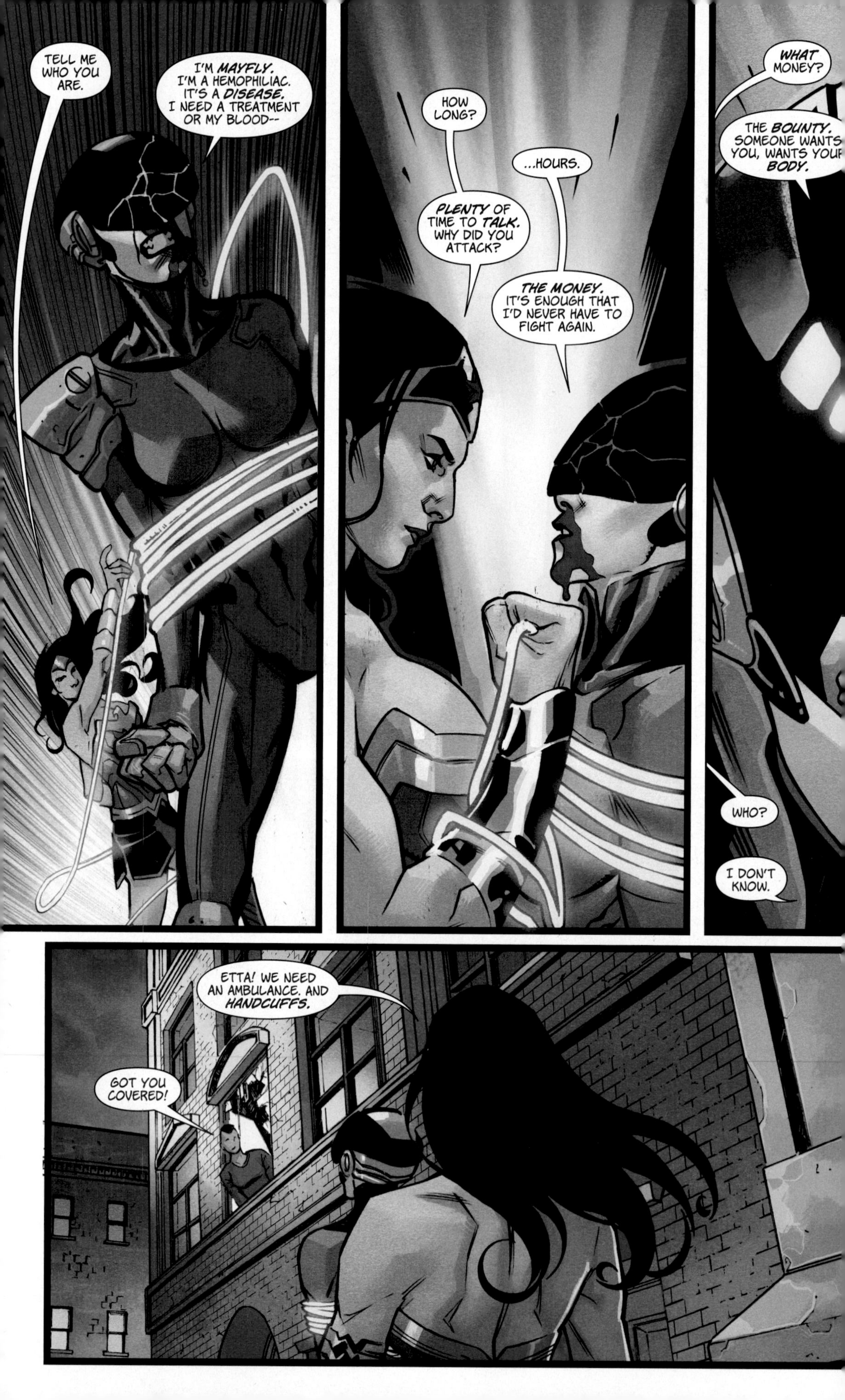
TELL ME WHO YOU ARE.
I'M MAYFLY. I'M A HEMOPHILIAC. IT'S A DISEASE. I NEED A TREATMENT OR MY BLOOD--
HOW LONG?
...HOURS.
PLENTY OF TIME TO TALK. WHY DID YOU ATTACK?
THE MONEY. IT'S ENOUGH THAT I'D NEVER HAVE TO FIGHT AGAIN.
WHAT MONEY?
THE BOUNTY. SOMEONE WANTS YOU, WANTS YOUR BODY.
WHO?
I DON'T KNOW.
ETTA! WE NEED AN AMBULANCE. AND HANDCUFFS.
GOT YOU COVERED!

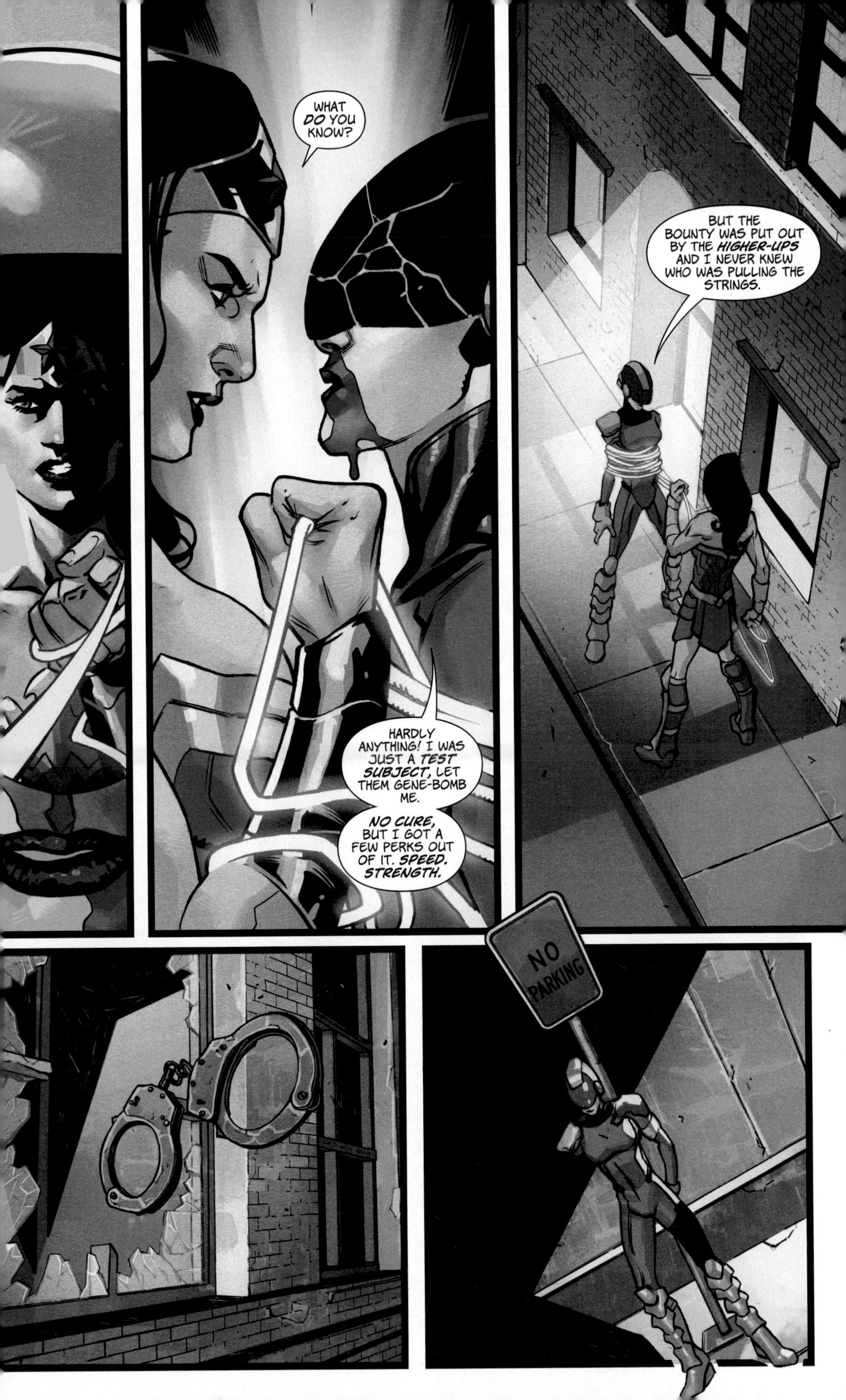

WHAT DO YOU KNOW?
HARDLY ANYTHING! I WAS JUST A TEST SUBJECT, LET THEM GENE-BOMB ME.
NO CURE, BUT I GOT A FEW PERKS OUT OF IT. SPEED. STRENGTH.
BUT THE BOUNTY WAS PUT OUT BY THE HIGHER-UPS AND I NEVER KNEW WHO WAS PULLING THE STRINGS.
NO PARKING

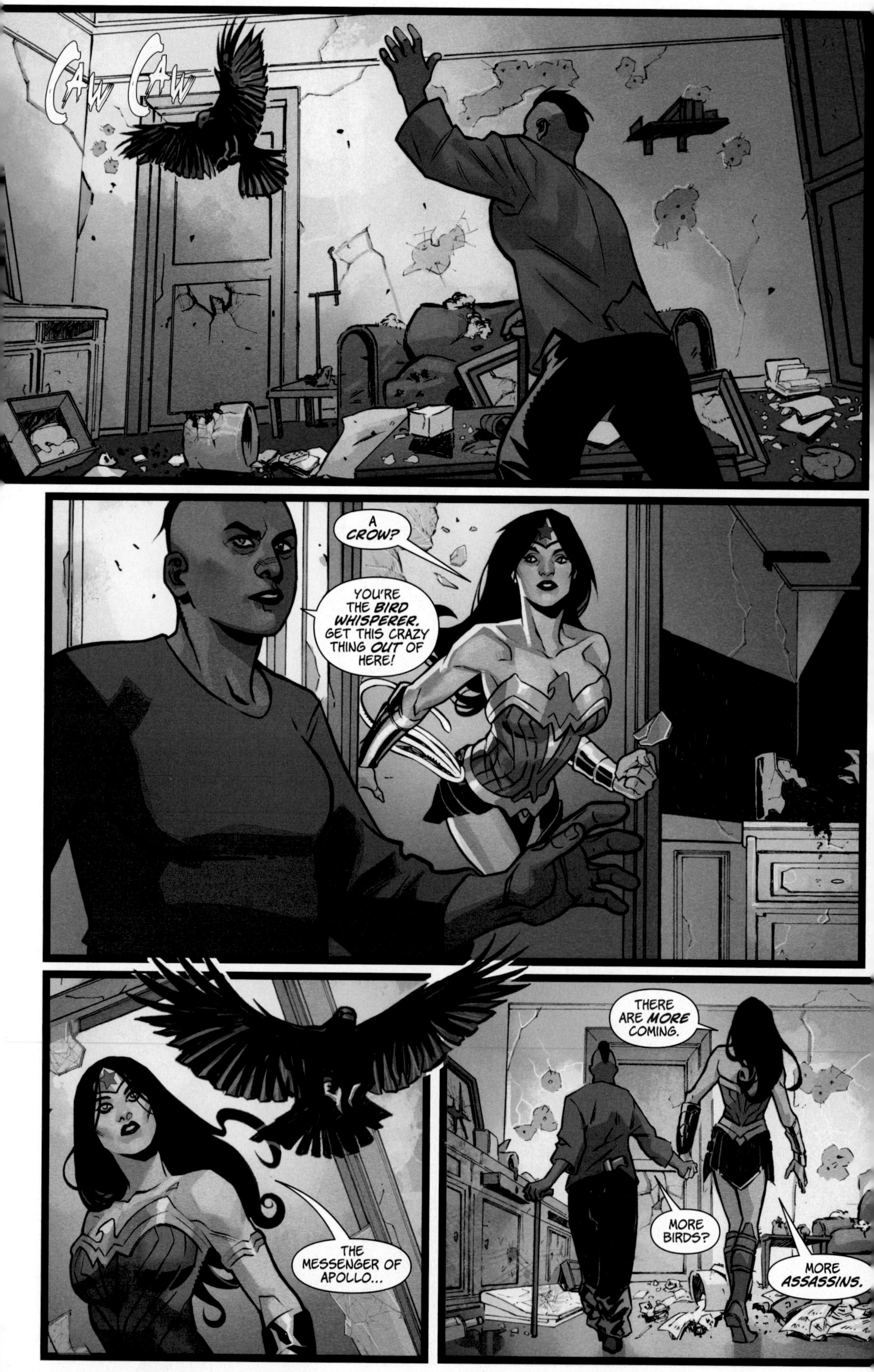
CAW CAW
A CROW?
YOU'RE THE BIRD WHISPERER. GET THIS CRAZY THING OUT OF HERE!
THE MESSENGER OF APOLLO...
THERE ARE MORE COMING.
MORE BIRDS?
MORE ASSASSINS.

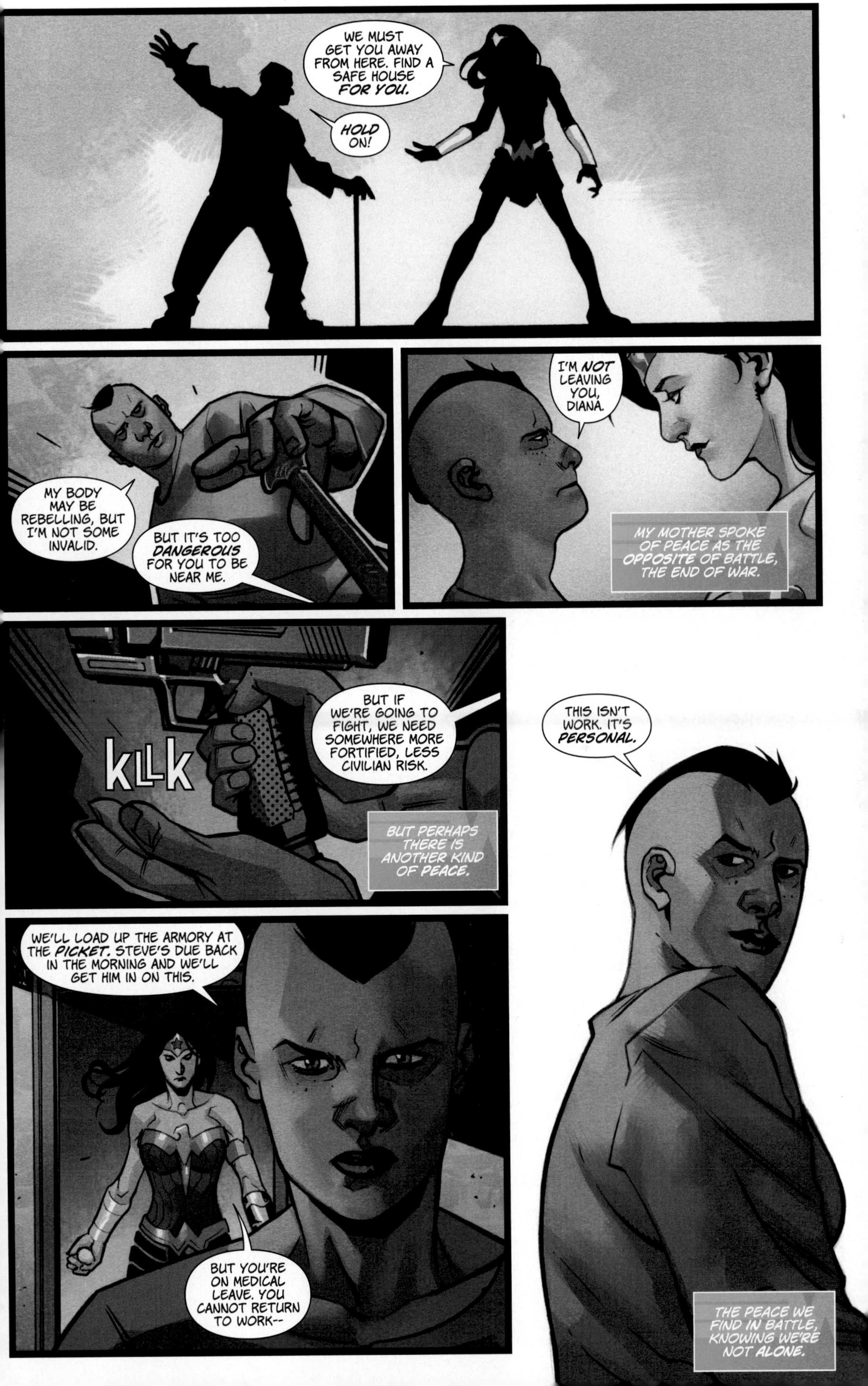
WE MUST GET YOU AWAY FROM HERE. FIND A SAFE HOUSE FOR YOU.
HOLD ON!
MY BODY MAY BE REBELLING, BUT I'M NOT SOME INVALID.
BUT IT'S TOO DANGEROUS FOR YOU TO BE NEAR ME.
I'M NOT LEAVING YOU, DIANA.
MY MOTHER SPOKE OF PEACE AS THE OPPOSITE OF BATTLE, THE END OF WAR.
KLLK
BUT IF WE'RE GOING TO FIGHT, WE NEED SOMEWHERE MORE FORTIFIED, LESS CIVILIAN RISK.
BUT PERHAPS THERE IS ANOTHER KIND OF PEACE.
WE'LL LOAD UP THE ARMORY AT THE PICKET. STEVE'S DUE BACK IN THE MORNING AND WE'LL GET HIM IN ON THIS.
BUT YOU'RE ON MEDICAL LEAVE. YOU CANNOT RETURN TO WORK--
THIS ISN'T WORK. IT'S PERSONAL.
THE PEACE WE FIND IN BATTLE, KNOWING WE'RE NOT ALONE.

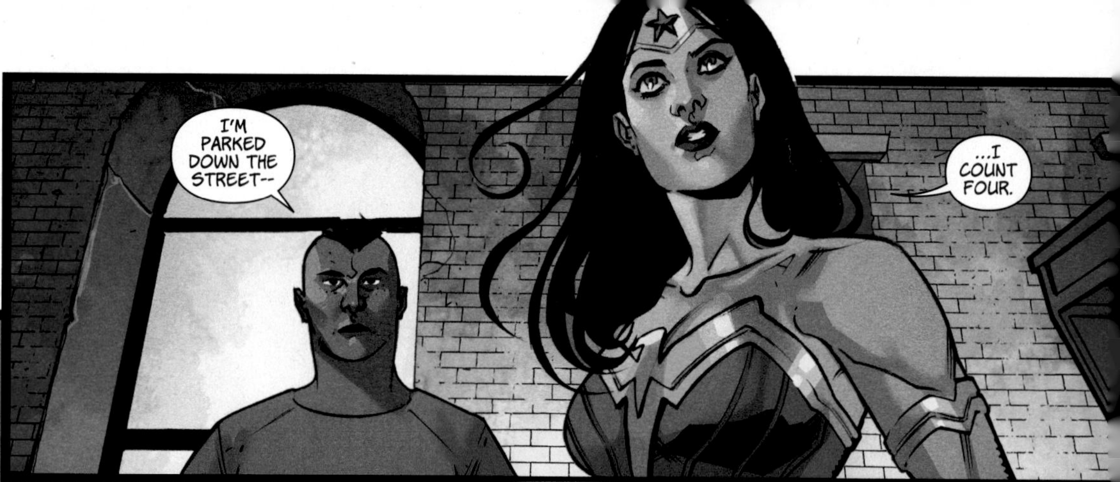
I'M PARKED DOWN THE STREET--
...I COUNT FOUR.

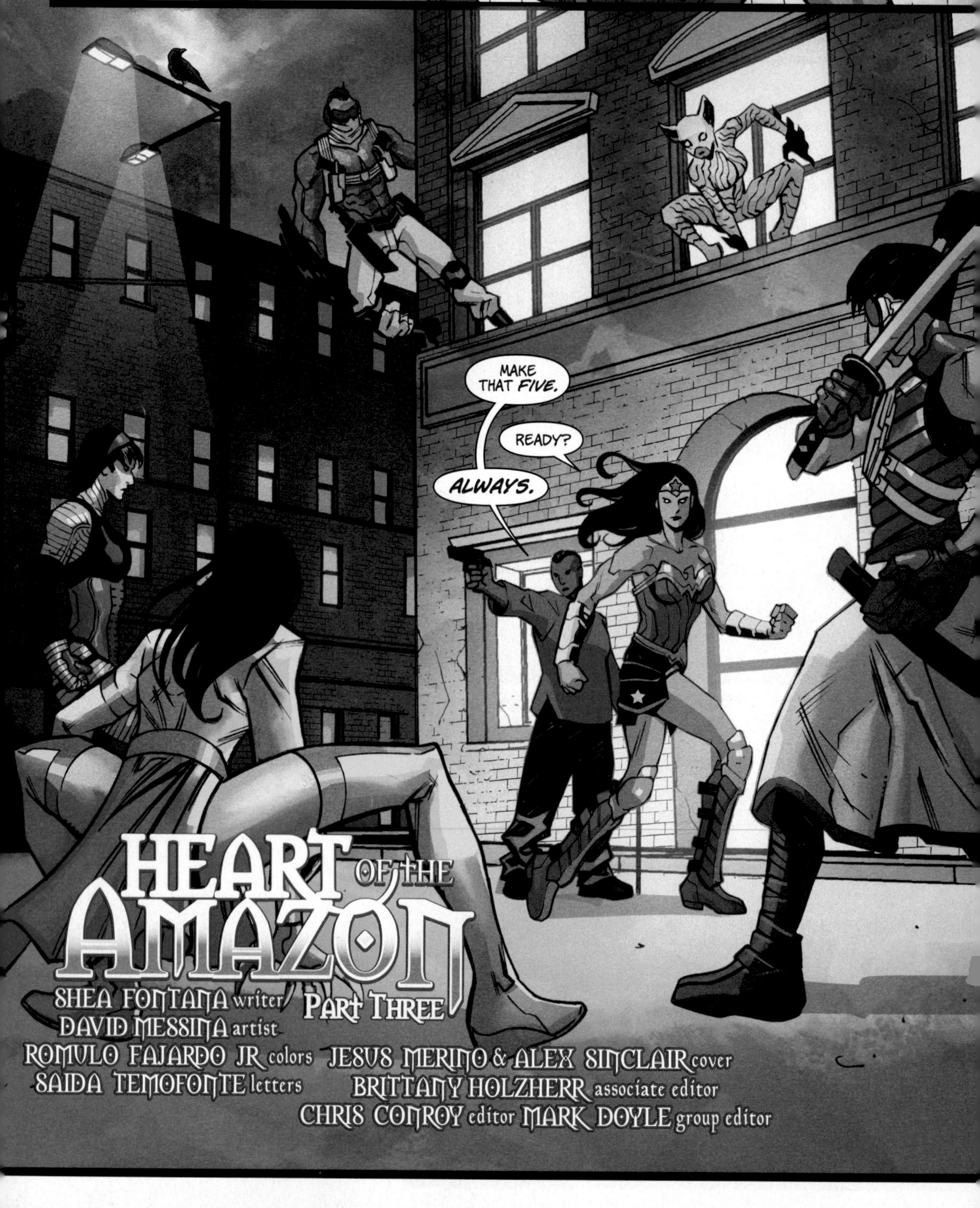
MAKE THAT FIVE.
READY?
ALWAYS.
HEART OF THE AMAZON
PART THREE
SHEA FONTANA writer
DAVID MESSINA artist
ROMULO FAJARDO JR colors
SAIDA TEMOFONTE letters
JESUS MERINO & ALEX SINCLAIR cover
BRITTANY HOLZHERR associate editor
CHRIS CONROY editor MARK DOYLE group editor

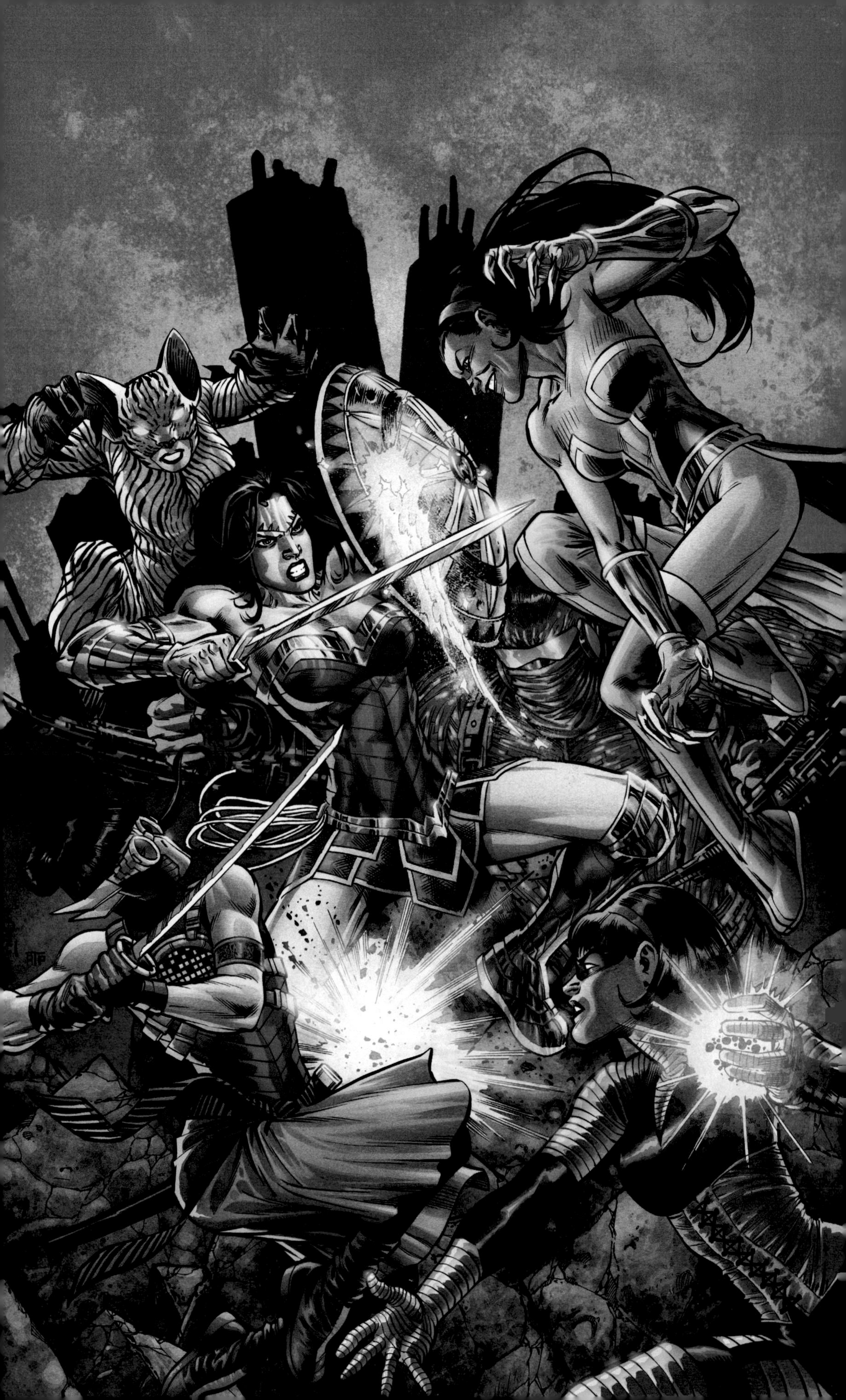

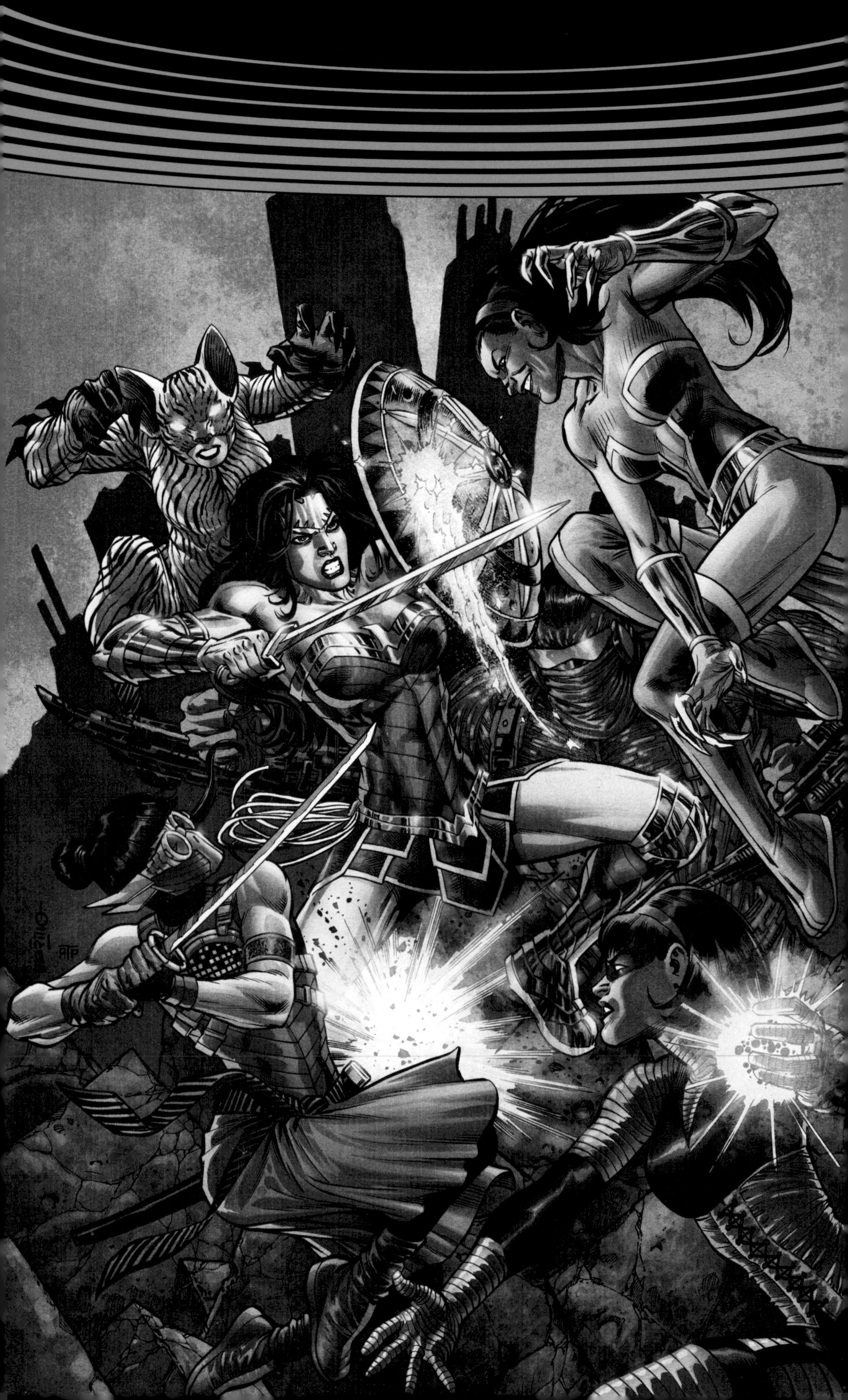

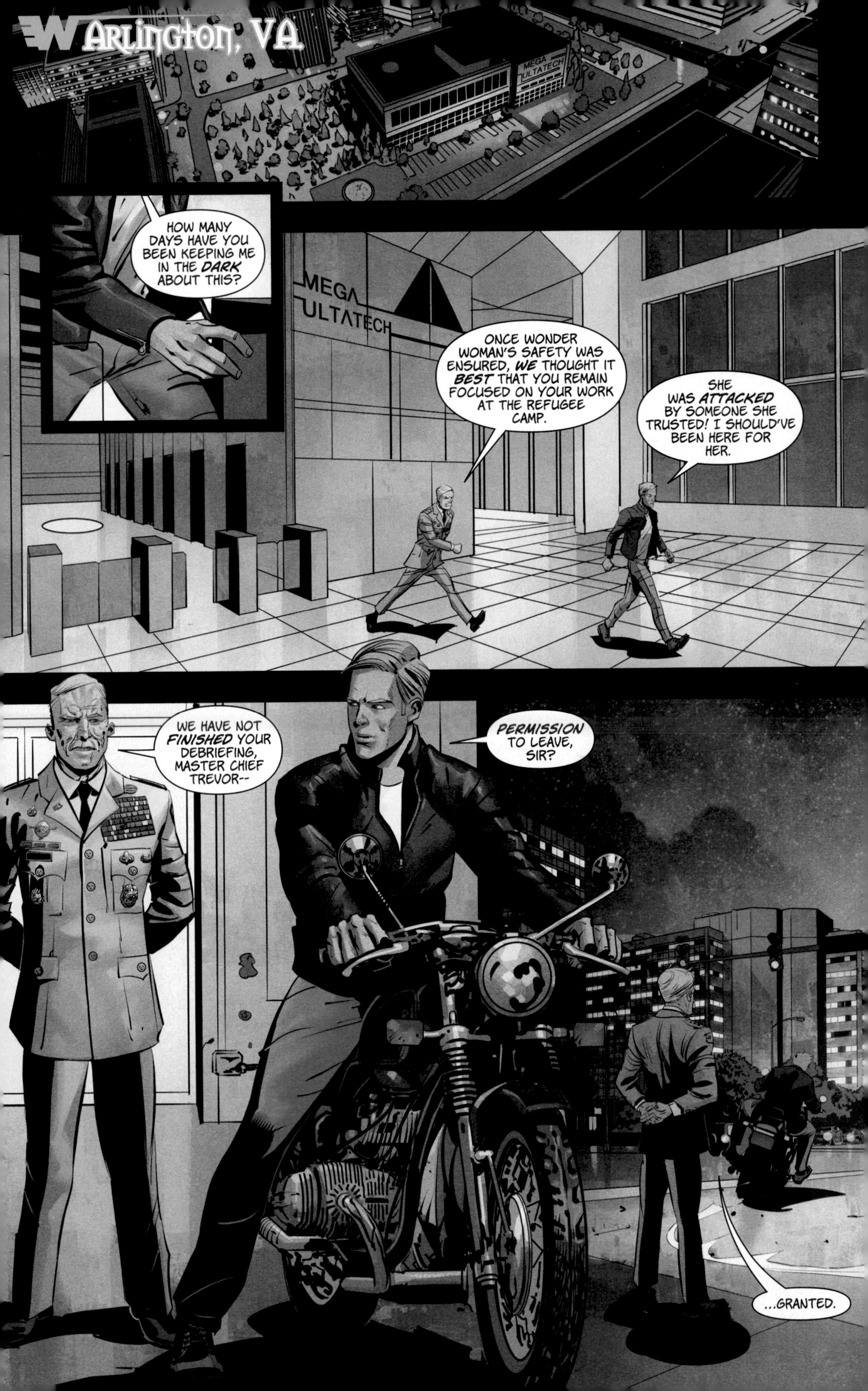
ARLINGTON, VA
MEGA ULTATECH
HOW MANY DAYS HAVE YOU BEEN KEEPING ME IN THE DARK ABOUT THIS?
MEGA ULTATECH
ONCE WONDER WOMAN'S SAFETY WAS ENSURED, WE THOUGHT IT BEST THAT YOU REMAIN FOCUSED ON YOUR WORK AT THE REFUGEE CAMP.
SHE WAS ATTACKED BY SOMEONE SHE TRUSTED! I SHOULD'VE BEEN HERE FOR HER.
WE HAVE NOT FINISHED YOUR DEBRIEFING, MASTER CHIEF TREVOR--
PERMISSION TO LEAVE, SIR?
...GRANTED.

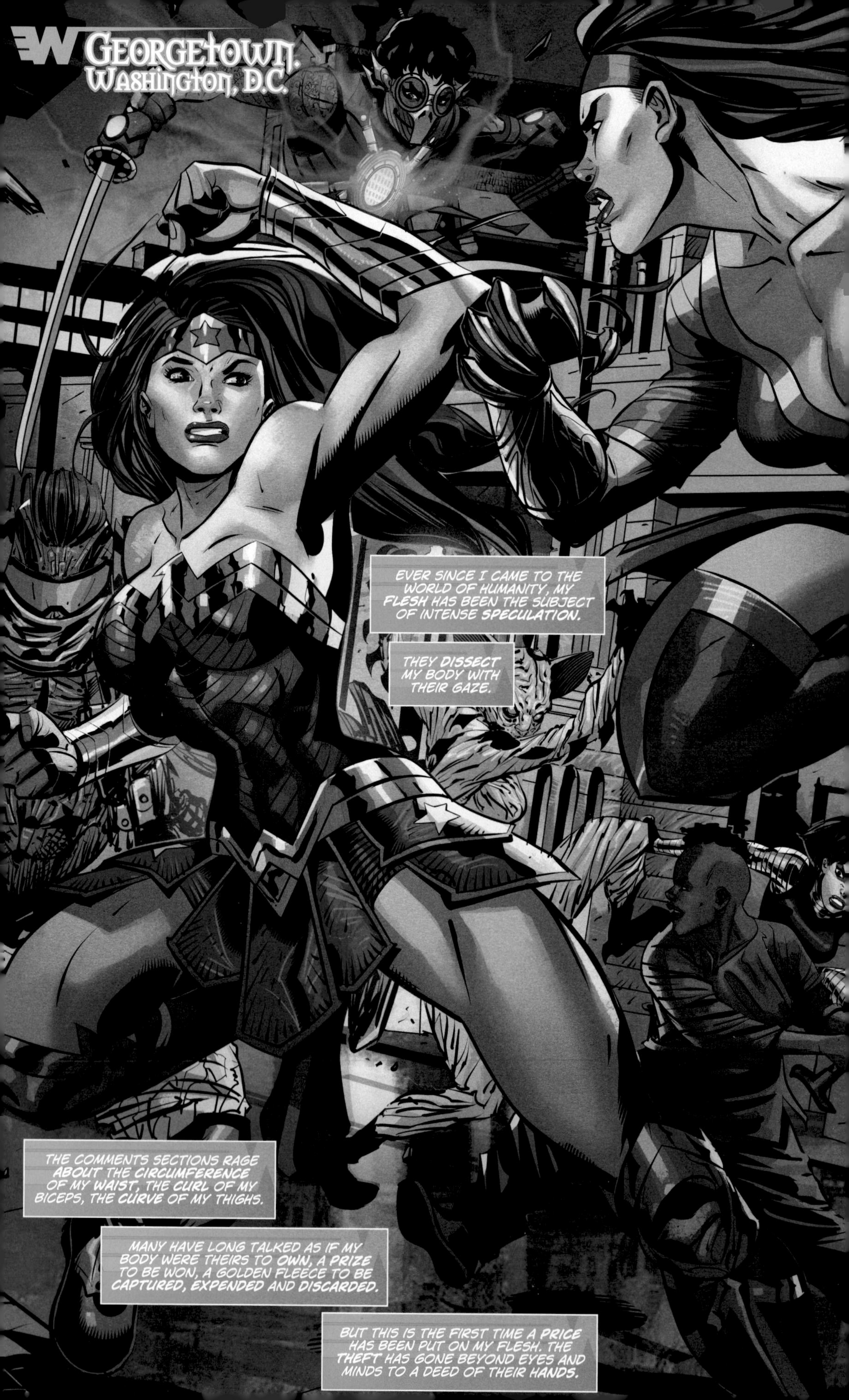
GEORGETOWN. WASHINGTON, D.C.
EVER SINCE I CAME TO THE WORLD OF HUMANITY, MY FLESH HAS BEEN THE SUBJECT OF INTENSE SPECULATION.
THEY DISSECT MY BODY WITH THEIR GAZE.
THE COMMENTS SECTIONS RAGE ABOUT THE CIRCUMFERENCE OF MY WAIST, THE CURL OF MY BICEPS, THE CURVE OF MY THIGHS.
MANY HAVE LONG TALKED AS IF MY BODY WERE THEIRS TO OWN, A PRIZE TO BE WON, A GOLDEN FLEECE TO BE CAPTURED, EXPENDED AND DISCARDED.
BUT THIS IS THE FIRST TIME A PRICE HAS BEEN PUT ON MY FLESH. THE THEFT HAS GONE BEYOND EYES AND MINDS TO A DEED OF THEIR HANDS.

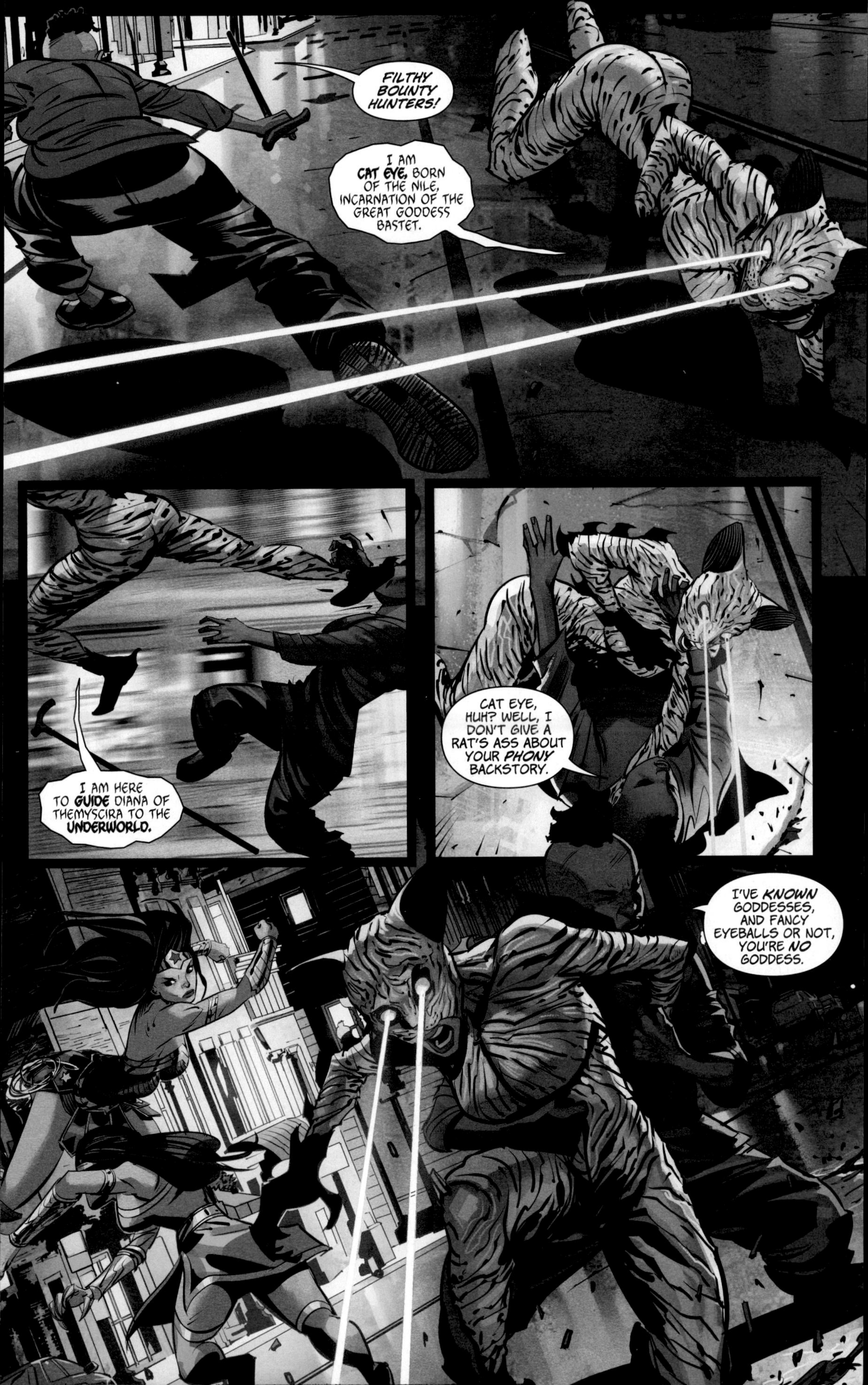
FILTHY BOUNTY HUNTERS!
I AM CAT EYE, BORN OF THE NILE, INCARNATION OF THE GREAT GODDESS BASTET.
I AM HERE TO GUIDE DIANA OF THEMYSCIRA TO THE UNDERWORLD.
CAT EYE, HUH? WELL, I DON'T GIVE A RAT'S ASS ABOUT YOUR PHONY BACKSTORY.
I'VE KNOWN GODDESSES, AND FANCY EYEBALLS OR NOT, YOU'RE NO GODDESS.

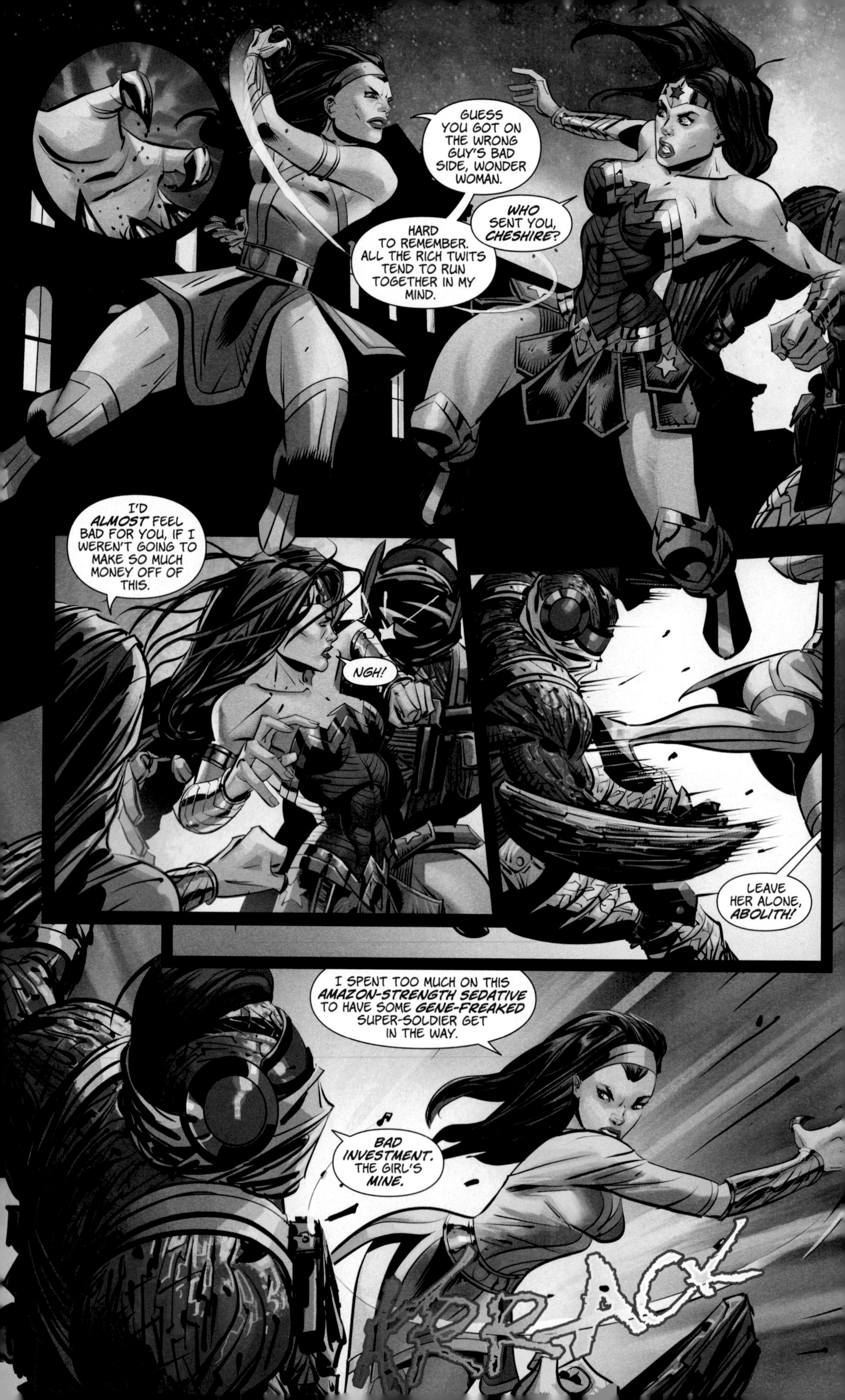
GUESS YOU GOT ON THE WRONG GUY'S BAD SIDE, WONDER WOMAN.
WHO SENT YOU, CHESHIRE?
HARD TO REMEMBER. ALL THE RICH TWITS TEND TO RUN TOGETHER IN MY MIND.
I'D ALMOST FEEL BAD FOR YOU, IF I WEREN'T GOING TO MAKE SO MUCH MONEY OFF OF THIS.
NGH!
LEAVE HER ALONE, ABOLITH!
I SPENT TOO MUCH ON THIS AMAZON-STRENGTH SEDATIVE TO HAVE SOME GENE-FREAKED SUPER-SOLDIER GET IN THE WAY.
BAD INVESTMENT. THE GIRL'S MINE.
KRRACK

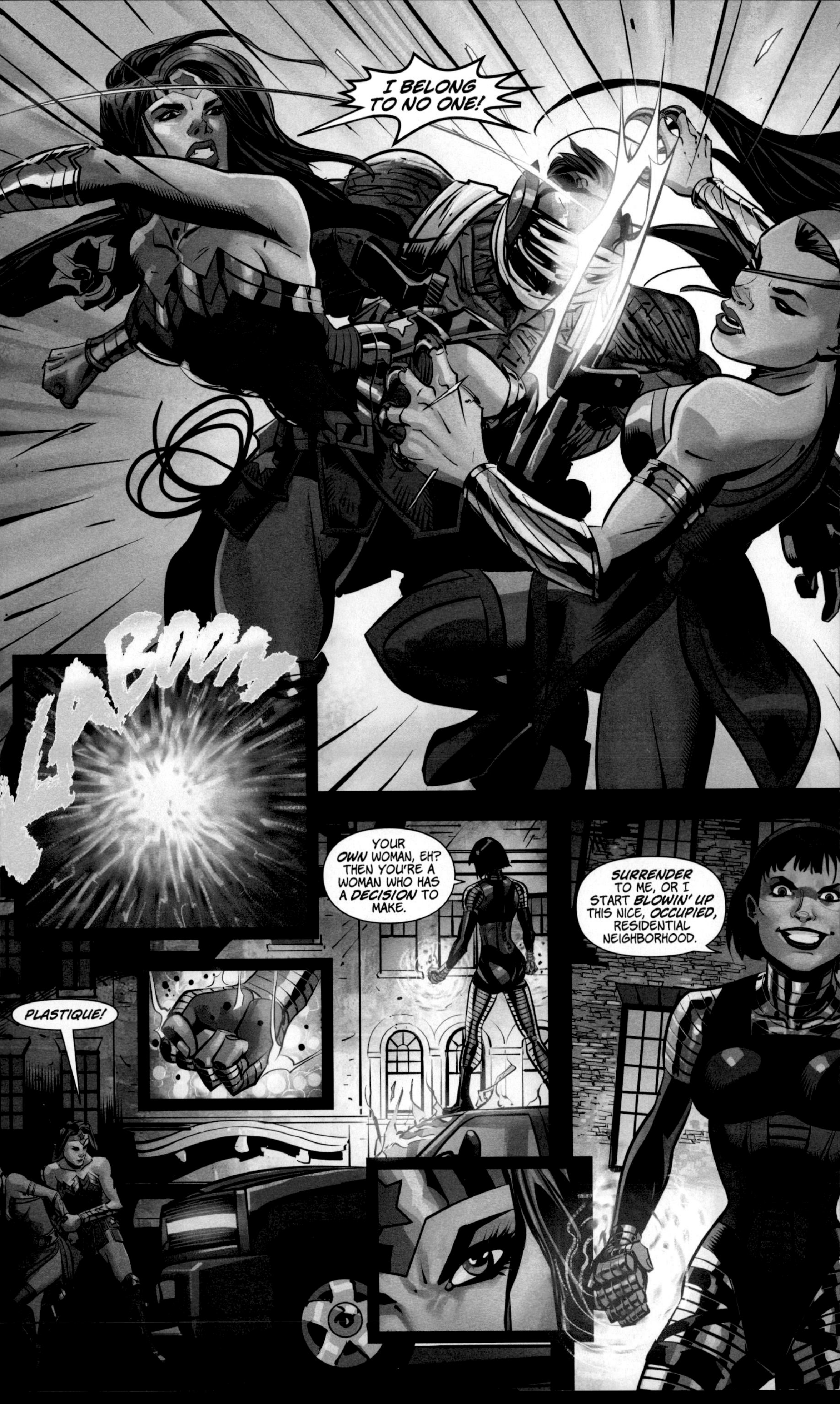
I BELONG TO NO ONE!
KLABOOM
PLASTIQUE!
YOUR OWN WOMAN, EH? THEN YOU'RE A WOMAN WHO HAS A DECISION TO MAKE.
SURRENDER TO ME, OR I START BLOWIN' UP THIS NICE, OCCUPIED, RESIDENTIAL NEIGHBORHOOD.

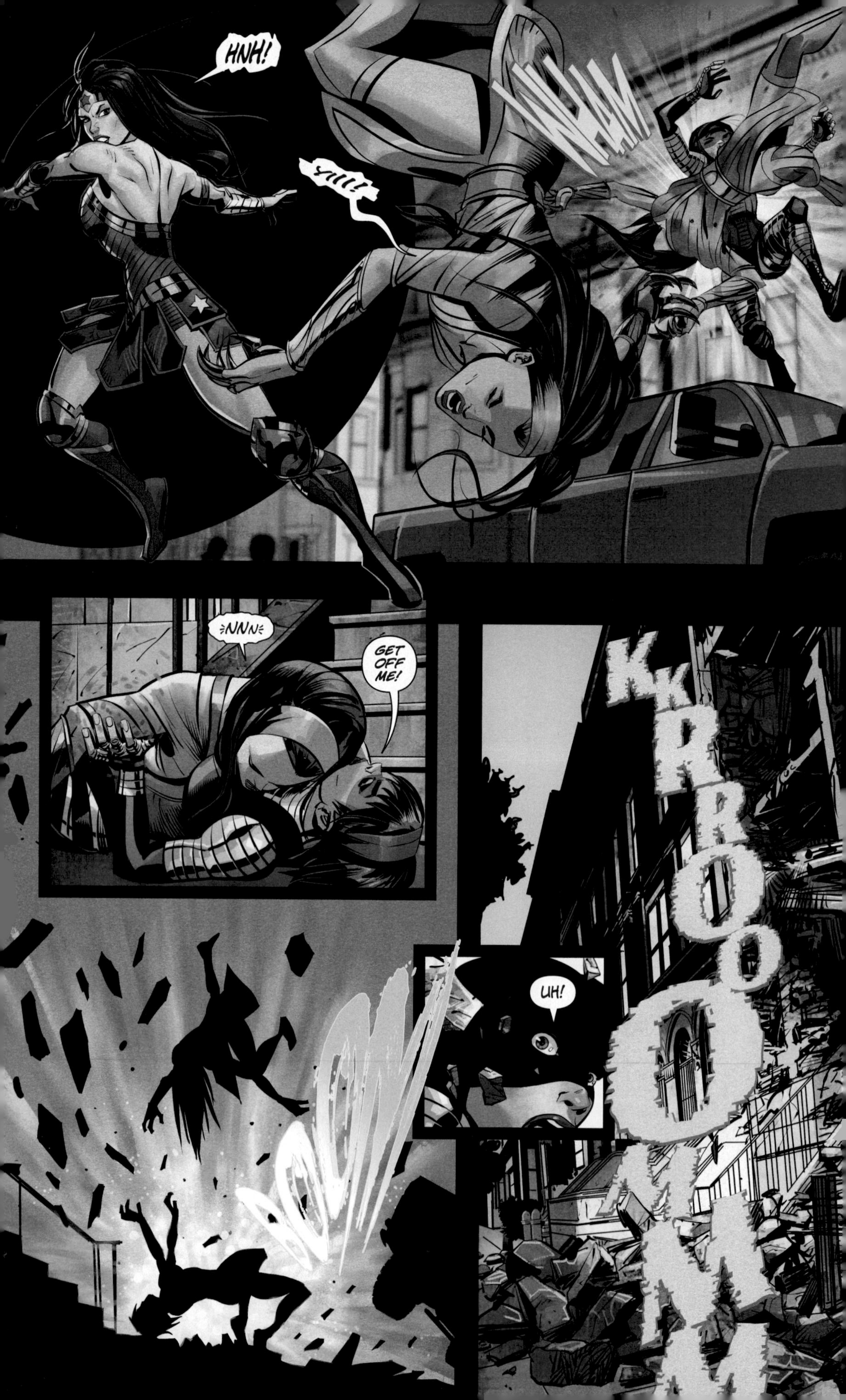
HNH!
WHAM
YIII!
NNN
GET OFF ME!
KKRROOOMM
UH!

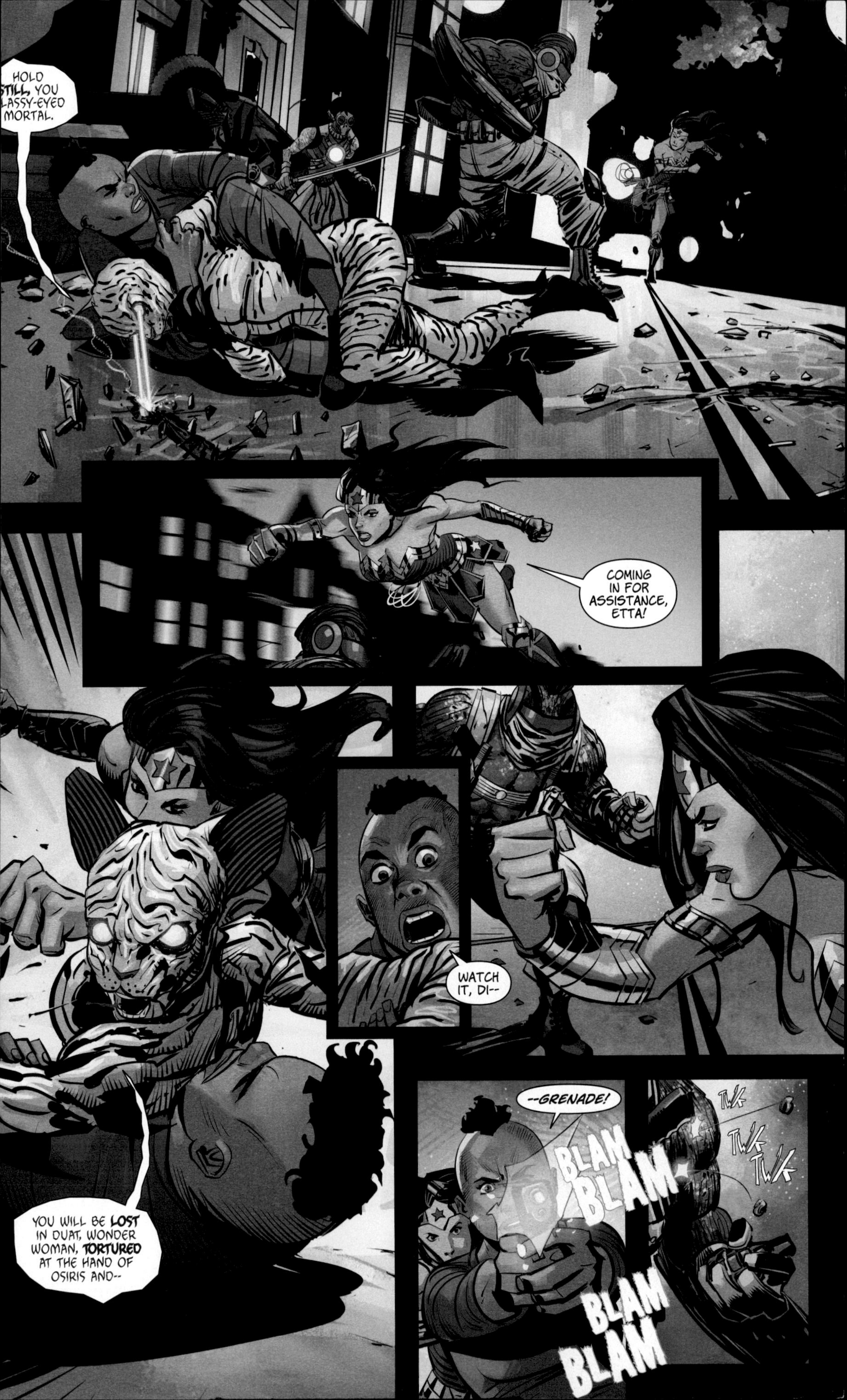
HOLD STILL, YOU LASSY-EYED MORTAL.
COMING IN FOR ASSISTANCE, ETTA!
YOU WILL BE LOST IN DUAT, WONDER WOMAN, TORTURED AT THE HAND OF OSIRIS AND--
WATCH IT, DI--
--GRENADE!
BLAM BLAM
TWK TWK TWK
BLAM BLAM

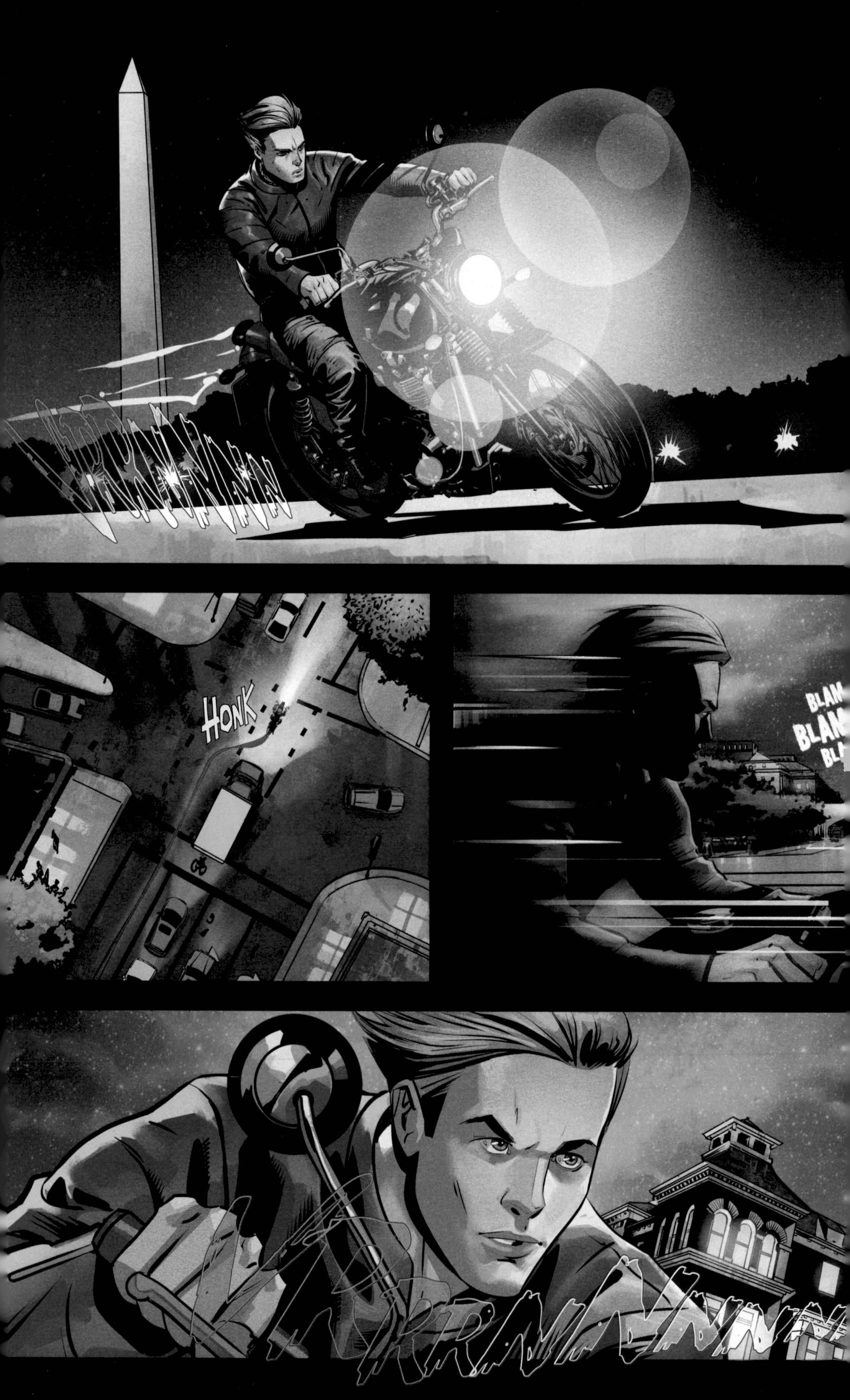
HONK
BLAM
BLAM
BLA

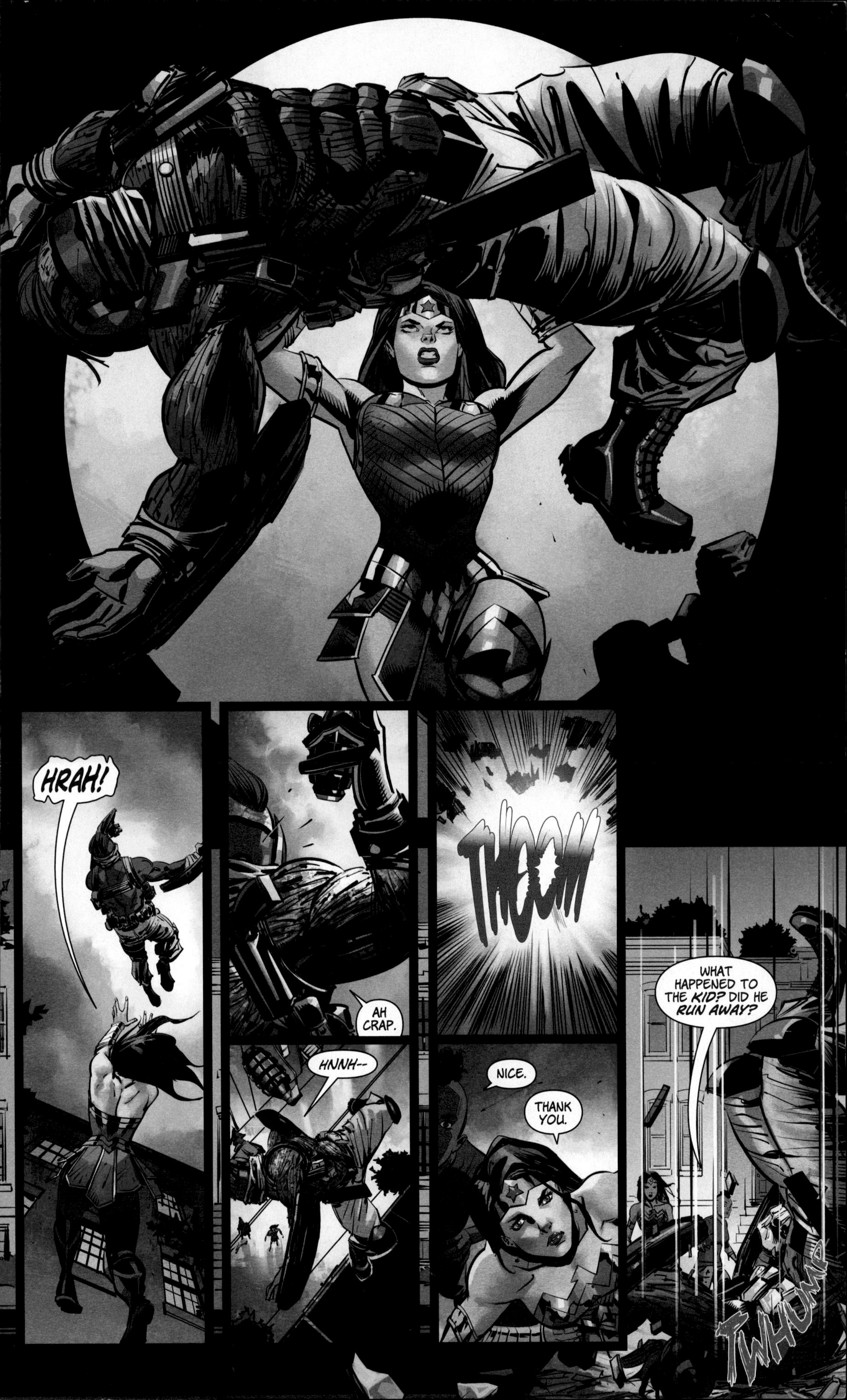
HRAH!
AH CRAP.
THOOM
HNNH--
NICE.
THANK YOU.
WHAT HAPPENED TO THE KID? DID HE RUN AWAY?
TWHUMP

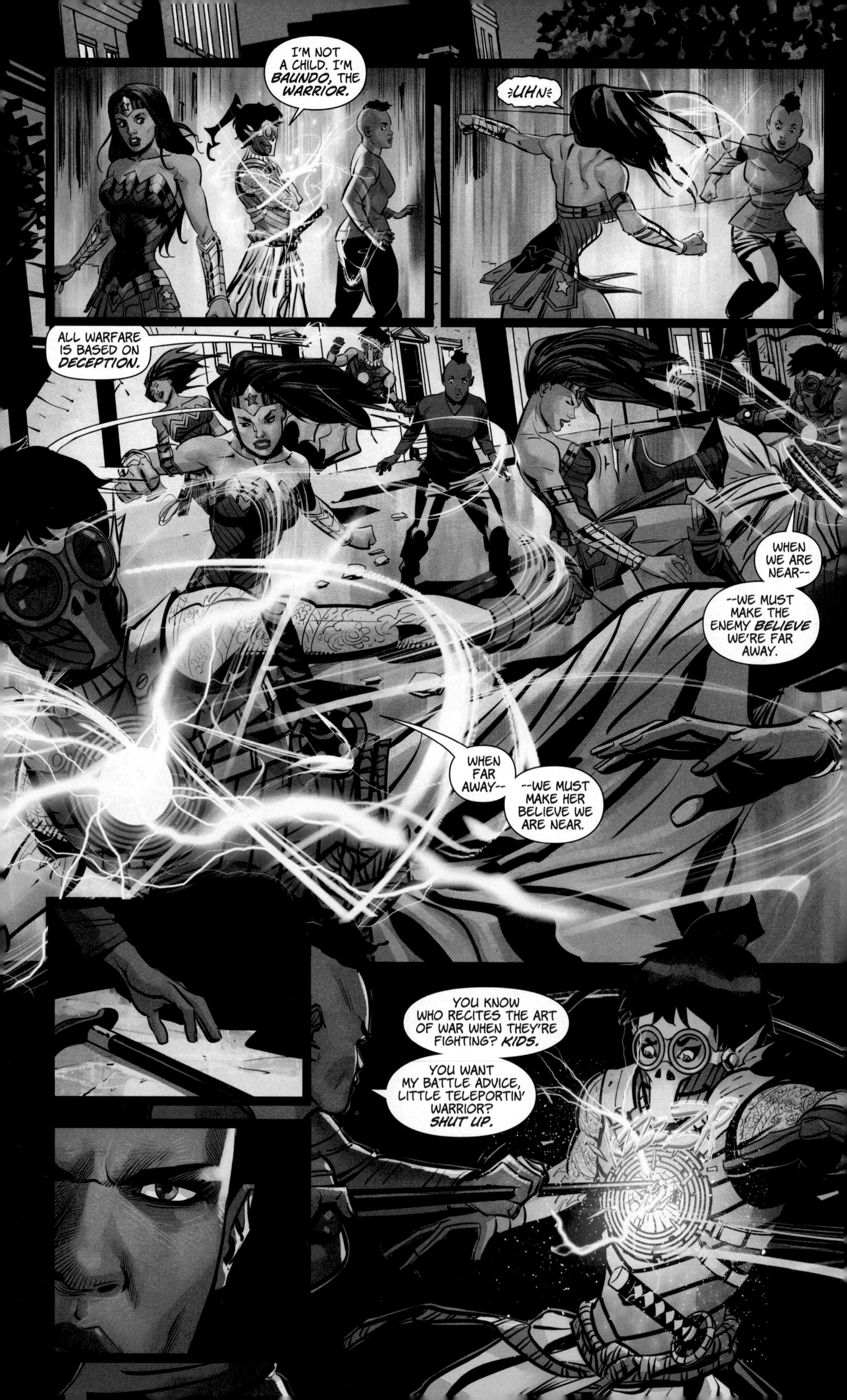
I'M NOT A CHILD. I'M BAUNDO, THE WARRIOR.
UHN
ALL WARFARE IS BASED ON DECEPTION.
WHEN WE ARE NEAR--
--WE MUST MAKE THE ENEMY BELIEVE WE'RE FAR AWAY.
WHEN FAR AWAY--
--WE MUST MAKE HER BELIEVE WE ARE NEAR.
YOU KNOW WHO RECITES THE ART OF WAR WHEN THEY'RE FIGHTING? KIDS.
YOU WANT MY BATTLE ADVICE, LITTLE TELEPORTIN' WARRIOR? SHUT UP.

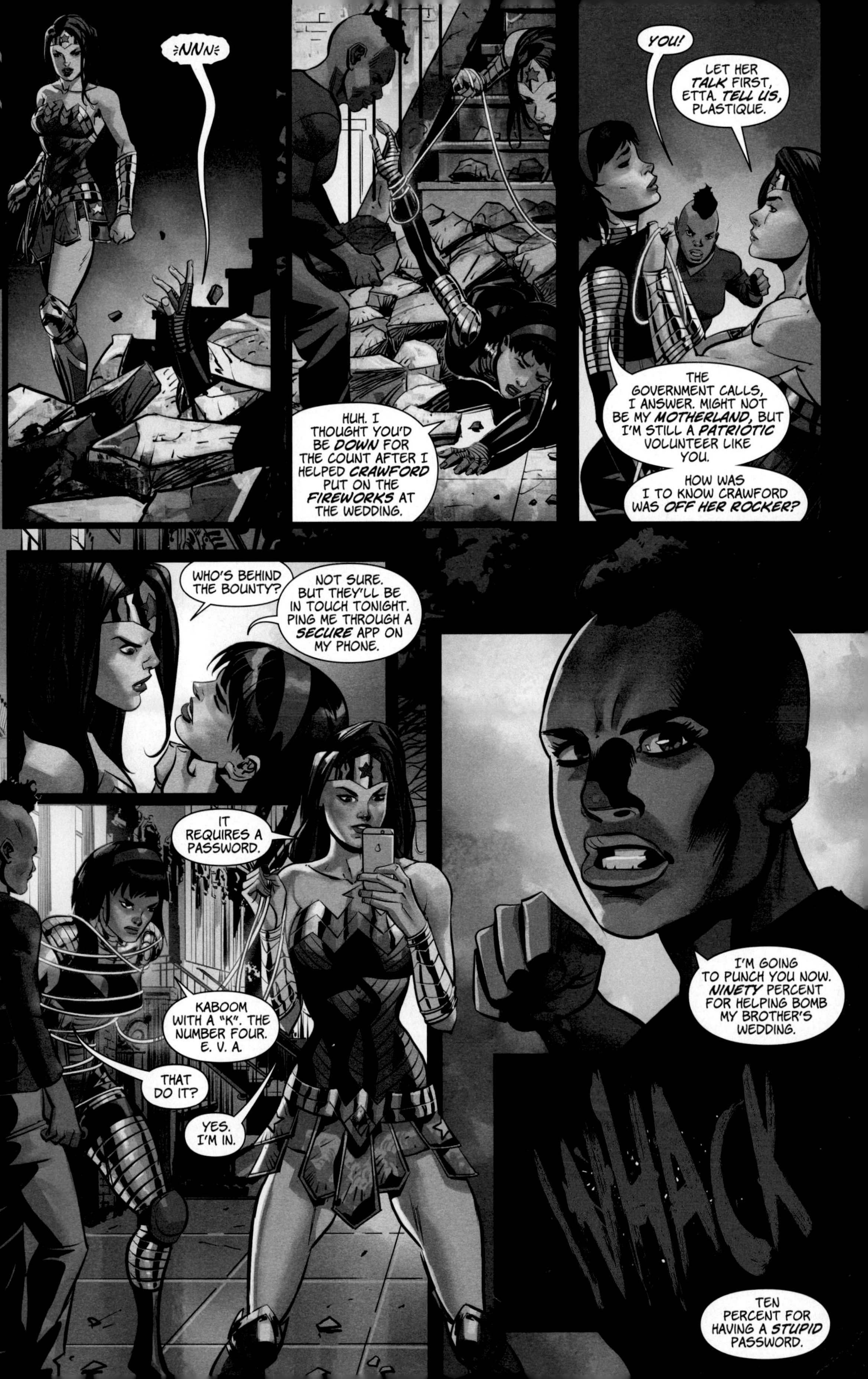
NNN
HUH. I THOUGHT YOU'D BE DOWN FOR THE COUNT AFTER I HELPED CRAWFORD PUT ON THE FIREWORKS AT THE WEDDING.
YOU!
LET HER TALK FIRST, ETTA. TELL US, PLASTIQUE.
THE GOVERNMENT CALLS, I ANSWER. MIGHT NOT BE MY MOTHERLAND, BUT I'M STILL A PATRIOTIC VOLUNTEER LIKE YOU.
HOW WAS I TO KNOW CRAWFORD WAS OFF HER ROCKER?
WHO'S BEHIND THE BOUNTY?
NOT SURE. BUT THEY'LL BE IN TOUCH TONIGHT. PING ME THROUGH A SECURE APP ON MY PHONE.
IT REQUIRES A PASSWORD.
KABOOM WITH A "K". THE NUMBER FOUR. E. V. A.
THAT DO IT?
YES. I'M IN.
I'M GOING TO PUNCH YOU NOW. NINETY PERCENT FOR HELPING BOMB MY BROTHER'S WEDDING.
WHACK
TEN PERCENT FOR HAVING A STUPID PASSWORD.

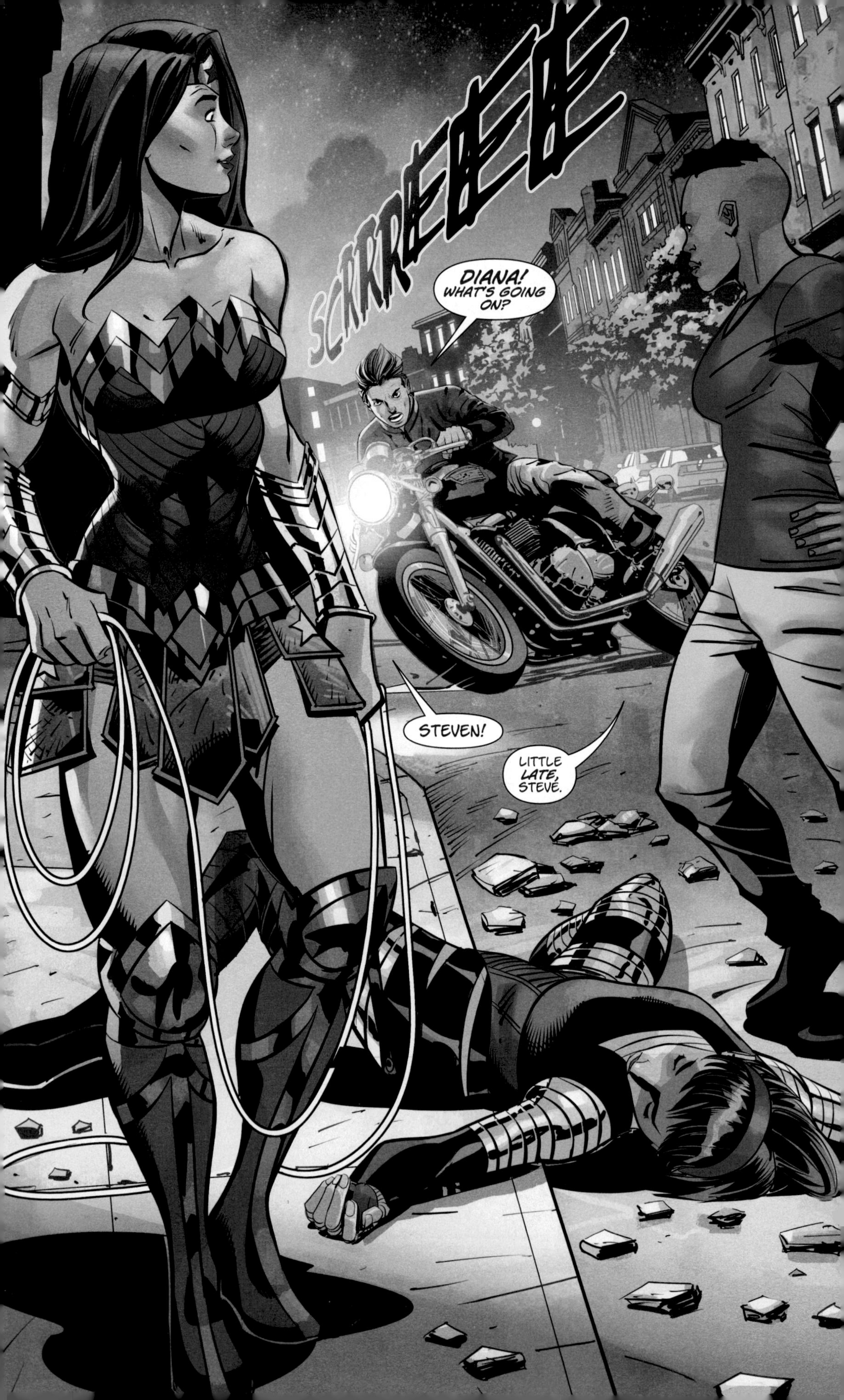
SCRRREEEEE
DIANA! WHAT'S GOING ON?
STEVEN!
LITTLE LATE, STEVE.

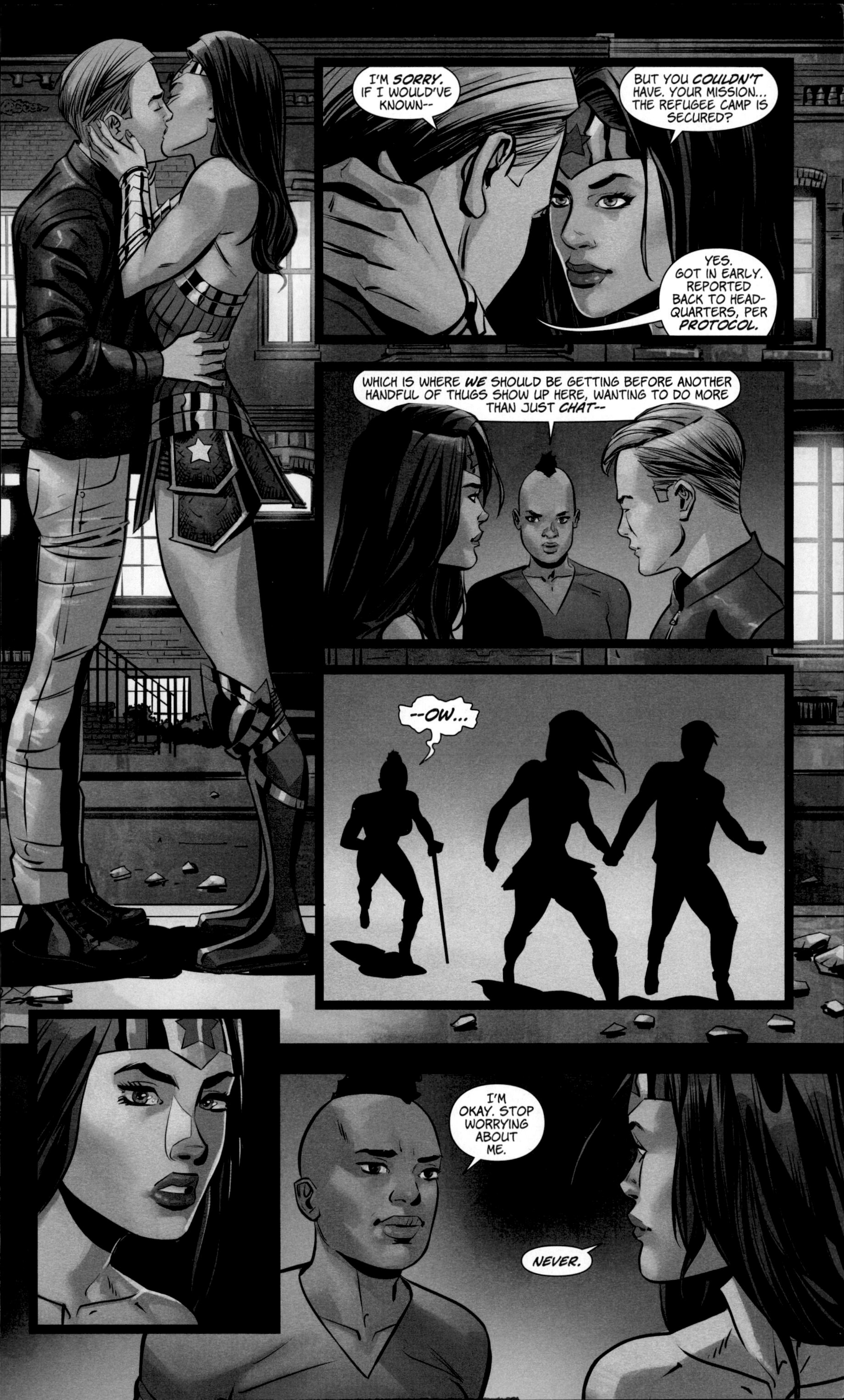

I'M SORRY. IF I WOULD'VE KNOWN--
BUT YOU COULDN'T HAVE. YOUR MISSION... THE REFUGEE CAMP IS SECURED?
YES. GOT IN EARLY. REPORTED BACK TO HEAD-QUARTERS, PER PROTOCOL.
WHICH IS WHERE WE SHOULD BE GETTING BEFORE ANOTHER HANDFUL OF THUGS SHOW UP HERE, WANTING TO DO MORE THAN JUST CHAT--
--OW...
I'M OKAY. STOP WORRYING ABOUT ME.
NEVER.

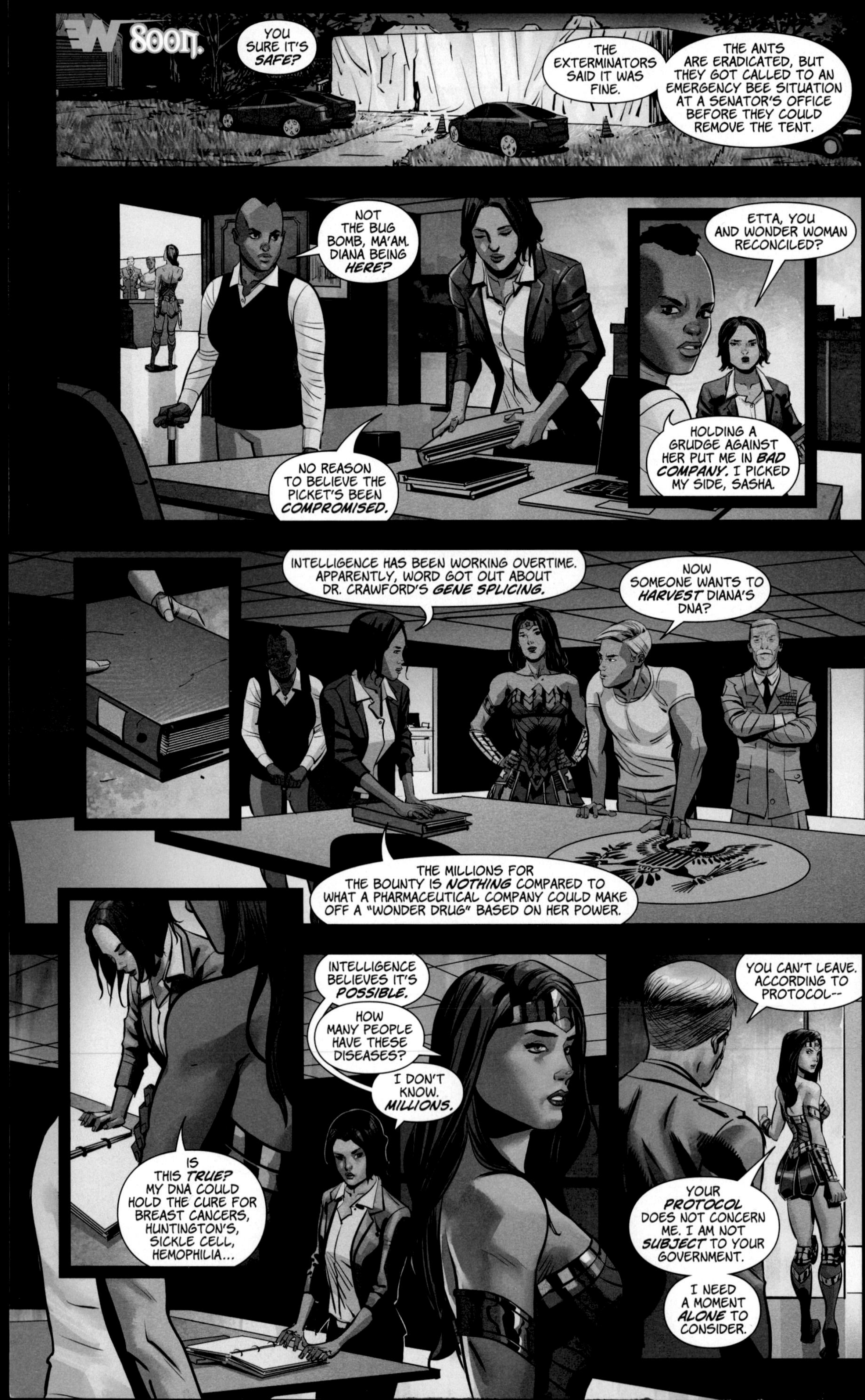
SOON.
YOU SURE IT'S SAFE?
THE EXTERMINATORS SAID IT WAS FINE.
THE ANTS ARE ERADICATED, BUT THEY GOT CALLED TO AN EMERGENCY BEE SITUATION AT A SENATOR'S OFFICE BEFORE THEY COULD REMOVE THE TENT.
NOT THE BUG BOMB, MA'AM. DIANA BEING HERE?
NO REASON TO BELIEVE THE PICKET'S BEEN COMPROMISED.
ETTA, YOU AND WONDER WOMAN RECONCILED?
HOLDING A GRUDGE AGAINST HER PUT ME IN BAD COMPANY. I PICKED MY SIDE, SASHA.
INTELLIGENCE HAS BEEN WORKING OVERTIME. APPARENTLY, WORD GOT OUT ABOUT DR. CRAWFORD'S GENE SPLICING.
NOW SOMEONE WANTS TO HARVEST DIANA'S DNA?
THE MILLIONS FOR THE BOUNTY IS NOTHING COMPARED TO WHAT A PHARMACEUTICAL COMPANY COULD MAKE OFF A "WONDER DRUG" BASED ON HER POWER.
IS THIS TRUE? MY DNA COULD HOLD THE CURE FOR BREAST CANCERS, HUNTINGTON'S, SICKLE CELL, HEMOPHILIA...
INTELLIGENCE BELIEVES IT'S POSSIBLE.
HOW MANY PEOPLE HAVE THESE DISEASES?
I DON'T KNOW. MILLIONS.
YOU CAN'T LEAVE. ACCORDING TO PROTOCOL--
YOUR PROTOCOL DOES NOT CONCERN ME. I AM NOT SUBJECT TO YOUR GOVERNMENT.
I NEED A MOMENT ALONE TO CONSIDER.

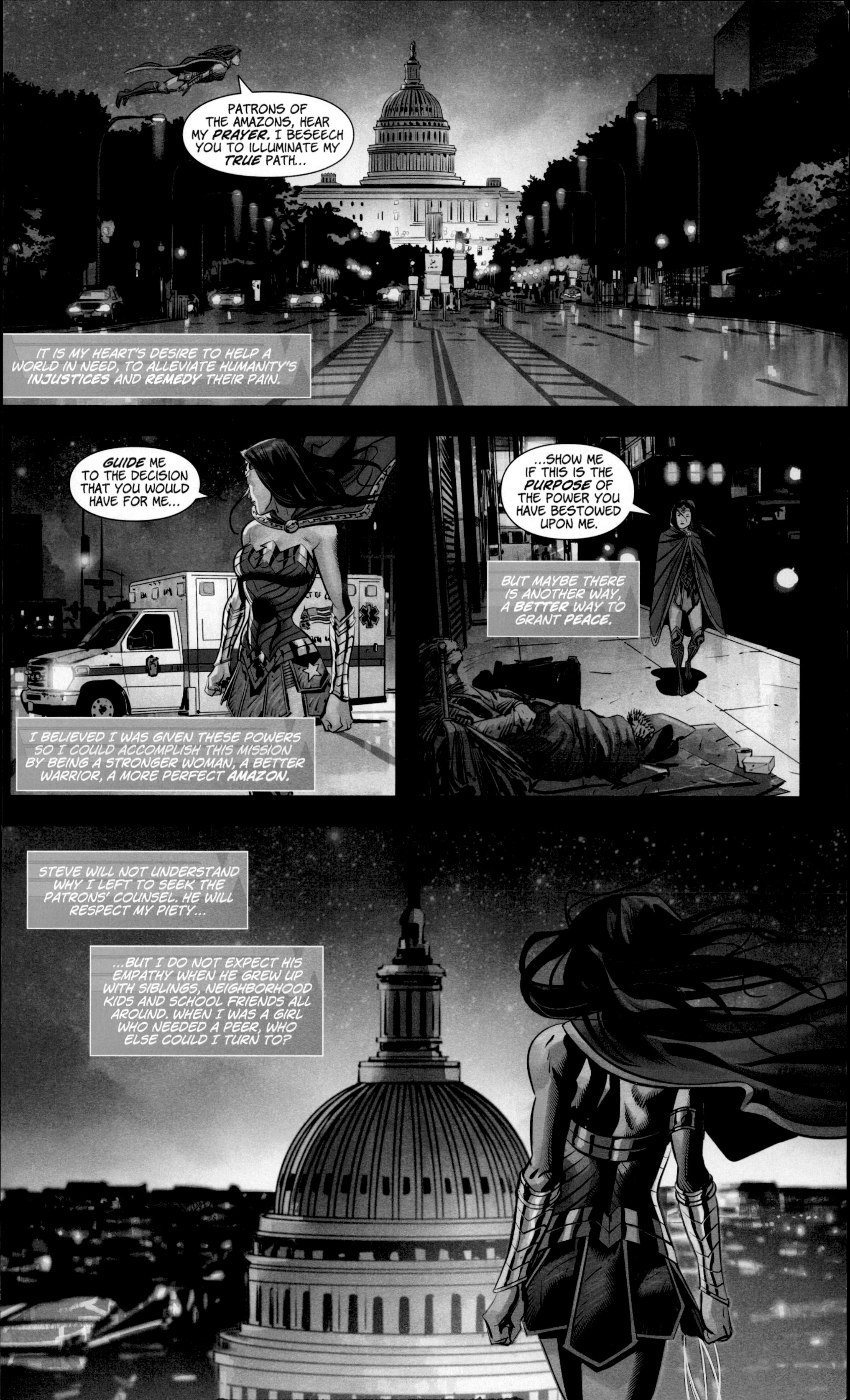
PATRONS OF THE AMAZONS, HEAR MY PRAYER. I BESEECH YOU TO ILLUMINATE MY TRUE PATH...
IT IS MY HEART'S DESIRE TO HELP A WORLD IN NEED, TO ALLEVIATE HUMANITY'S INJUSTICES AND REMEDY THEIR PAIN.
GUIDE ME TO THE DECISION THAT YOU WOULD HAVE FOR ME...
I BELIEVED I WAS GIVEN THESE POWERS SO I COULD ACCOMPLISH THIS MISSION BY BEING A STRONGER WOMAN, A BETTER WARRIOR, A MORE PERFECT AMAZON.
...SHOW ME IF THIS IS THE PURPOSE OF THE POWER YOU HAVE BESTOWED UPON ME.
BUT MAYBE THERE IS ANOTHER WAY, A BETTER WAY TO GRANT PEACE.
STEVE WILL NOT UNDERSTAND WHY I LEFT TO SEEK THE PATRONS' COUNSEL. HE WILL RESPECT MY PIETY...
...BUT I DO NOT EXPECT HIS EMPATHY WHEN HE GREW UP WITH SIBLINGS, NEIGHBORHOOD KIDS AND SCHOOL FRIENDS ALL AROUND. WHEN I WAS A GIRL WHO NEEDED A PEER, WHO ELSE COULD I TURN TO?

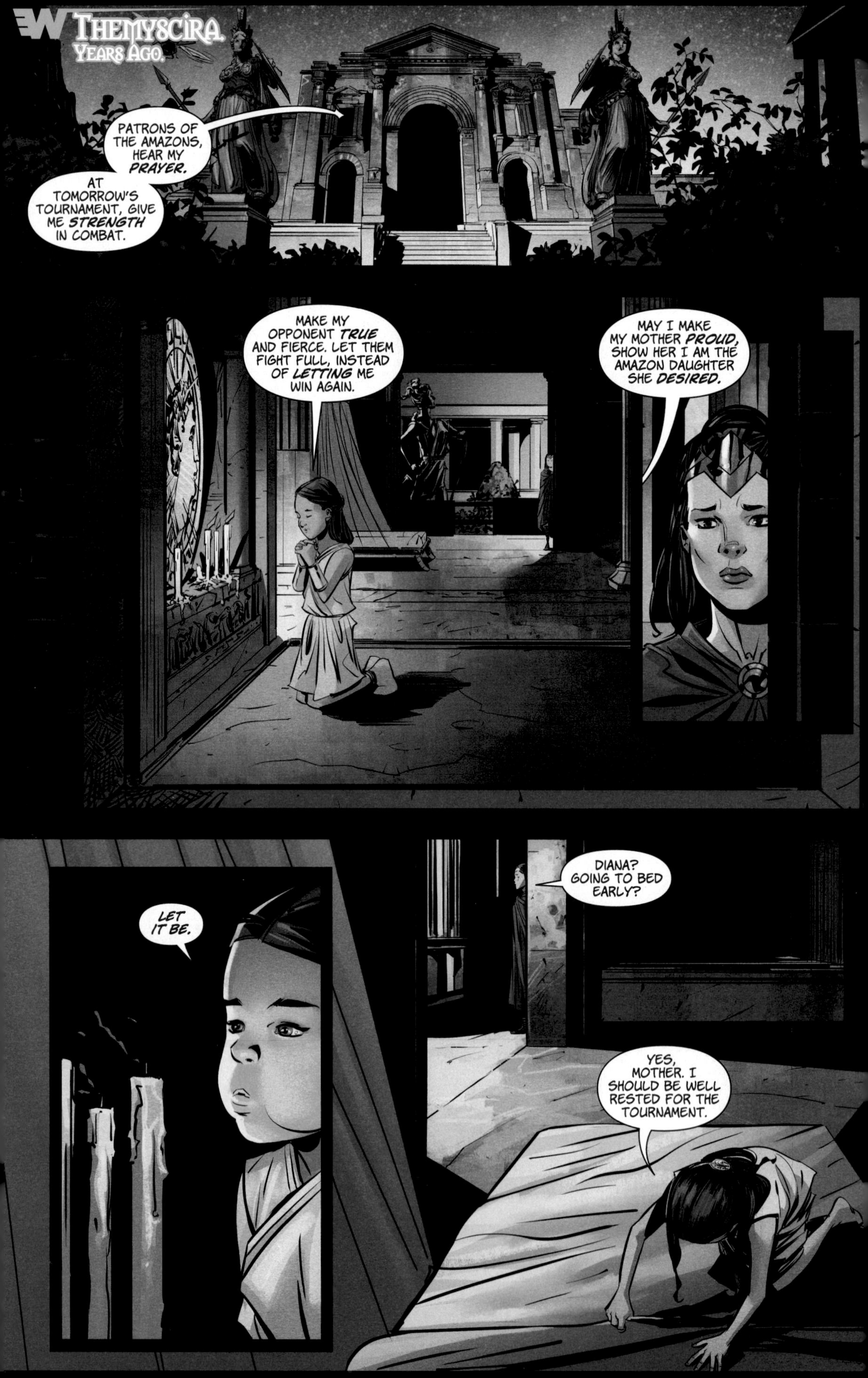
THEMYSCIRA. YEARS AGO.
PATRONS OF THE AMAZONS, HEAR MY PRAYER.
AT TOMORROW'S TOURNAMENT, GIVE ME STRENGTH IN COMBAT.
MAKE MY OPPONENT TRUE AND FIERCE. LET THEM FIGHT FULL, INSTEAD OF LETTING ME WIN AGAIN.
MAY I MAKE MY MOTHER PROUD, SHOW HER I AM THE AMAZON DAUGHTER SHE DESIRED.
LET IT BE.
DIANA? GOING TO BED EARLY?
YES, MOTHER. I SHOULD BE WELL RESTED FOR THE TOURNAMENT.

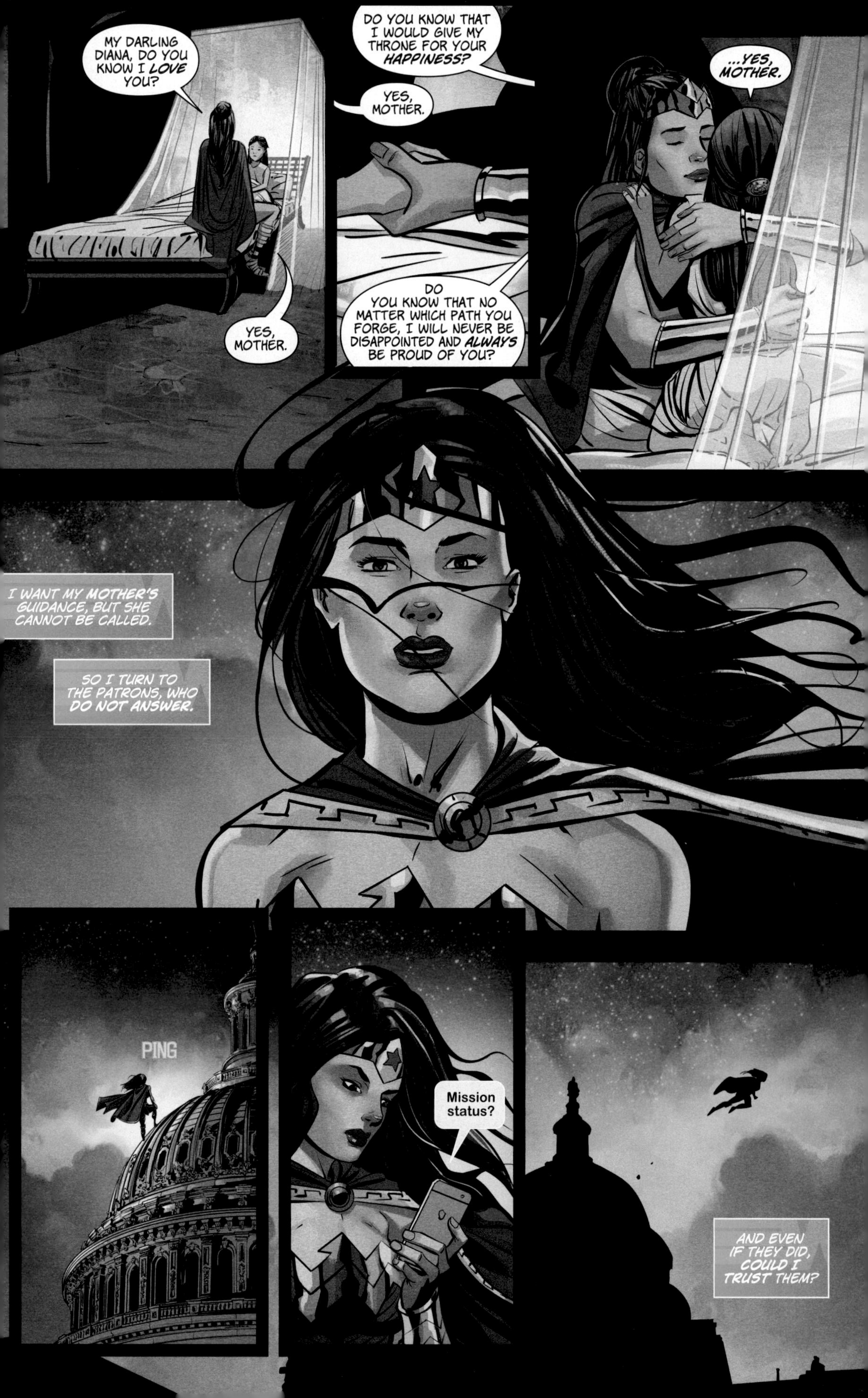
MY DARLING DIANA, DO YOU KNOW I LOVE YOU?
YES, MOTHER.
DO YOU KNOW THAT I WOULD GIVE MY THRONE FOR YOUR HAPPINESS?
YES, MOTHER.
DO YOU KNOW THAT NO MATTER WHICH PATH YOU FORGE, I WILL NEVER BE DISAPPOINTED AND ALWAYS BE PROUD OF YOU?
...YES, MOTHER.
I WANT MY MOTHER'S GUIDANCE, BUT SHE CANNOT BE CALLED.
SO I TURN TO THE PATRONS, WHO DO NOT ANSWER.
PING
Mission status?
AND EVEN IF THEY DID, COULD I TRUST THEM?

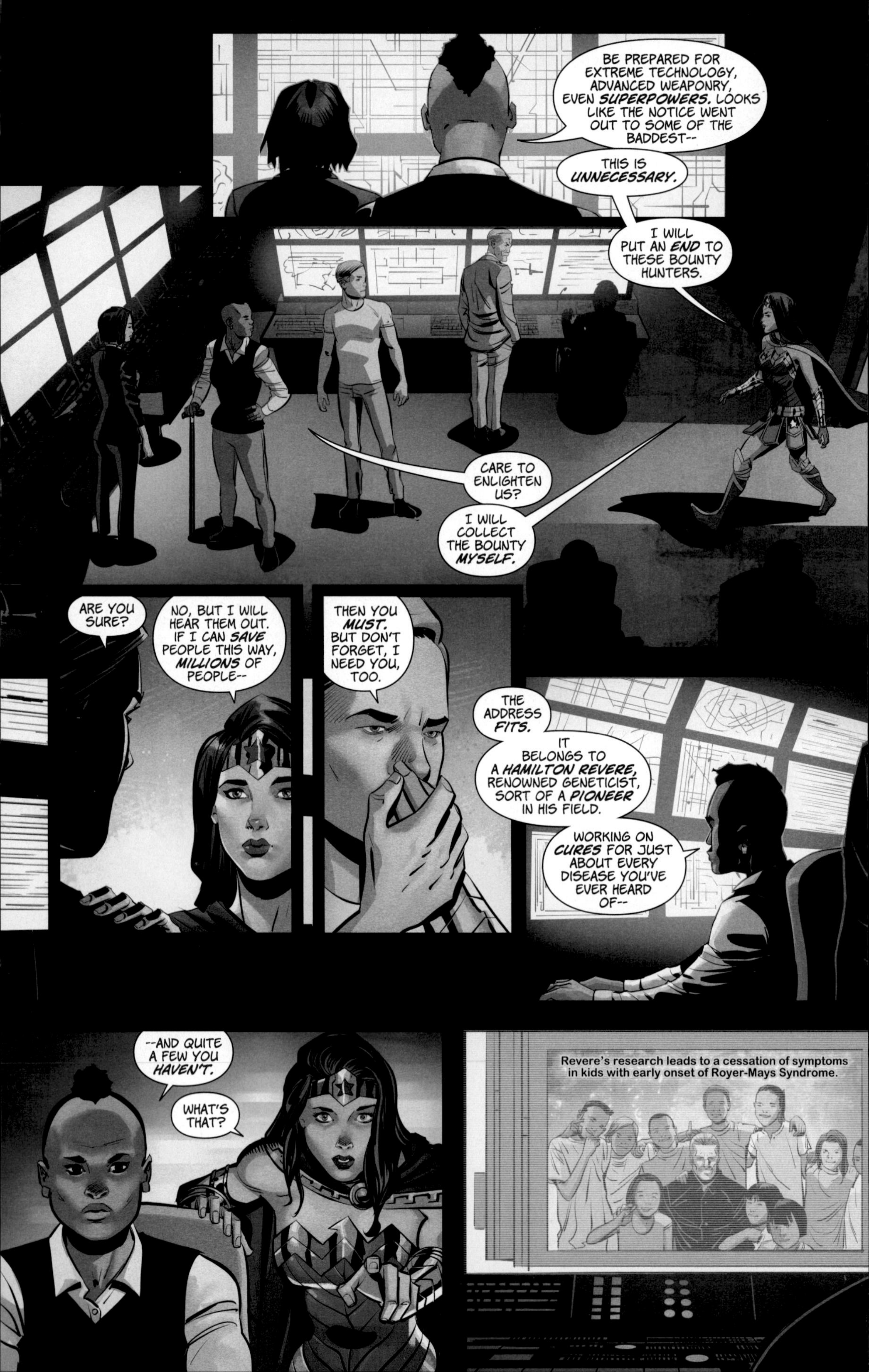
BE PREPARED FOR EXTREME TECHNOLOGY, ADVANCED WEAPONRY, EVEN *SUPERPOWERS.* LOOKS LIKE THE NOTICE WENT OUT TO SOME OF THE BADDEST--
THIS IS *UNNECESSARY.*
I WILL PUT AN *END* TO THESE BOUNTY HUNTERS.
CARE TO ENLIGHTEN US?
I WILL COLLECT THE BOUNTY *MYSELF.*
ARE YOU SURE?
NO, BUT I WILL HEAR THEM OUT. IF I CAN *SAVE* PEOPLE THIS WAY, *MILLIONS* OF PEOPLE--
THEN YOU *MUST.* BUT DON'T FORGET, I NEED YOU, TOO.
THE ADDRESS *FITS.*
IT BELONGS TO A *HAMILTON REVERE,* RENOWNED GENETICIST, SORT OF A *PIONEER* IN HIS FIELD.
WORKING ON *CURES* FOR JUST ABOUT EVERY DISEASE YOU'VE EVER HEARD OF--
--AND QUITE A FEW YOU *HAVEN'T.*
WHAT'S THAT?
Revere's research leads to a cessation of symptoms in kids with early onset of Royer-Mays Syndrome.

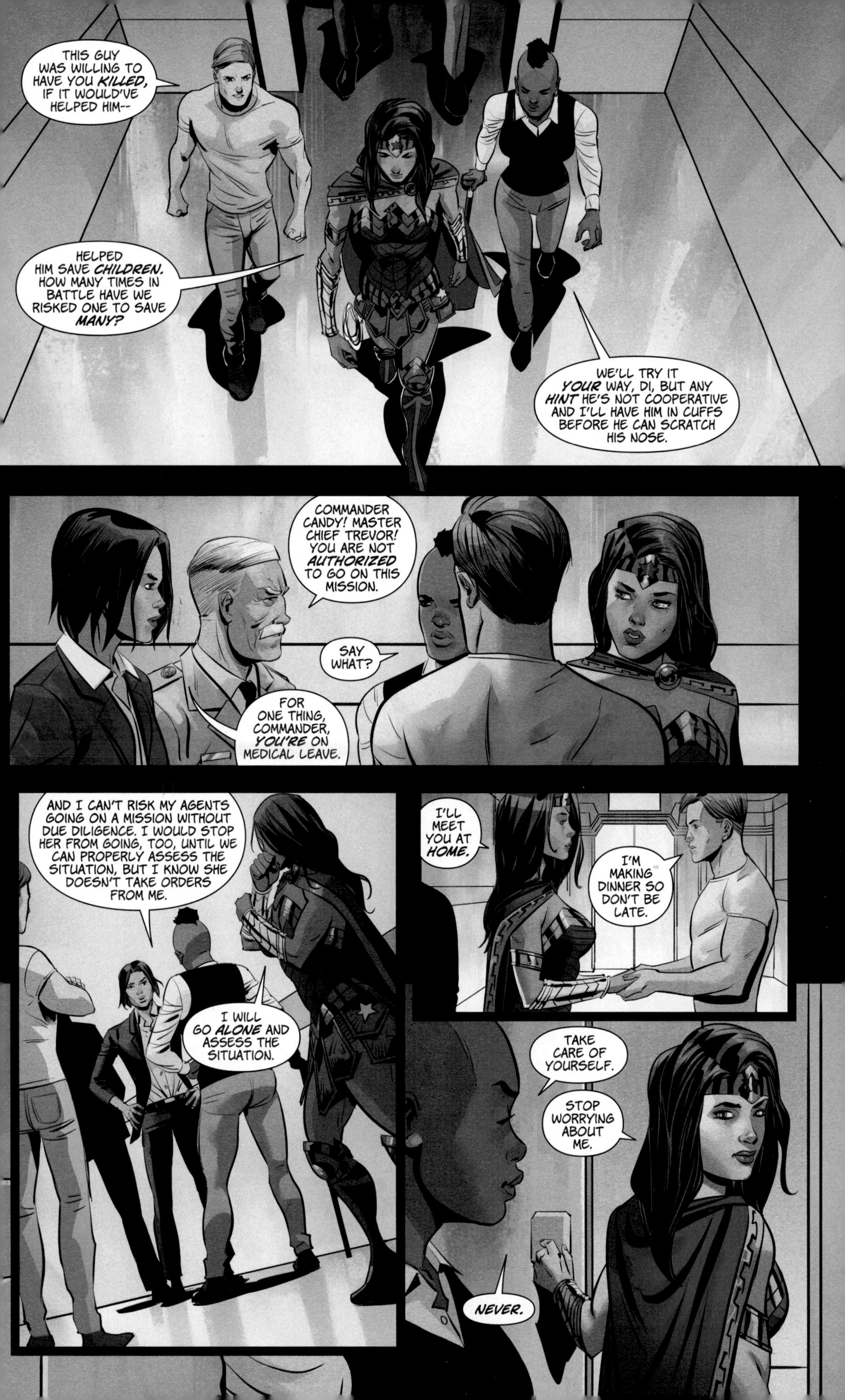

THIS GUY WAS WILLING TO HAVE YOU KILLED, IF IT WOULD'VE HELPED HIM--
HELPED HIM SAVE CHILDREN. HOW MANY TIMES IN BATTLE HAVE WE RISKED ONE TO SAVE MANY?
WE'LL TRY IT YOUR WAY, DI, BUT ANY HINT HE'S NOT COOPERATIVE AND I'LL HAVE HIM IN CUFFS BEFORE HE CAN SCRATCH HIS NOSE.
COMMANDER CANDY! MASTER CHIEF TREVOR! YOU ARE NOT AUTHORIZED TO GO ON THIS MISSION.
SAY WHAT?
FOR ONE THING, COMMANDER, YOU'RE ON MEDICAL LEAVE.
AND I CAN'T RISK MY AGENTS GOING ON A MISSION WITHOUT DUE DILIGENCE. I WOULD STOP HER FROM GOING, TOO, UNTIL WE CAN PROPERLY ASSESS THE SITUATION, BUT I KNOW SHE DOESN'T TAKE ORDERS FROM ME.
I WILL GO ALONE AND ASSESS THE SITUATION.
I'LL MEET YOU AT HOME.
I'M MAKING DINNER SO DON'T BE LATE.
TAKE CARE OF YOURSELF.
STOP WORRYING ABOUT ME.
NEVER.

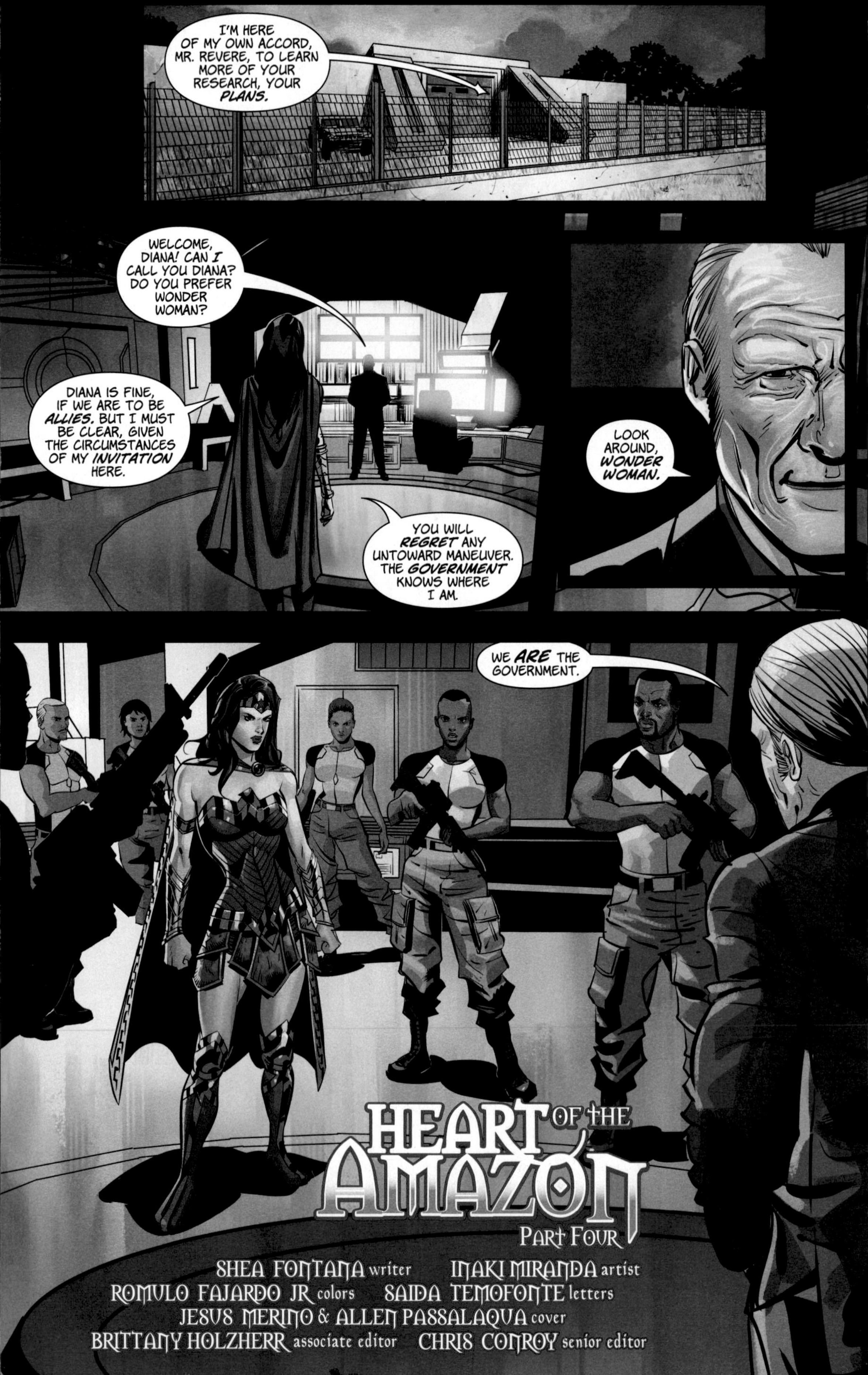

I'M HERE OF MY OWN ACCORD, MR. REVERE, TO LEARN MORE OF YOUR RESEARCH, YOUR PLANS.
WELCOME, DIANA! CAN I CALL YOU DIANA? DO YOU PREFER WONDER WOMAN?
DIANA IS FINE, IF WE ARE TO BE ALLIES. BUT I MUST BE CLEAR, GIVEN THE CIRCUMSTANCES OF MY INVITATION HERE.
YOU WILL REGRET ANY UNTOWARD MANEUVER. THE GOVERNMENT KNOWS WHERE I AM.
LOOK AROUND, WONDER WOMAN.
WE ARE THE GOVERNMENT.
HEART OF THE AMAZON
PART FOUR
SHEA FONTANA writer
INAKI MIRANDA artist
ROMULO FAJARDO JR colors
SAIDA TEMOFONTE letters
JESUS MERINO & ALLEN PASSALAQUA cover
BRITTANY HOLZHERR associate editor
CHRIS CONROY senior editor

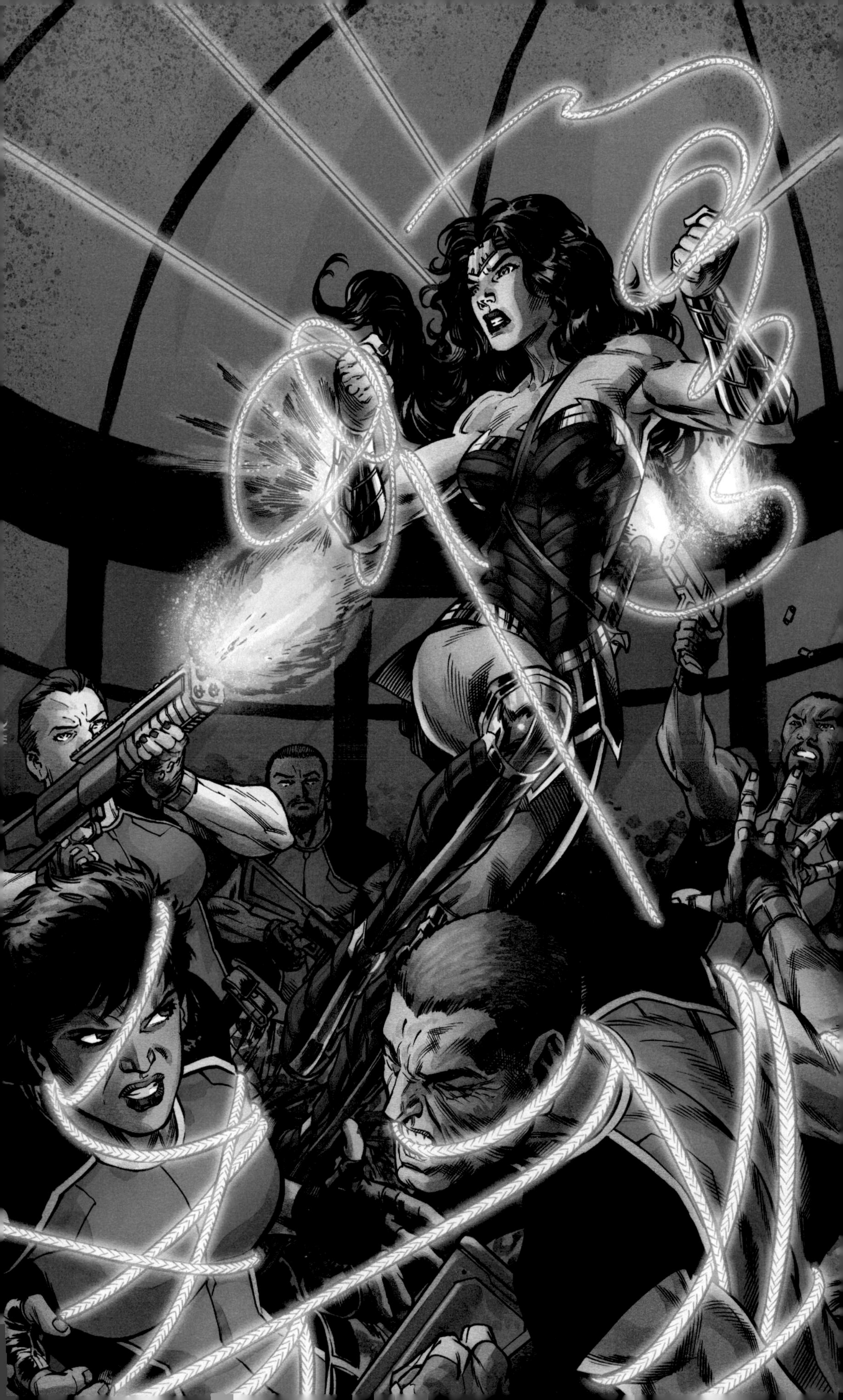

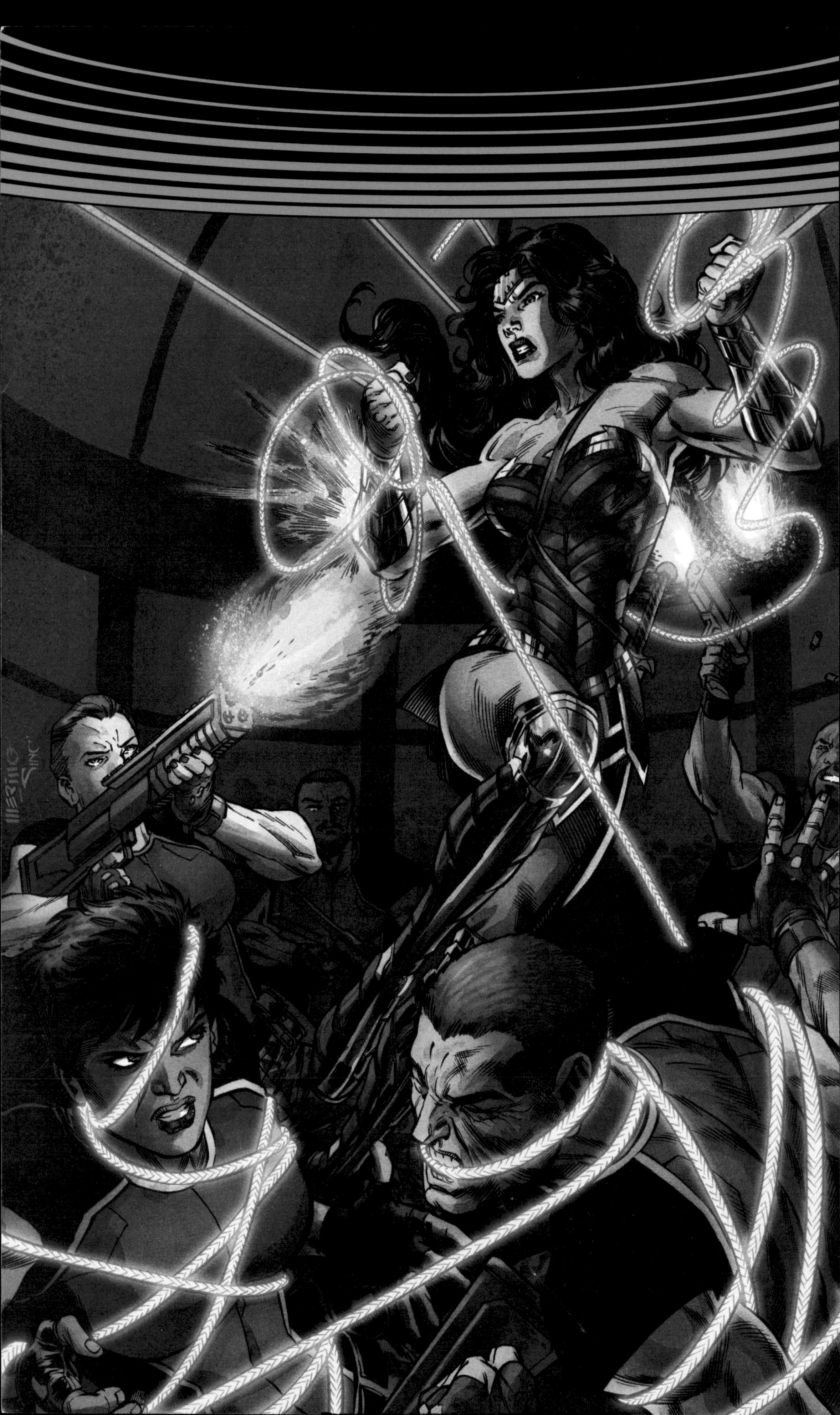

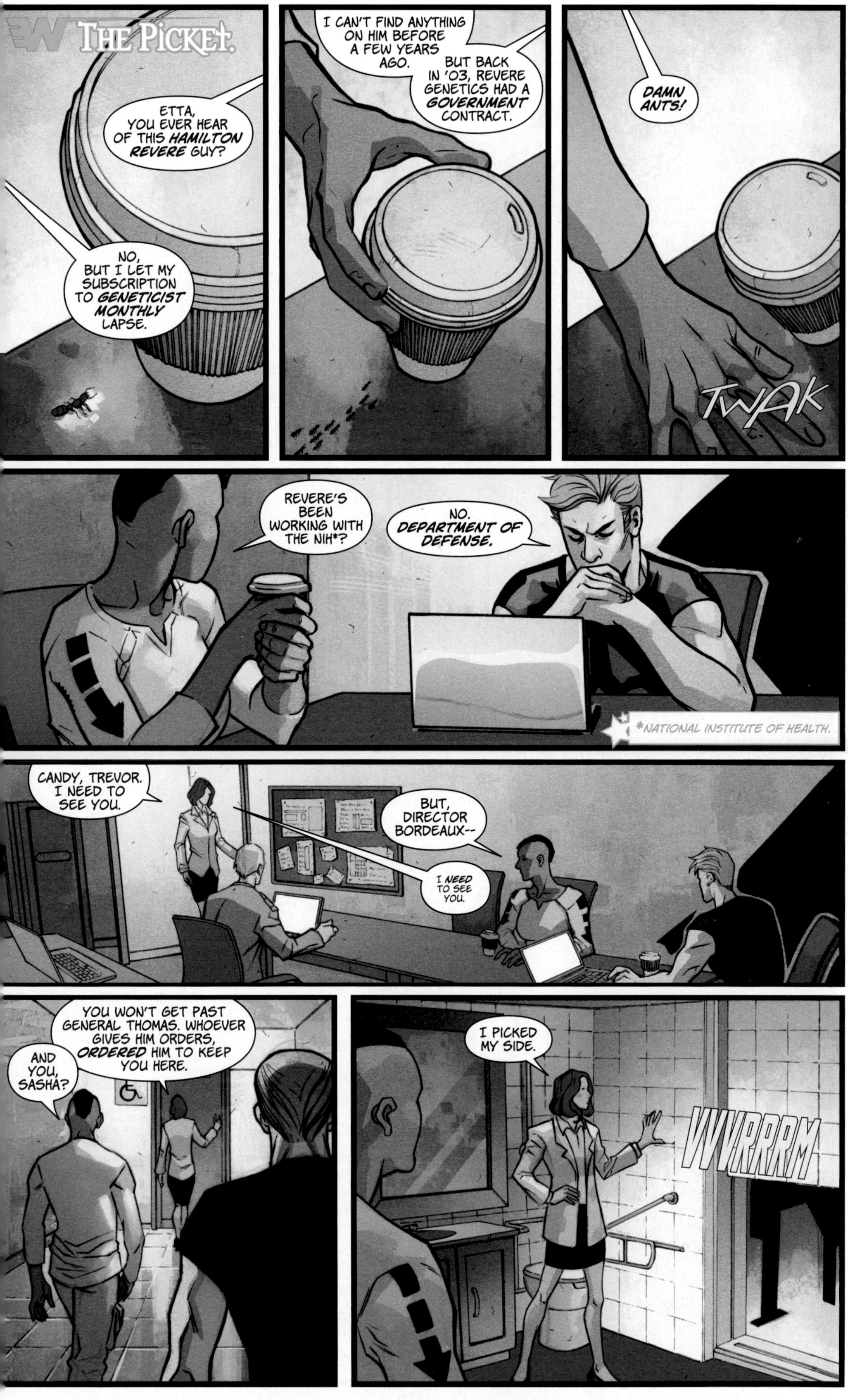
THE PICKET.
ETTA, YOU EVER HEAR OF THIS HAMILTON REVERE GUY?
NO, BUT I LET MY SUBSCRIPTION TO GENETICIST MONTHLY LAPSE.
I CAN'T FIND ANYTHING ON HIM BEFORE A FEW YEARS AGO.
BUT BACK IN '03, REVERE GENETICS HAD A GOVERNMENT CONTRACT.
DAMN ANTS!
TWAK
REVERE'S BEEN WORKING WITH THE NIH*?
NO. DEPARTMENT OF DEFENSE.
*NATIONAL INSTITUTE OF HEALTH.
CANDY, TREVOR. I NEED TO SEE YOU.
BUT, DIRECTOR BORDEAUX--
I NEED TO SEE YOU.
YOU WON'T GET PAST GENERAL THOMAS. WHOEVER GIVES HIM ORDERS, ORDERED HIM TO KEEP YOU HERE.
AND YOU, SASHA?
I PICKED MY SIDE.
VVVRRRM

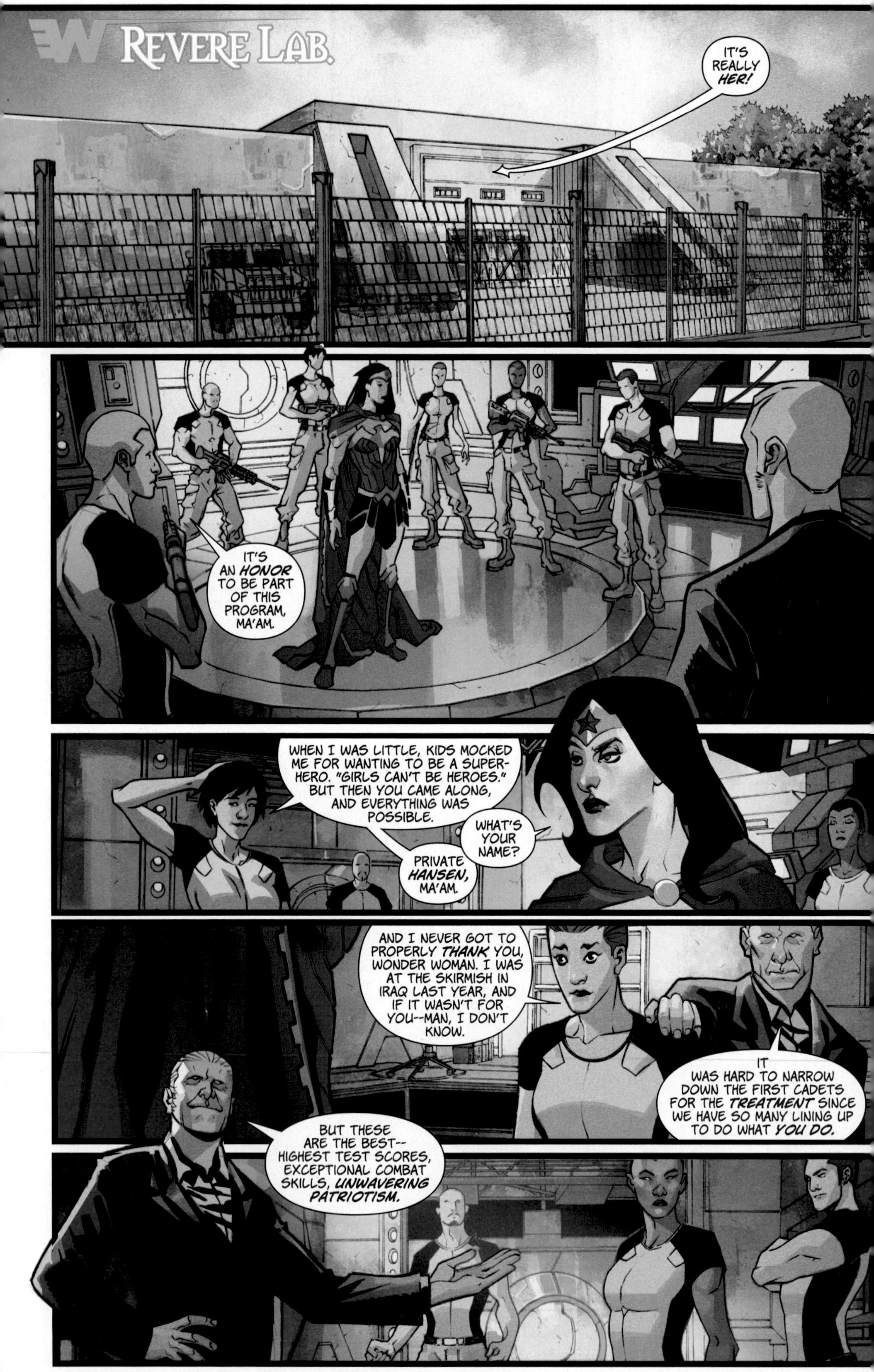
REVERE LAB.
IT'S REALLY HER!
IT'S AN HONOR TO BE PART OF THIS PROGRAM, MA'AM.
WHEN I WAS LITTLE, KIDS MOCKED ME FOR WANTING TO BE A SUPERHERO. "GIRLS CAN'T BE HEROES." BUT THEN YOU CAME ALONG, AND EVERYTHING WAS POSSIBLE.
WHAT'S YOUR NAME?
PRIVATE HANSEN, MA'AM.
AND I NEVER GOT TO PROPERLY THANK YOU, WONDER WOMAN. I WAS AT THE SKIRMISH IN IRAQ LAST YEAR, AND IF IT WASN'T FOR YOU--MAN, I DON'T KNOW.
IT WAS HARD TO NARROW DOWN THE FIRST CADETS FOR THE TREATMENT SINCE WE HAVE SO MANY LINING UP TO DO WHAT YOU DO.
BUT THESE ARE THE BEST--HIGHEST TEST SCORES, EXCEPTIONAL COMBAT SKILLS, UNWAVERING PATRIOTISM.

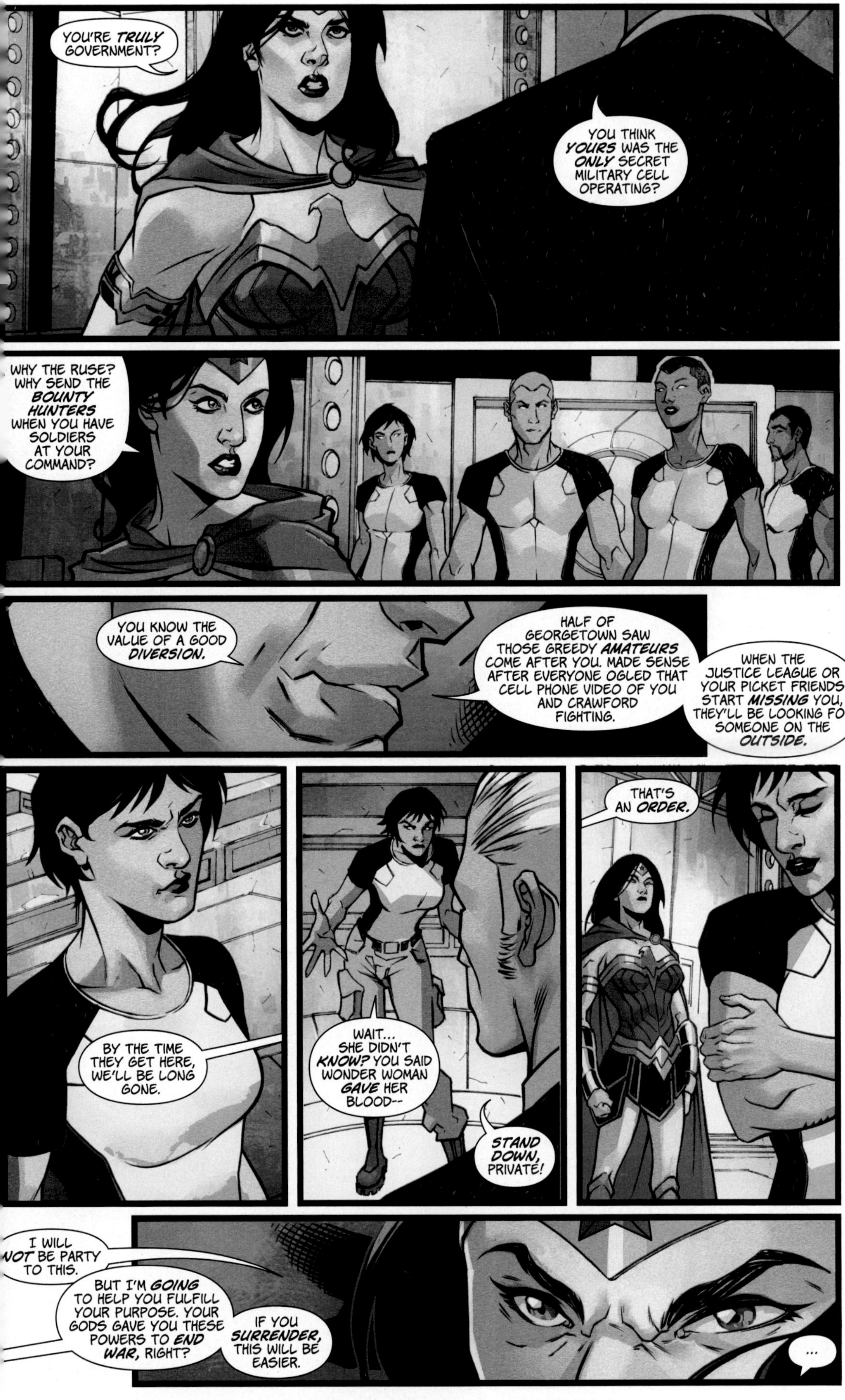
YOU'RE TRULY GOVERNMENT?
YOU THINK YOURS WAS THE ONLY SECRET MILITARY CELL OPERATING?
WHY THE RUSE? WHY SEND THE BOUNTY HUNTERS WHEN YOU HAVE SOLDIERS AT YOUR COMMAND?
YOU KNOW THE VALUE OF A GOOD DIVERSION.
HALF OF GEORGETOWN SAW THOSE GREEDY AMATEURS COME AFTER YOU. MADE SENSE AFTER EVERYONE OGLED THAT CELL PHONE VIDEO OF YOU AND CRAWFORD FIGHTING.
WHEN THE JUSTICE LEAGUE OR YOUR PICKET FRIENDS START MISSING YOU, THEY'LL BE LOOKING FOR SOMEONE ON THE OUTSIDE.
BY THE TIME THEY GET HERE, WE'LL BE LONG GONE.
WAIT... SHE DIDN'T KNOW? YOU SAID WONDER WOMAN GAVE HER BLOOD--
STAND DOWN, PRIVATE!
THAT'S AN ORDER.
I WILL NOT BE PARTY TO THIS.
BUT I'M GOING TO HELP YOU FULFILL YOUR PURPOSE. YOUR GODS GAVE YOU THESE POWERS TO END WAR, RIGHT?
IF YOU SURRENDER, THIS WILL BE EASIER.
...

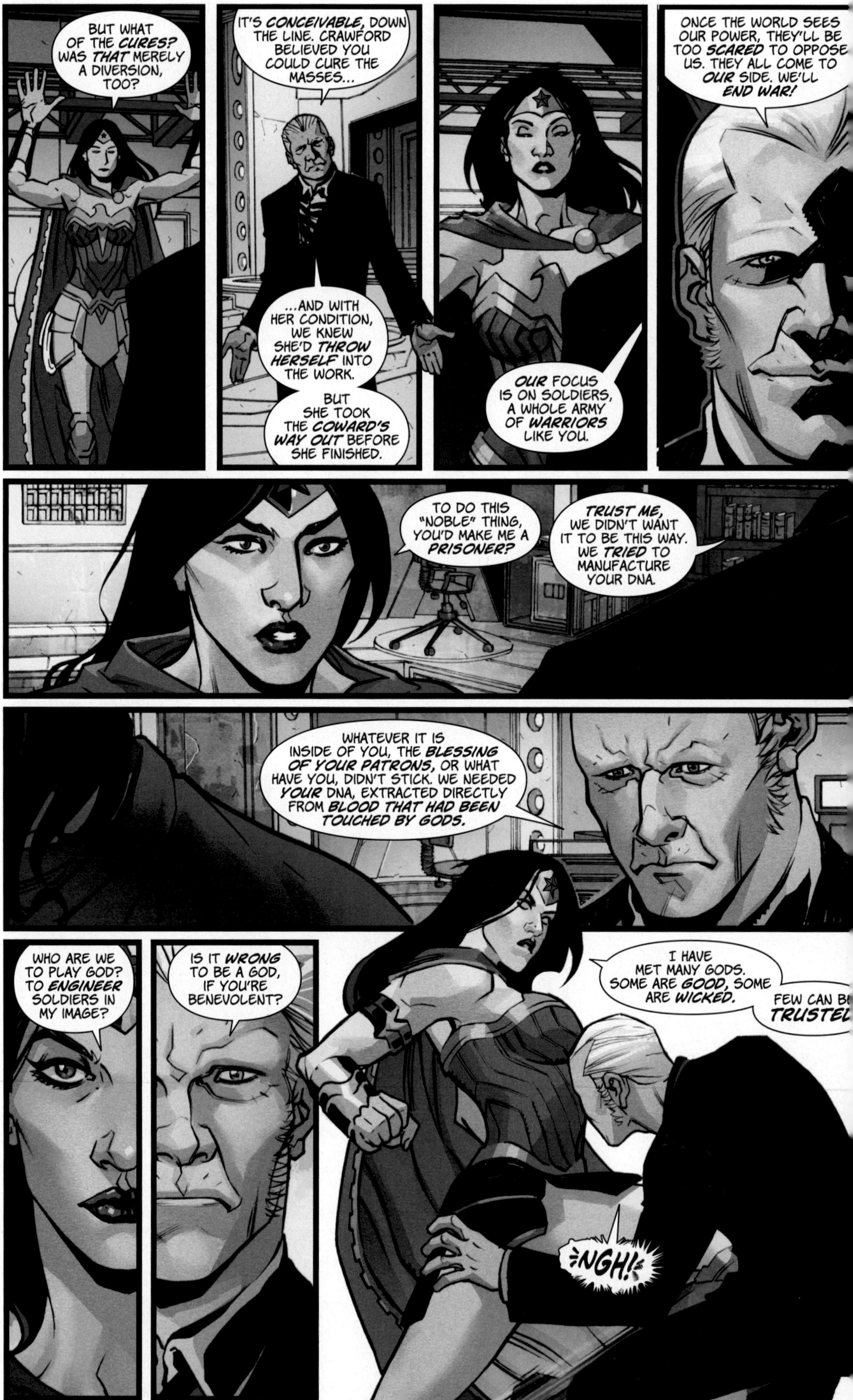

BUT WHAT OF THE CURES? WAS THAT MERELY A DIVERSION, TOO?
IT'S CONCEIVABLE, DOWN THE LINE. CRAWFORD BELIEVED YOU COULD CURE THE MASSES...
...AND WITH HER CONDITION, WE KNEW SHE'D THROW HERSELF INTO THE WORK.
BUT SHE TOOK THE COWARD'S WAY OUT BEFORE SHE FINISHED.
OUR FOCUS IS ON SOLDIERS, A WHOLE ARMY OF WARRIORS LIKE YOU.
ONCE THE WORLD SEES OUR POWER, THEY'LL BE TOO SCARED TO OPPOSE US. THEY ALL COME TO OUR SIDE. WE'LL END WAR!
TO DO THIS "NOBLE" THING, YOU'D MAKE ME A PRISONER?
TRUST ME, WE DIDN'T WANT IT TO BE THIS WAY. WE TRIED TO MANUFACTURE YOUR DNA.
WHATEVER IT IS INSIDE OF YOU, THE BLESSING OF YOUR PATRONS, OR WHAT HAVE YOU, DIDN'T STICK. WE NEEDED YOUR DNA, EXTRACTED DIRECTLY FROM BLOOD THAT HAD BEEN TOUCHED BY GODS.
WHO ARE WE TO PLAY GOD? TO ENGINEER SOLDIERS IN MY IMAGE?
IS IT WRONG TO BE A GOD, IF YOU'RE BENEVOLENT?
I HAVE MET MANY GODS. SOME ARE GOOD, SOME ARE WICKED.
FEW CAN BE TRUSTED
NGH!

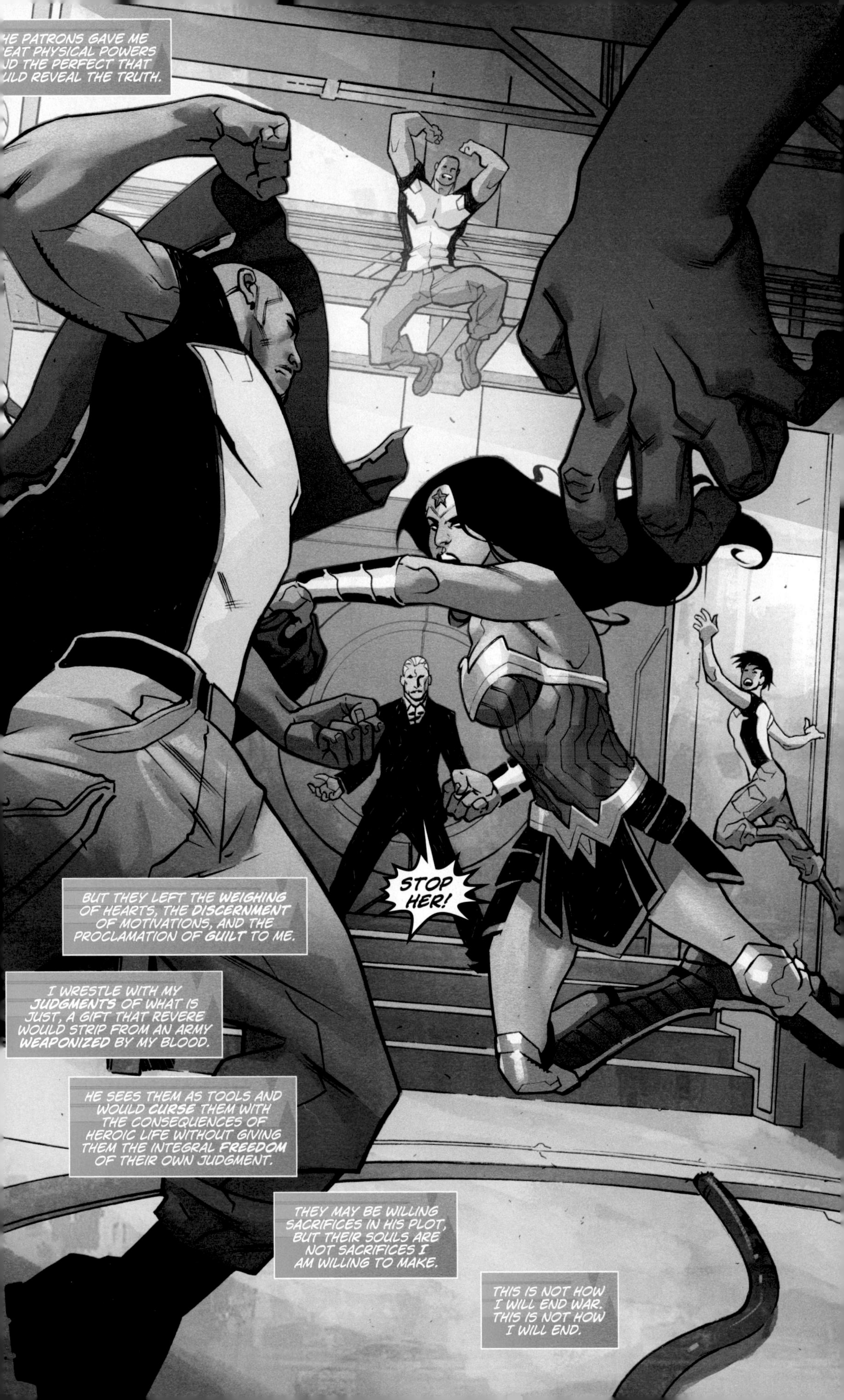
HE PATRONS GAVE ME
EAT PHYSICAL POWERS
ND THE PERFECT THAT
ULD REVEAL THE TRUTH.
BUT THEY LEFT THE WEIGHING OF HEARTS, THE DISCERNMENT OF MOTIVATIONS, AND THE PROCLAMATION OF GUILT TO ME.
STOP HER!
I WRESTLE WITH MY JUDGMENTS OF WHAT IS JUST, A GIFT THAT REVERE WOULD STRIP FROM AN ARMY WEAPONIZED BY MY BLOOD.
HE SEES THEM AS TOOLS AND WOULD CURSE THEM WITH THE CONSEQUENCES OF HEROIC LIFE WITHOUT GIVING THEM THE INTEGRAL FREEDOM OF THEIR OWN JUDGMENT.
THEY MAY BE WILLING SACRIFICES IN HIS PLOT, BUT THEIR SOULS ARE NOT SACRIFICES I AM WILLING TO MAKE.
THIS IS NOT HOW I WILL END WAR. THIS IS NOT HOW I WILL END.

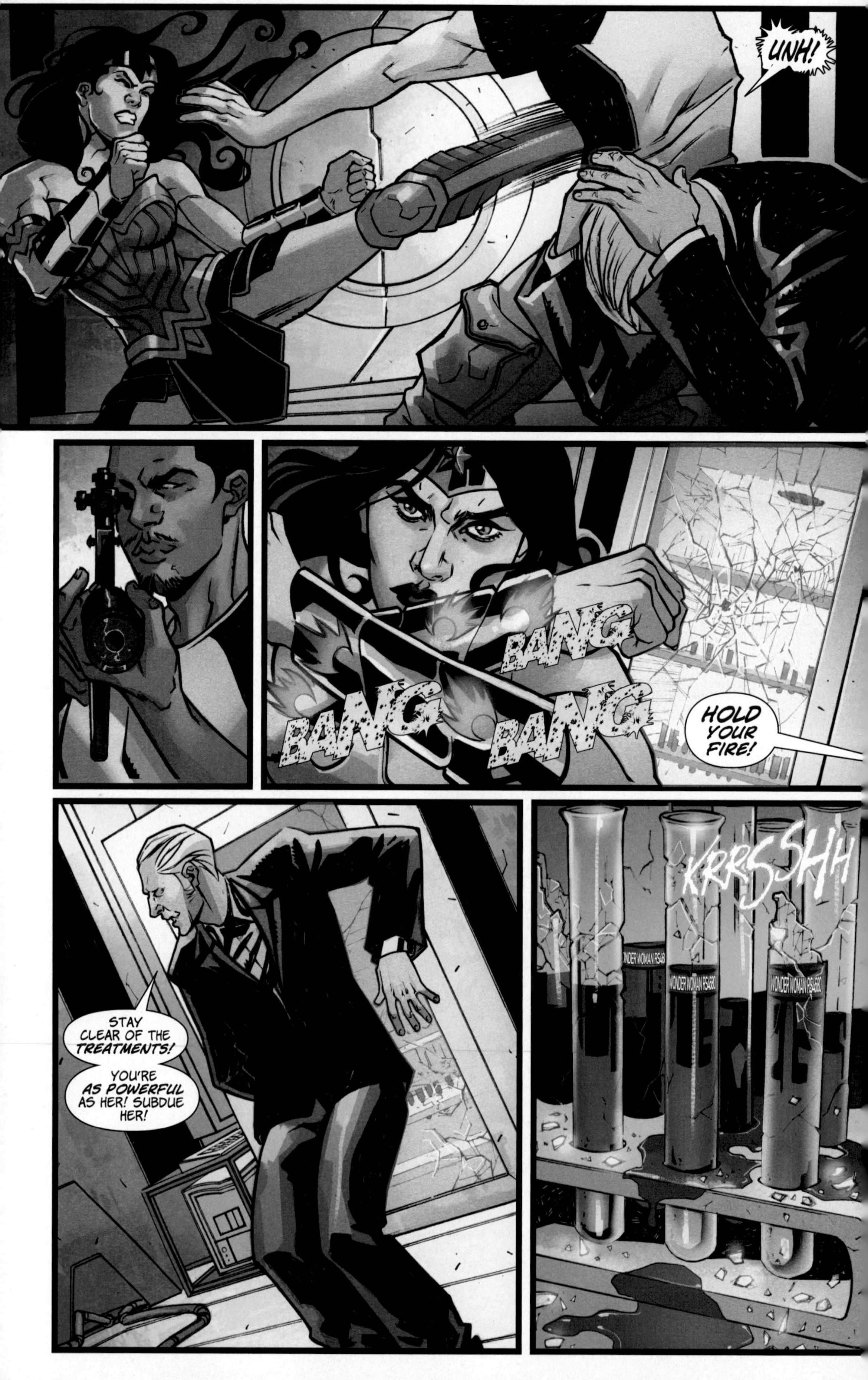
UNH!
BANG
BANG
BANG
HOLD YOUR FIRE!
STAY CLEAR OF THE TREATMENTS!
YOU'RE AS POWERFUL AS HER! SUBDUE HER!
KRRSSHH

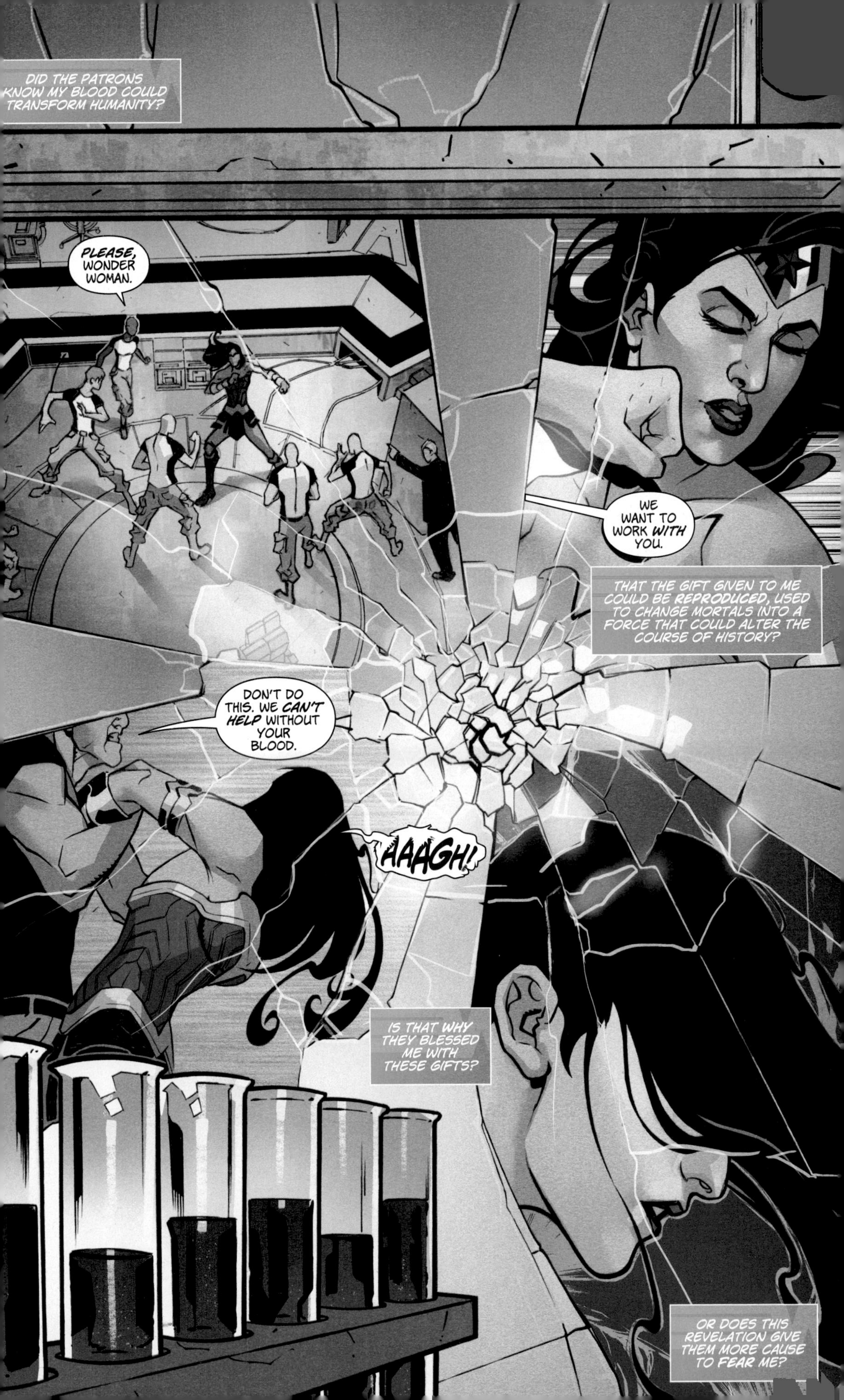

DID THE PATRONS KNOW MY BLOOD COULD TRANSFORM HUMANITY?
PLEASE, WONDER WOMAN.
WE WANT TO WORK WITH YOU.
THAT THE GIFT GIVEN TO ME COULD BE REPRODUCED, USED TO CHANGE MORTALS INTO A FORCE THAT COULD ALTER THE COURSE OF HISTORY?
DON'T DO THIS. WE CAN'T HELP WITHOUT YOUR BLOOD.
HAAAGH!
IS THAT WHY THEY BLESSED ME WITH THESE GIFTS?
OR DOES THIS REVELATION GIVE THEM MORE CAUSE TO FEAR ME?

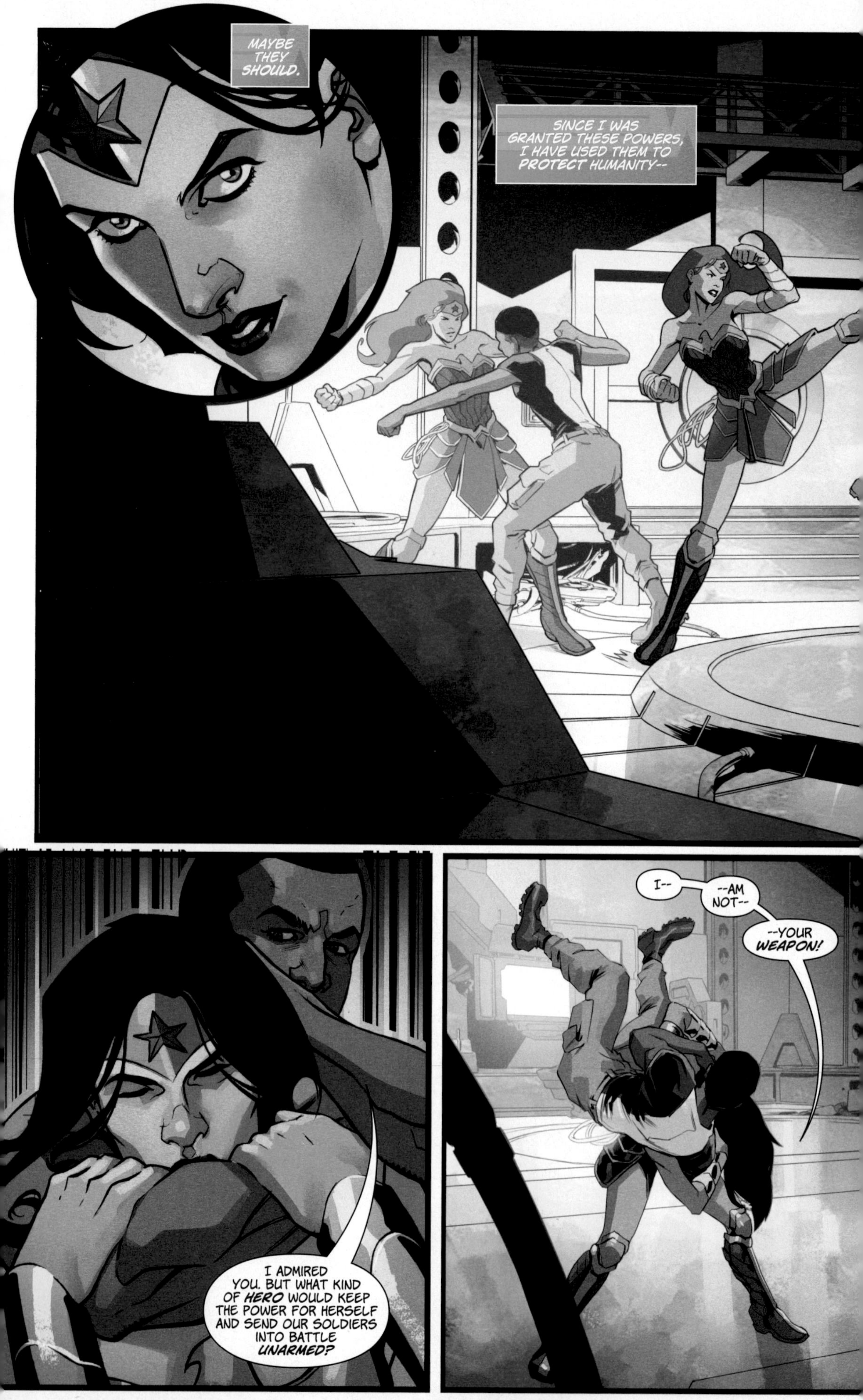
MAYBE THEY SHOULD.
SINCE I WAS GRANTED THESE POWERS, I HAVE USED THEM TO PROTECT HUMANITY--
I ADMIRED YOU. BUT WHAT KIND OF HERO WOULD KEEP THE POWER FOR HERSELF AND SEND OUR SOLDIERS INTO BATTLE UNARMED?
I--
--AM NOT--
--YOUR WEAPON!

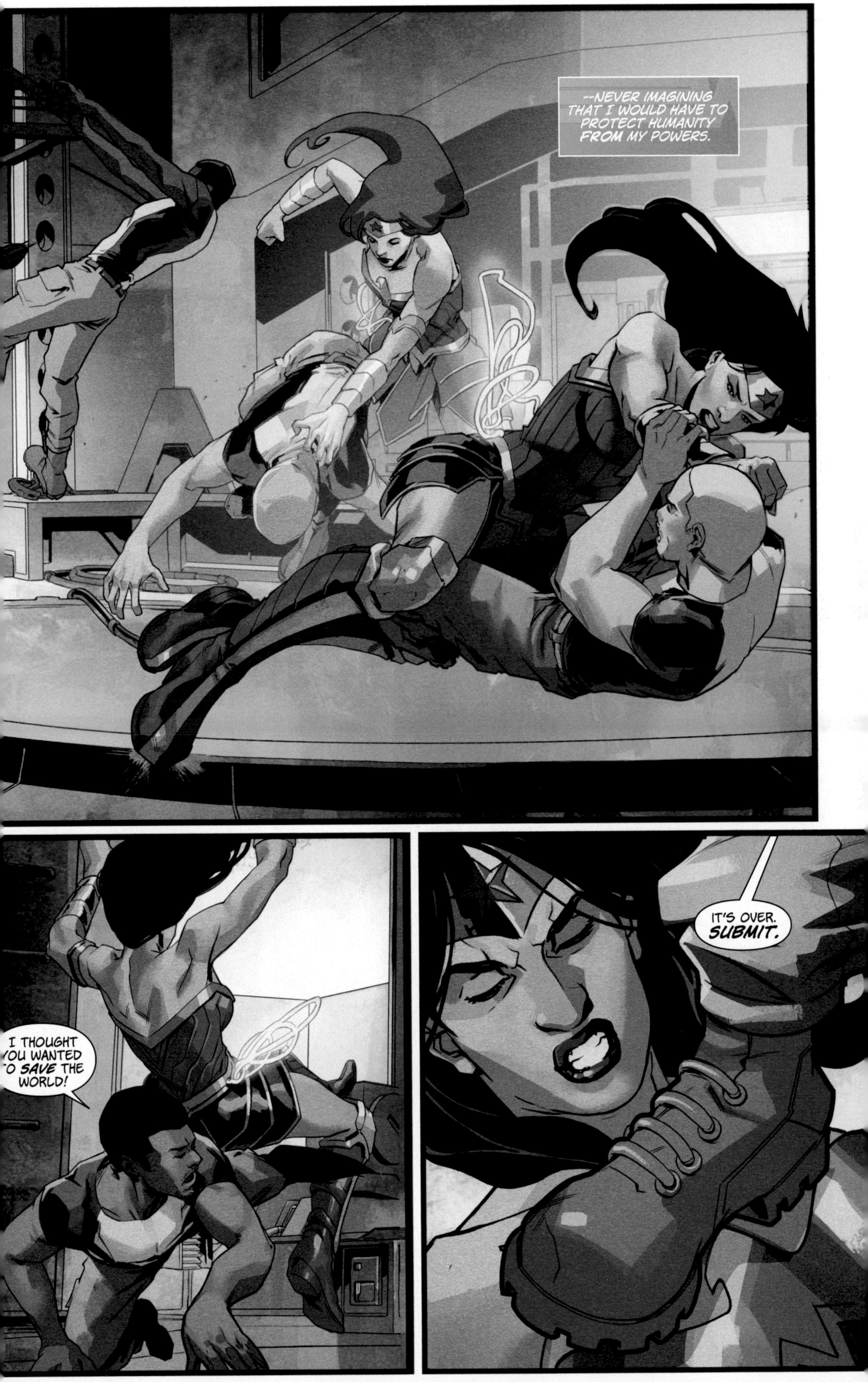
--NEVER IMAGINING THAT I WOULD HAVE TO PROTECT HUMANITY FROM MY POWERS.
I THOUGHT OU WANTED O *SAVE* THE WORLD!
IT'S OVER. **SUBMIT.**

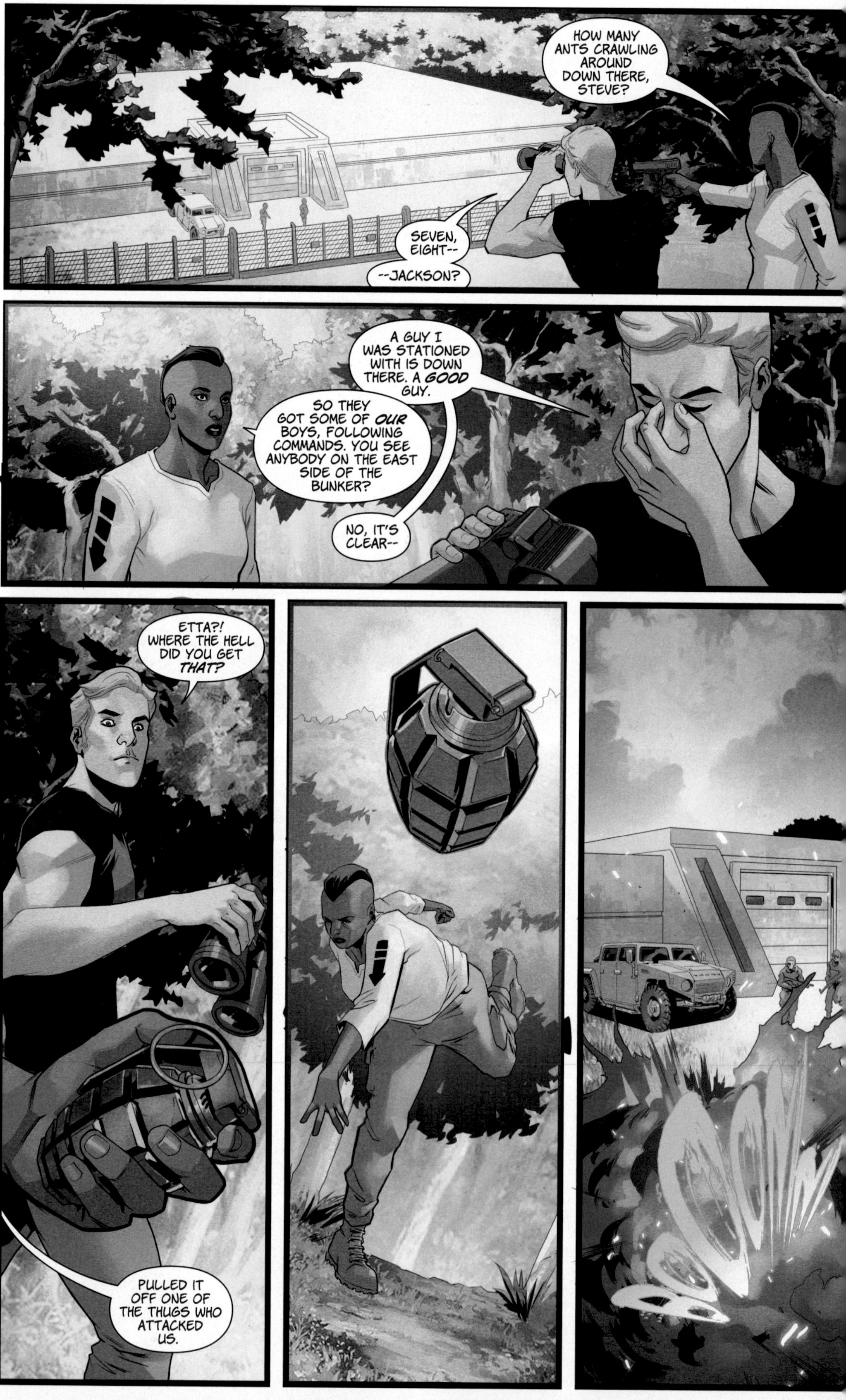
HOW MANY ANTS CRAWLING AROUND DOWN THERE, STEVE?
SEVEN, EIGHT--
--JACKSON?
A GUY I WAS STATIONED WITH IS DOWN THERE. A *GOOD* GUY.
SO THEY GOT SOME OF *OUR* BOYS, FOLLOWING COMMANDS. YOU SEE ANYBODY ON THE EAST SIDE OF THE BUNKER?
NO, IT'S CLEAR--
ETTA?! WHERE THE HELL DID YOU GET *THAT?*
PULLED IT OFF ONE OF THE THUGS WHO ATTACKED US.

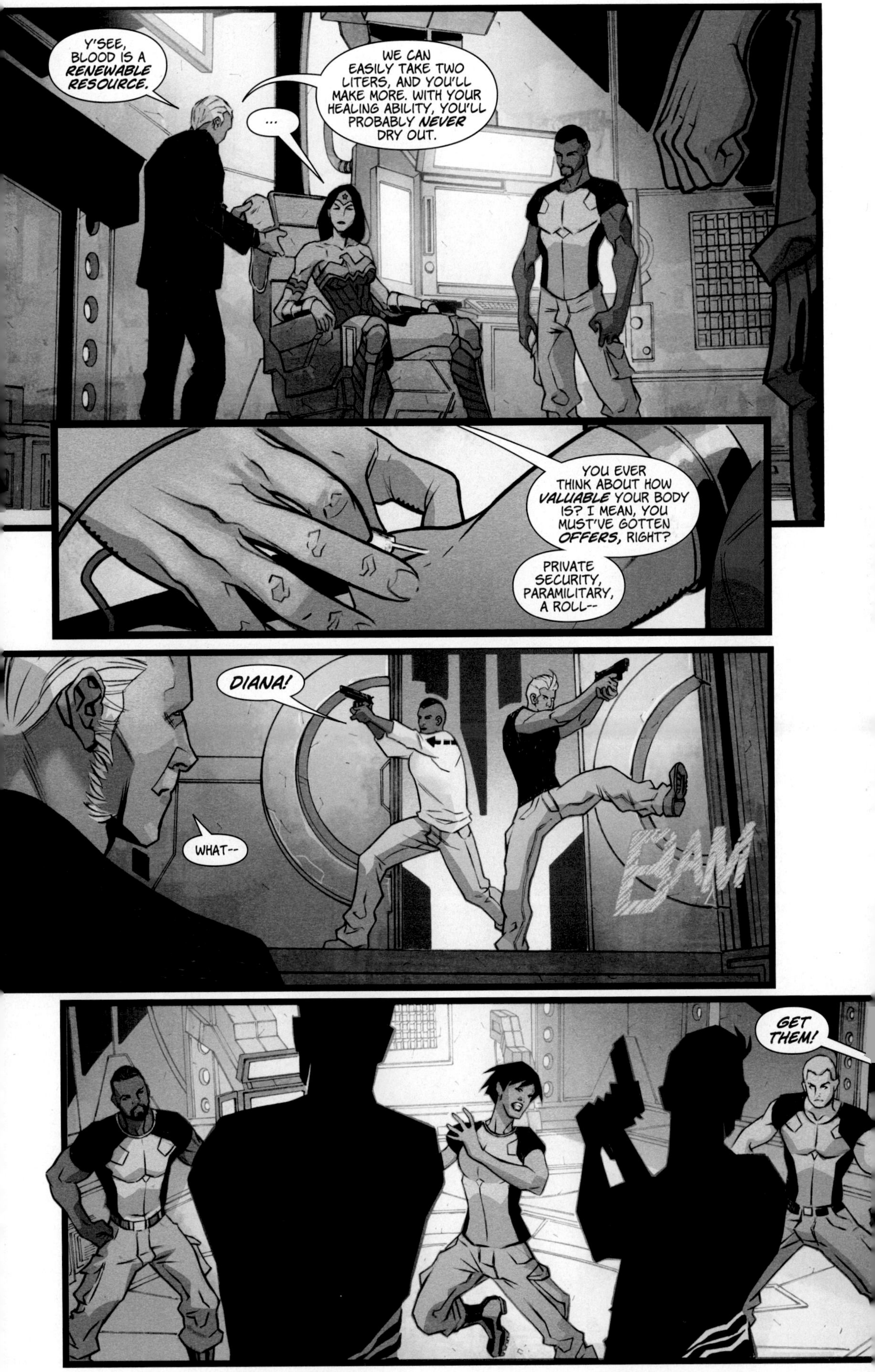
Y'SEE, BLOOD IS A RENEWABLE RESOURCE.
...
WE CAN EASILY TAKE TWO LITERS, AND YOU'LL MAKE MORE. WITH YOUR HEALING ABILITY, YOU'LL PROBABLY NEVER DRY OUT.
YOU EVER THINK ABOUT HOW VALUABLE YOUR BODY IS? I MEAN, YOU MUST'VE GOTTEN OFFERS, RIGHT?
PRIVATE SECURITY, PARAMILITARY, A ROLL--
DIANA!
WHAT--
BAM
GET THEM!

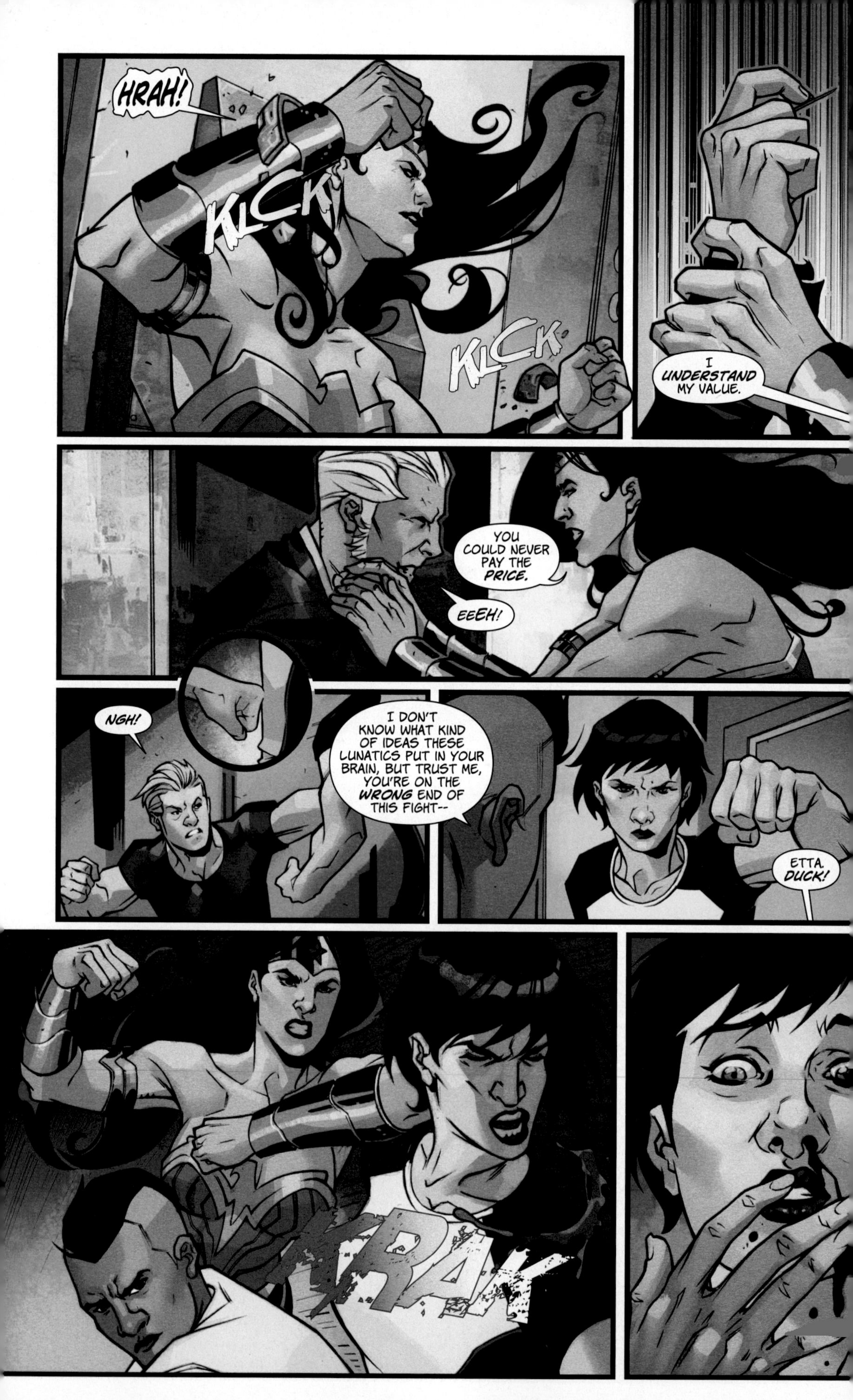
HRAH!
KLCK
KLCK
I UNDERSTAND MY VALUE.
YOU COULD NEVER PAY THE PRICE.
EEEH!
NGH!
I DON'T KNOW WHAT KIND OF IDEAS THESE LUNATICS PUT IN YOUR BRAIN, BUT TRUST ME, YOU'RE ON THE WRONG END OF THIS FIGHT--
ETTA. DUCK!
KRAK

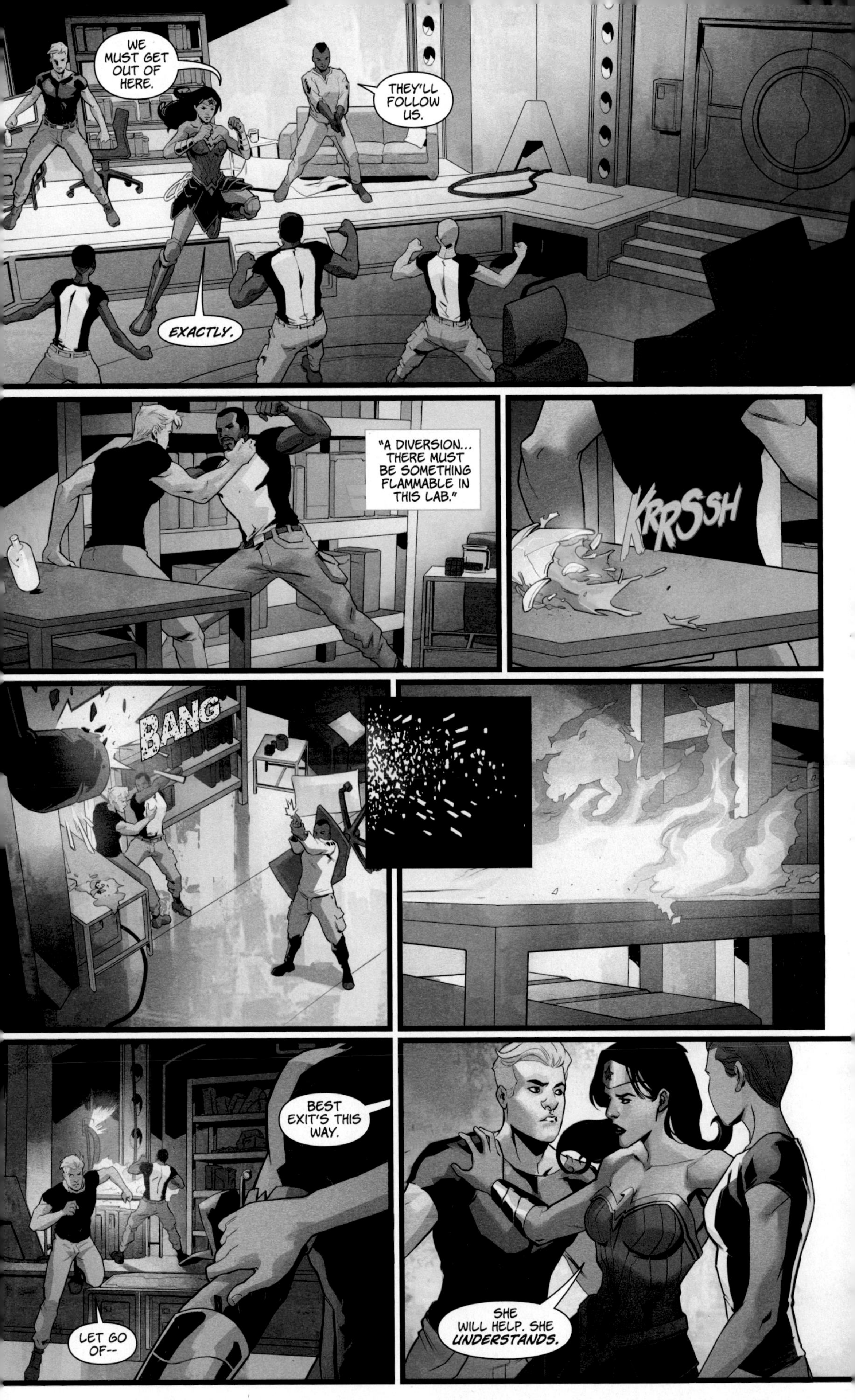
WE MUST GET OUT OF HERE.
THEY'LL FOLLOW US.
EXACTLY.
"A DIVERSION... THERE MUST BE SOMETHING FLAMMABLE IN THIS LAB."
KRRSSH
BANG
BEST EXIT'S THIS WAY.
LET GO OF--
SHE WILL HELP. SHE UNDERSTANDS.

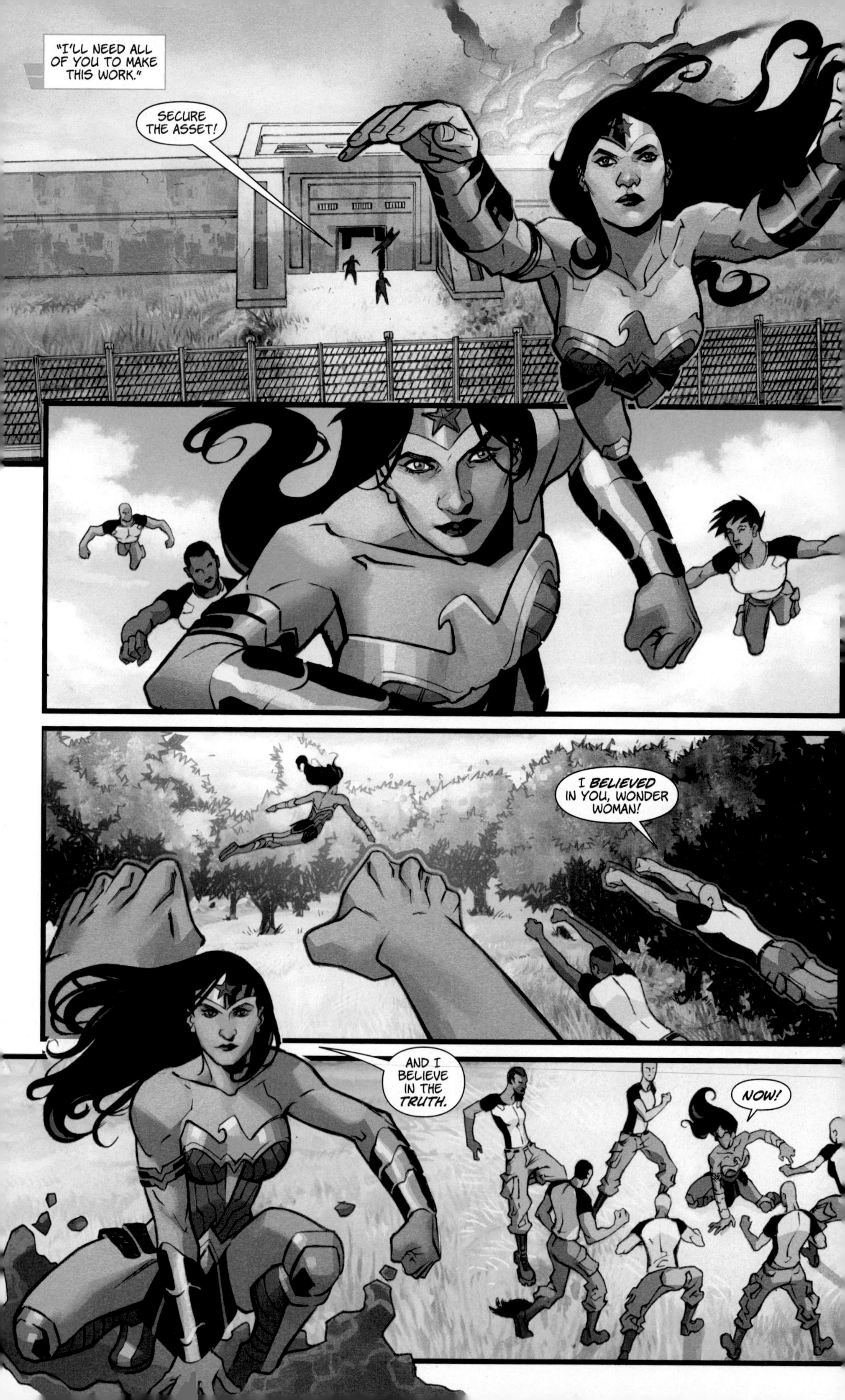
"I'LL NEED ALL OF YOU TO MAKE THIS WORK."
SECURE THE ASSET!
I BELIEVED IN YOU, WONDER WOMAN!
AND I BELIEVE IN THE TRUTH.
NOW!

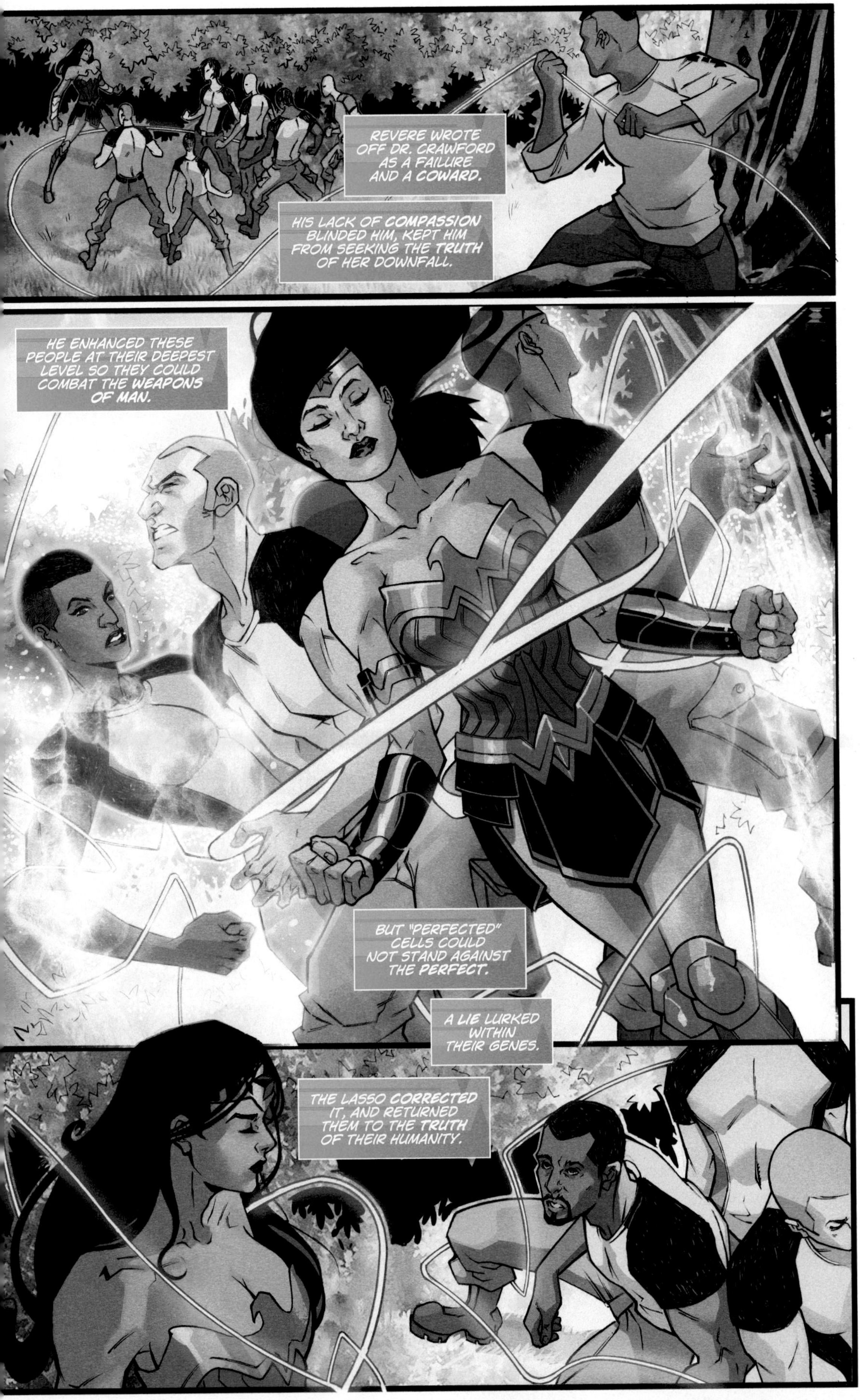
REVERE WROTE OFF DR. CRAWFORD AS A FAILURE AND A COWARD.
HIS LACK OF COMPASSION BLINDED HIM, KEPT HIM FROM SEEKING THE TRUTH OF HER DOWNFALL.
HE ENHANCED THESE PEOPLE AT THEIR DEEPEST LEVEL SO THEY COULD COMBAT THE WEAPONS OF MAN.
BUT "PERFECTED" CELLS COULD NOT STAND AGAINST THE PERFECT.
A LIE LURKED WITHIN THEIR GENES.
THE LASSO CORRECTED IT, AND RETURNED THEM TO THE TRUTH OF THEIR HUMANITY.

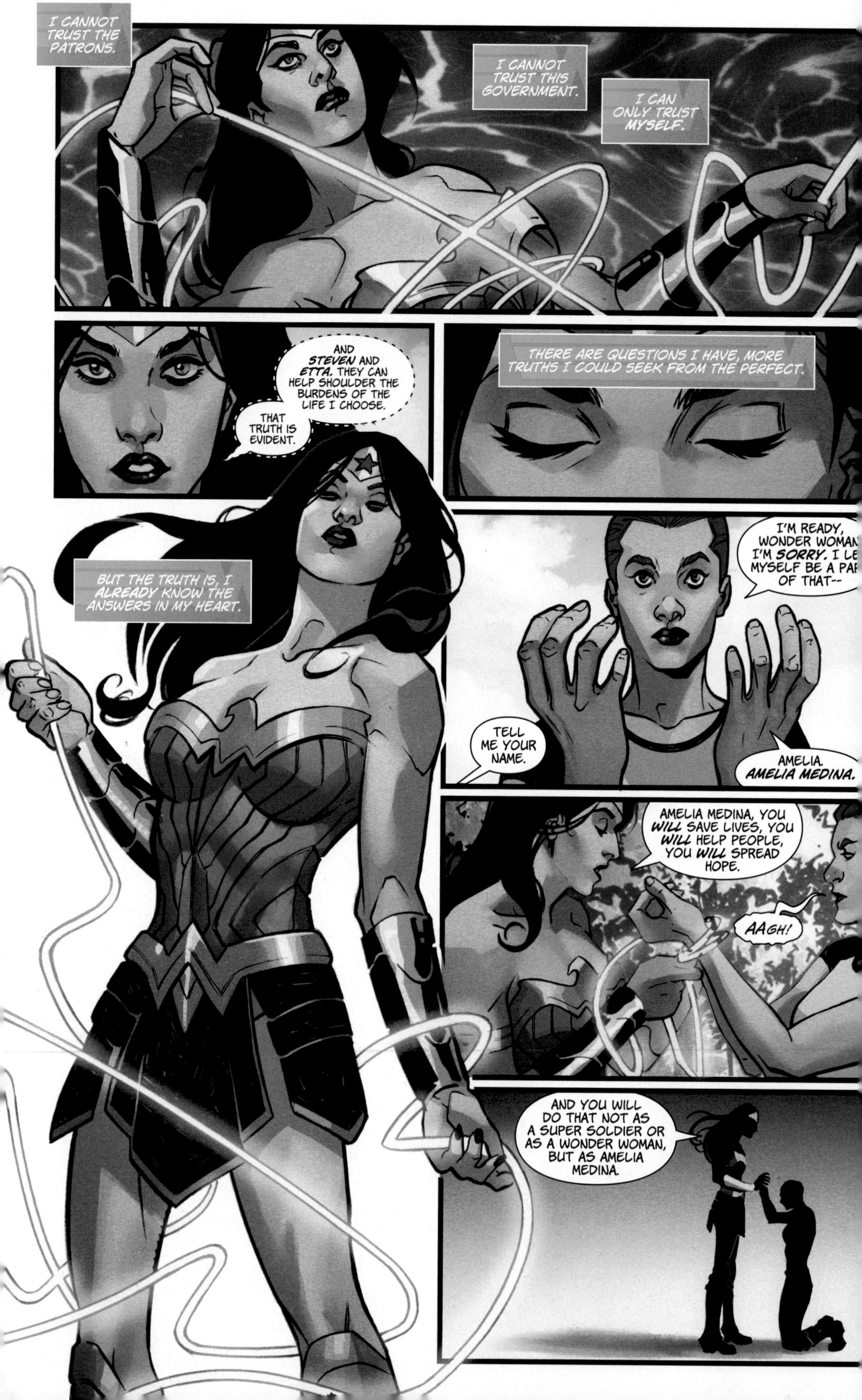
I CANNOT TRUST THE PATRONS.
I CANNOT TRUST THIS GOVERNMENT.
I CAN ONLY TRUST MYSELF.
AND STEVEN AND ETTA. THEY CAN HELP SHOULDER THE BURDENS OF THE LIFE I CHOOSE.
THAT TRUTH IS EVIDENT.
THERE ARE QUESTIONS I HAVE, MORE TRUTHS I COULD SEEK FROM THE PERFECT.
BUT THE TRUTH IS, I ALREADY KNOW THE ANSWERS IN MY HEART.
I'M READY, WONDER WOMAN. I'M SORRY. I LET MYSELF BE A PART OF THAT--
TELL ME YOUR NAME.
AMELIA. AMELIA MEDINA.
AMELIA MEDINA, YOU WILL SAVE LIVES, YOU WILL HELP PEOPLE, YOU WILL SPREAD HOPE.
AAGH!
AND YOU WILL DO THAT NOT AS A SUPER SOLDIER OR AS A WONDER WOMAN, BUT AS AMELIA MEDINA.

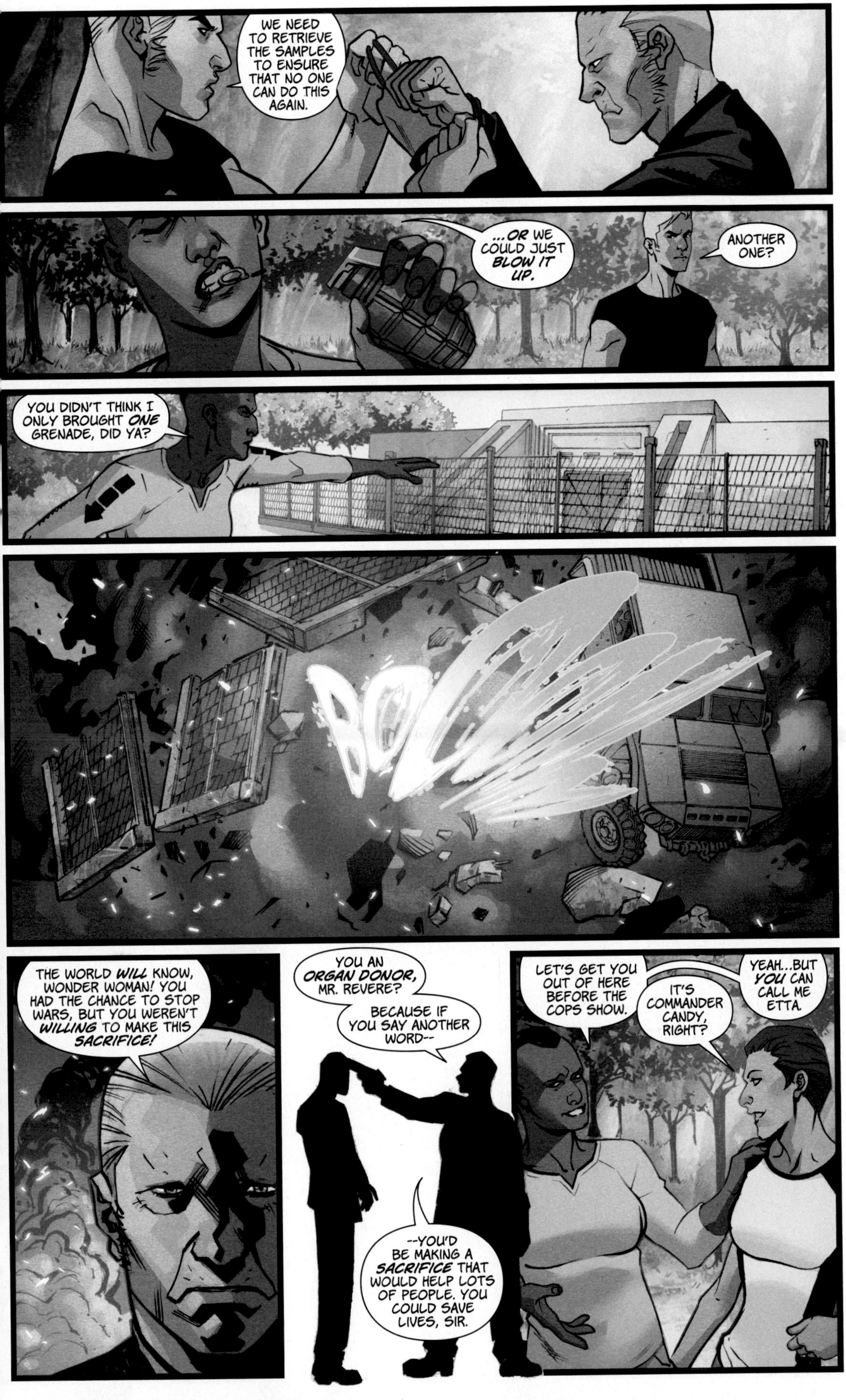
WE NEED TO RETRIEVE THE SAMPLES TO ENSURE THAT NO ONE CAN DO THIS AGAIN.
...OR WE COULD JUST BLOW IT UP.
ANOTHER ONE?
YOU DIDN'T THINK I ONLY BROUGHT ONE GRENADE, DID YA?
BOOM
THE WORLD WILL KNOW, WONDER WOMAN! YOU HAD THE CHANCE TO STOP WARS, BUT YOU WEREN'T WILLING TO MAKE THIS SACRIFICE!
YOU AN ORGAN DONOR, MR. REVERE?
BECAUSE IF YOU SAY ANOTHER WORD--
--YOU'D BE MAKING A SACRIFICE THAT WOULD HELP LOTS OF PEOPLE. YOU COULD SAVE LIVES, SIR.
LET'S GET YOU OUT OF HERE BEFORE THE COPS SHOW.
IT'S COMMANDER CANDY, RIGHT?
YEAH...BUT YOU CAN CALL ME ETTA.

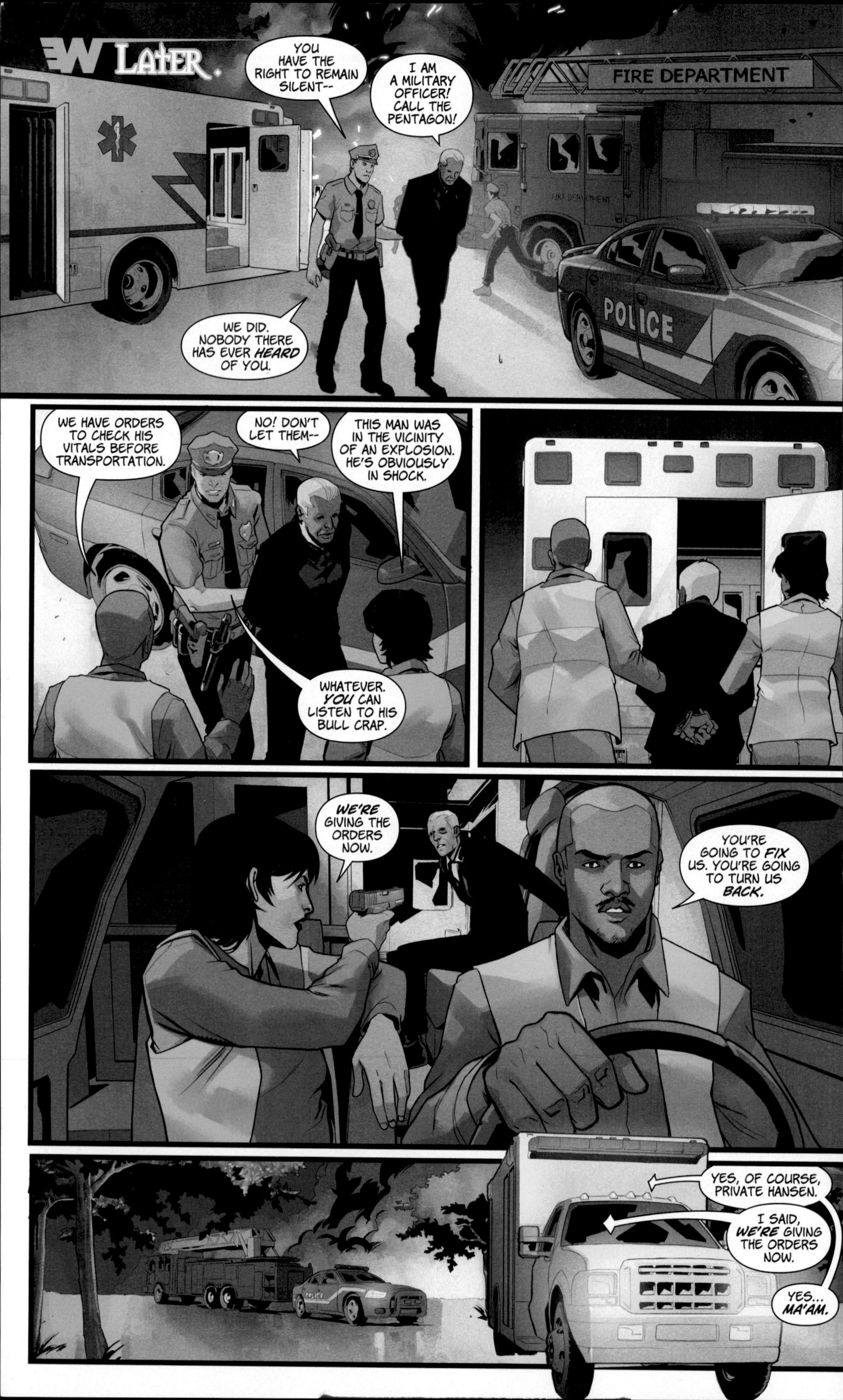

LATER.
YOU HAVE THE RIGHT TO REMAIN SILENT--
I AM A MILITARY OFFICER! CALL THE PENTAGON!
FIRE DEPARTMENT
WE DID. NOBODY THERE HAS EVER HEARD OF YOU.
POLICE
WE HAVE ORDERS TO CHECK HIS VITALS BEFORE TRANSPORTATION.
NO! DON'T LET THEM--
THIS MAN WAS IN THE VICINITY OF AN EXPLOSION. HE'S OBVIOUSLY IN SHOCK.
WHATEVER. YOU CAN LISTEN TO HIS BULL CRAP.
WE'RE GIVING THE ORDERS NOW.
YOU'RE GOING TO FIX US. YOU'RE GOING TO TURN US BACK.
YES, OF COURSE, PRIVATE HANSEN.
I SAID, WE'RE GIVING THE ORDERS NOW.
YES... MA'AM.

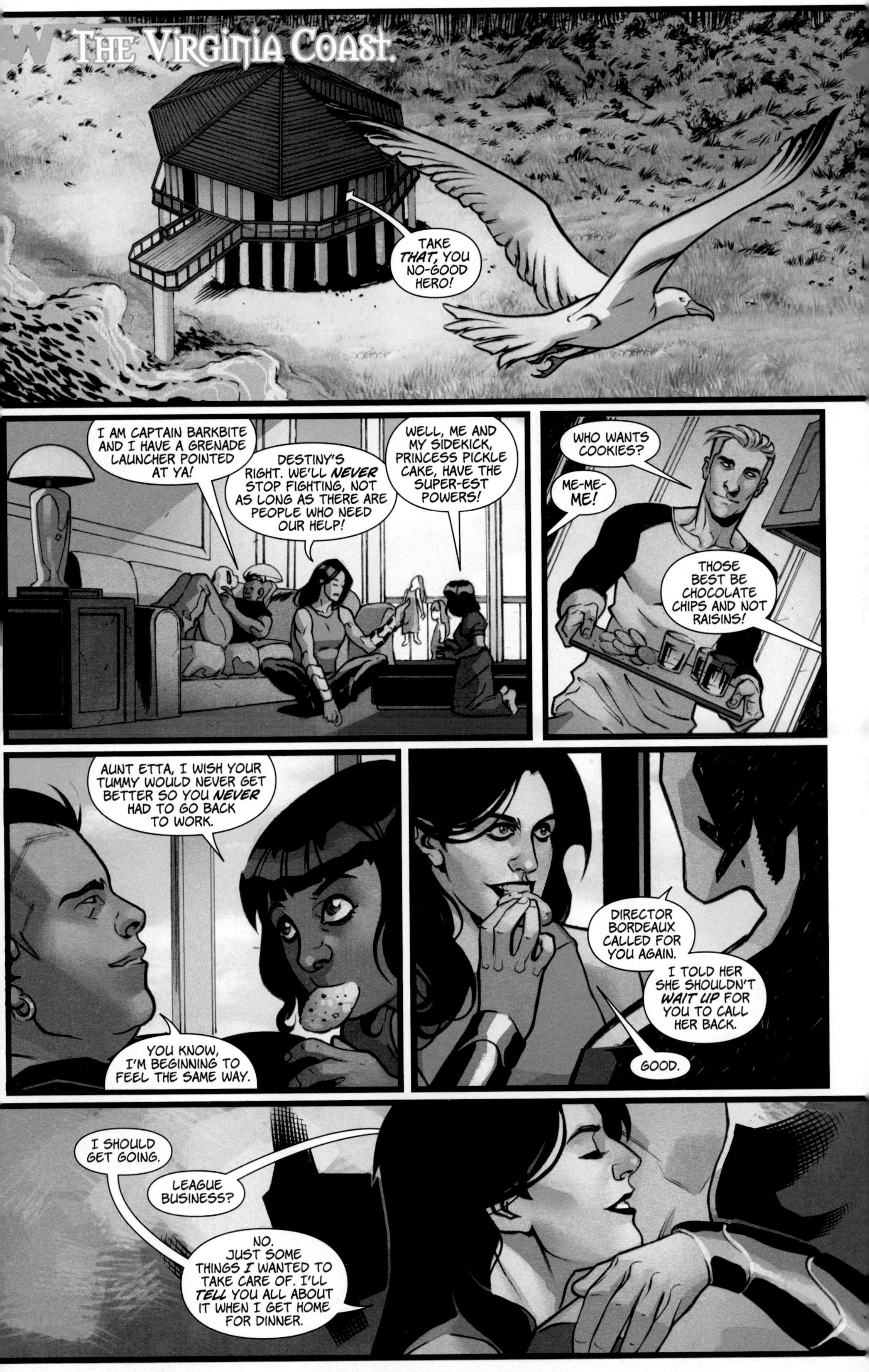
THE VIRGINIA COAST.
TAKE THAT, YOU NO-GOOD HERO!
I AM CAPTAIN BARKBITE AND I HAVE A GRENADE LAUNCHER POINTED AT YA!
DESTINY'S RIGHT. WE'LL NEVER STOP FIGHTING, NOT AS LONG AS THERE ARE PEOPLE WHO NEED OUR HELP!
WELL, ME AND MY SIDEKICK, PRINCESS PICKLE CAKE, HAVE THE SUPER-EST POWERS!
WHO WANTS COOKIES?
ME-ME-ME!
THOSE BEST BE CHOCOLATE CHIPS AND NOT RAISINS!
AUNT ETTA, I WISH YOUR TUMMY WOULD NEVER GET BETTER SO YOU NEVER HAD TO GO BACK TO WORK.
YOU KNOW, I'M BEGINNING TO FEEL THE SAME WAY.
DIRECTOR BORDEAUX CALLED FOR YOU AGAIN.
I TOLD HER SHE SHOULDN'T WAIT UP FOR YOU TO CALL HER BACK.
GOOD.
I SHOULD GET GOING.
LEAGUE BUSINESS?
NO. JUST SOME THINGS I WANTED TO TAKE CARE OF. I'LL TELL YOU ALL ABOUT IT WHEN I GET HOME FOR DINNER.

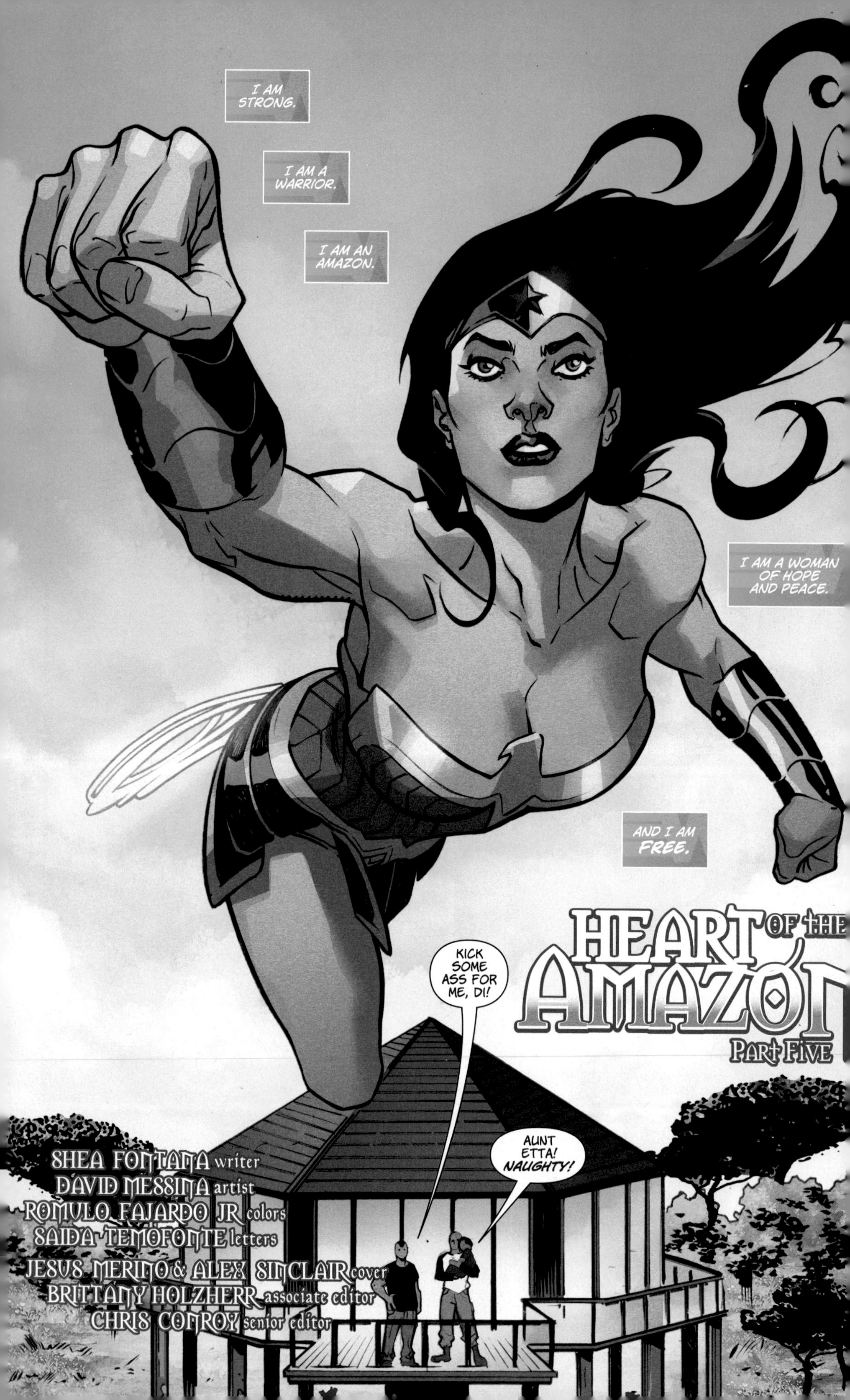
I AM STRONG.
I AM A WARRIOR.
I AM AN AMAZON.
I AM A WOMAN OF HOPE AND PEACE.
AND I AM FREE.
HEART OF THE AMAZON
PART FIVE
KICK SOME ASS FOR ME, DI!
AUNT ETTA! NAUGHTY!
SHEA FONTANA writer
DAVID MESSINA artist
ROMULO FAJARDO JR colors
SAIDA TEMOFONTE letters
JESUS MERINO & ALEX SINCLAIR cover
BRITTANY HOLZHERR associate editor
CHRIS CONROY senior editor

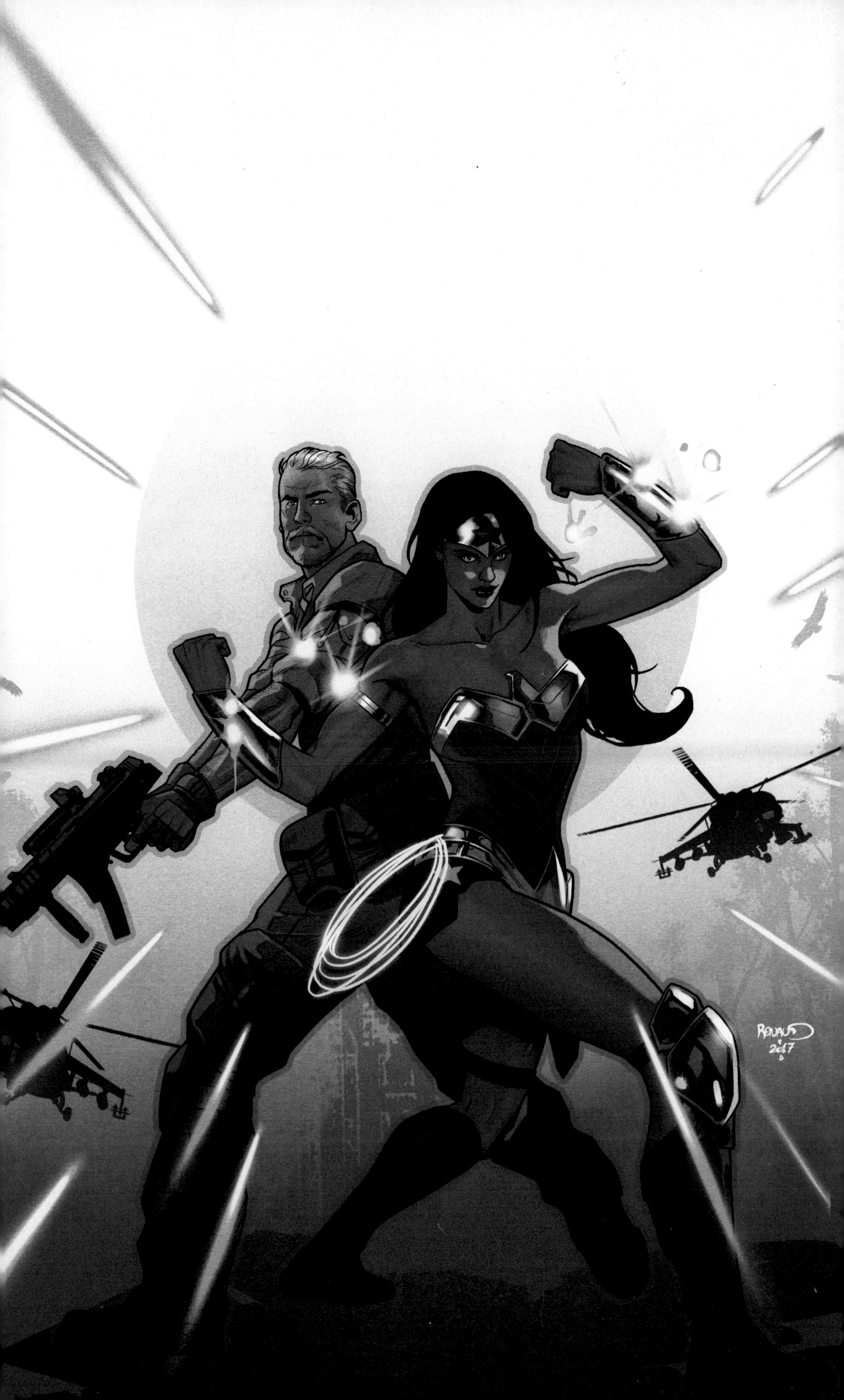
RENAUD
2017

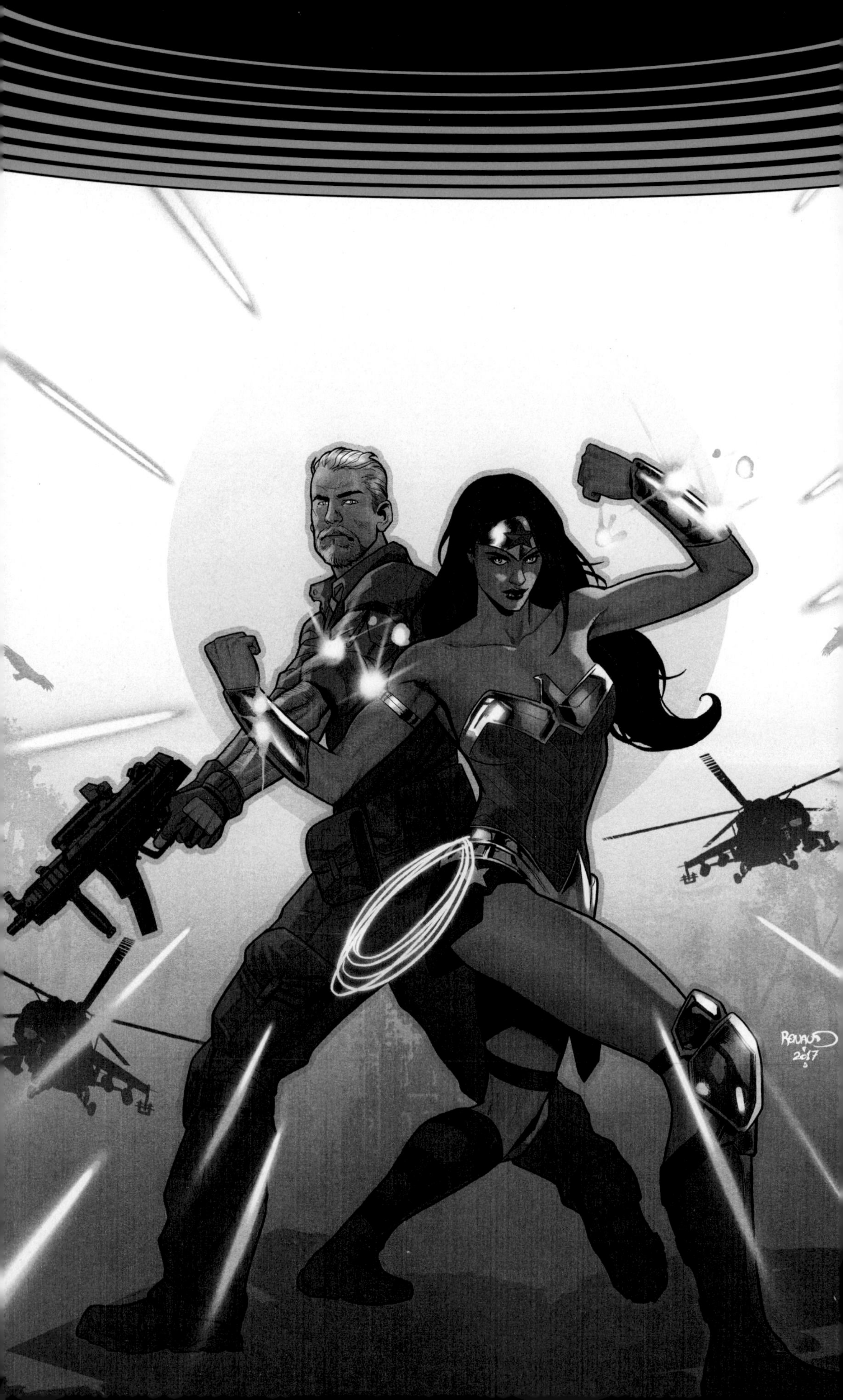
RENAUD
2017

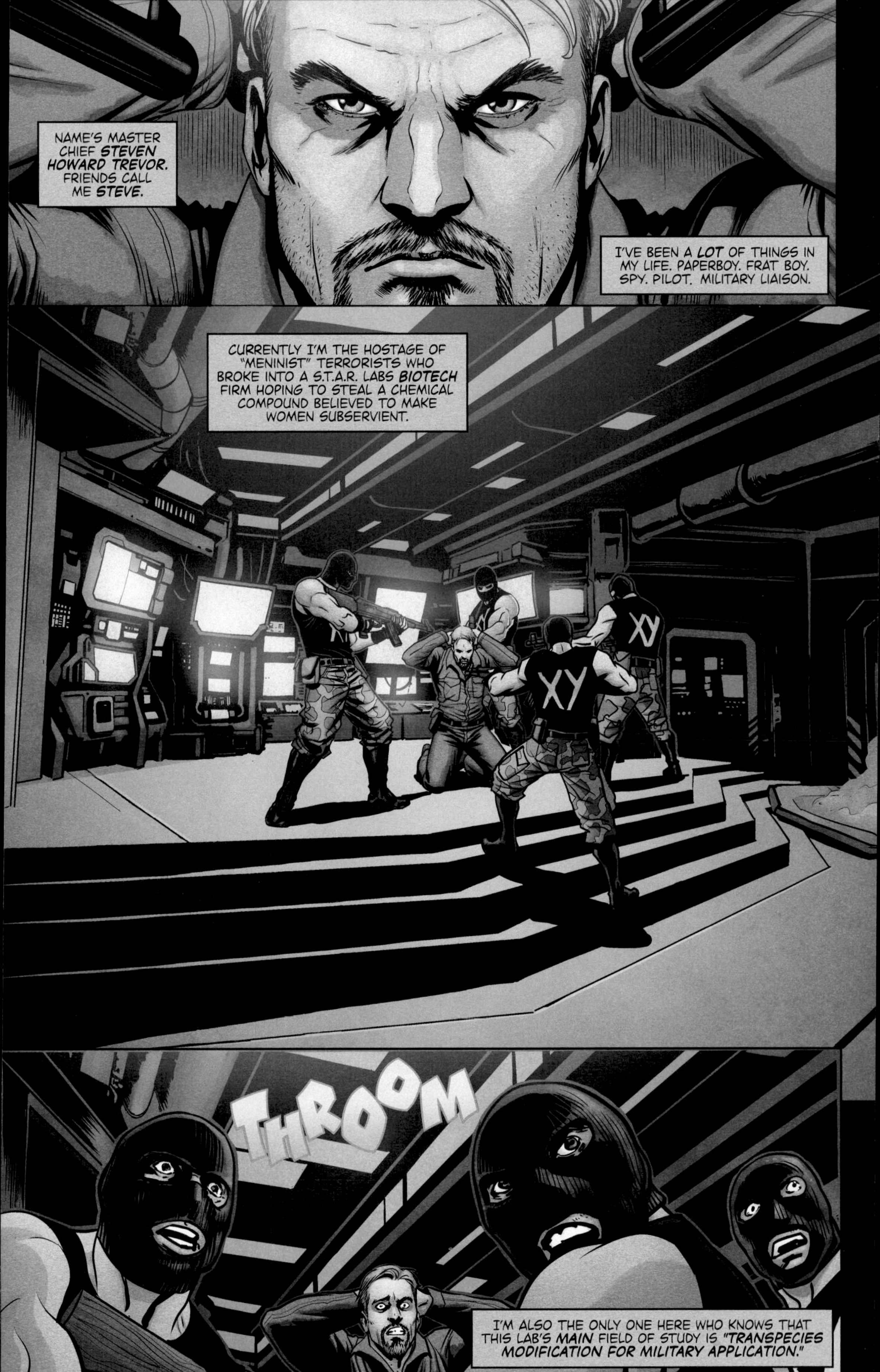

NAME'S MASTER CHIEF **STEVEN HOWARD TREVOR.** FRIENDS CALL ME **STEVE.**
I'VE BEEN A **LOT** OF THINGS IN MY LIFE. PAPERBOY. FRAT BOY. SPY. PILOT. MILITARY LIAISON.
CURRENTLY I'M THE HOSTAGE OF "MENINIST" TERRORISTS WHO BROKE INTO A S.T.A.R. LABS **BIOTECH** FIRM HOPING TO STEAL A CHEMICAL COMPOUND BELIEVED TO MAKE WOMEN SUBSERVIENT.
XY
XY
THROOM
I'M ALSO THE ONLY ONE HERE WHO KNOWS THAT THIS LAB'S **MAIN** FIELD OF STUDY IS *"TRANSPECIES MODIFICATION FOR MILITARY APPLICATION."*

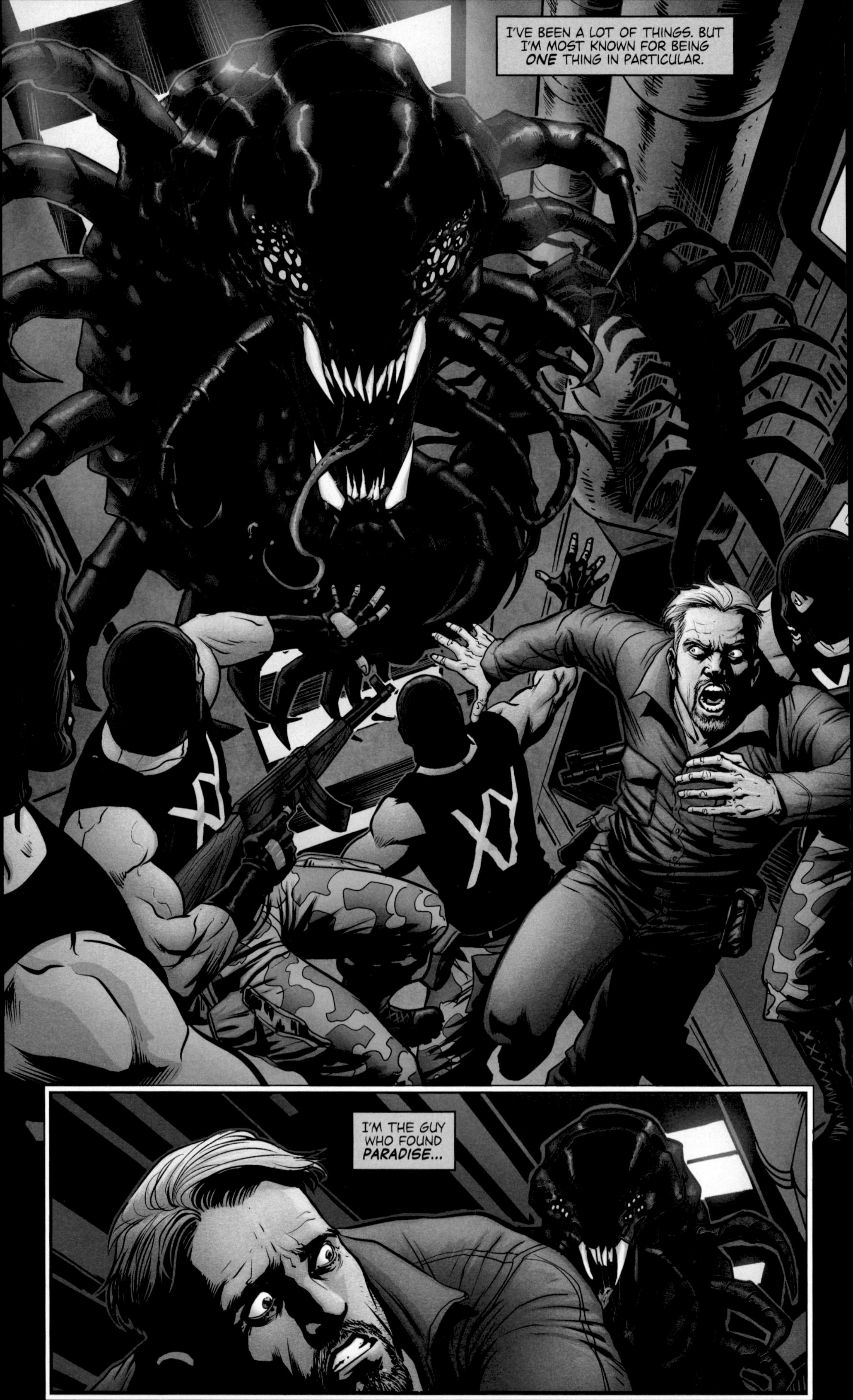
I'VE BEEN A LOT OF THINGS. BUT I'M MOST KNOWN FOR BEING ONE THING IN PARTICULAR.
I'M THE GUY WHO FOUND PARADISE...

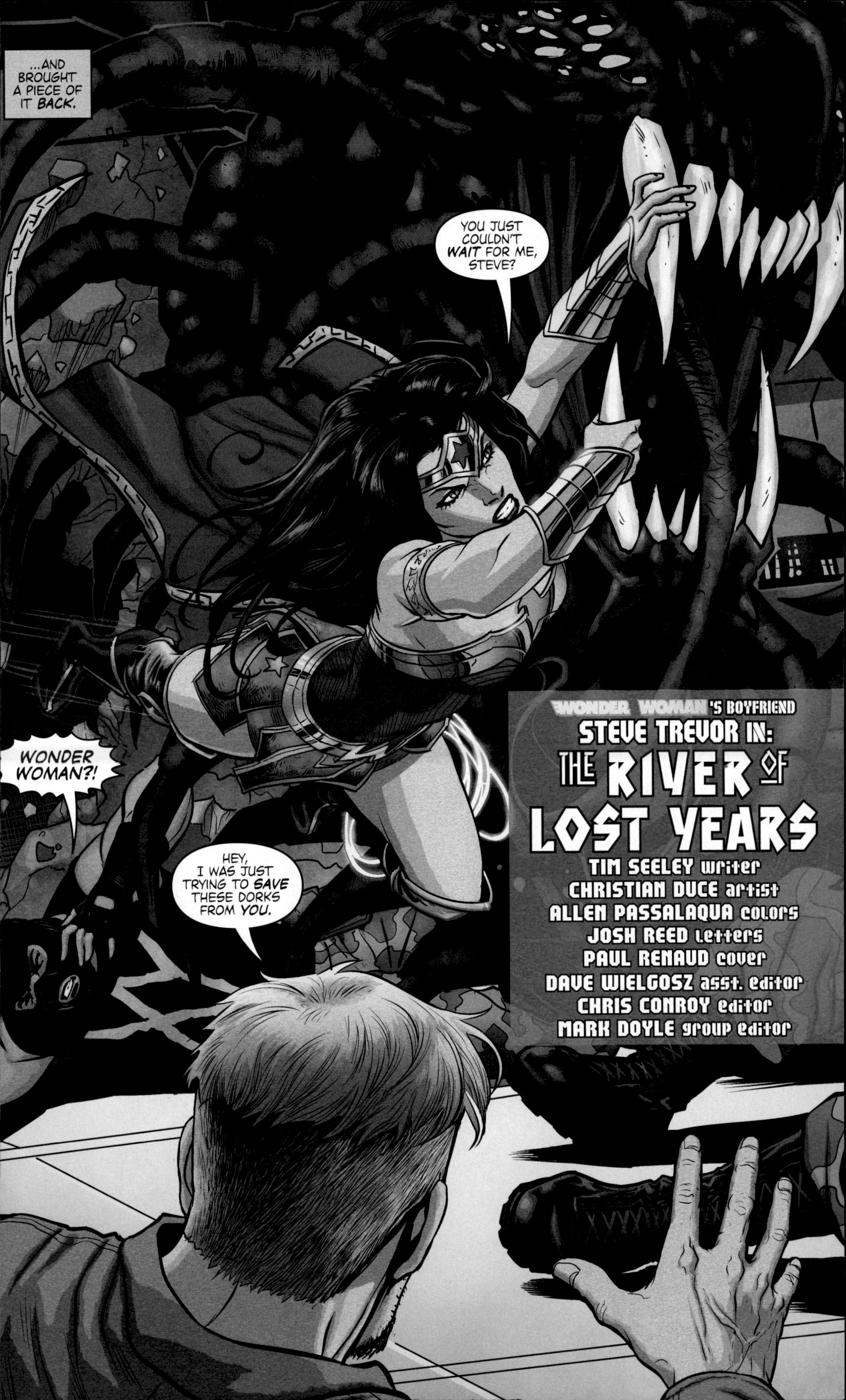

...AND BROUGHT A PIECE OF IT BACK.
YOU JUST COULDN'T WAIT FOR ME, STEVE?
WONDER WOMAN?!
HEY, I WAS JUST TRYING TO SAVE THESE DORKS FROM YOU.
WONDER WOMAN'S BOYFRIEND
STEVE TREVOR IN:
THE RIVER OF LOST YEARS
TIM SEELEY writer
CHRISTIAN DUCE artist
ALLEN PASSALAQUA colors
JOSH REED letters
PAUL RENAUD cover
DAVE WIELGOSZ asst. editor
CHRIS CONROY editor
MARK DOYLE group editor

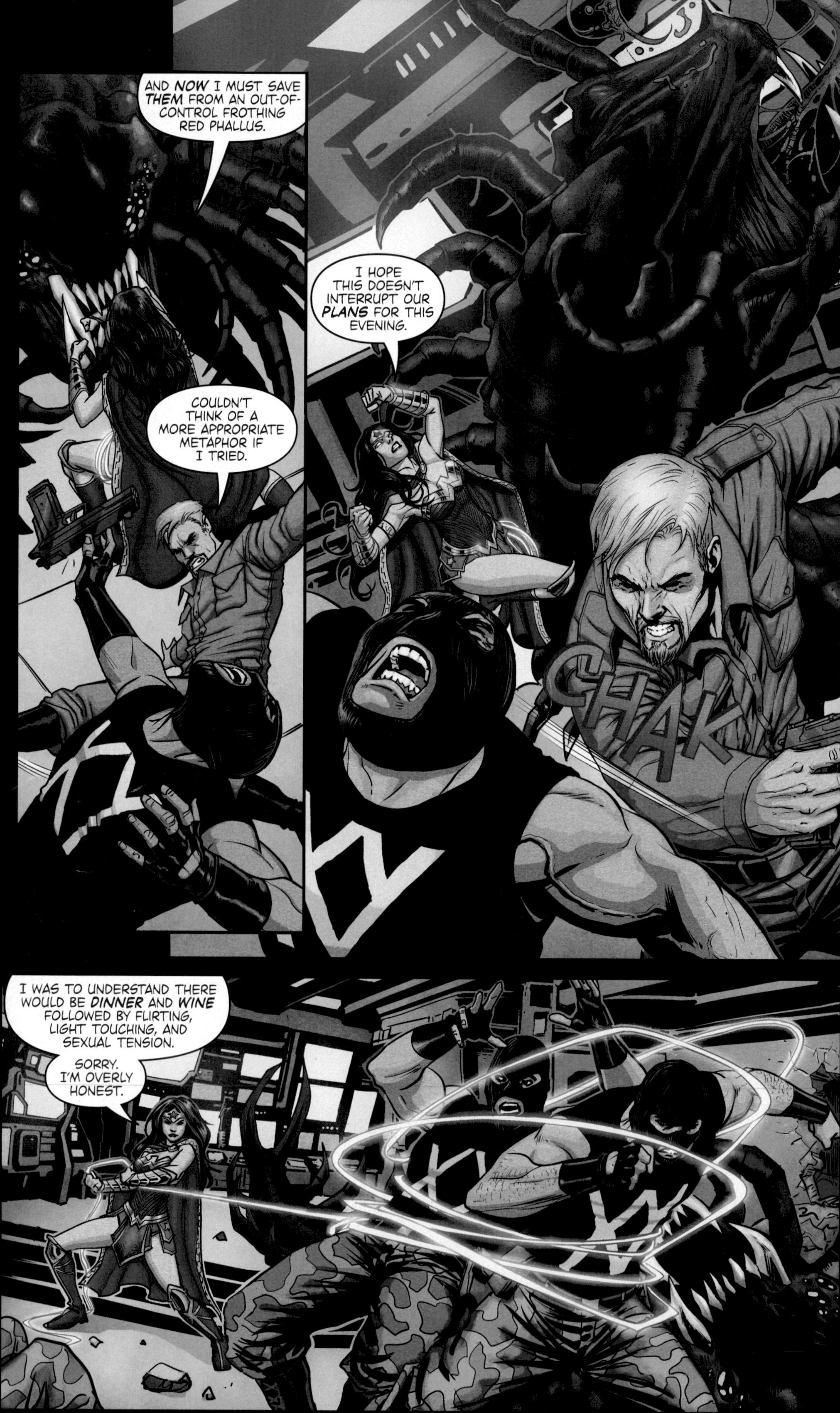
AND NOW I MUST SAVE THEM FROM AN OUT-OF-CONTROL FROTHING RED PHALLUS.
COULDN'T THINK OF A MORE APPROPRIATE METAPHOR IF I TRIED.
I HOPE THIS DOESN'T INTERRUPT OUR PLANS FOR THIS EVENING.
CHAK
I WAS TO UNDERSTAND THERE WOULD BE DINNER AND WINE FOLLOWED BY FLIRTING, LIGHT TOUCHING, AND SEXUAL TENSION.
SORRY. I'M OVERLY HONEST.

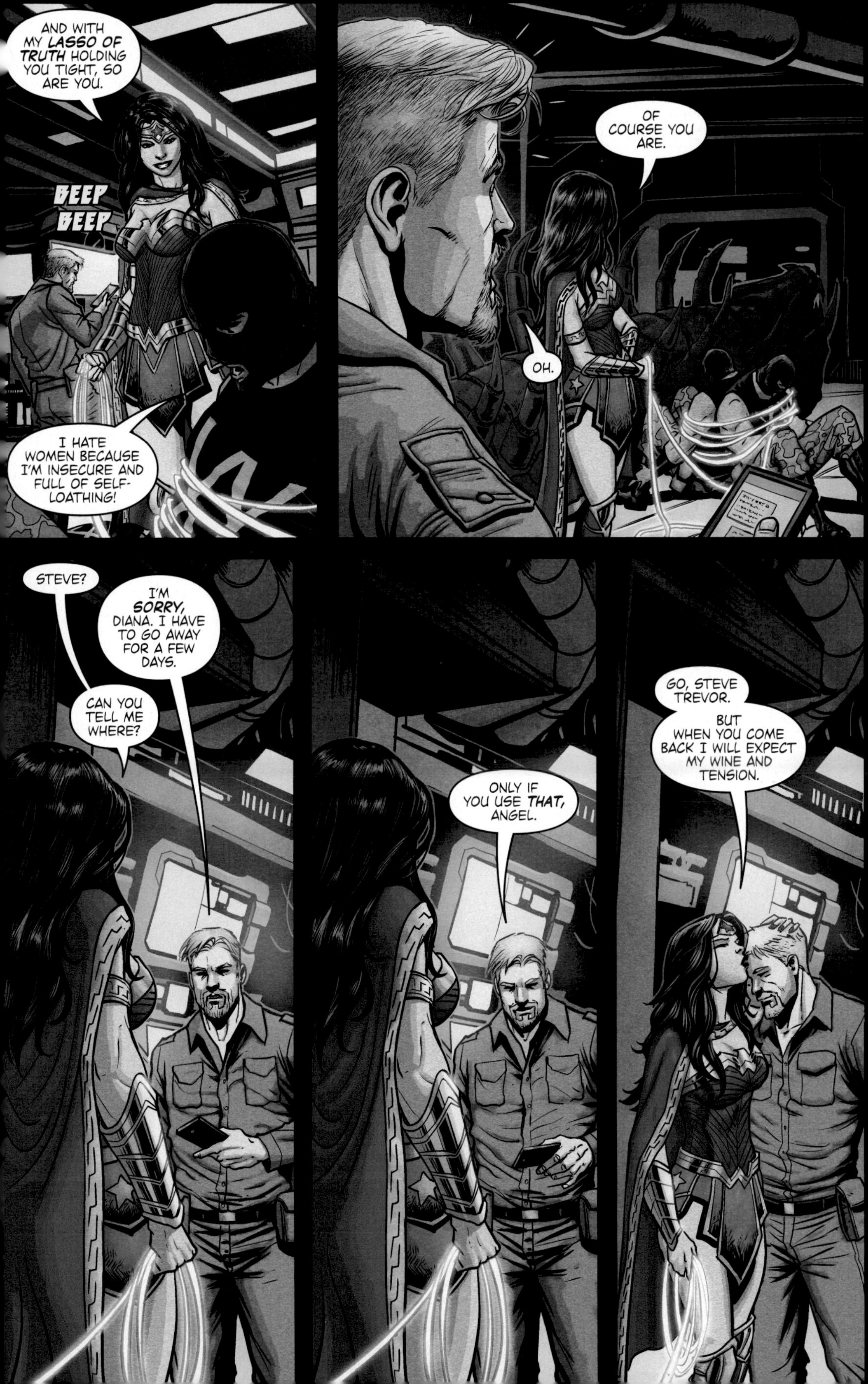
AND WITH MY LASSO OF TRUTH HOLDING YOU TIGHT, SO ARE YOU.
BEEP BEEP
I HATE WOMEN BECAUSE I'M INSECURE AND FULL OF SELF-LOATHING!
OF COURSE YOU ARE.
OH.
STEVE?
I'M SORRY, DIANA. I HAVE TO GO AWAY FOR A FEW DAYS.
CAN YOU TELL ME WHERE?
ONLY IF YOU USE THAT, ANGEL.
GO, STEVE TREVOR.
BUT WHEN YOU COME BACK I WILL EXPECT MY WINE AND TENSION.

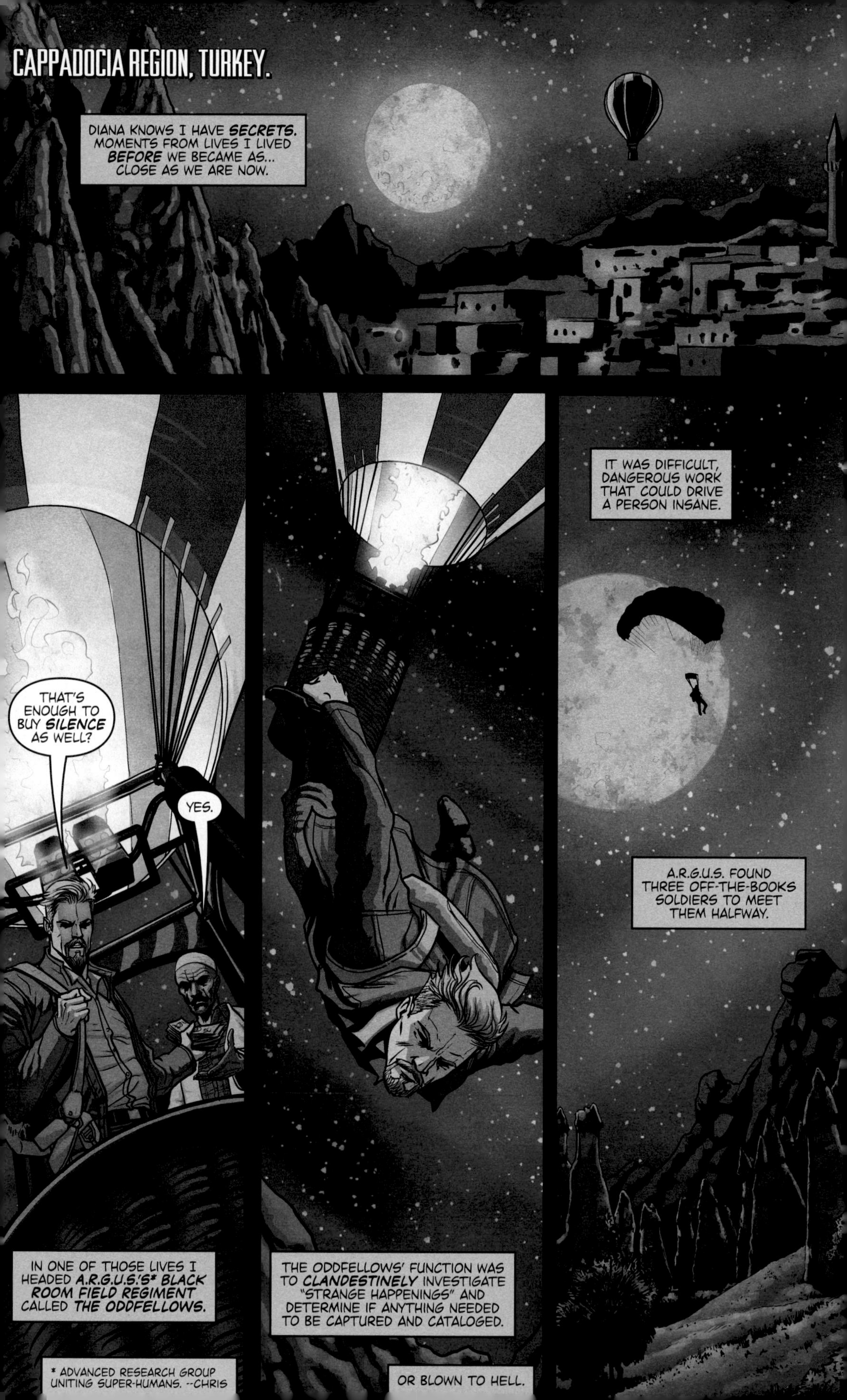

CAPPADOCIA REGION, TURKEY.
DIANA KNOWS I HAVE SECRETS. MOMENTS FROM LIVES I LIVED BEFORE WE BECAME AS... CLOSE AS WE ARE NOW.
THAT'S ENOUGH TO BUY SILENCE AS WELL?
YES.
IN ONE OF THOSE LIVES I HEADED A.R.G.U.S.'S* BLACK ROOM FIELD REGIMENT CALLED THE ODDFELLOWS.
* ADVANCED RESEARCH GROUP UNITING SUPER-HUMANS. --CHRIS
THE ODDFELLOWS' FUNCTION WAS TO CLANDESTINELY INVESTIGATE "STRANGE HAPPENINGS" AND DETERMINE IF ANYTHING NEEDED TO BE CAPTURED AND CATALOGED.
OR BLOWN TO HELL.
IT WAS DIFFICULT, DANGEROUS WORK THAT COULD DRIVE A PERSON INSANE.
A.R.G.U.S. FOUND THREE OFF-THE-BOOKS SOLDIERS TO MEET THEM HALFWAY.

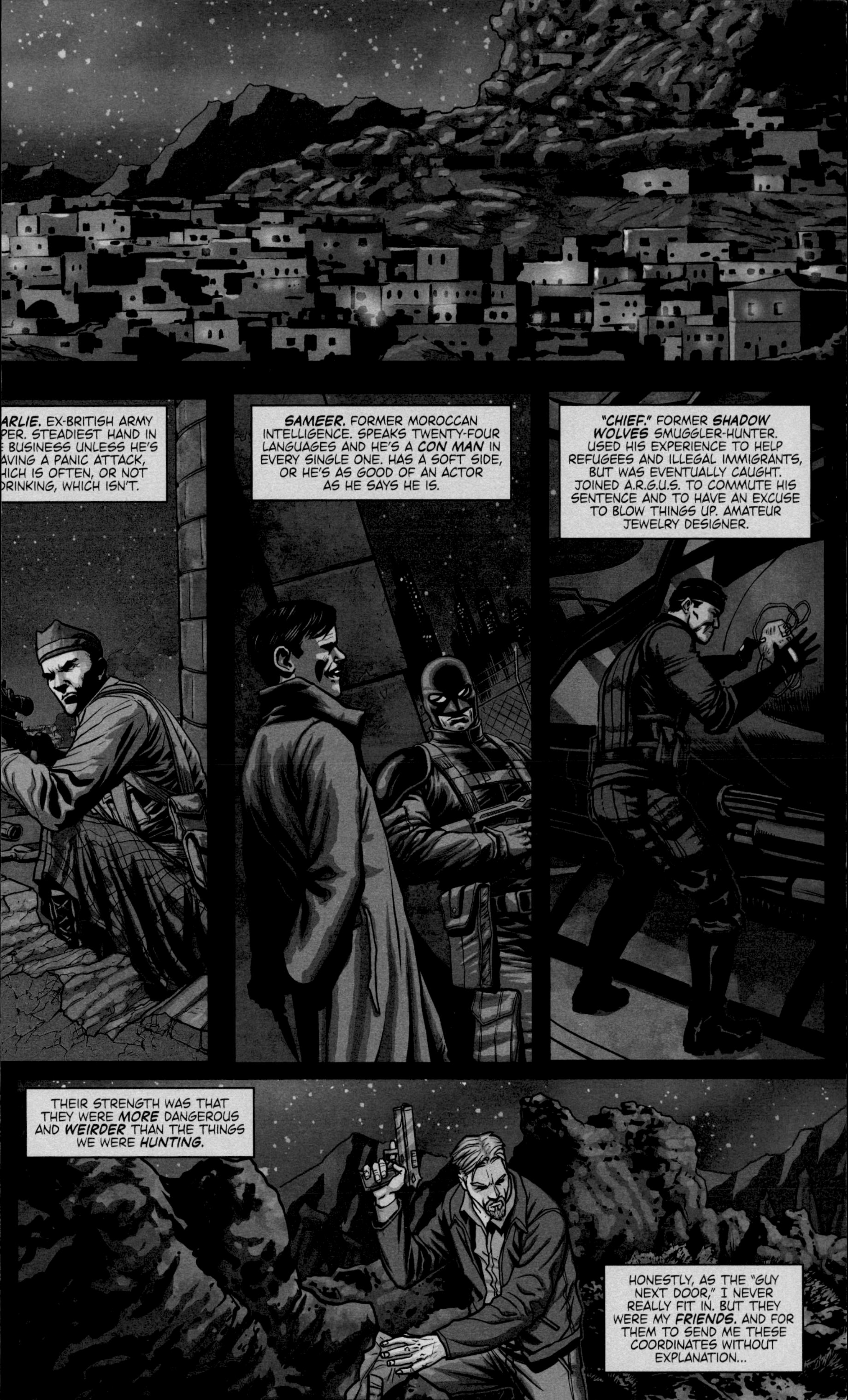
ARLIE. EX-BRITISH ARMY PER. STEADIEST HAND IN E BUSINESS UNLESS HE'S AVING A PANIC ATTACK, HICH IS OFTEN, OR NOT DRINKING, WHICH ISN'T.
SAMEER. FORMER MOROCCAN INTELLIGENCE. SPEAKS TWENTY-FOUR LANGUAGES AND HE'S A CON MAN IN EVERY SINGLE ONE. HAS A SOFT SIDE, OR HE'S AS GOOD OF AN ACTOR AS HE SAYS HE IS.
"CHIEF." FORMER SHADOW WOLVES SMUGGLER-HUNTER. USED HIS EXPERIENCE TO HELP REFUGEES AND ILLEGAL IMMIGRANTS, BUT WAS EVENTUALLY CAUGHT. JOINED A.R.G.U.S. TO COMMUTE HIS SENTENCE AND TO HAVE AN EXCUSE TO BLOW THINGS UP. AMATEUR JEWELRY DESIGNER.
THEIR STRENGTH WAS THAT THEY WERE MORE DANGEROUS AND WEIRDER THAN THE THINGS WE WERE HUNTING.
HONESTLY, AS THE "GUY NEXT DOOR," I NEVER REALLY FIT IN. BUT THEY WERE MY FRIENDS. AND FOR THEM TO SEND ME THESE COORDINATES WITHOUT EXPLANATION...

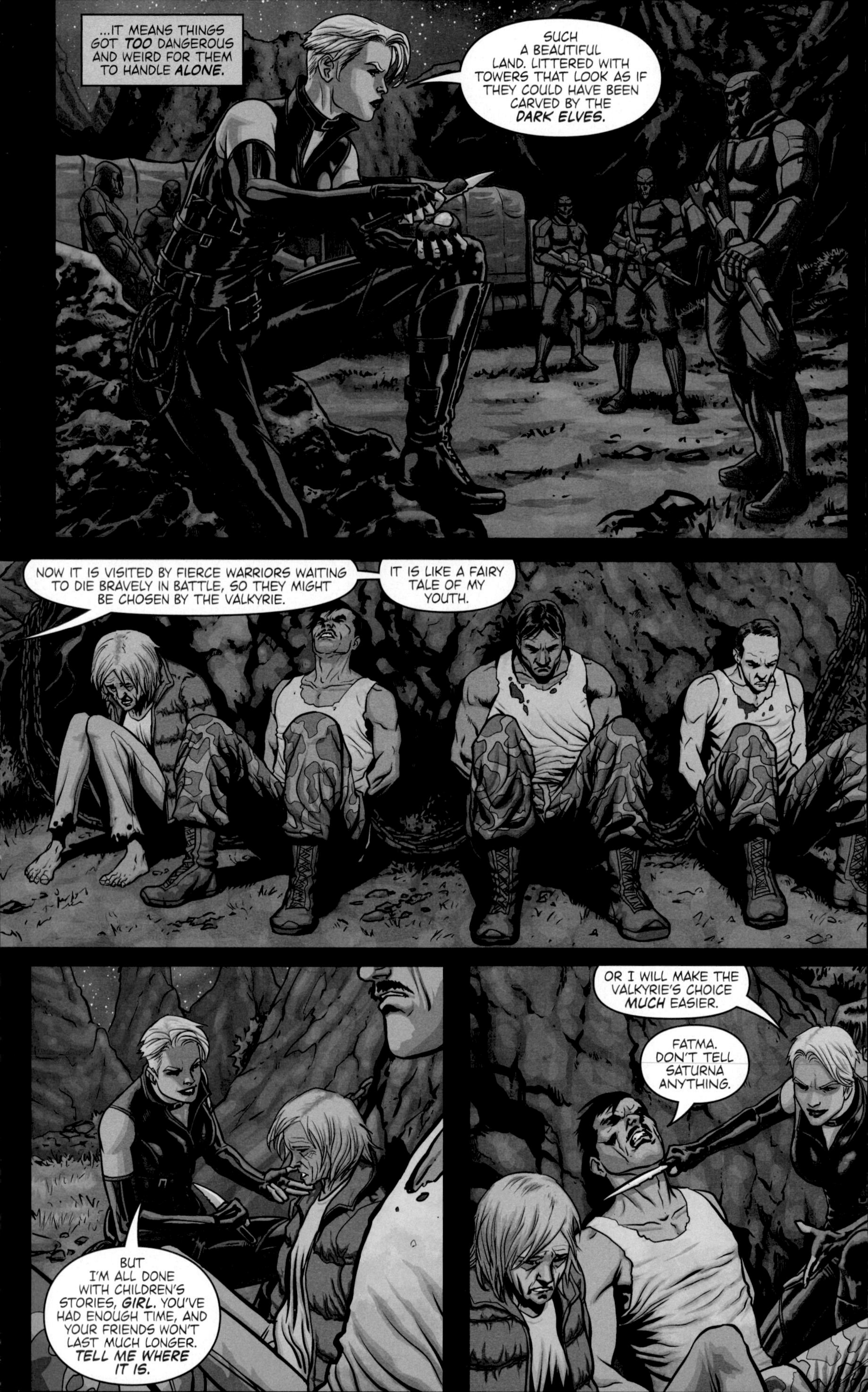
...IT MEANS THINGS GOT TOO DANGEROUS AND WEIRD FOR THEM TO HANDLE ALONE.
SUCH A BEAUTIFUL LAND. LITTERED WITH TOWERS THAT LOOK AS IF THEY COULD HAVE BEEN CARVED BY THE DARK ELVES.
NOW IT IS VISITED BY FIERCE WARRIORS WAITING TO DIE BRAVELY IN BATTLE, SO THEY MIGHT BE CHOSEN BY THE VALKYRIE.
IT IS LIKE A FAIRY TALE OF MY YOUTH.
BUT I'M ALL DONE WITH CHILDREN'S STORIES, GIRL. YOU'VE HAD ENOUGH TIME, AND YOUR FRIENDS WON'T LAST MUCH LONGER. TELL ME WHERE IT IS.
OR I WILL MAKE THE VALKYRIE'S CHOICE MUCH EASIER.
FATMA. DON'T TELL SATURNA ANYTHING.

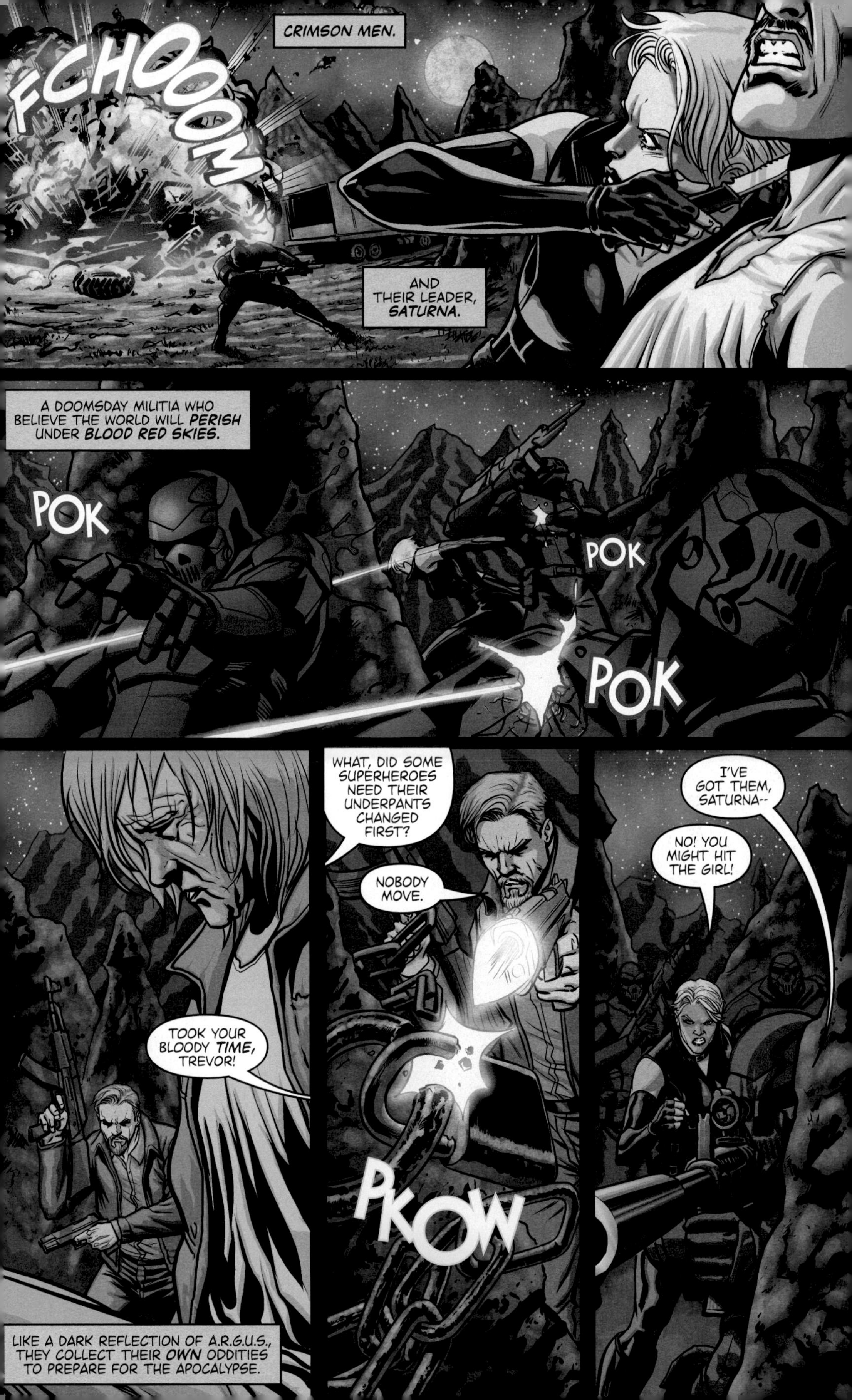
FCHOOOM
CRIMSON MEN.
AND THEIR LEADER, SATURNA.
A DOOMSDAY MILITIA WHO BELIEVE THE WORLD WILL PERISH UNDER BLOOD RED SKIES.
POK
POK
POK
TOOK YOUR BLOODY TIME, TREVOR!
LIKE A DARK REFLECTION OF A.R.G.U.S., THEY COLLECT THEIR OWN ODDITIES TO PREPARE FOR THE APOCALYPSE.
WHAT, DID SOME SUPERHEROES NEED THEIR UNDERPANTS CHANGED FIRST?
NOBODY MOVE.
PKOW
I'VE GOT THEM, SATURNA--
NO! YOU MIGHT HIT THE GIRL!

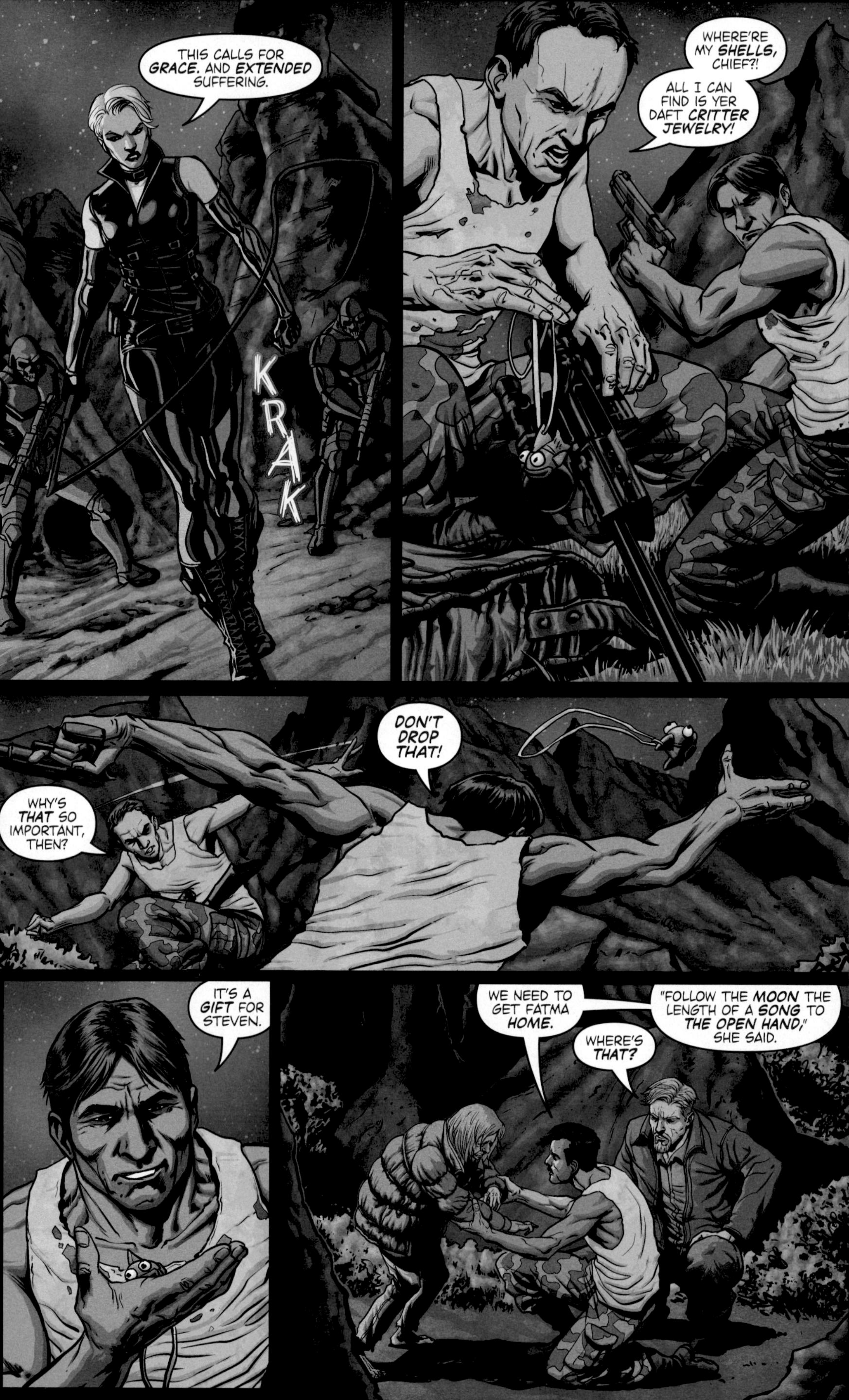
THIS CALLS FOR GRACE. AND EXTENDED SUFFERING.
KRAK
WHERE'RE MY SHELLS, CHIEF?!
ALL I CAN FIND IS YER DAFT CRITTER JEWELRY!
WHY'S THAT SO IMPORTANT, THEN?
DON'T DROP THAT!
IT'S A GIFT FOR STEVEN.
WE NEED TO GET FATMA HOME.
"FOLLOW THE MOON THE LENGTH OF A SONG TO THE OPEN HAND," SHE SAID.
WHERE'S THAT?

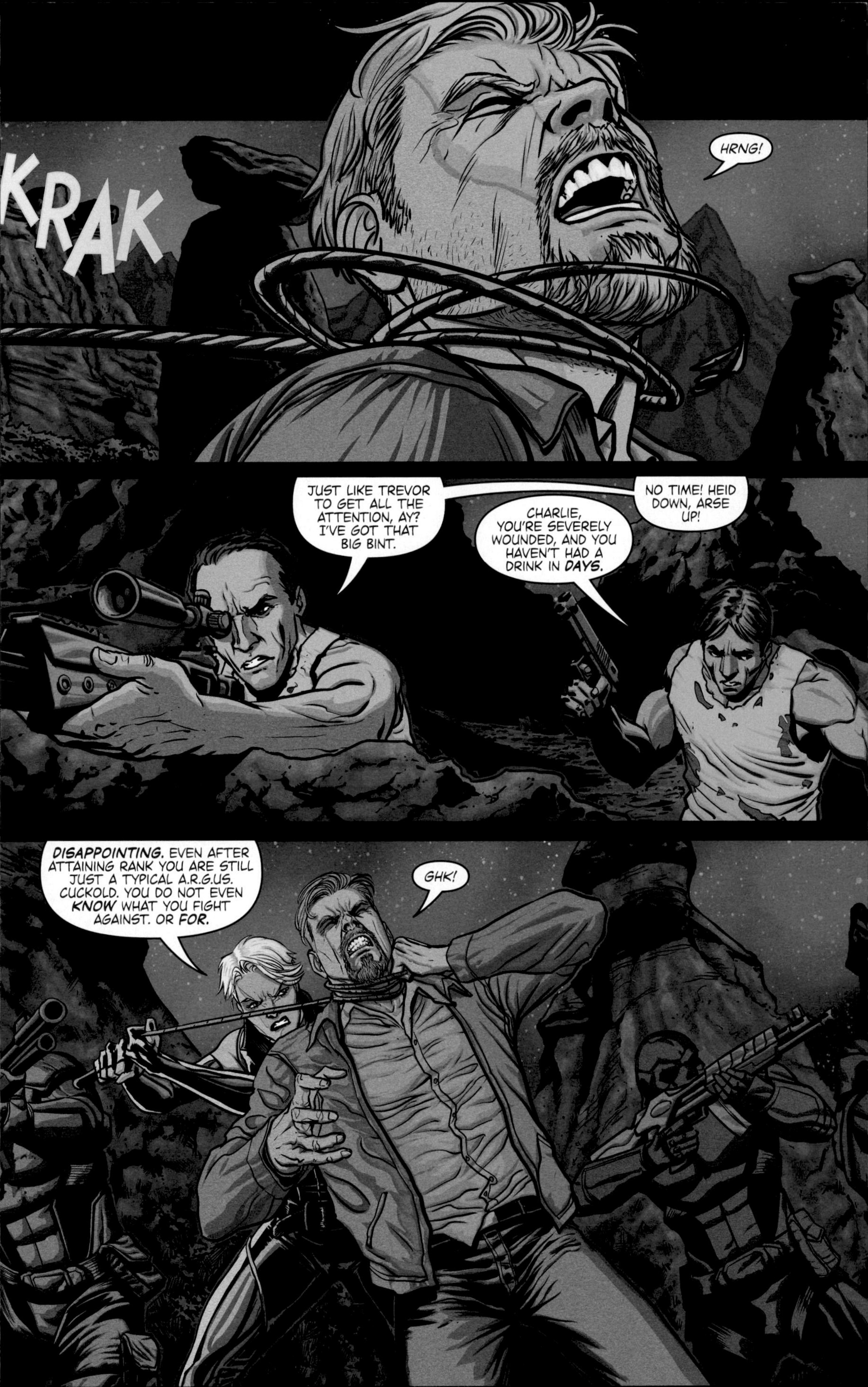

KRAK
HRNG!
JUST LIKE TREVOR TO GET ALL THE ATTENTION, AY? I'VE GOT THAT BIG BINT.
NO TIME! HEID DOWN, ARSE UP!
CHARLIE, YOU'RE SEVERELY WOUNDED, AND YOU HAVEN'T HAD A DRINK IN DAYS.
DISAPPOINTING. EVEN AFTER ATTAINING RANK YOU ARE STILL JUST A TYPICAL A.R.G.US. CUCKOLD. YOU DO NOT EVEN KNOW WHAT YOU FIGHT AGAINST. OR FOR.
GHK!

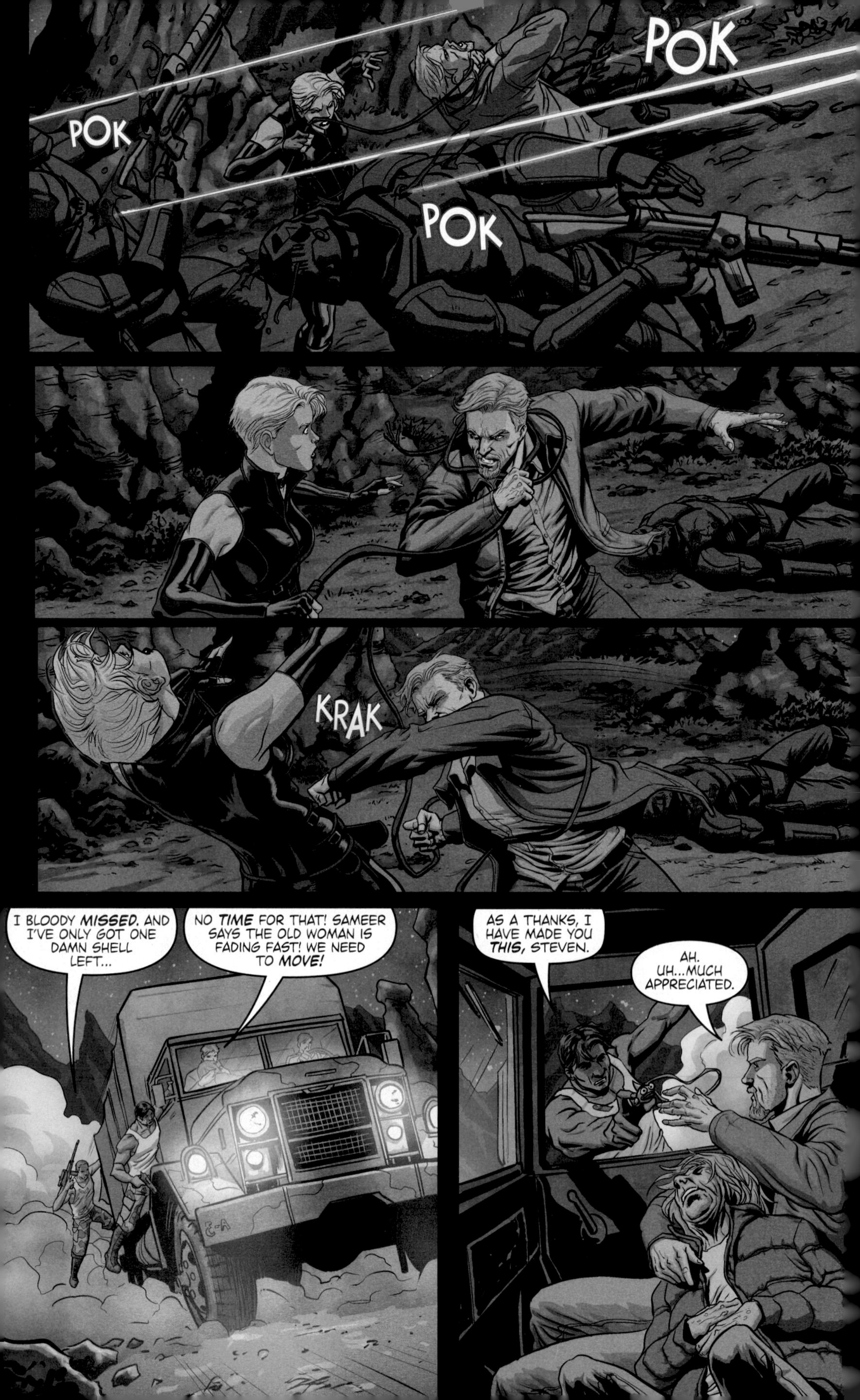
POK
POK
POK
KRAK
I BLOODY MISSED. AND I'VE ONLY GOT ONE DAMN SHELL LEFT...
NO TIME FOR THAT! SAMEER SAYS THE OLD WOMAN IS FADING FAST! WE NEED TO MOVE!
AS A THANKS, I HAVE MADE YOU THIS, STEVEN.
AH. UH...MUCH APPRECIATED.

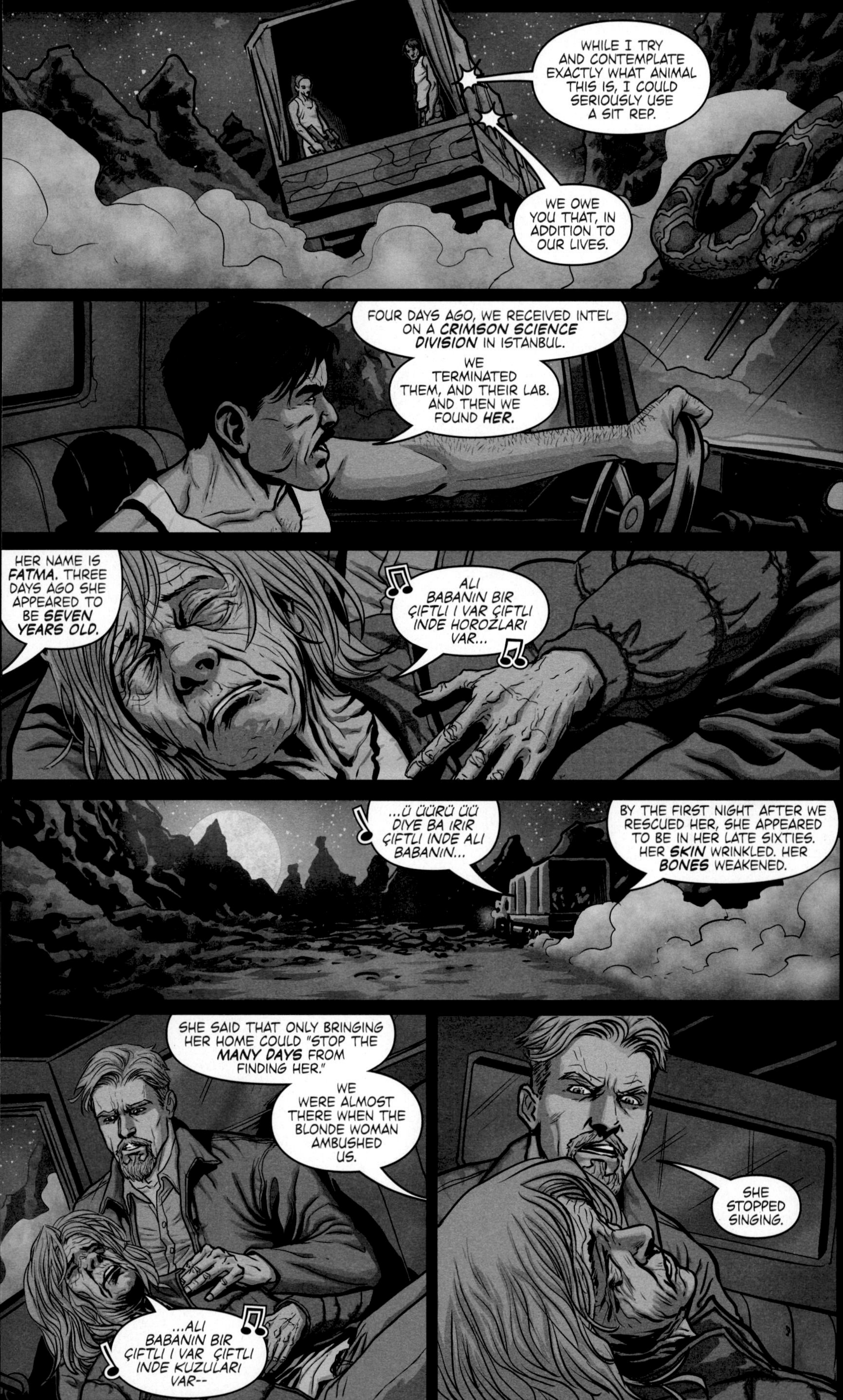
WHILE I TRY AND CONTEMPLATE EXACTLY WHAT ANIMAL THIS IS, I COULD SERIOUSLY USE A SIT REP.
WE OWE YOU THAT, IN ADDITION TO OUR LIVES.
FOUR DAYS AGO, WE RECEIVED INTEL ON A CRIMSON SCIENCE DIVISION IN ISTANBUL.
WE TERMINATED THEM, AND THEIR LAB. AND THEN WE FOUND HER.
HER NAME IS FATMA. THREE DAYS AGO SHE APPEARED TO BE SEVEN YEARS OLD.
ALI BABANIN BIR ÇIFTLI I VAR ÇIFTLI INDE HOROZLARI VAR...
...Ü ÜÜRÜ ÜÜ DIYE BA IRIR ÇIFTLI INDE ALI BABANIN...
BY THE FIRST NIGHT AFTER WE RESCUED HER, SHE APPEARED TO BE IN HER LATE SIXTIES. HER SKIN WRINKLED. HER BONES WEAKENED.
SHE SAID THAT ONLY BRINGING HER HOME COULD "STOP THE MANY DAYS FROM FINDING HER."
WE WERE ALMOST THERE WHEN THE BLONDE WOMAN AMBUSHED US.
...ALI BABANIN BIR ÇIFTLI I VAR ÇIFTLI INDE KUZULARI VAR--
SHE STOPPED SINGING.

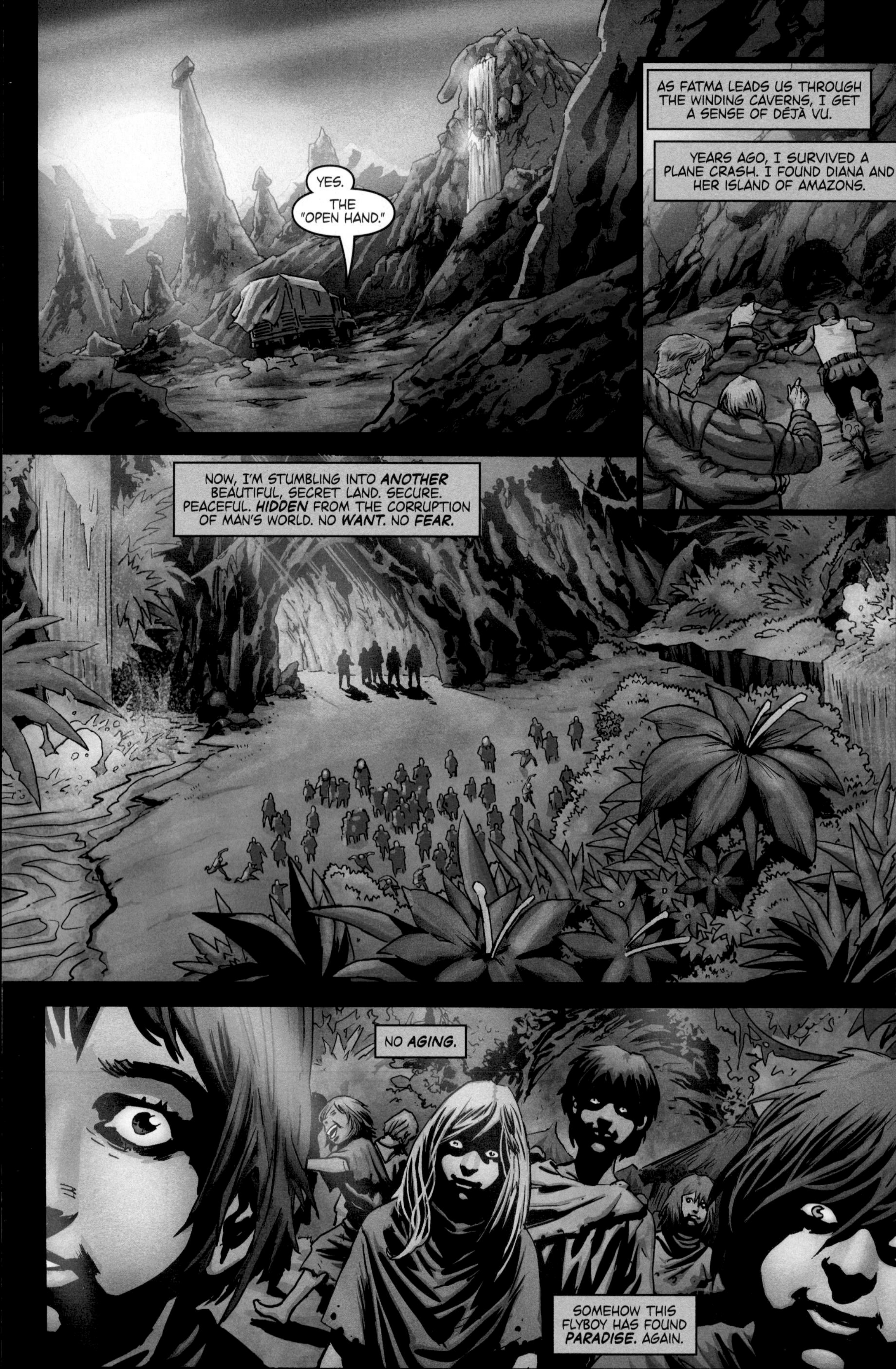
YES.
THE "OPEN HAND."
AS FATMA LEADS US THROUGH THE WINDING CAVERNS, I GET A SENSE OF DÉJÀ VU.
YEARS AGO, I SURVIVED A PLANE CRASH. I FOUND DIANA AND HER ISLAND OF AMAZONS.
NOW, I'M STUMBLING INTO ANOTHER BEAUTIFUL, SECRET LAND. SECURE. PEACEFUL. HIDDEN FROM THE CORRUPTION OF MAN'S WORLD. NO WANT. NO FEAR.
NO AGING.
SOMEHOW THIS FLYBOY HAS FOUND PARADISE. AGAIN.

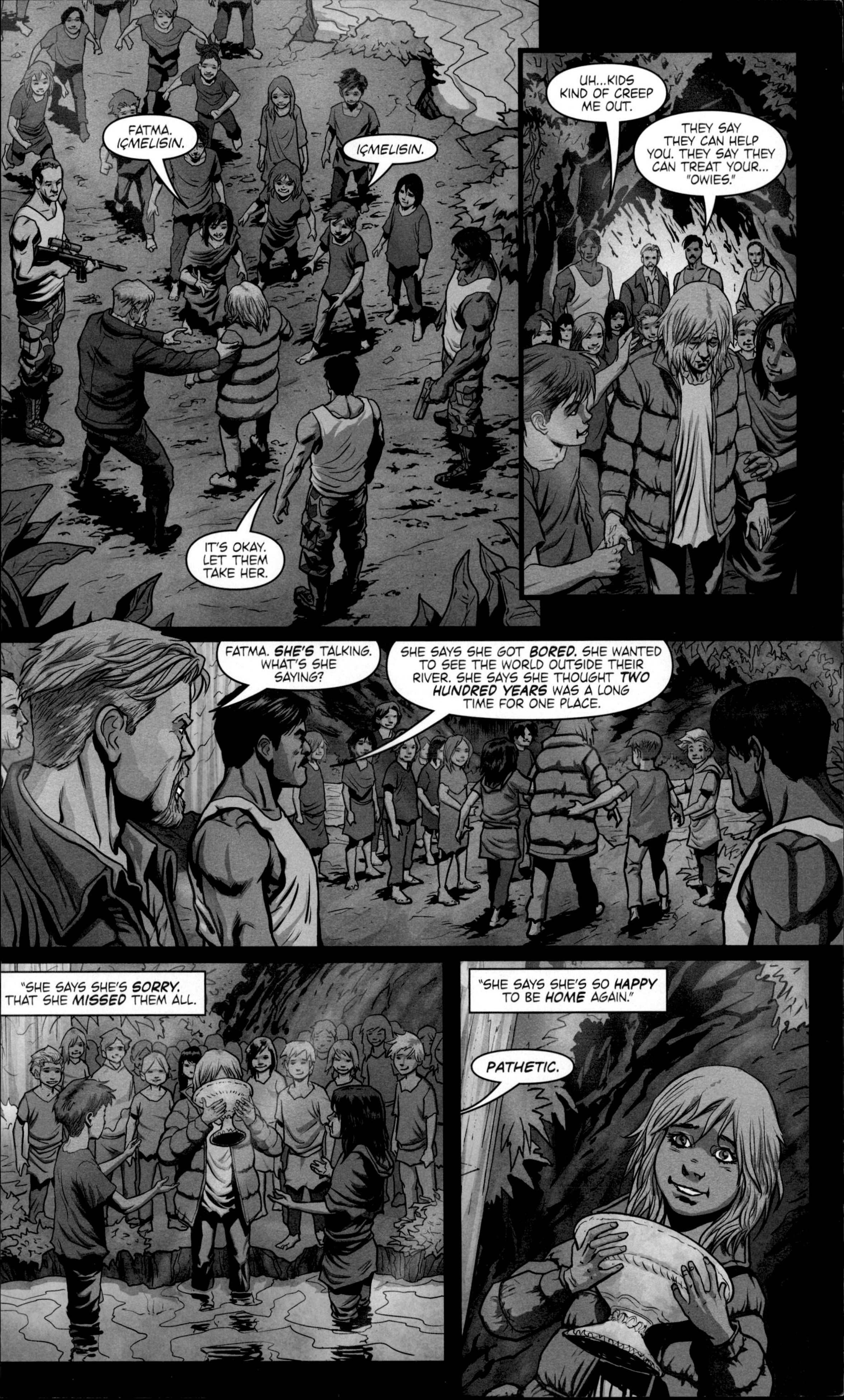
FATMA. IÇMELISIN.
IÇMELISIN.
UH...KIDS KIND OF CREEP ME OUT.
THEY SAY THEY CAN HELP YOU. THEY SAY THEY CAN TREAT YOUR... "OWIES."
IT'S OKAY. LET THEM TAKE HER.
FATMA. SHE'S TALKING. WHAT'S SHE SAYING?
SHE SAYS SHE GOT BORED. SHE WANTED TO SEE THE WORLD OUTSIDE THEIR RIVER. SHE SAYS SHE THOUGHT TWO HUNDRED YEARS WAS A LONG TIME FOR ONE PLACE.
"SHE SAYS SHE'S SORRY. THAT SHE MISSED THEM ALL.
"SHE SAYS SHE'S SO HAPPY TO BE HOME AGAIN."
PATHETIC.

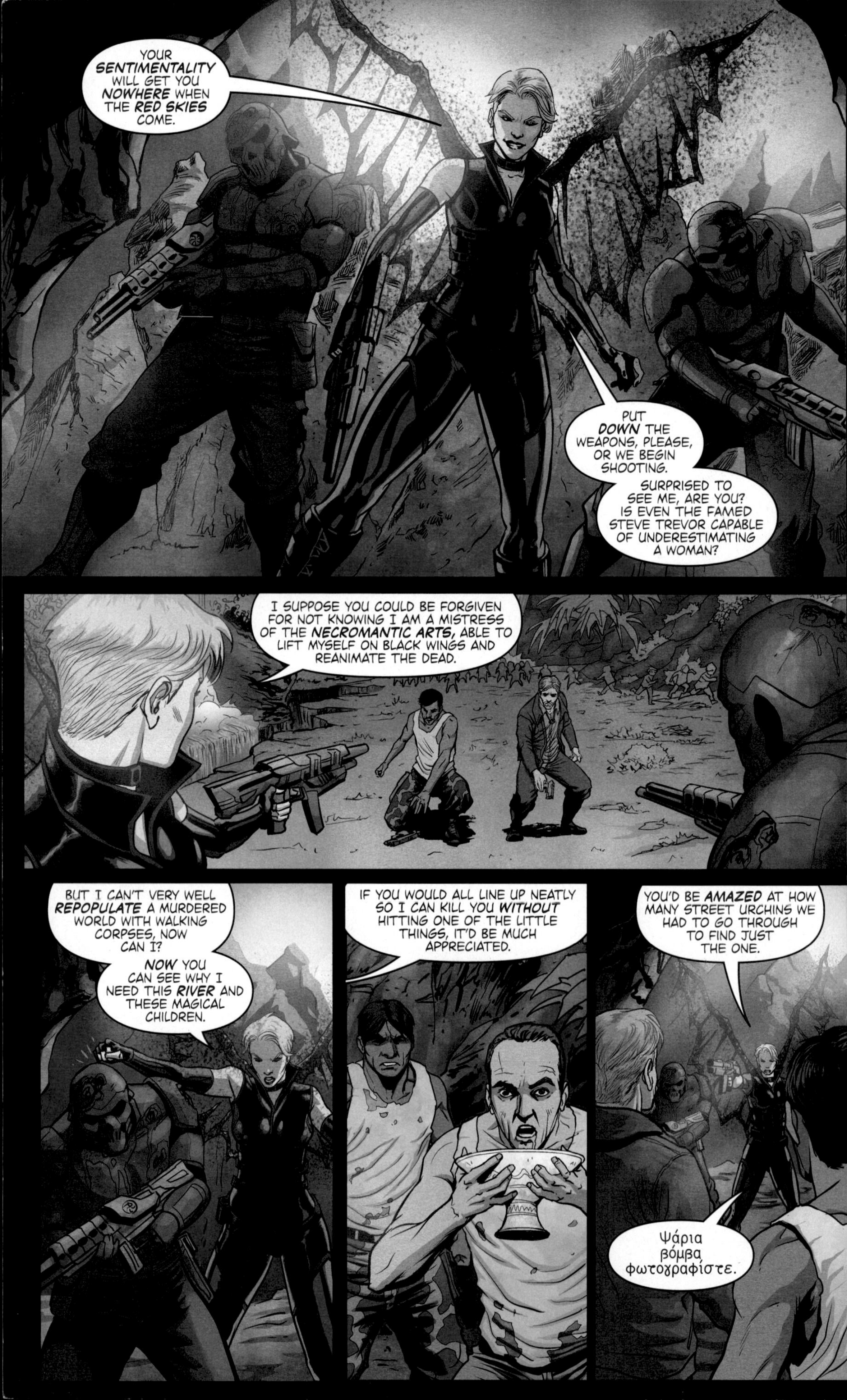
YOUR SENTIMENTALITY WILL GET YOU NOWHERE WHEN THE RED SKIES COME.
PUT DOWN THE WEAPONS, PLEASE, OR WE BEGIN SHOOTING.
SURPRISED TO SEE ME, ARE YOU? IS EVEN THE FAMED STEVE TREVOR CAPABLE OF UNDERESTIMATING A WOMAN?
I SUPPOSE YOU COULD BE FORGIVEN FOR NOT KNOWING I AM A MISTRESS OF THE NECROMANTIC ARTS, ABLE TO LIFT MYSELF ON BLACK WINGS AND REANIMATE THE DEAD.
BUT I CAN'T VERY WELL REPOPULATE A MURDERED WORLD WITH WALKING CORPSES, NOW CAN I?
NOW YOU CAN SEE WHY I NEED THIS RIVER AND THESE MAGICAL CHILDREN.
IF YOU WOULD ALL LINE UP NEATLY SO I CAN KILL YOU WITHOUT HITTING ONE OF THE LITTLE THINGS, IT'D BE MUCH APPRECIATED.
YOU'D BE AMAZED AT HOW MANY STREET URCHINS WE HAD TO GO THROUGH TO FIND JUST THE ONE.
Ψάρια βόμβα φωτογραφίστε.

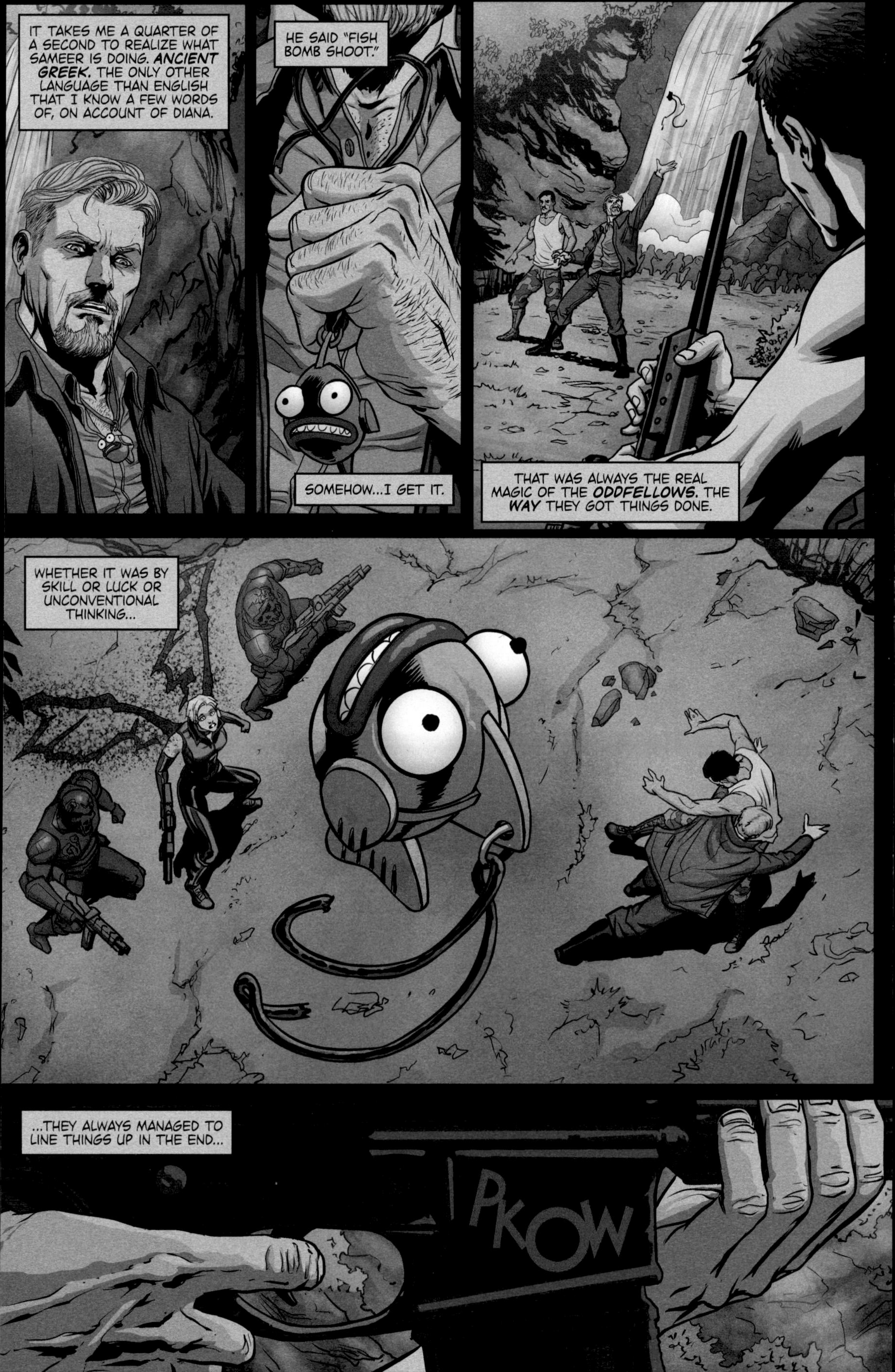
IT TAKES ME A QUARTER OF A SECOND TO REALIZE WHAT SAMEER IS DOING. ANCIENT GREEK. THE ONLY OTHER LANGUAGE THAN ENGLISH THAT I KNOW A FEW WORDS OF, ON ACCOUNT OF DIANA.
HE SAID "FISH BOMB SHOOT."
SOMEHOW...I GET IT.
THAT WAS ALWAYS THE REAL MAGIC OF THE ODDFELLOWS. THE WAY THEY GOT THINGS DONE.
WHETHER IT WAS BY SKILL OR LUCK OR UNCONVENTIONAL THINKING...
...THEY ALWAYS MANAGED TO LINE THINGS UP IN THE END...
PKOW

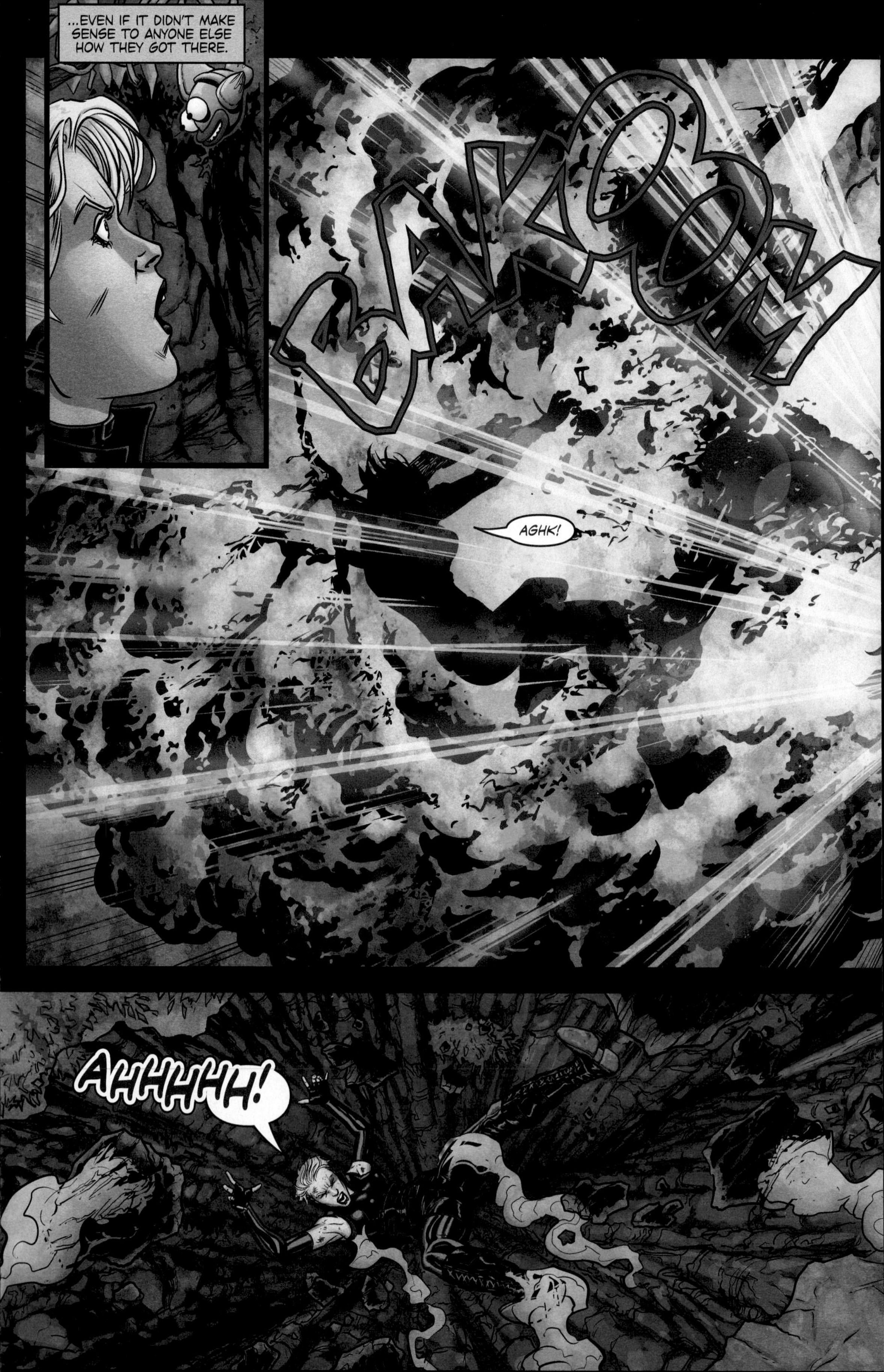
...EVEN IF IT DIDN'T MAKE SENSE TO ANYONE ELSE HOW THEY GOT THERE.
KA-BOOM
AGHK!
AHHHHH!

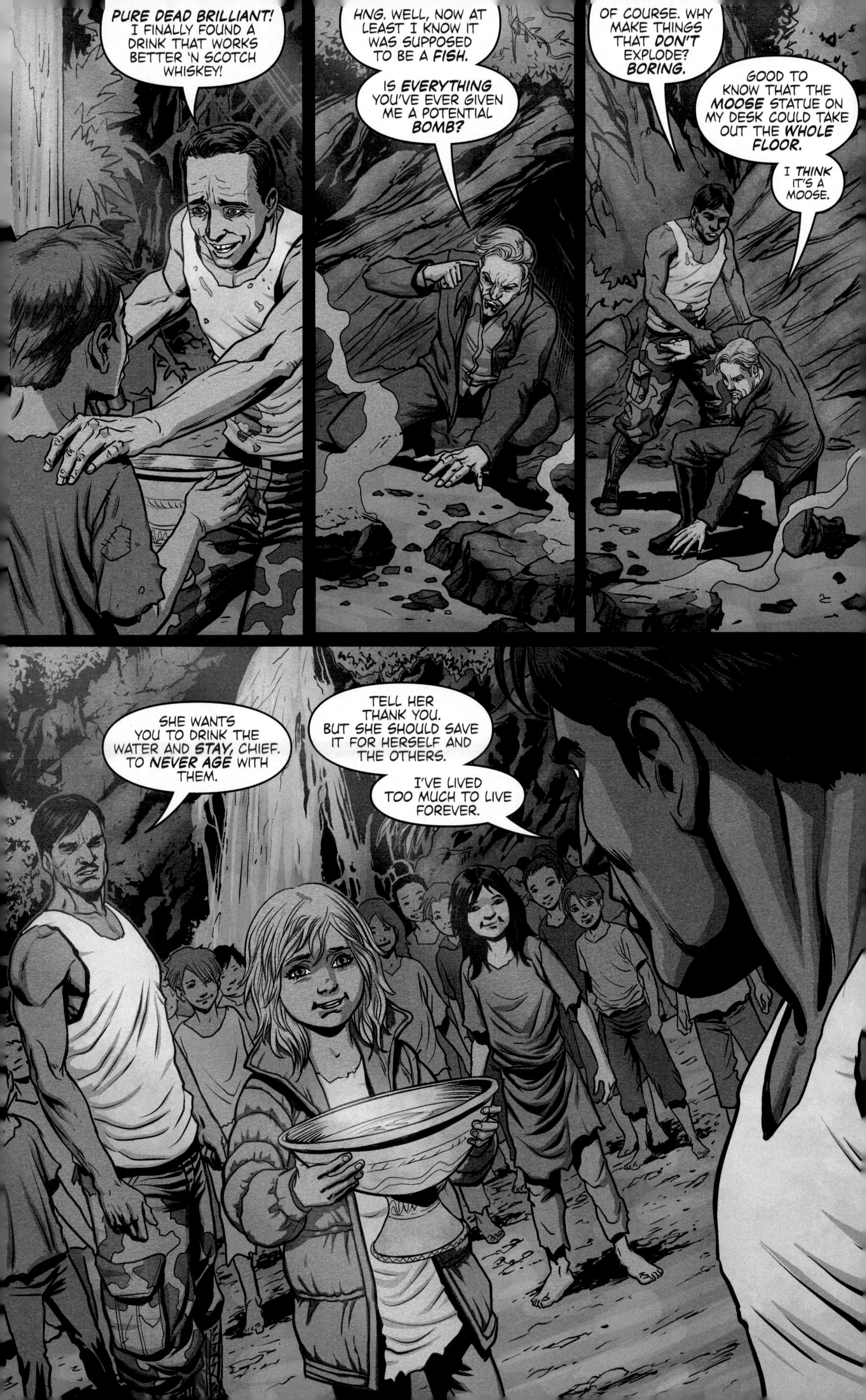
PURE DEAD BRILLIANT! I FINALLY FOUND A DRINK THAT WORKS BETTER 'N SCOTCH WHISKEY!
HNG. WELL, NOW AT LEAST I KNOW IT WAS SUPPOSED TO BE A FISH.
IS EVERYTHING YOU'VE EVER GIVEN ME A POTENTIAL BOMB?
OF COURSE. WHY MAKE THINGS THAT DON'T EXPLODE? BORING.
GOOD TO KNOW THAT THE MOOSE STATUE ON MY DESK COULD TAKE OUT THE WHOLE FLOOR.
I THINK IT'S A MOOSE.
SHE WANTS YOU TO DRINK THE WATER AND STAY, CHIEF. TO NEVER AGE WITH THEM.
TELL HER THANK YOU. BUT SHE SHOULD SAVE IT FOR HERSELF AND THE OTHERS.
I'VE LIVED TOO MUCH TO LIVE FOREVER.

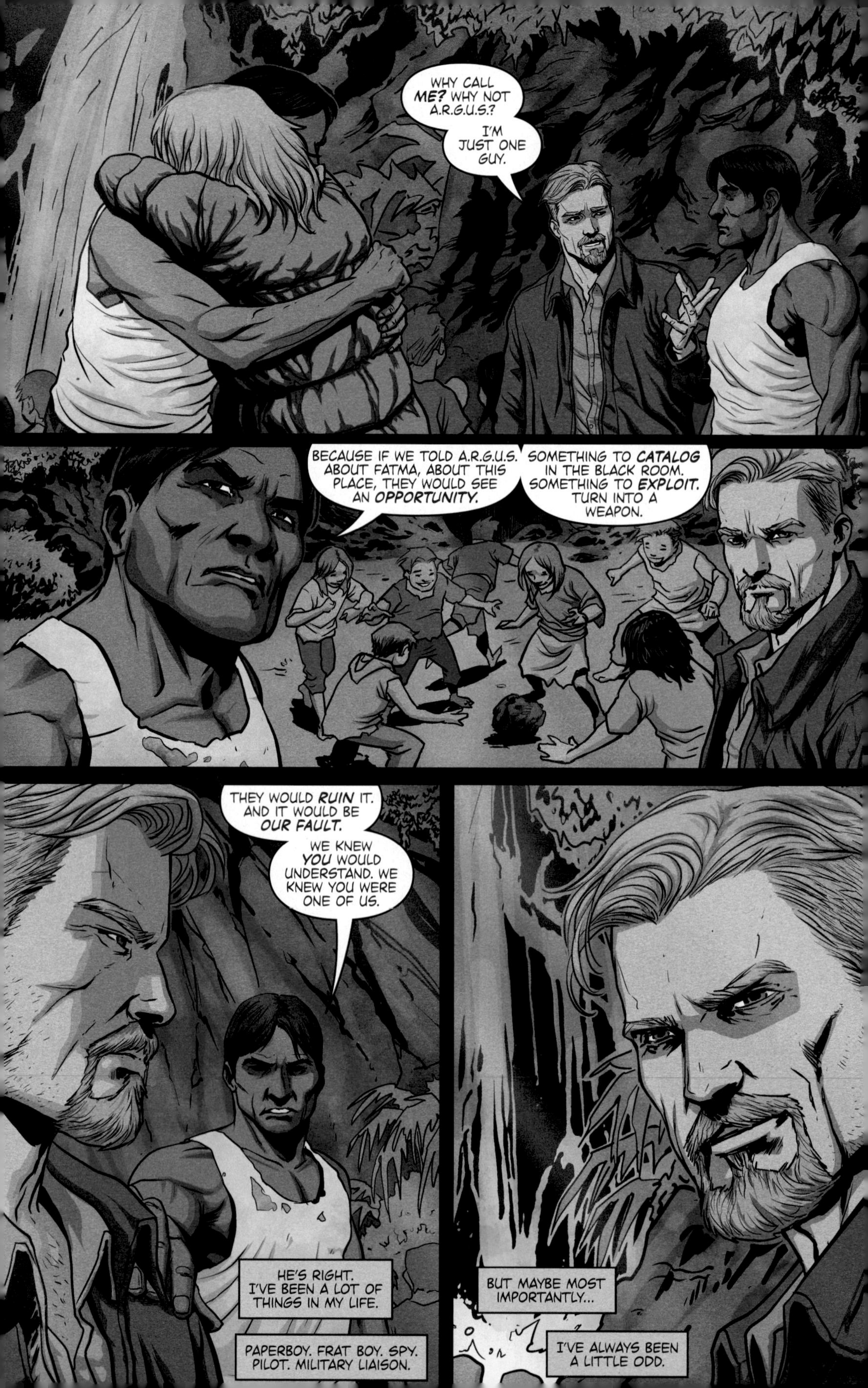
WHY CALL ME? WHY NOT A.R.G.U.S.?
I'M JUST ONE GUY.
BECAUSE IF WE TOLD A.R.G.U.S. ABOUT FATMA, ABOUT THIS PLACE, THEY WOULD SEE AN OPPORTUNITY.
SOMETHING TO CATALOG IN THE BLACK ROOM. SOMETHING TO EXPLOIT. TURN INTO A WEAPON.
THEY WOULD RUIN IT. AND IT WOULD BE OUR FAULT.
WE KNEW YOU WOULD UNDERSTAND. WE KNEW YOU WERE ONE OF US.
HE'S RIGHT. I'VE BEEN A LOT OF THINGS IN MY LIFE.
PAPERBOY. FRAT BOY. SPY. PILOT. MILITARY LIAISON.
BUT MAYBE MOST IMPORTANTLY...
I'VE ALWAYS BEEN A LITTLE ODD.

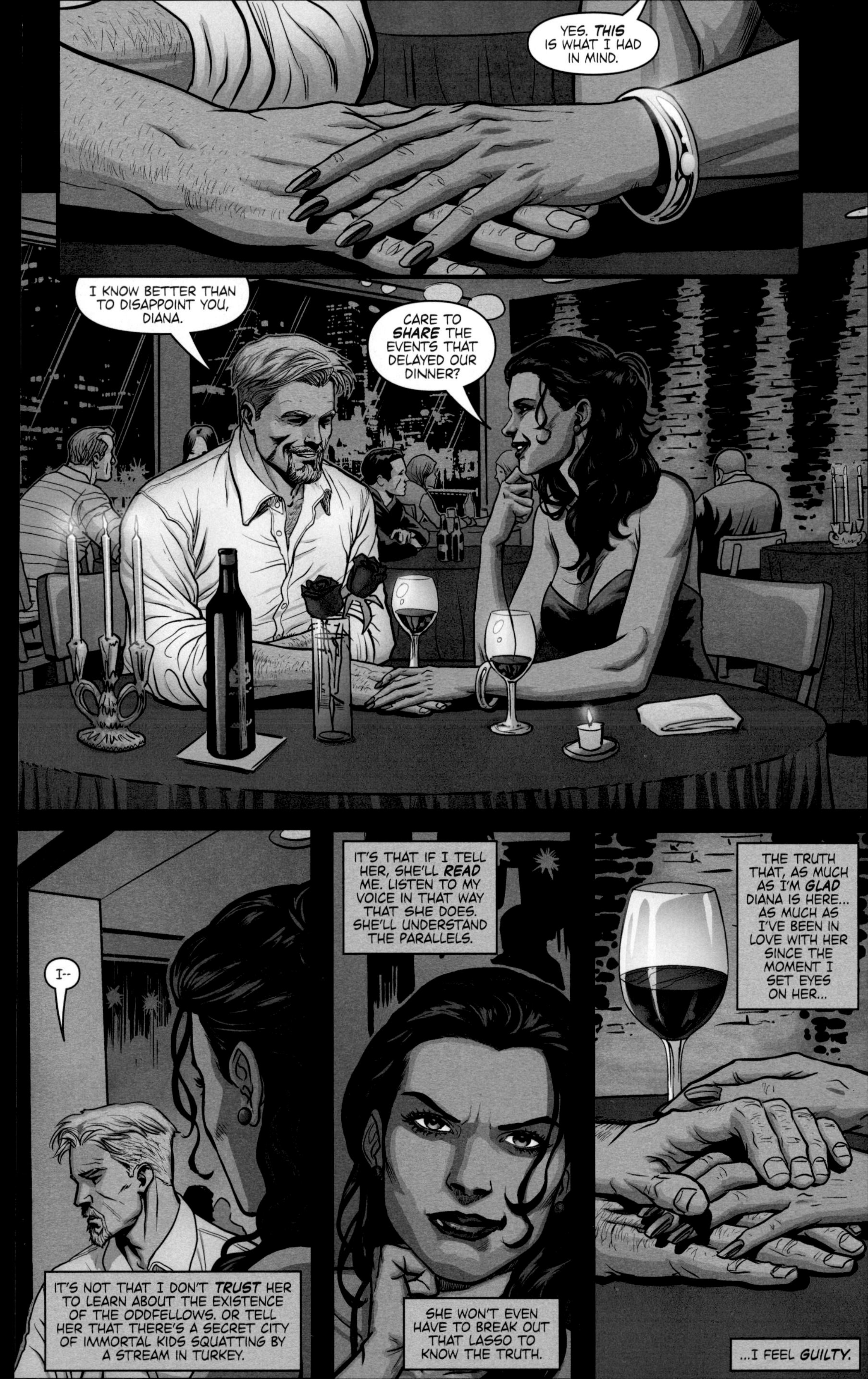
YES. THIS IS WHAT I HAD IN MIND.
I KNOW BETTER THAN TO DISAPPOINT YOU, DIANA.
CARE TO SHARE THE EVENTS THAT DELAYED OUR DINNER?
I--
IT'S NOT THAT I DON'T TRUST HER TO LEARN ABOUT THE EXISTENCE OF THE ODDFELLOWS. OR TELL HER THAT THERE'S A SECRET CITY OF IMMORTAL KIDS SQUATTING BY A STREAM IN TURKEY.
IT'S THAT IF I TELL HER, SHE'LL READ ME. LISTEN TO MY VOICE IN THAT WAY THAT SHE DOES. SHE'LL UNDERSTAND THE PARALLELS.
SHE WON'T EVEN HAVE TO BREAK OUT THAT LASSO TO KNOW THE TRUTH.
THE TRUTH THAT, AS MUCH AS I'M GLAD DIANA IS HERE... AS MUCH AS I'VE BEEN IN LOVE WITH HER SINCE THE MOMENT I SET EYES ON HER...
...I FEEL GUILTY.

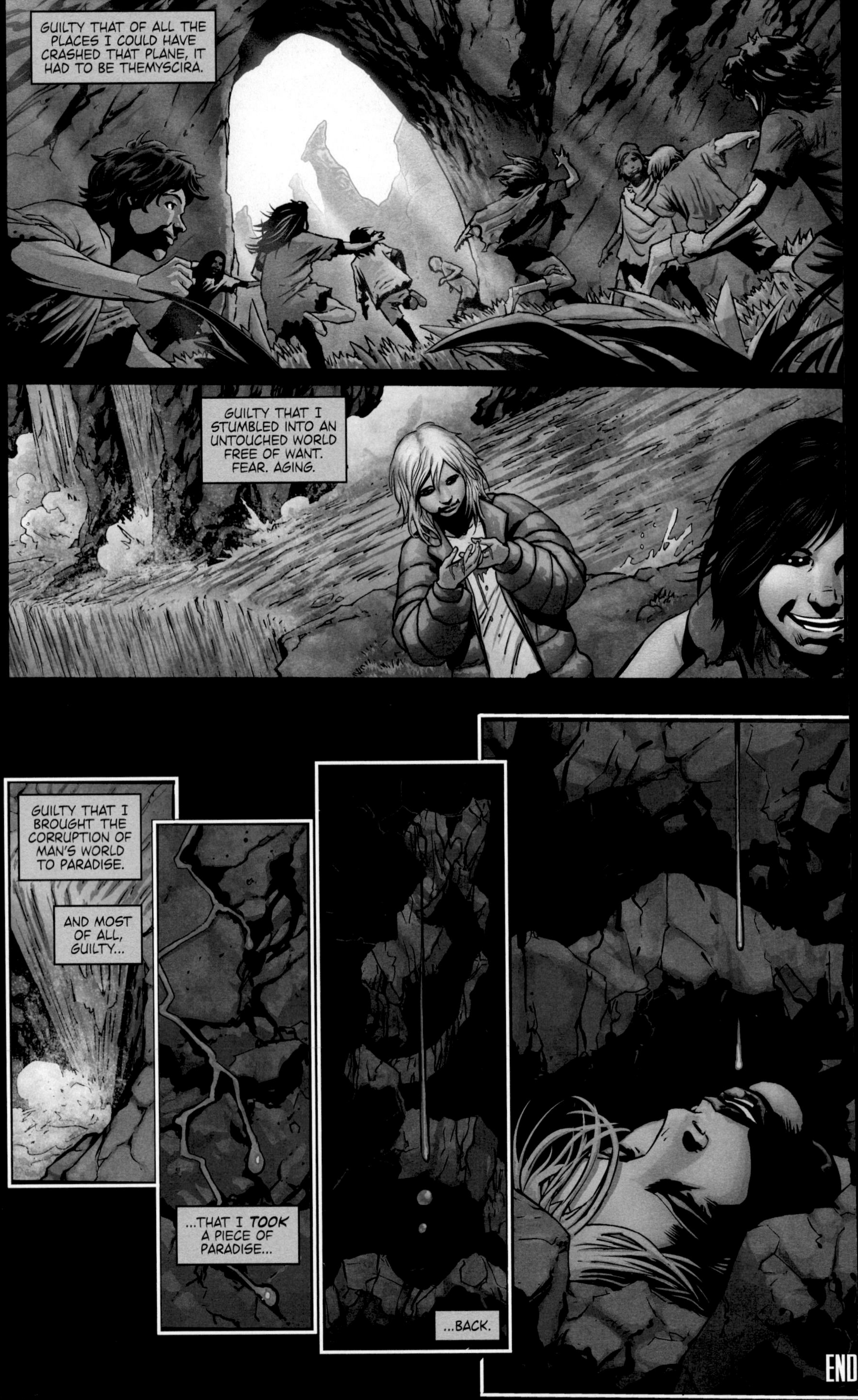
GUILTY THAT OF ALL THE PLACES I COULD HAVE CRASHED THAT PLANE, IT HAD TO BE THEMYSCIRA.
GUILTY THAT I STUMBLED INTO AN UNTOUCHED WORLD FREE OF WANT. FEAR. AGING.
GUILTY THAT I BROUGHT THE CORRUPTION OF MAN'S WORLD TO PARADISE.
AND MOST OF ALL, GUILTY...
...THAT I *TOOK* A PIECE OF PARADISE...
...BACK.
END

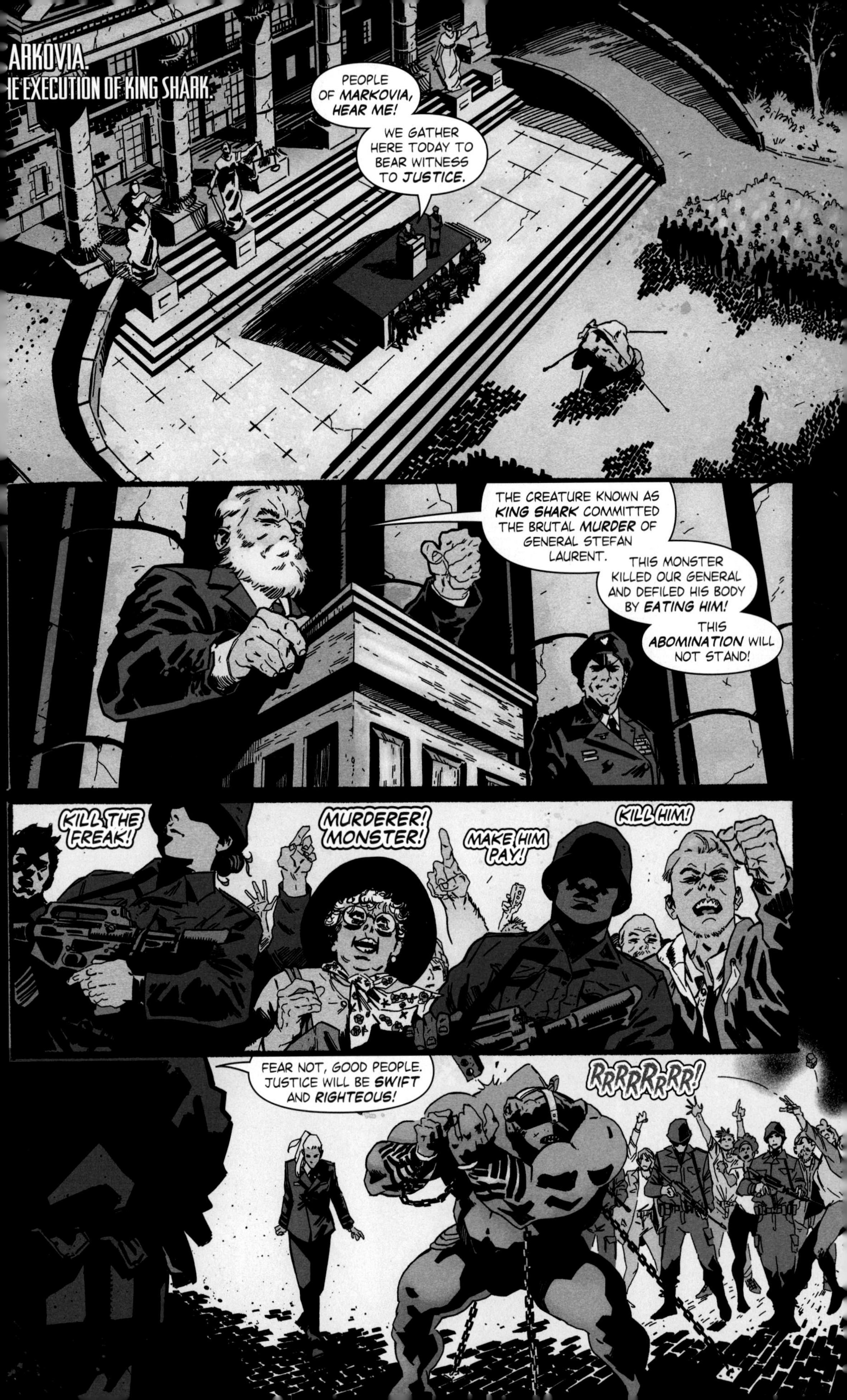
ARKOVIA.
IE EXECUTION OF KING SHARK.
PEOPLE OF MARKOVIA, HEAR ME!
WE GATHER HERE TODAY TO BEAR WITNESS TO JUSTICE.
THE CREATURE KNOWN AS KING SHARK COMMITTED THE BRUTAL MURDER OF GENERAL STEFAN LAURENT.
THIS MONSTER KILLED OUR GENERAL AND DEFILED HIS BODY BY EATING HIM!
THIS ABOMINATION WILL NOT STAND!
KILL THE FREAK!
MURDERER! MONSTER!
MAKE HIM PAY!
KILL HIM!
FEAR NOT, GOOD PEOPLE. JUSTICE WILL BE SWIFT AND RIGHTEOUS!
RRRRRRRR!

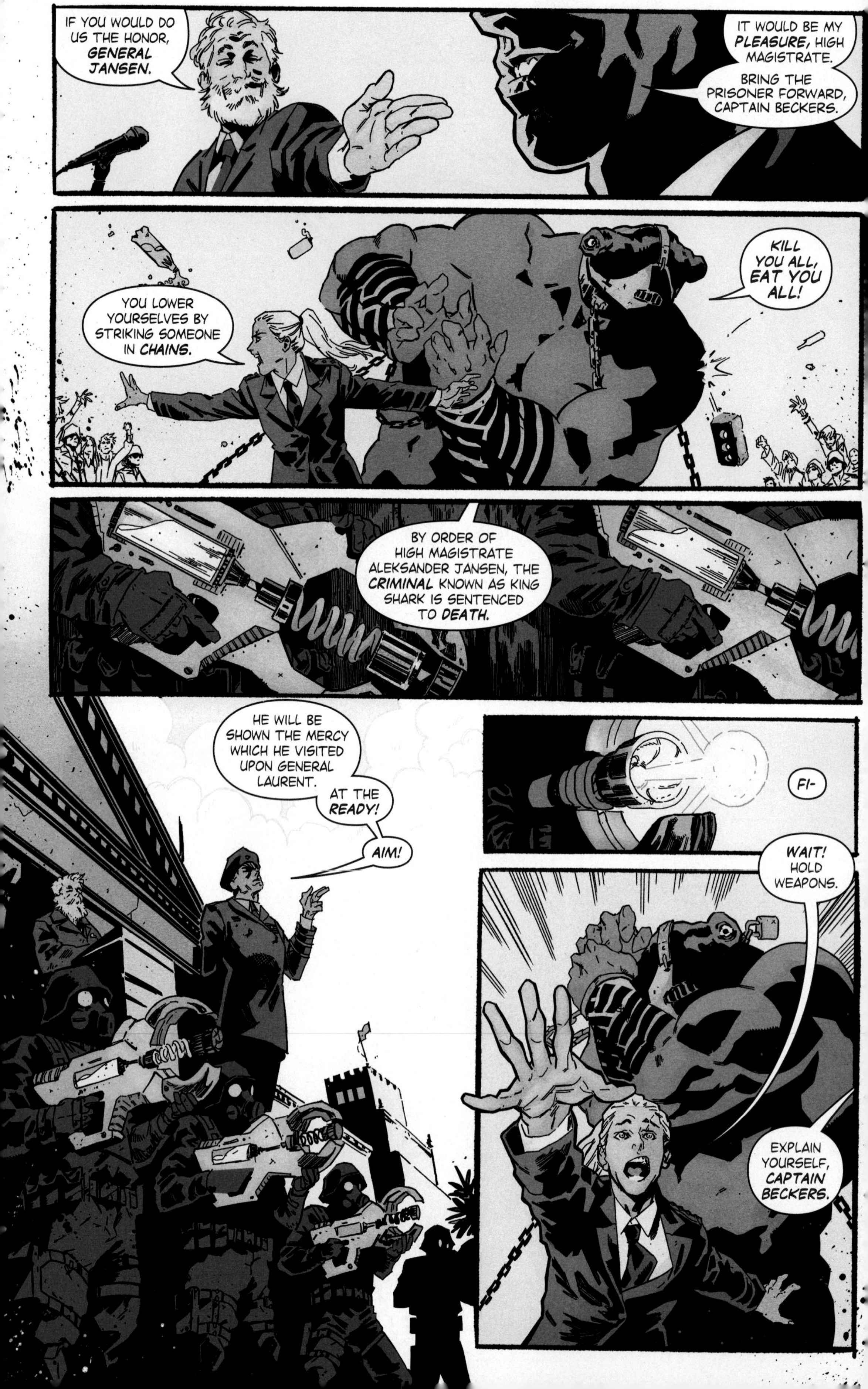

IF YOU WOULD DO US THE HONOR, GENERAL JANSEN.
IT WOULD BE MY PLEASURE, HIGH MAGISTRATE.
BRING THE PRISONER FORWARD, CAPTAIN BECKERS.
YOU LOWER YOURSELVES BY STRIKING SOMEONE IN CHAINS.
KILL YOU ALL, EAT YOU ALL!
BY ORDER OF HIGH MAGISTRATE ALEKSANDER JANSEN, THE CRIMINAL KNOWN AS KING SHARK IS SENTENCED TO DEATH.
HE WILL BE SHOWN THE MERCY WHICH HE VISITED UPON GENERAL LAURENT.
AT THE READY!
AIM!
FI-
WAIT! HOLD WEAPONS.
EXPLAIN YOURSELF, CAPTAIN BECKERS.

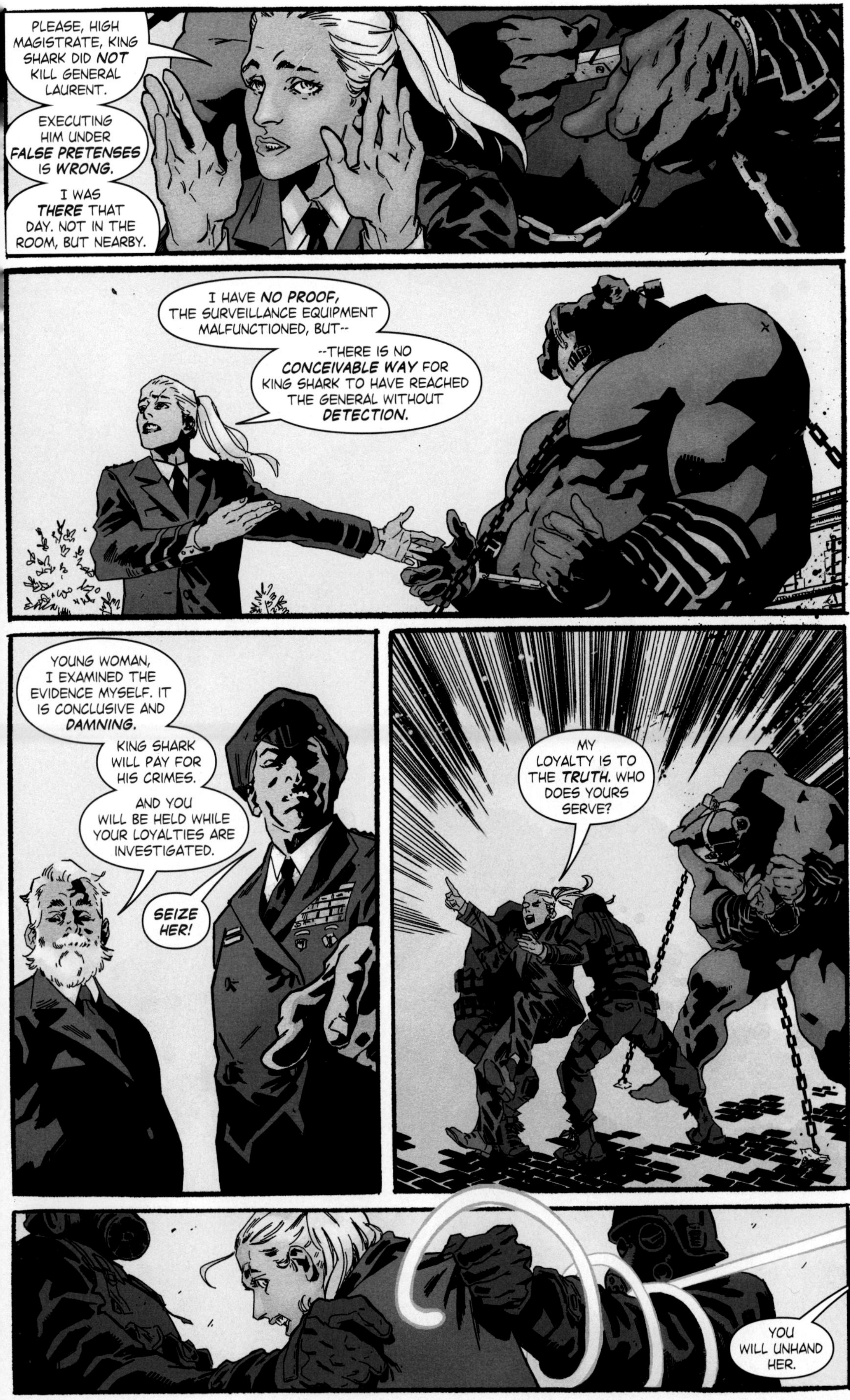
PLEASE, HIGH MAGISTRATE, KING SHARK DID NOT KILL GENERAL LAURENT.
EXECUTING HIM UNDER FALSE PRETENSES IS WRONG.
I WAS THERE THAT DAY. NOT IN THE ROOM, BUT NEARBY.
I HAVE NO PROOF, THE SURVEILLANCE EQUIPMENT MALFUNCTIONED, BUT--
--THERE IS NO CONCEIVABLE WAY FOR KING SHARK TO HAVE REACHED THE GENERAL WITHOUT DETECTION.
YOUNG WOMAN, I EXAMINED THE EVIDENCE MYSELF. IT IS CONCLUSIVE AND DAMNING.
KING SHARK WILL PAY FOR HIS CRIMES.
AND YOU WILL BE HELD WHILE YOUR LOYALTIES ARE INVESTIGATED.
SEIZE HER!
MY LOYALTY IS TO THE TRUTH. WHO DOES YOURS SERVE?
YOU WILL UNHAND HER.

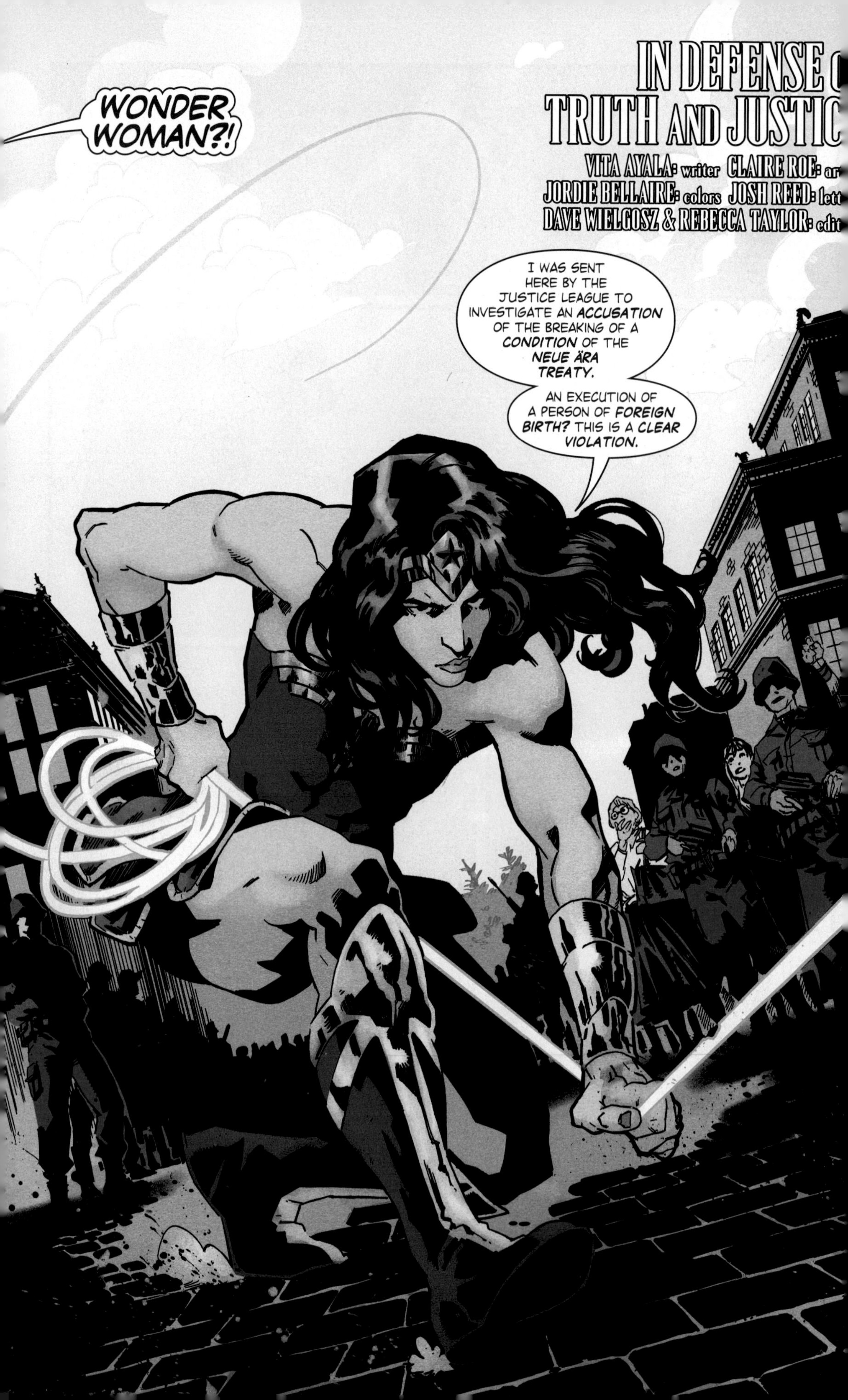
WONDER WOMAN?!
IN DEFENSE
TRUTH AND JUSTIC
VITA AYALA: writer CLAIRE ROE: ar
JORDIE BELLAIRE: colors JOSH REED: lett
DAVE WIELGOSZ & REBECCA TAYLOR: edit
I WAS SENT HERE BY THE JUSTICE LEAGUE TO INVESTIGATE AN ACCUSATION OF THE BREAKING OF A CONDITION OF THE NEUE ÄRA TREATY.
AN EXECUTION OF A PERSON OF FOREIGN BIRTH? THIS IS A CLEAR VIOLATION.

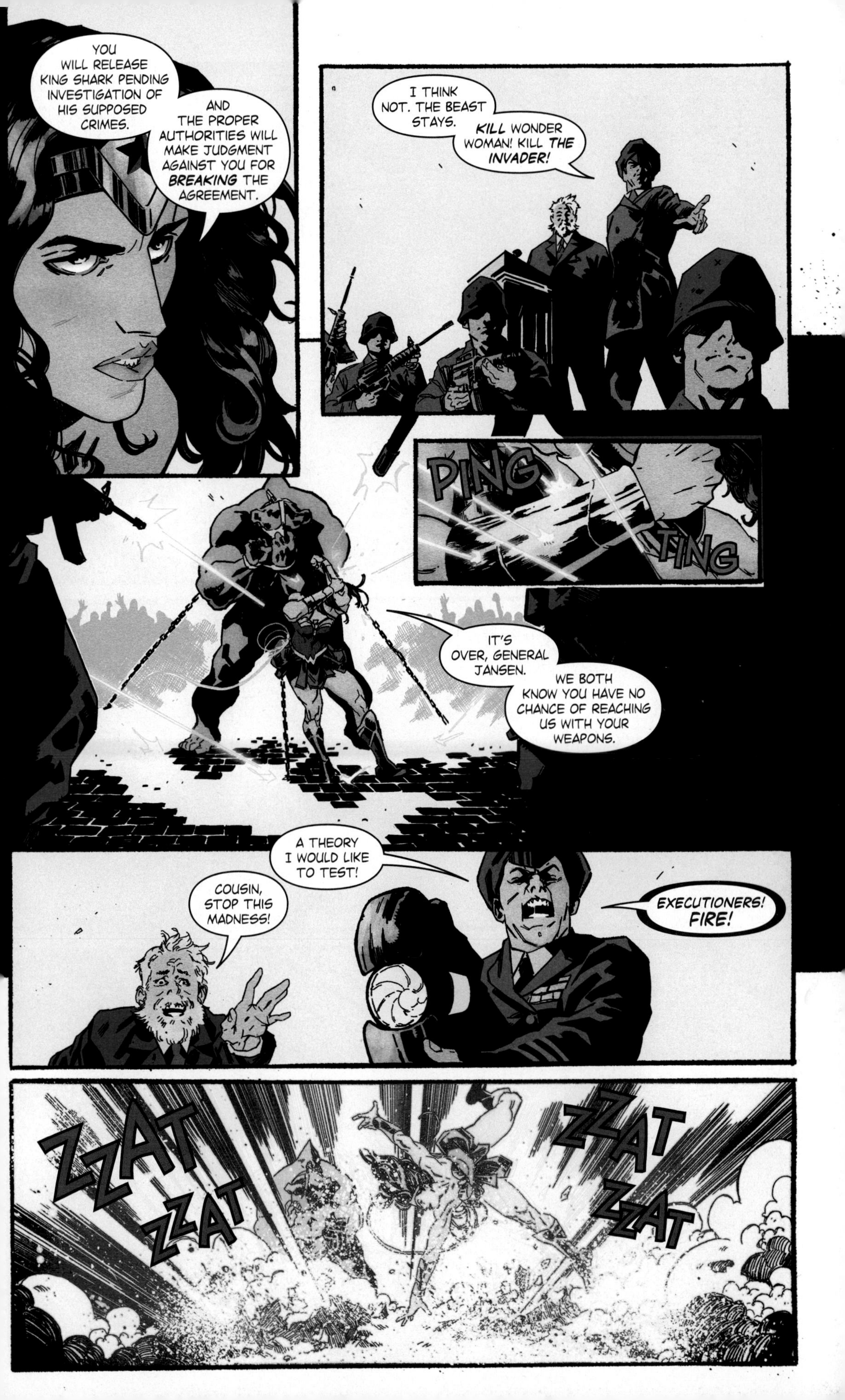
YOU WILL RELEASE KING SHARK PENDING INVESTIGATION OF HIS SUPPOSED CRIMES.
AND THE PROPER AUTHORITIES WILL MAKE JUDGMENT AGAINST YOU FOR BREAKING THE AGREEMENT.
I THINK NOT. THE BEAST STAYS.
KILL WONDER WOMAN! KILL THE INVADER!
PING
TING
IT'S OVER, GENERAL JANSEN.
WE BOTH KNOW YOU HAVE NO CHANCE OF REACHING US WITH YOUR WEAPONS.
A THEORY I WOULD LIKE TO TEST!
COUSIN, STOP THIS MADNESS!
EXECUTIONERS! FIRE!
ZZAT
ZZAT
ZZAT
ZZAT

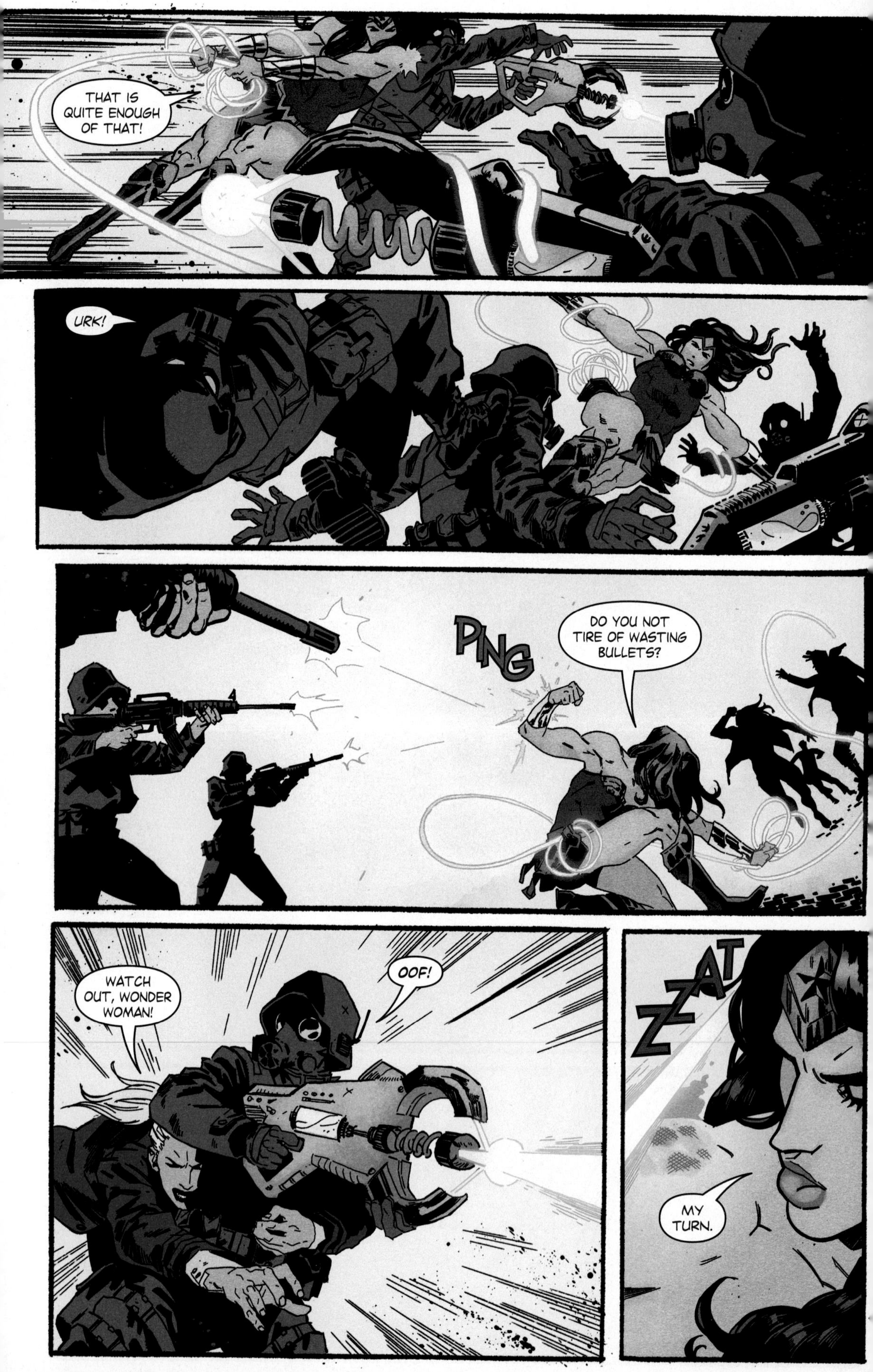
THAT IS QUITE ENOUGH OF THAT!
URK!
PING
DO YOU NOT TIRE OF WASTING BULLETS?
WATCH OUT, WONDER WOMAN!
OOF!
ZZZAT
MY TURN.

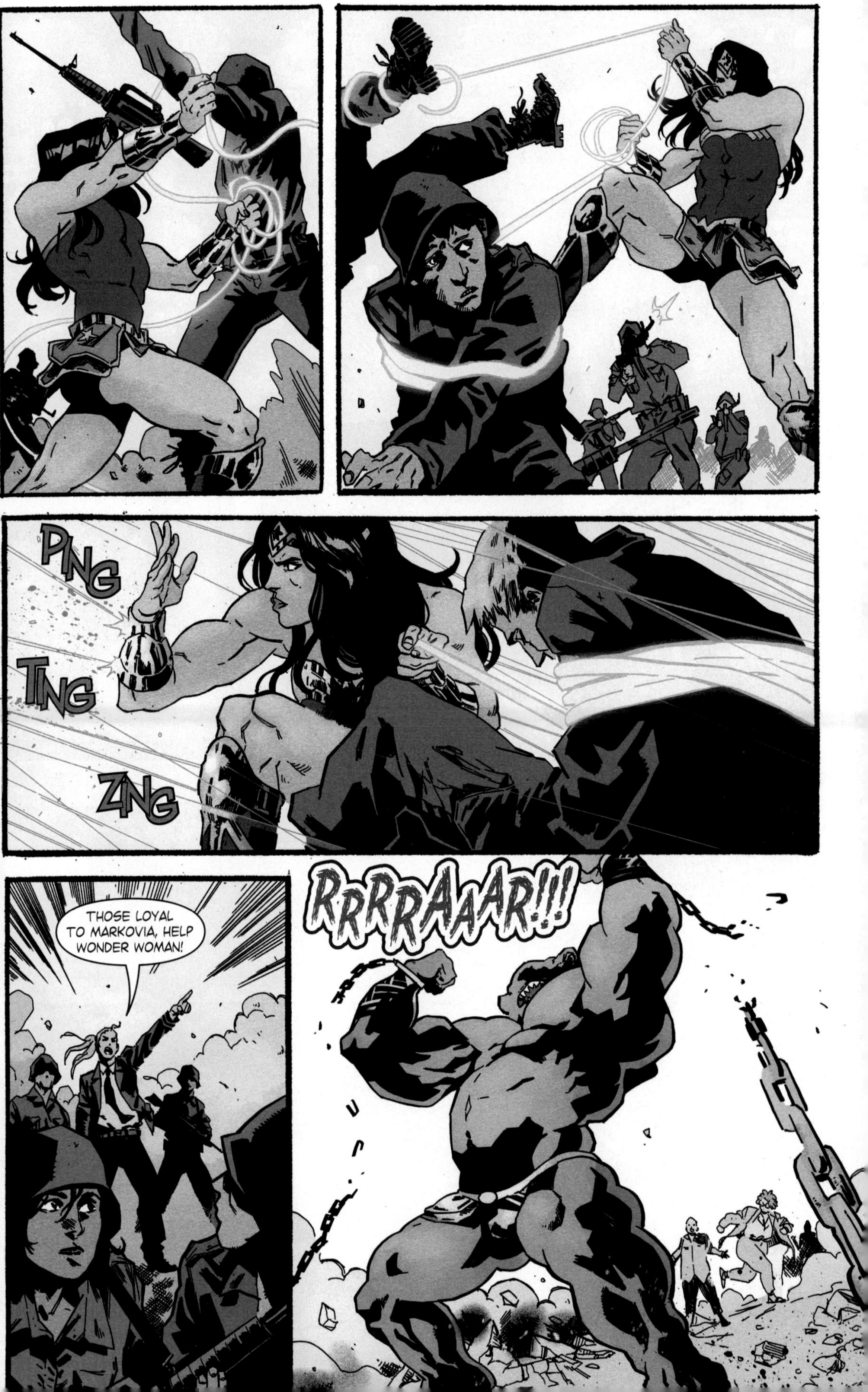
PING
TING
ZING
THOSE LOYAL TO MARKOVIA, HELP WONDER WOMAN!
RRRRAAAR!!!

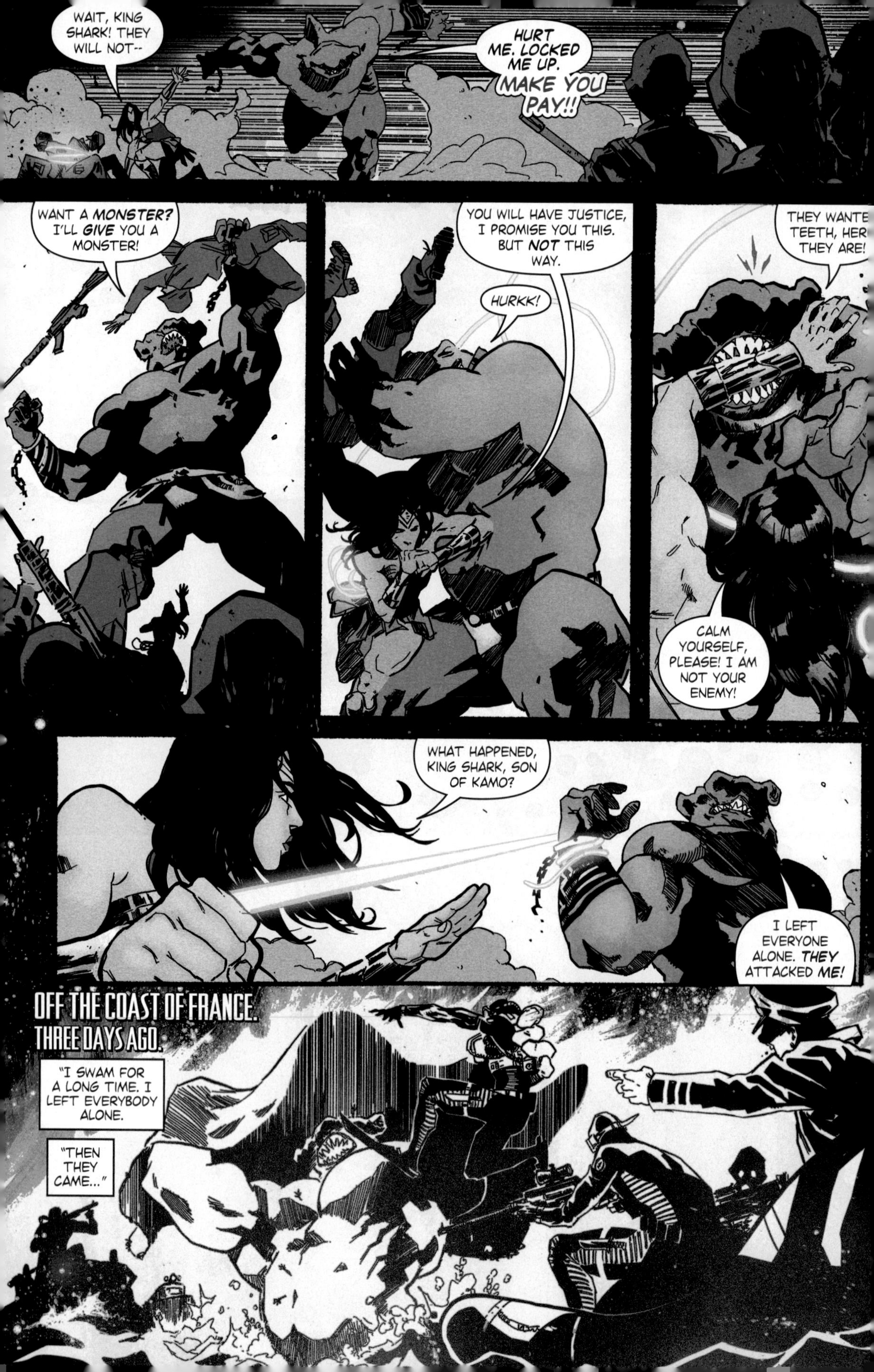
WAIT, KING SHARK! THEY WILL NOT--
HURT ME. LOCKED ME UP. MAKE YOU PAY!!
WANT A MONSTER? I'LL GIVE YOU A MONSTER!
YOU WILL HAVE JUSTICE, I PROMISE YOU THIS. BUT NOT THIS WAY.
HURKK!
THEY WANTE TEETH, HER THEY ARE!
CALM YOURSELF, PLEASE! I AM NOT YOUR ENEMY!
WHAT HAPPENED, KING SHARK, SON OF KAMO?
I LEFT EVERYONE ALONE. THEY ATTACKED ME!
OFF THE COAST OF FRANCE. THREE DAYS AGO.
"I SWAM FOR A LONG TIME. I LEFT EVERYBODY ALONE.
"THEN THEY CAME..."

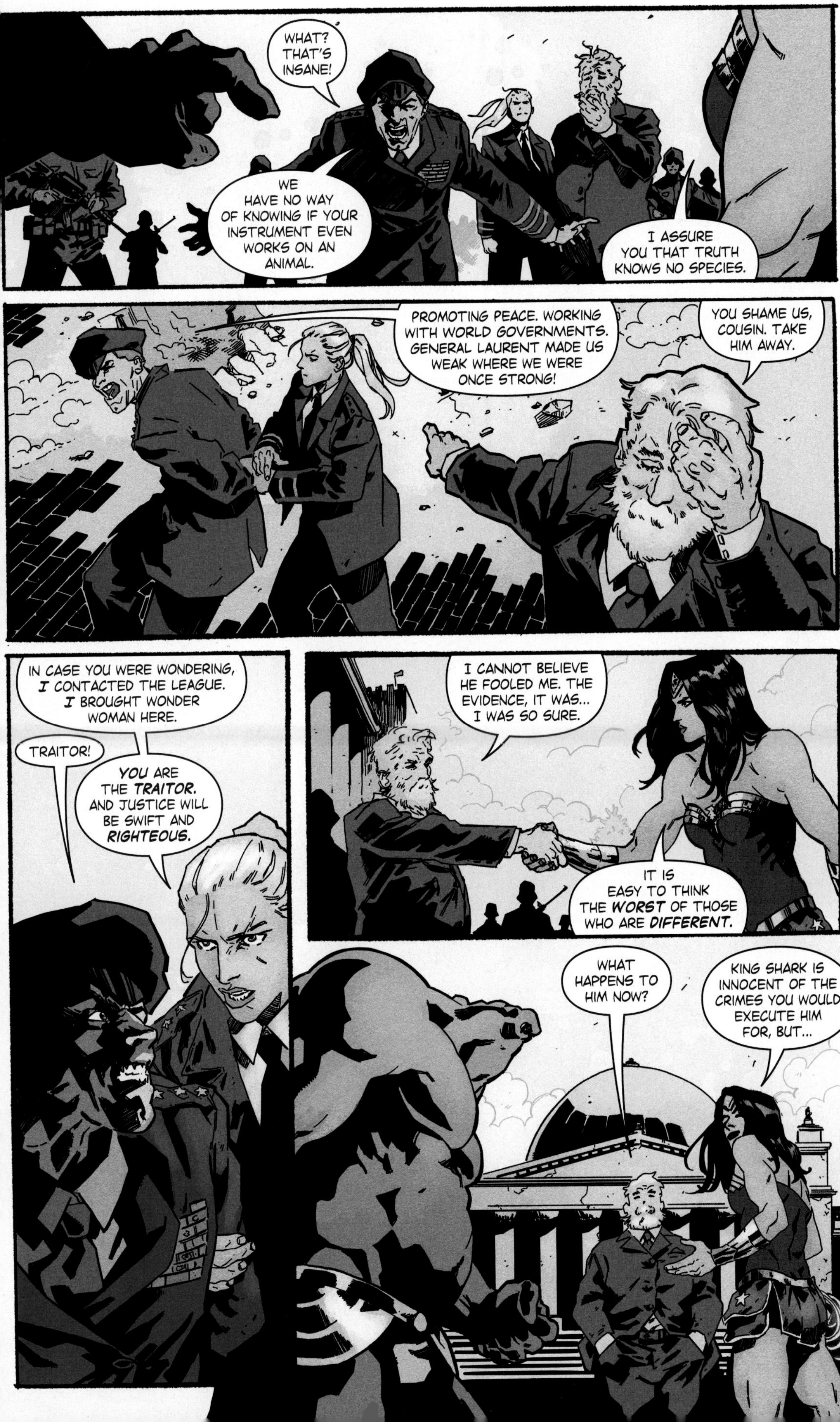
WHAT? THAT'S INSANE!
WE HAVE NO WAY OF KNOWING IF YOUR INSTRUMENT EVEN WORKS ON AN ANIMAL.
I ASSURE YOU THAT TRUTH KNOWS NO SPECIES.
PROMOTING PEACE. WORKING WITH WORLD GOVERNMENTS. GENERAL LAURENT MADE US WEAK WHERE WE WERE ONCE STRONG!
YOU SHAME US, COUSIN. TAKE HIM AWAY.
IN CASE YOU WERE WONDERING, I CONTACTED THE LEAGUE. I BROUGHT WONDER WOMAN HERE.
TRAITOR!
YOU ARE THE TRAITOR. AND JUSTICE WILL BE SWIFT AND RIGHTEOUS.
I CANNOT BELIEVE HE FOOLED ME. THE EVIDENCE, IT WAS... I WAS SO SURE.
IT IS EASY TO THINK THE WORST OF THOSE WHO ARE DIFFERENT.
WHAT HAPPENS TO HIM NOW?
KING SHARK IS INNOCENT OF THE CRIMES YOU WOULD EXECUTE HIM FOR, BUT...

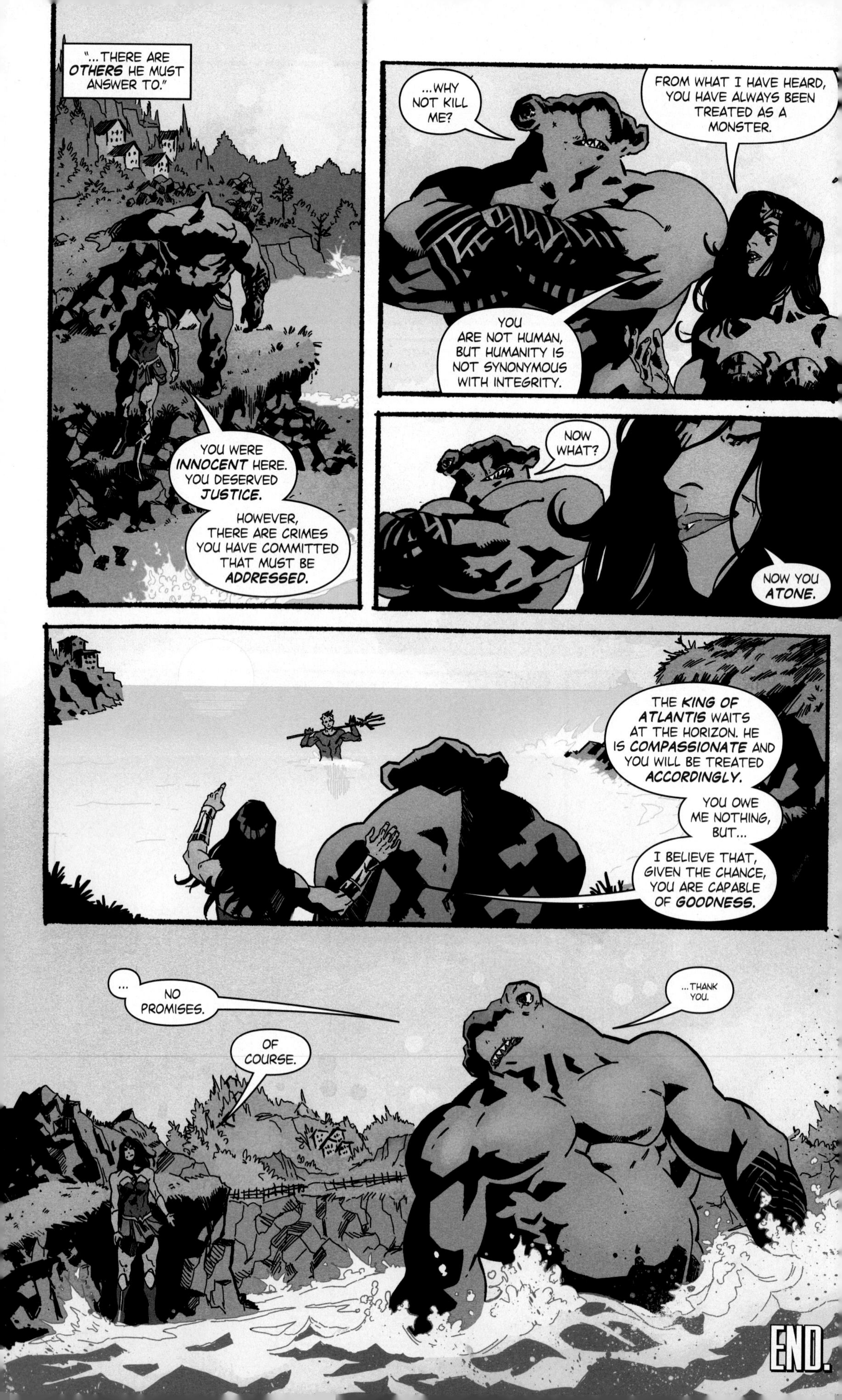
"...THERE ARE OTHERS HE MUST ANSWER TO."
YOU WERE INNOCENT HERE. YOU DESERVED JUSTICE.
HOWEVER, THERE ARE CRIMES YOU HAVE COMMITTED THAT MUST BE ADDRESSED.
...WHY NOT KILL ME?
FROM WHAT I HAVE HEARD, YOU HAVE ALWAYS BEEN TREATED AS A MONSTER.
YOU ARE NOT HUMAN, BUT HUMANITY IS NOT SYNONYMOUS WITH INTEGRITY.
NOW WHAT?
NOW YOU ATONE.
THE KING OF ATLANTIS WAITS AT THE HORIZON. HE IS COMPASSIONATE AND YOU WILL BE TREATED ACCORDINGLY.
YOU OWE ME NOTHING, BUT...
I BELIEVE THAT, GIVEN THE CHANCE, YOU ARE CAPABLE OF GOODNESS.
...
NO PROMISES.
OF COURSE.
...THANK YOU.
END.

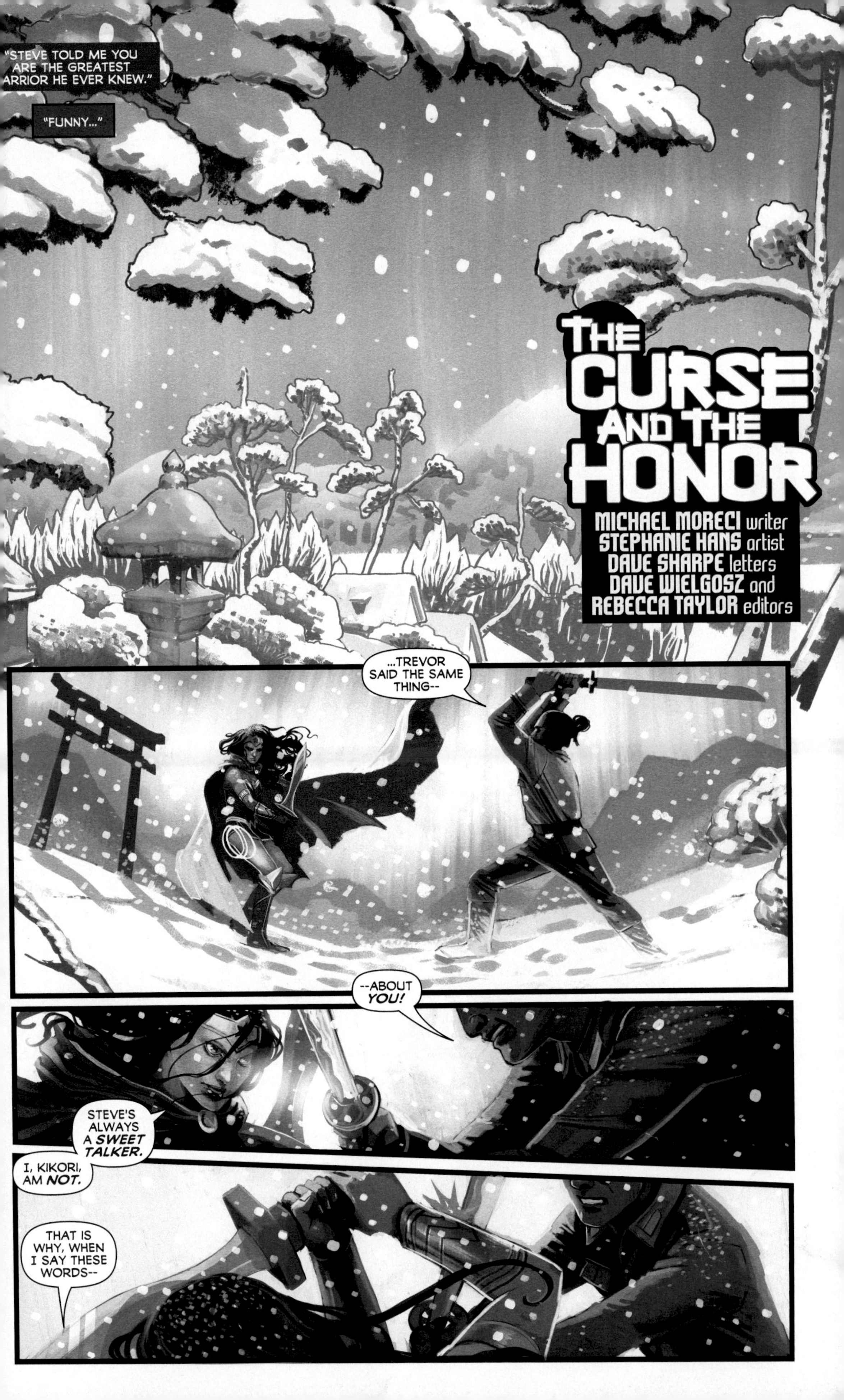

"STEVE TOLD ME YOU ARE THE GREATEST ARRIOR HE EVER KNEW."
"FUNNY..."
THE CURSE AND THE HONOR
MICHAEL MORECI writer
STEPHANIE HANS artist
DAVE SHARPE letters
DAVE WIELGOSZ and REBECCA TAYLOR editors
...TREVOR SAID THE SAME THING--
--ABOUT *YOU!*
STEVE'S ALWAYS A ***SWEET TALKER.***
I, KIKORI, AM ***NOT.***
THAT IS WHY, WHEN I SAY THESE WORDS--

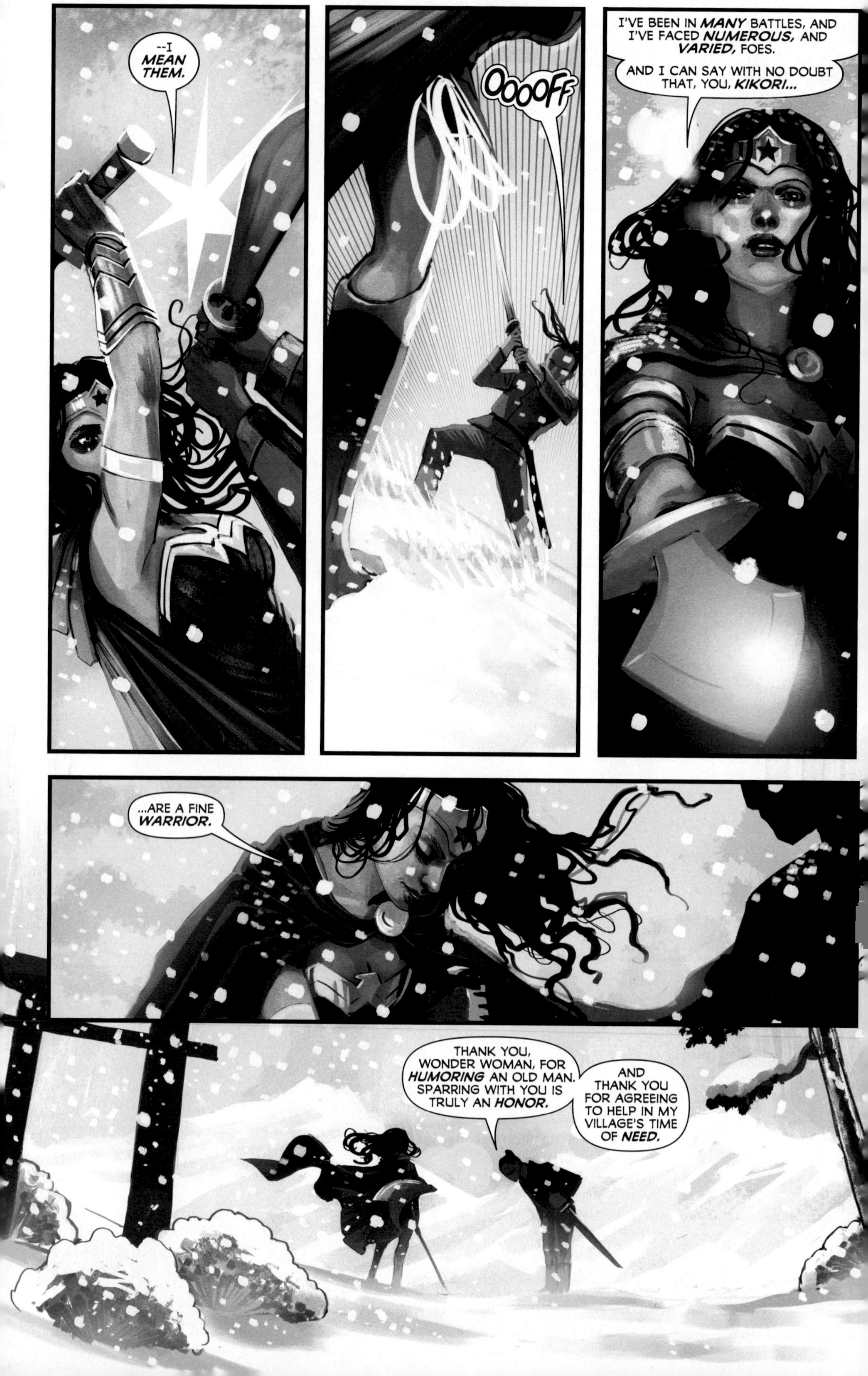
--I MEAN THEM.
OOOOFF
I'VE BEEN IN MANY BATTLES, AND I'VE FACED NUMEROUS, AND VARIED, FOES.
AND I CAN SAY WITH NO DOUBT THAT, YOU, KIKORI...
...ARE A FINE WARRIOR.
THANK YOU, WONDER WOMAN, FOR HUMORING AN OLD MAN. SPARRING WITH YOU IS TRULY AN HONOR.
AND THANK YOU FOR AGREEING TO HELP IN MY VILLAGE'S TIME OF NEED.

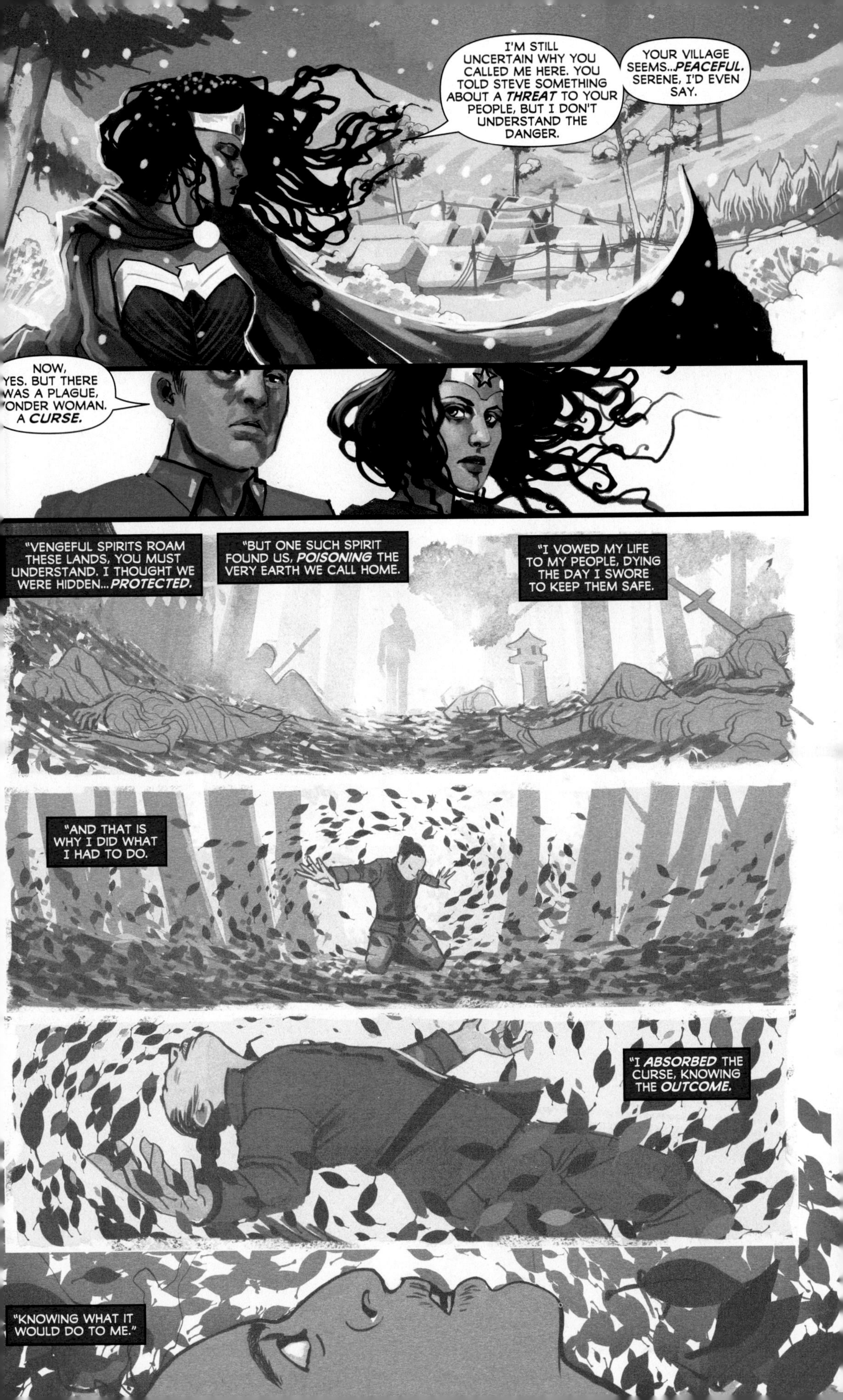
I'M STILL UNCERTAIN WHY YOU CALLED ME HERE. YOU TOLD STEVE SOMETHING ABOUT A THREAT TO YOUR PEOPLE, BUT I DON'T UNDERSTAND THE DANGER.
YOUR VILLAGE SEEMS...PEACEFUL. SERENE, I'D EVEN SAY.
NOW, YES. BUT THERE WAS A PLAGUE, WONDER WOMAN. A CURSE.
"VENGEFUL SPIRITS ROAM THESE LANDS, YOU MUST UNDERSTAND. I THOUGHT WE WERE HIDDEN...PROTECTED.
"BUT ONE SUCH SPIRIT FOUND US, POISONING THE VERY EARTH WE CALL HOME.
"I VOWED MY LIFE TO MY PEOPLE, DYING THE DAY I SWORE TO KEEP THEM SAFE.
"AND THAT IS WHY I DID WHAT I HAD TO DO.
"I ABSORBED THE CURSE, KNOWING THE OUTCOME.
"KNOWING WHAT IT WOULD DO TO ME."

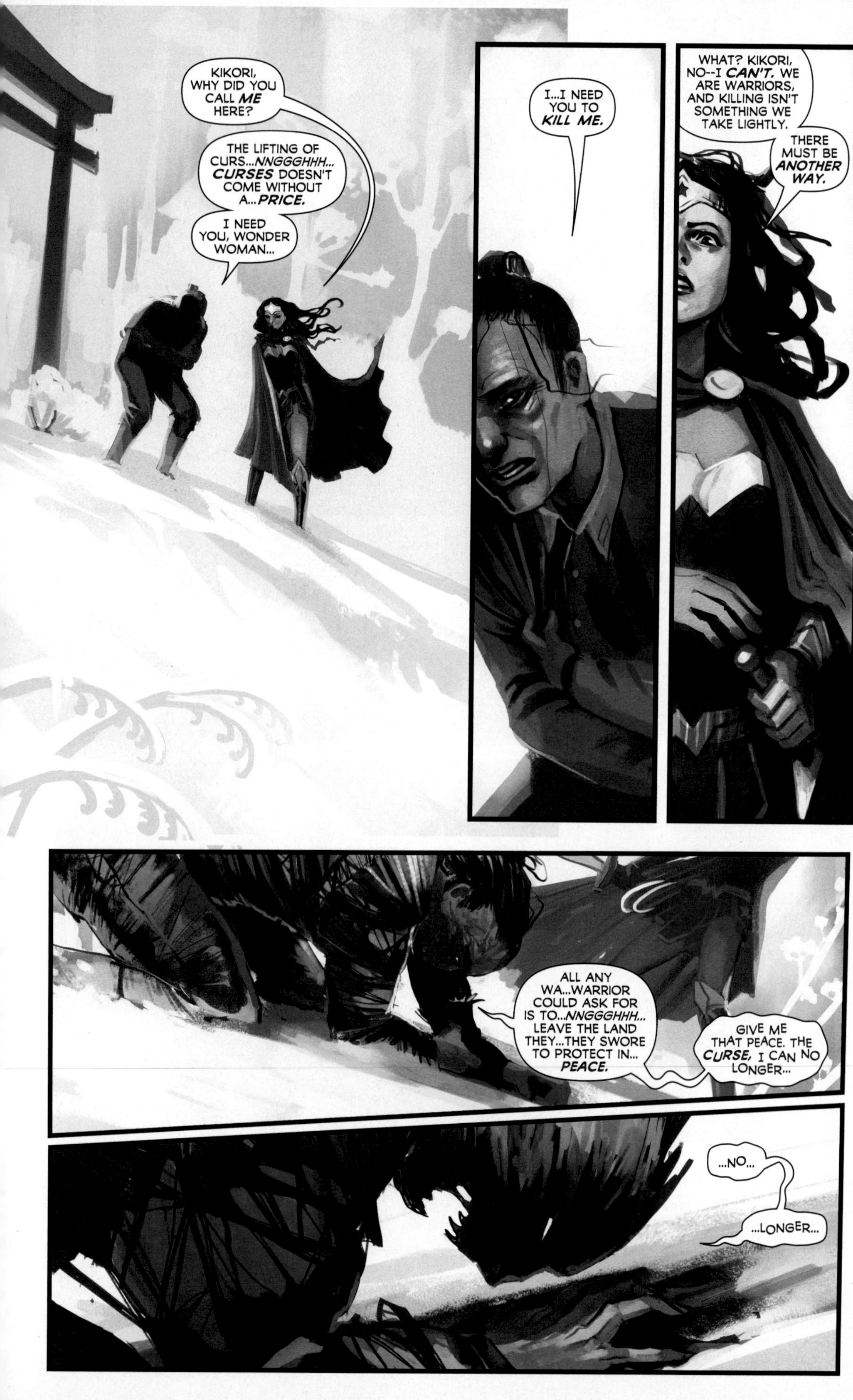
KIKORI, WHY DID YOU CALL *ME* HERE?
THE LIFTING OF CURS...*NNGGGHHH*... ***CURSES*** DOESN'T COME WITHOUT A...***PRICE.***
I NEED YOU, WONDER WOMAN...
I...I NEED YOU TO ***KILL ME.***
WHAT? KIKORI, NO--I ***CAN'T.*** WE ARE WARRIORS, AND KILLING ISN'T SOMETHING WE TAKE LIGHTLY.
THERE MUST BE ***ANOTHER WAY.***
ALL ANY WA...WARRIOR COULD ASK FOR IS TO...*NNGGGHHH*... LEAVE THE LAND THEY...THEY SWORE TO PROTECT IN... ***PEACE.***
GIVE ME THAT PEACE. THE ***CURSE,*** I CAN NO LONGER...
...NO...
...LONGER...

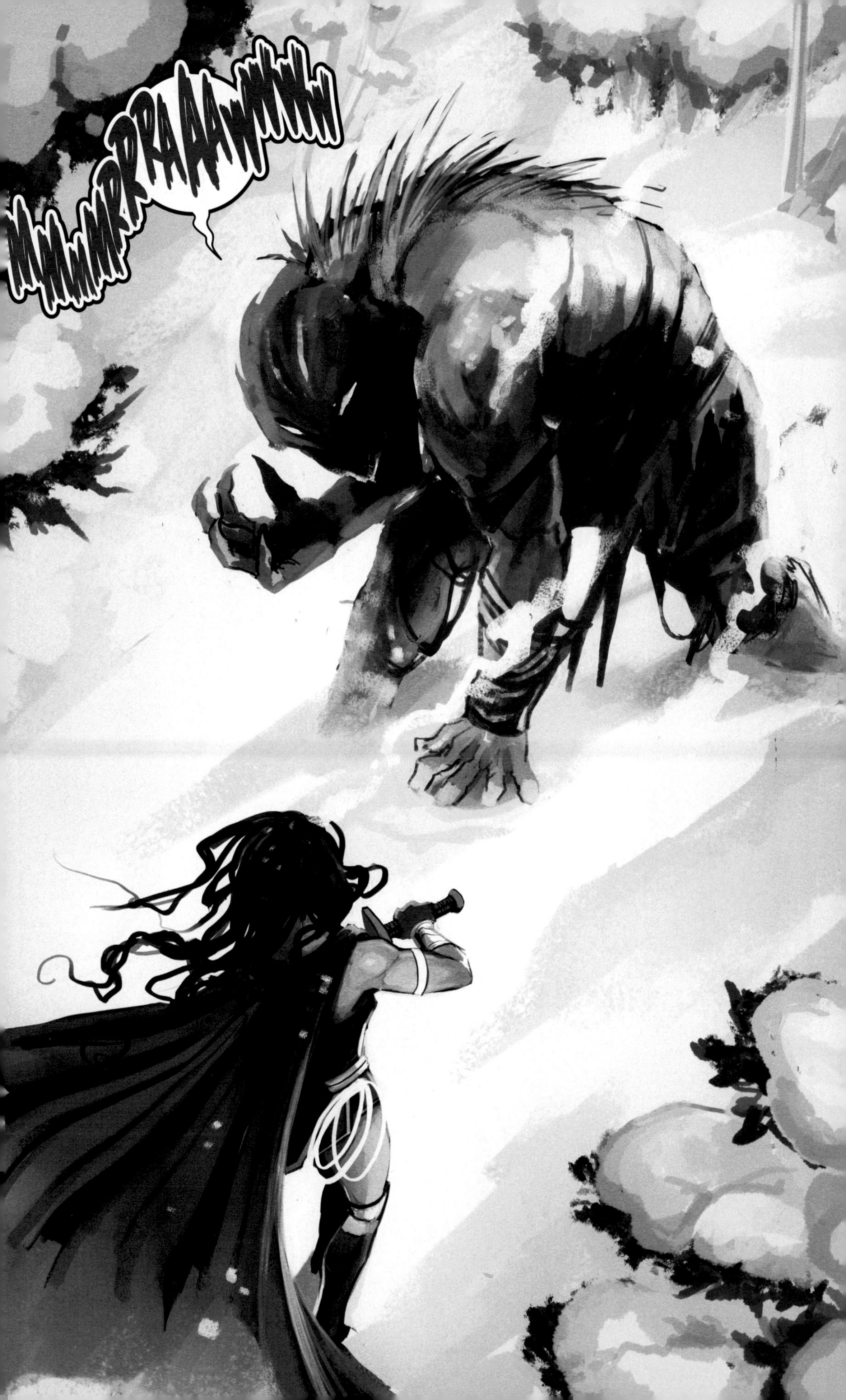
MMMMMRRAAAWWWWW

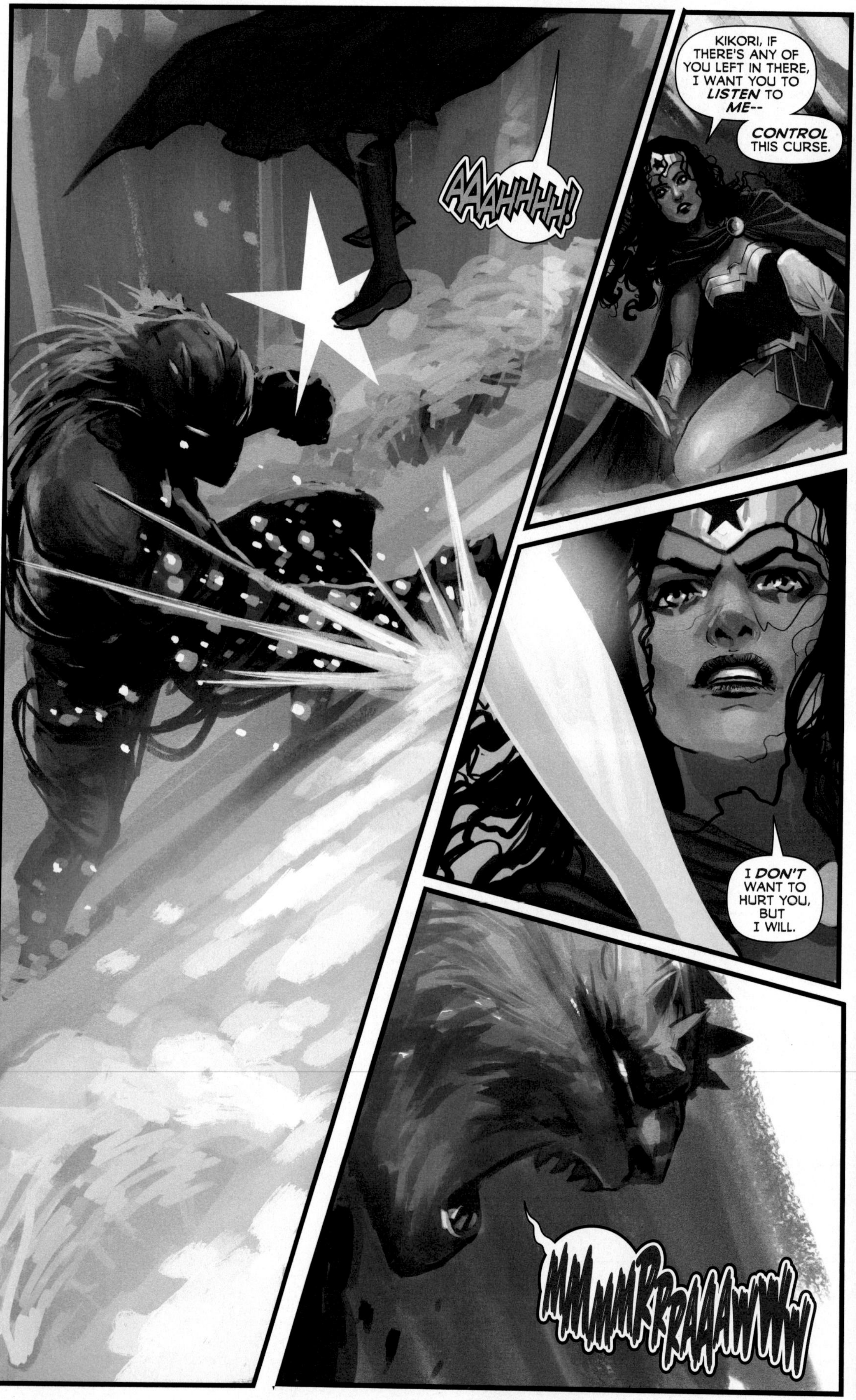
AAAHHHH!
KIKORI, IF THERE'S ANY OF YOU LEFT IN THERE, I WANT YOU TO LISTEN TO ME--
CONTROL THIS CURSE.
I DON'T WANT TO HURT YOU, BUT I WILL.
MMMMRRRAAAWWW

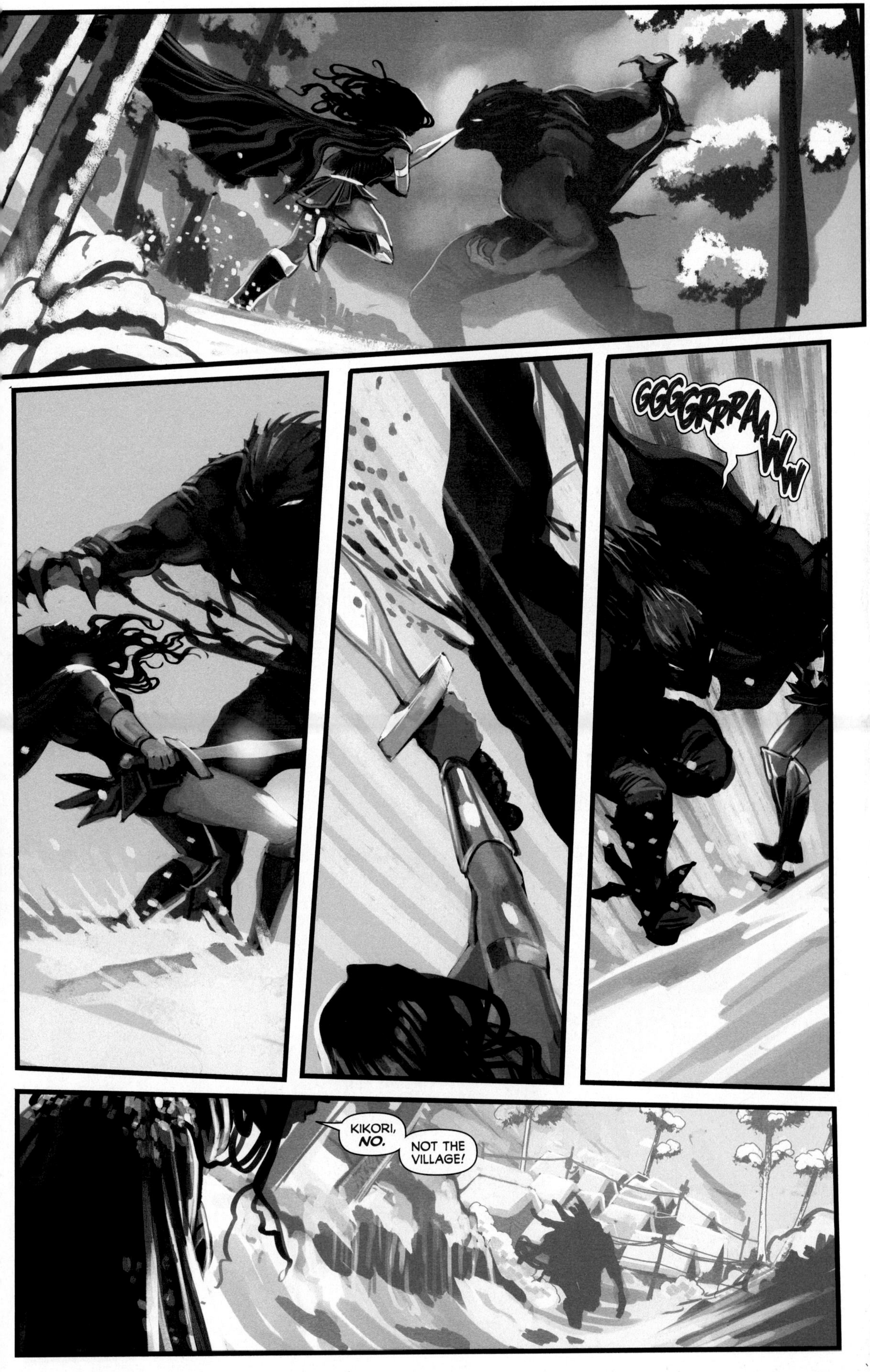
GGGGRRRAAWW
KIKORI, *NO.*
NOT THE VILLAGE!

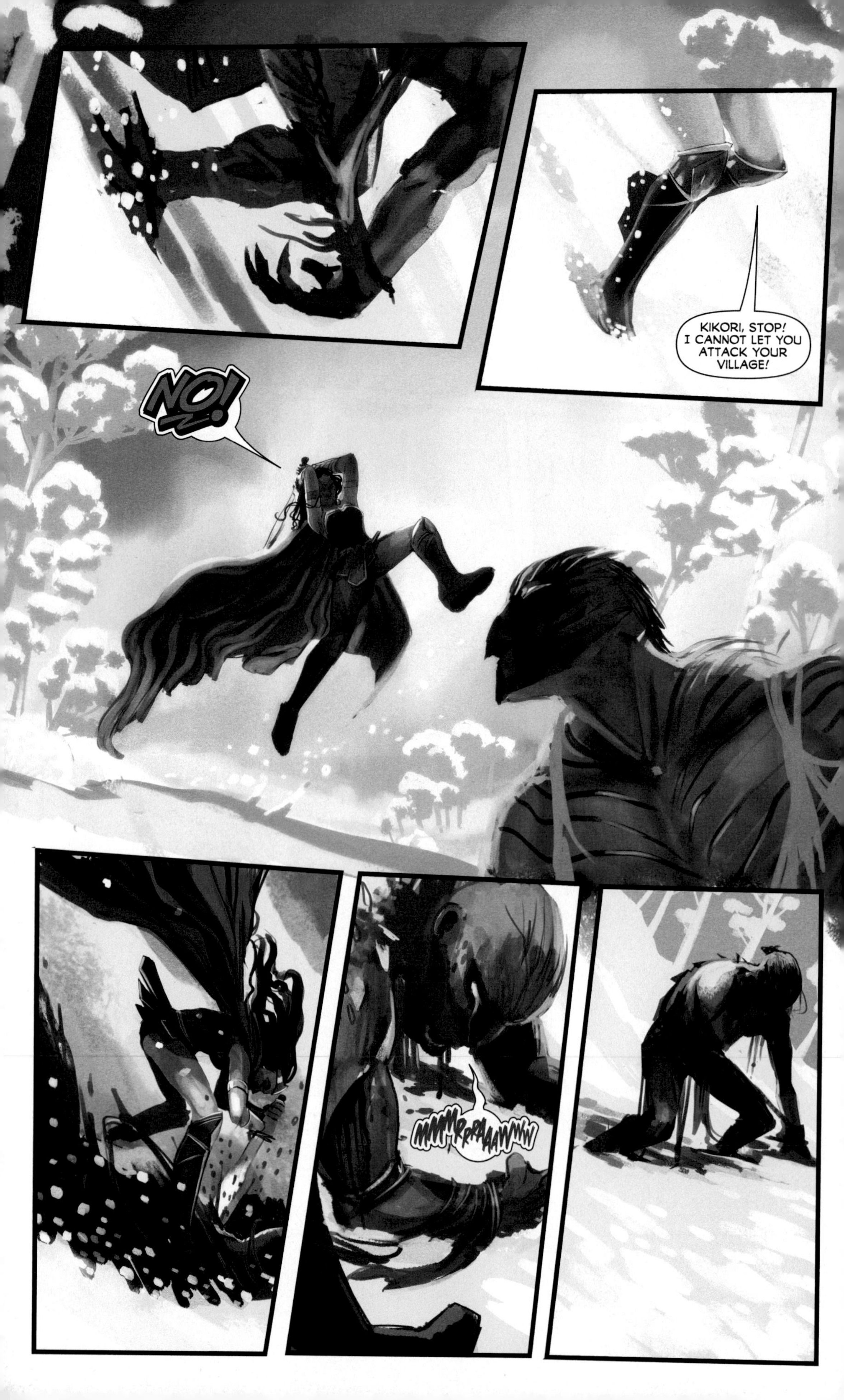
KIKORI, STOP! I CANNOT LET YOU ATTACK YOUR VILLAGE!
NO!
MMMRRRAAAWWW

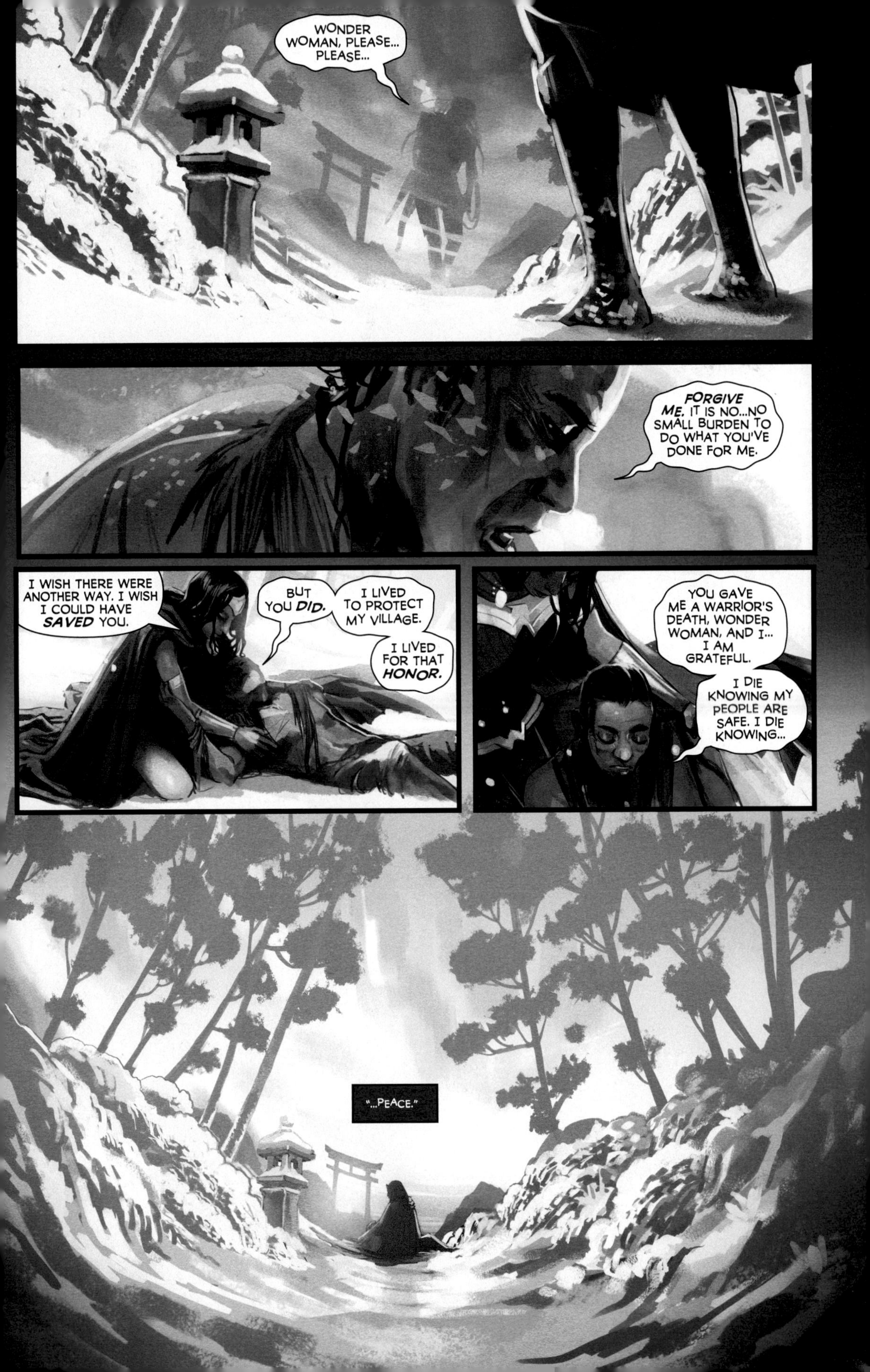

WONDER WOMAN, PLEASE... PLEASE...
FORGIVE ME. IT IS NO...NO SMALL BURDEN TO DO WHAT YOU'VE DONE FOR ME.
I WISH THERE WERE ANOTHER WAY. I WISH I COULD HAVE SAVED YOU.
BUT YOU DID.
I LIVED TO PROTECT MY VILLAGE.
I LIVED FOR THAT HONOR.
YOU GAVE ME A WARRIOR'S DEATH, WONDER WOMAN, AND I... I AM GRATEFUL.
I DIE KNOWING MY PEOPLE ARE SAFE. I DIE KNOWING...
"...PEACE."

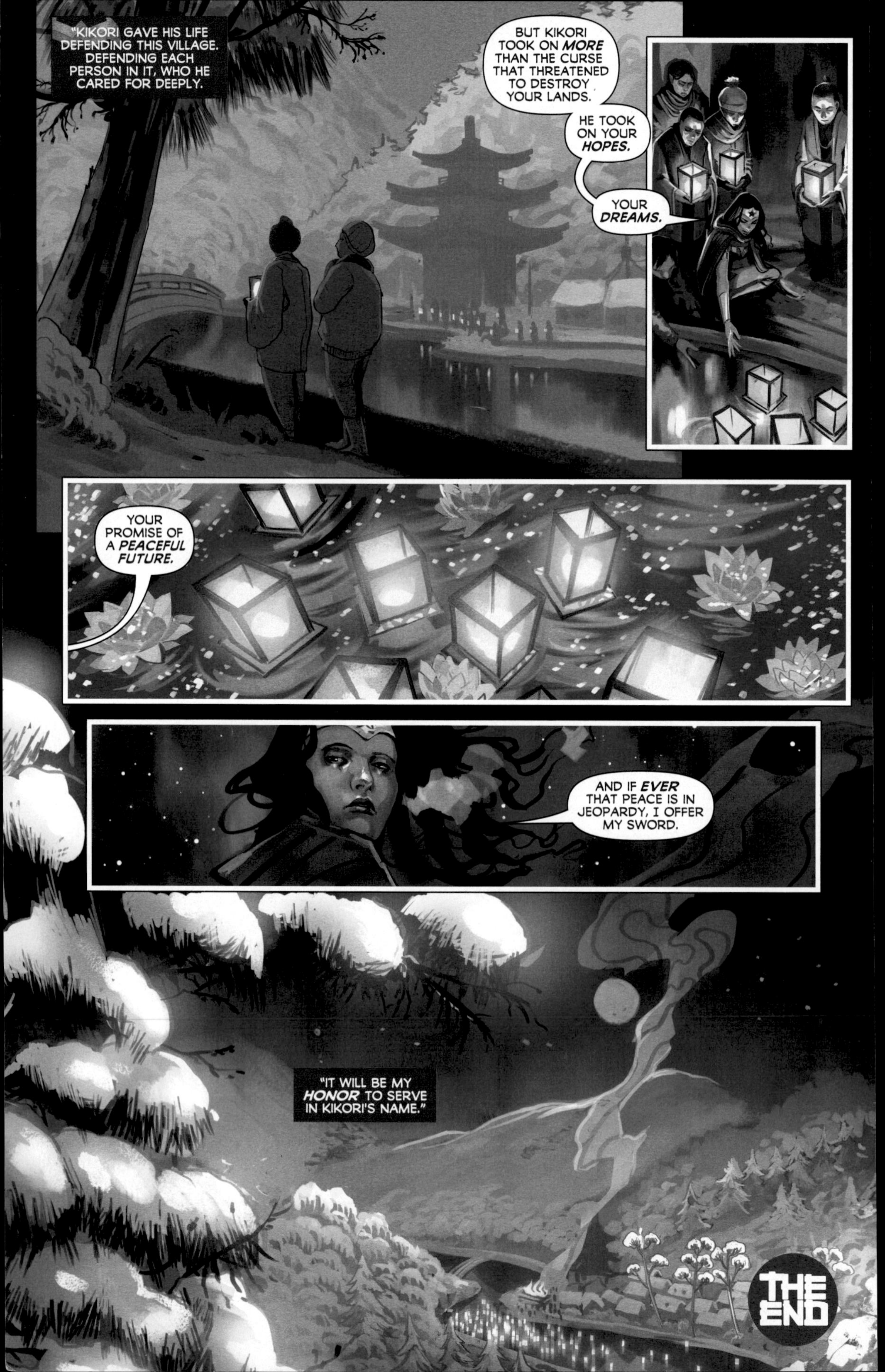
"KIKORI GAVE HIS LIFE DEFENDING THIS VILLAGE. DEFENDING EACH PERSON IN IT, WHO HE CARED FOR DEEPLY.
BUT KIKORI TOOK ON *MORE* THAN THE CURSE THAT THREATENED TO DESTROY YOUR LANDS.
HE TOOK ON YOUR ***HOPES.***
YOUR ***DREAMS.***
YOUR PROMISE OF A ***PEACEFUL FUTURE.***
AND IF ***EVER*** THAT PEACE IS IN JEOPARDY, I OFFER MY SWORD.
"IT WILL BE MY ***HONOR*** TO SERVE IN KIKORI'S NAME."
THE END

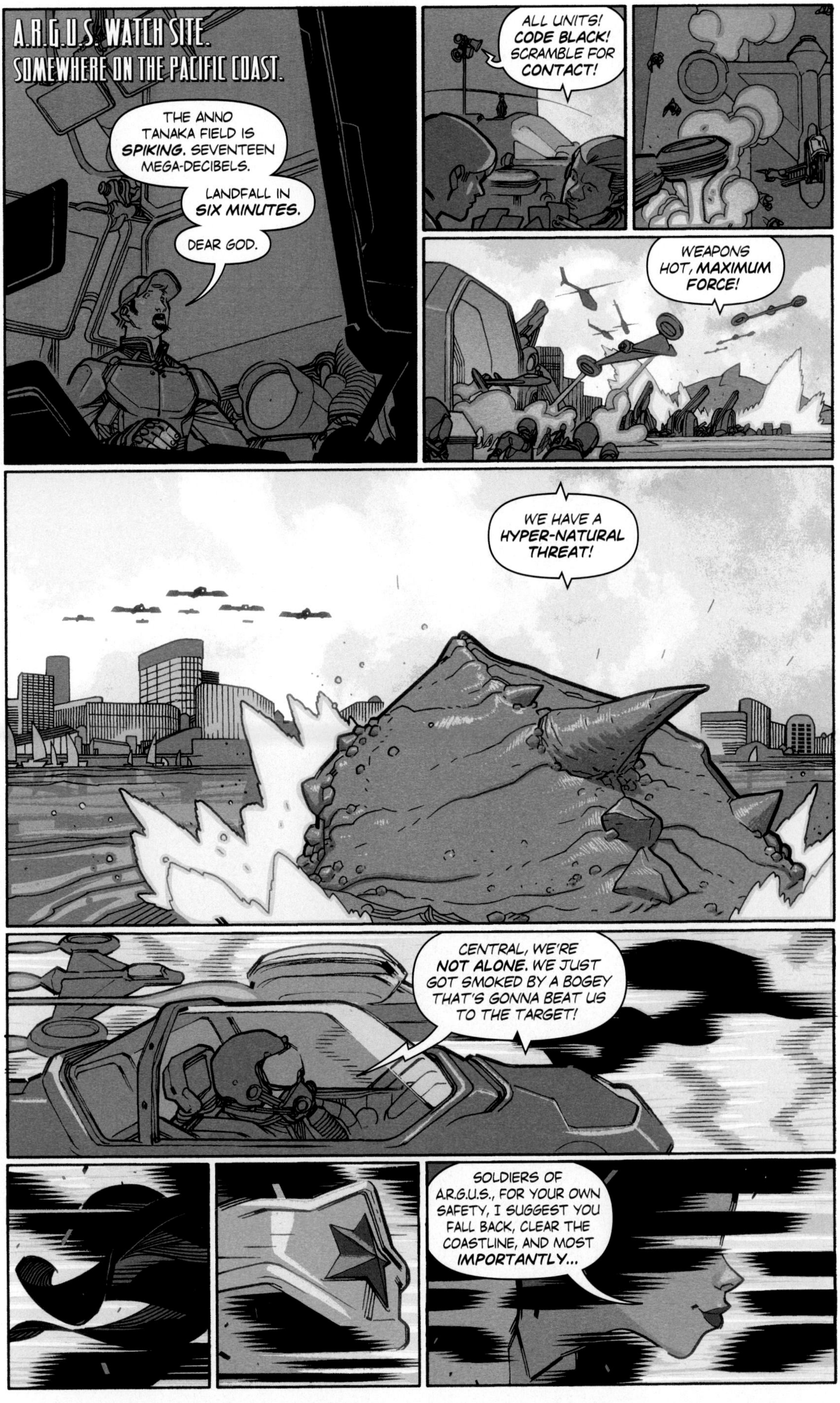
A.R.G.U.S. WATCH SITE.
SOMEWHERE ON THE PACIFIC COAST.
THE ANNO TANAKA FIELD IS SPIKING. SEVENTEEN MEGA-DECIBELS.
LANDFALL IN SIX MINUTES.
DEAR GOD.
ALL UNITS! CODE BLACK! SCRAMBLE FOR CONTACT!
WEAPONS HOT, MAXIMUM FORCE!
WE HAVE A HYPER-NATURAL THREAT!
CENTRAL, WE'RE NOT ALONE. WE JUST GOT SMOKED BY A BOGEY THAT'S GONNA BEAT US TO THE TARGET!
SOLDIERS OF A.R.G.U.S., FOR YOUR OWN SAFETY, I SUGGEST YOU FALL BACK, CLEAR THE COASTLINE, AND MOST IMPORTANTLY...

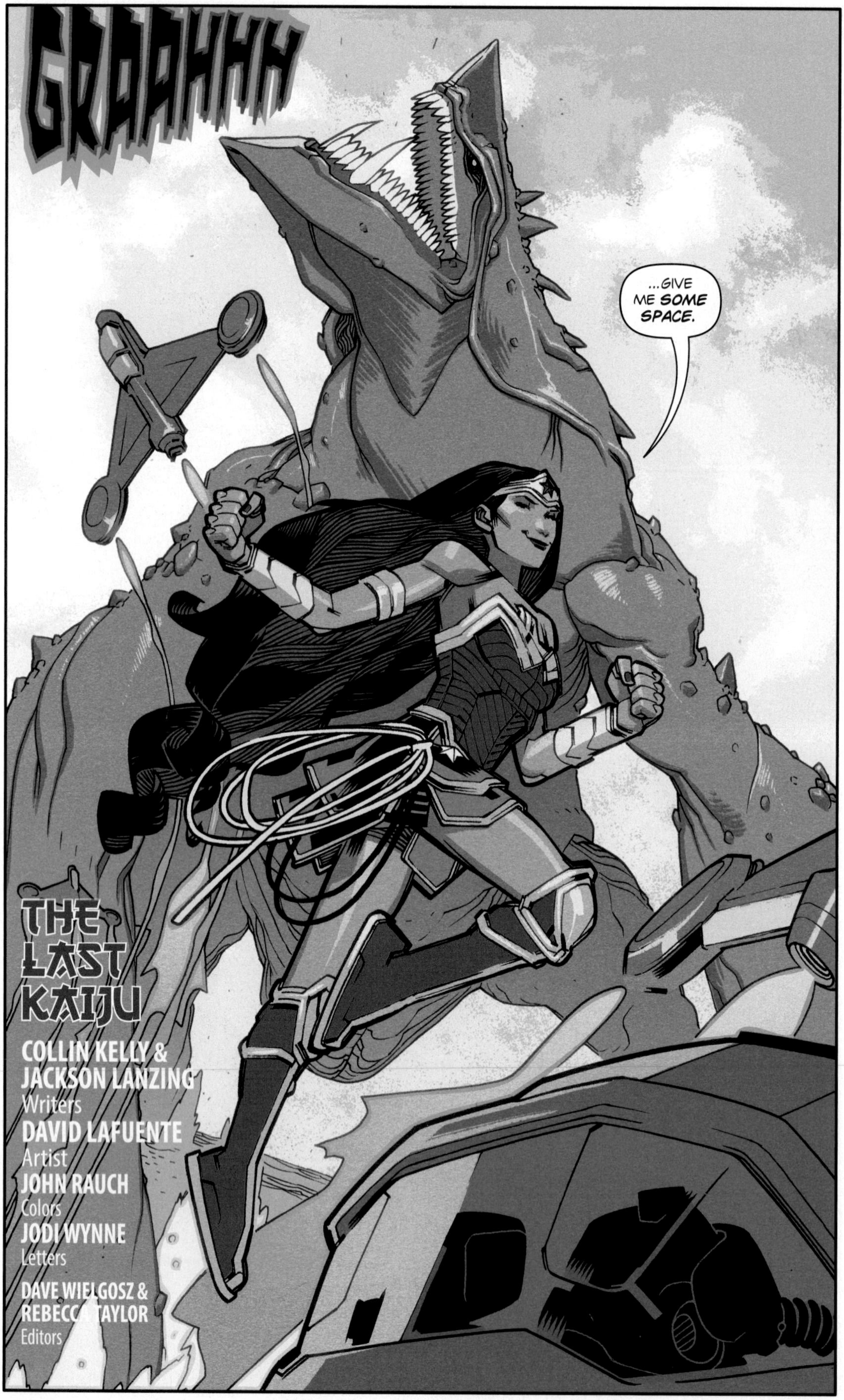
GRAAHHH
...GIVE ME SOME SPACE.
THE LAST KAIJU
COLLIN KELLY & JACKSON LANZING
Writers
DAVID LAFUENTE
Artist
JOHN RAUCH
Colors
JODI WYNNE
Letters
DAVE WIELGOSZ & REBECCA TAYLOR
Editors

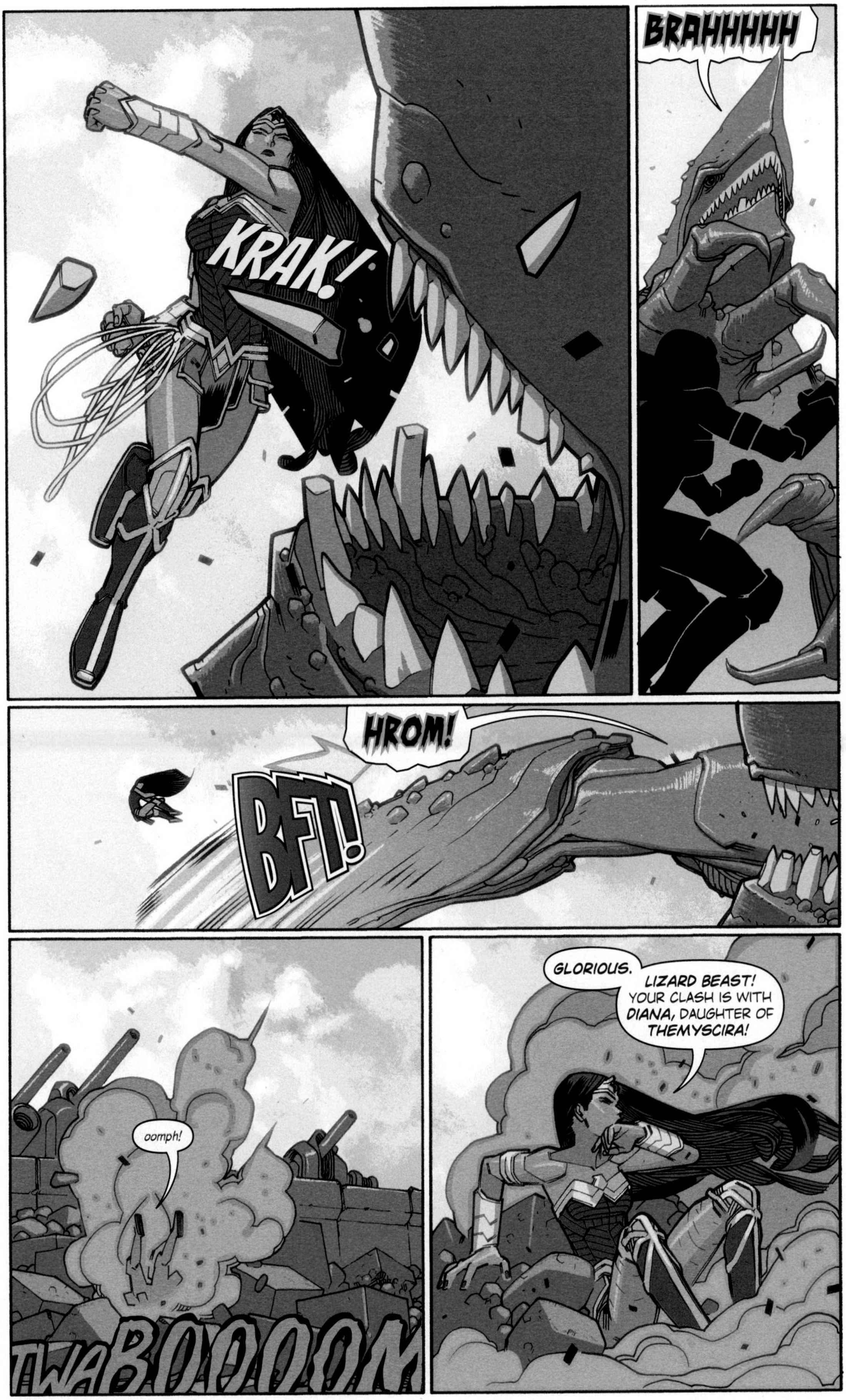
KRAK!
BRAHHHHH
HROM!
BFT!
oomph!
TWABOOOOM
GLORIOUS.
LIZARD BEAST! YOUR CLASH IS WITH DIANA, DAUGHTER OF THEMYSCIRA!

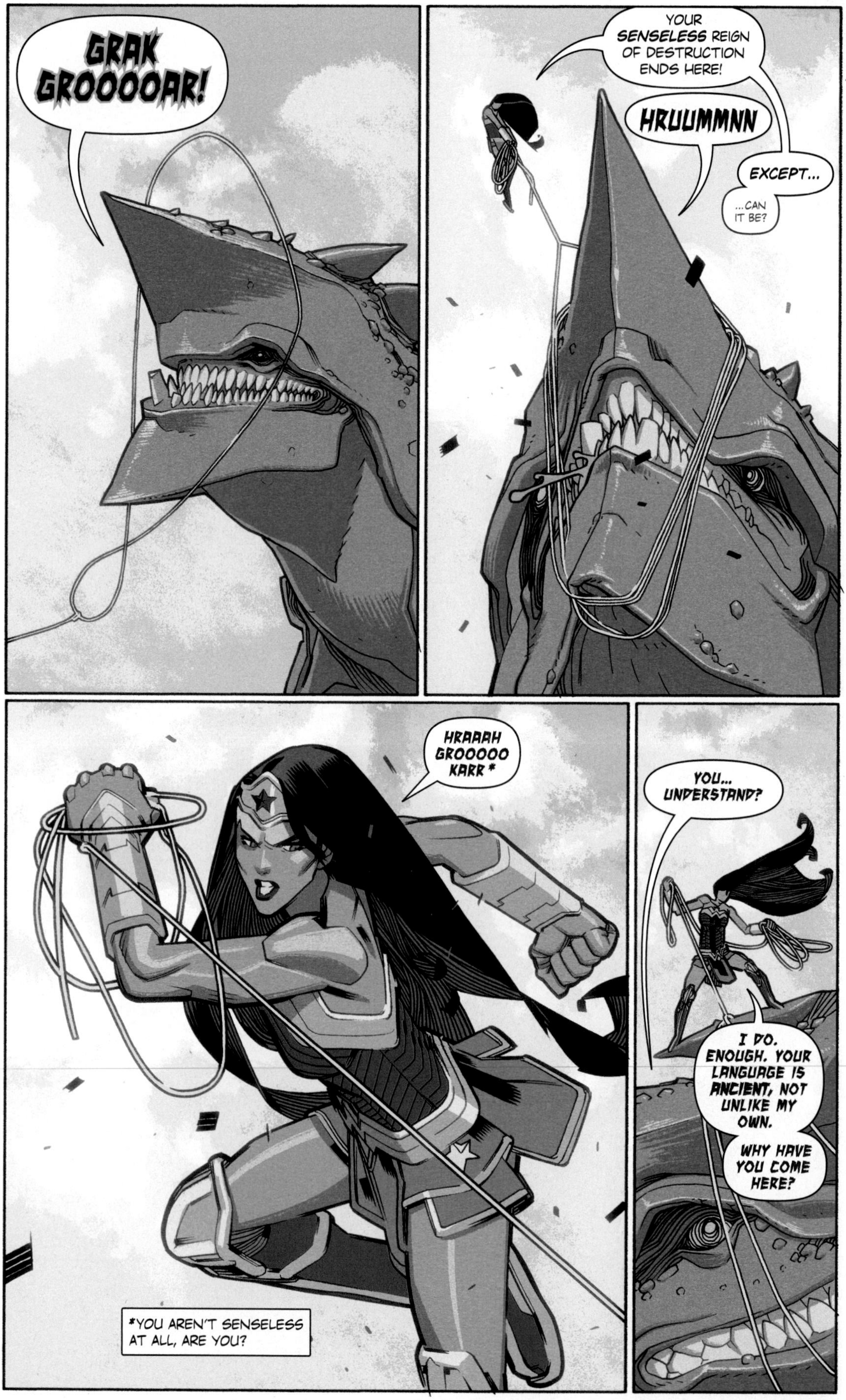
GRAK GROOOOAR!
YOUR SENSELESS REIGN OF DESTRUCTION ENDS HERE!
HRUUMMNN
EXCEPT...
...CAN IT BE?
HRAAAH GROOOOO KARR *
*YOU AREN'T SENSELESS AT ALL, ARE YOU?
YOU... UNDERSTAND?
I DO. ENOUGH. YOUR LANGUAGE IS ANCIENT, NOT UNLIKE MY OWN.
WHY HAVE YOU COME HERE?

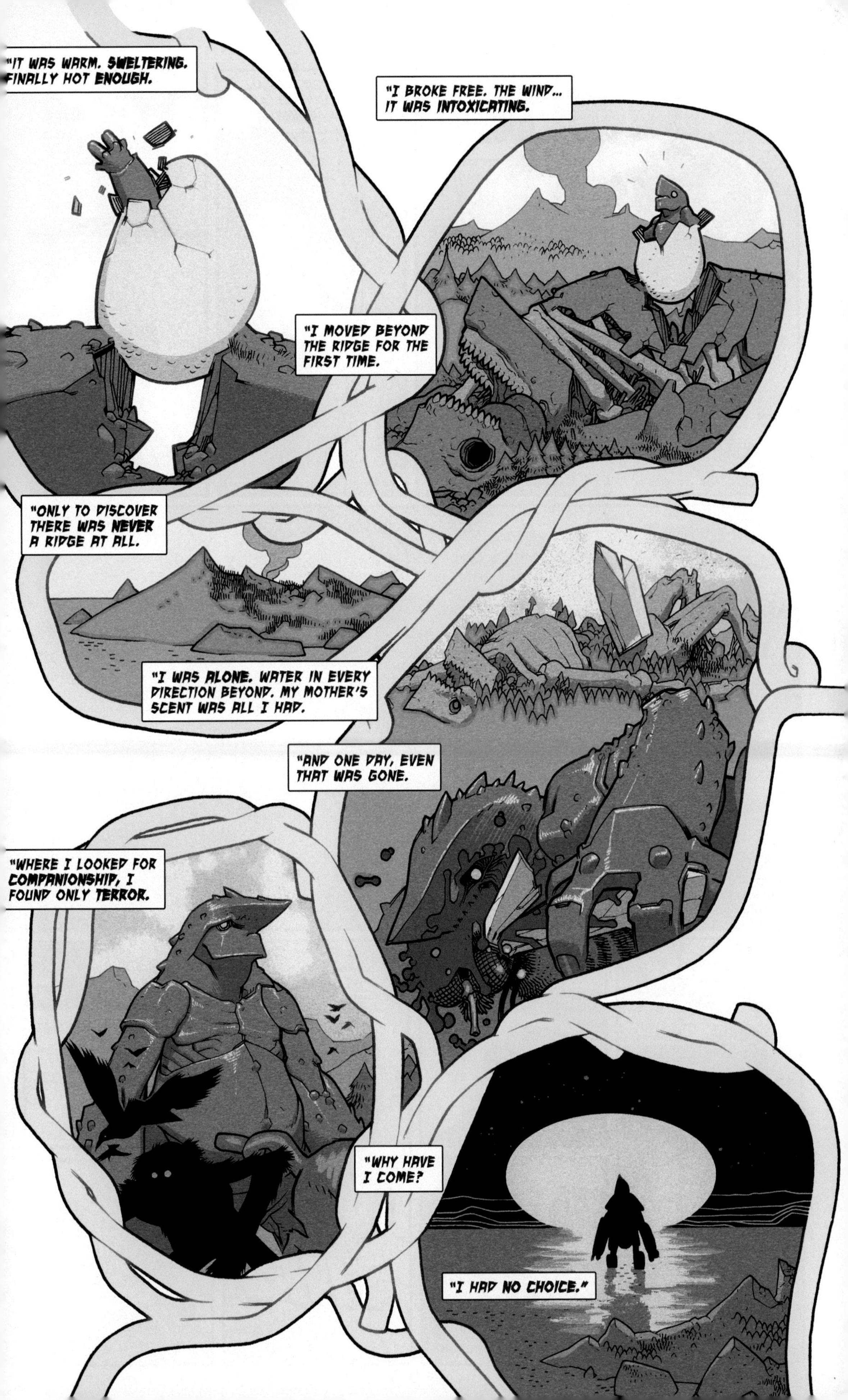
"IT WAS WARM. SWELTERING. FINALLY HOT ENOUGH.
"I BROKE FREE. THE WIND... IT WAS INTOXICATING.
"I MOVED BEYOND THE RIDGE FOR THE FIRST TIME.
"ONLY TO DISCOVER THERE WAS NEVER A RIDGE AT ALL.
"I WAS ALONE. WATER IN EVERY DIRECTION BEYOND. MY MOTHER'S SCENT WAS ALL I HAD.
"AND ONE DAY, EVEN THAT WAS GONE.
"WHERE I LOOKED FOR COMPANIONSHIP, I FOUND ONLY TERROR.
"WHY HAVE I COME?
"I HAD NO CHOICE."

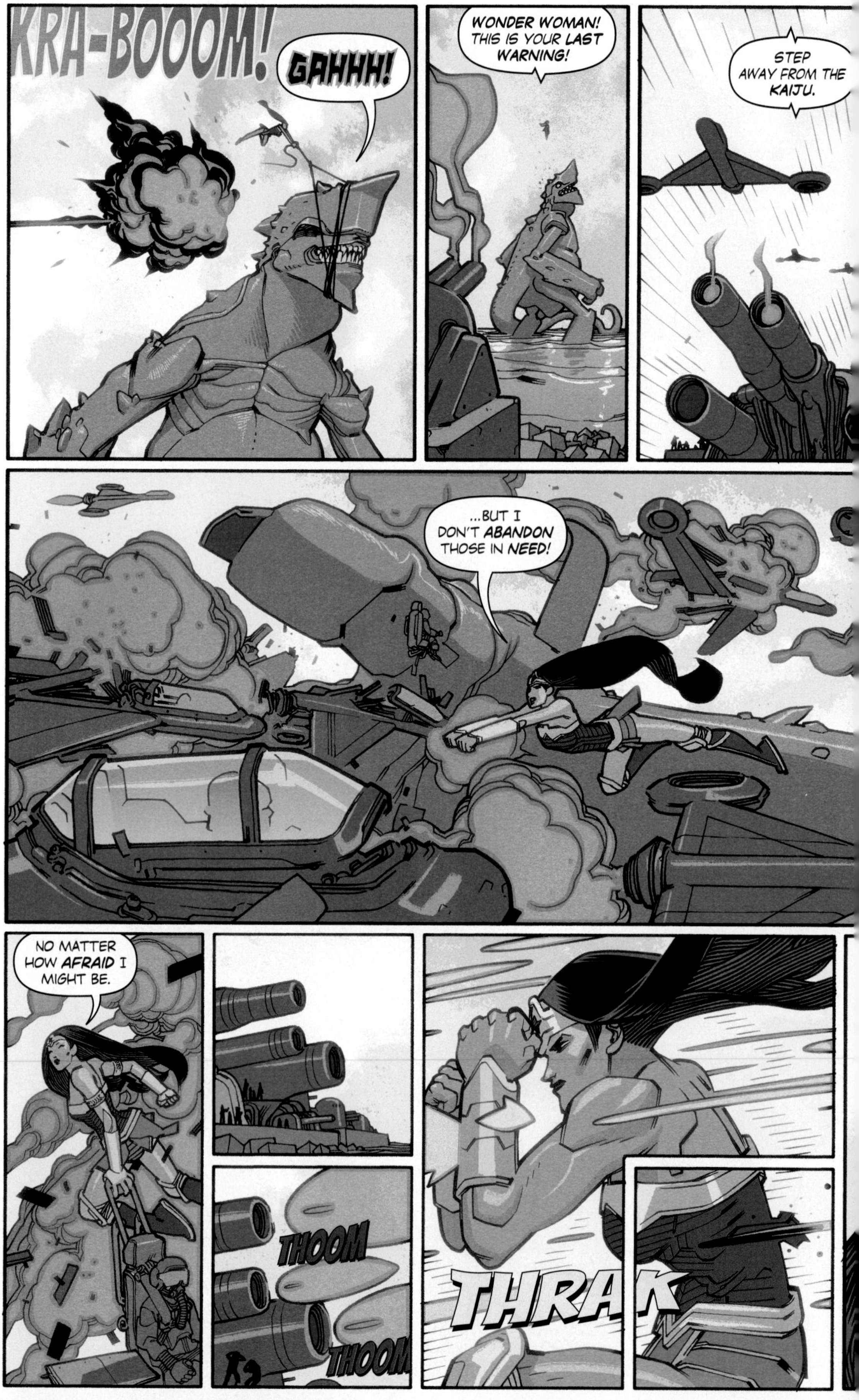
KRA-BOOOM!
GAHHH!
WONDER WOMAN! THIS IS YOUR LAST WARNING!
STEP AWAY FROM THE KAIJU.
...BUT I DON'T ABANDON THOSE IN NEED!
NO MATTER HOW AFRAID I MIGHT BE.
THOOM
THOOM
THRAK

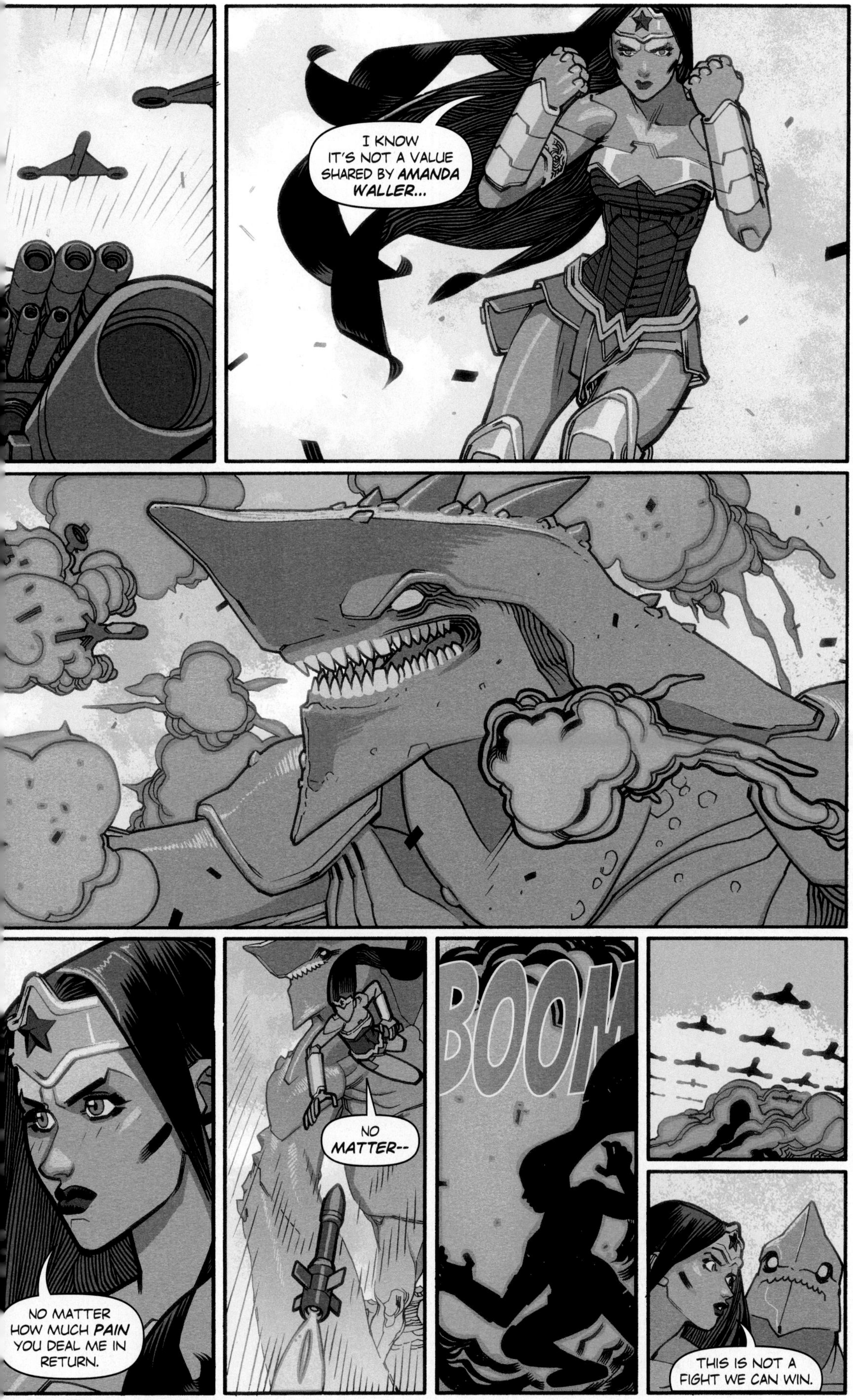
I KNOW IT'S NOT A VALUE SHARED BY AMANDA WALLER...
NO MATTER HOW MUCH PAIN YOU DEAL ME IN RETURN.
NO MATTER--
BOOM
THIS IS NOT A FIGHT WE CAN WIN.

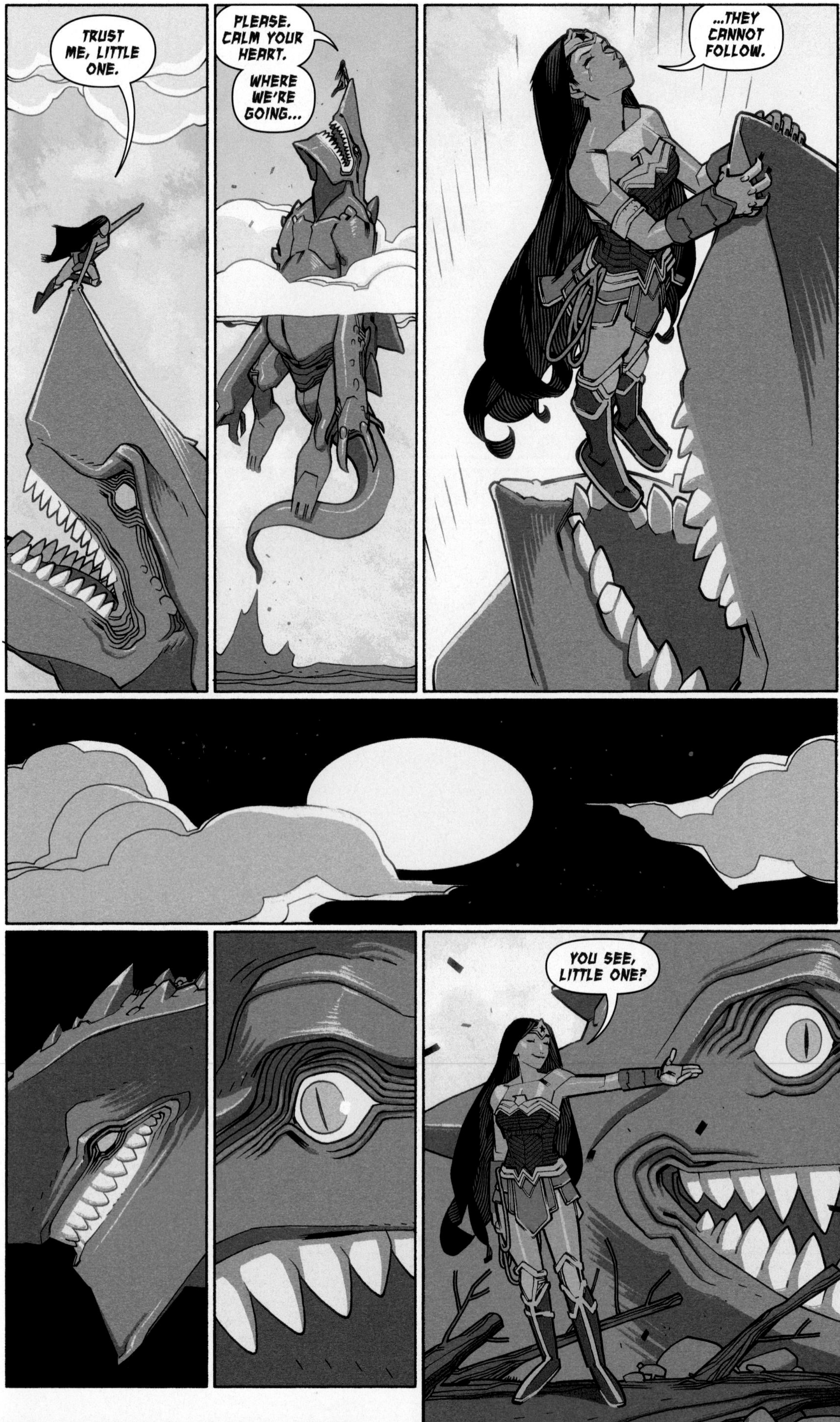
TRUST ME, LITTLE ONE.
PLEASE. CALM YOUR HEART.
WHERE WE'RE GOING...
...THEY CANNOT FOLLOW.
YOU SEE, LITTLE ONE?

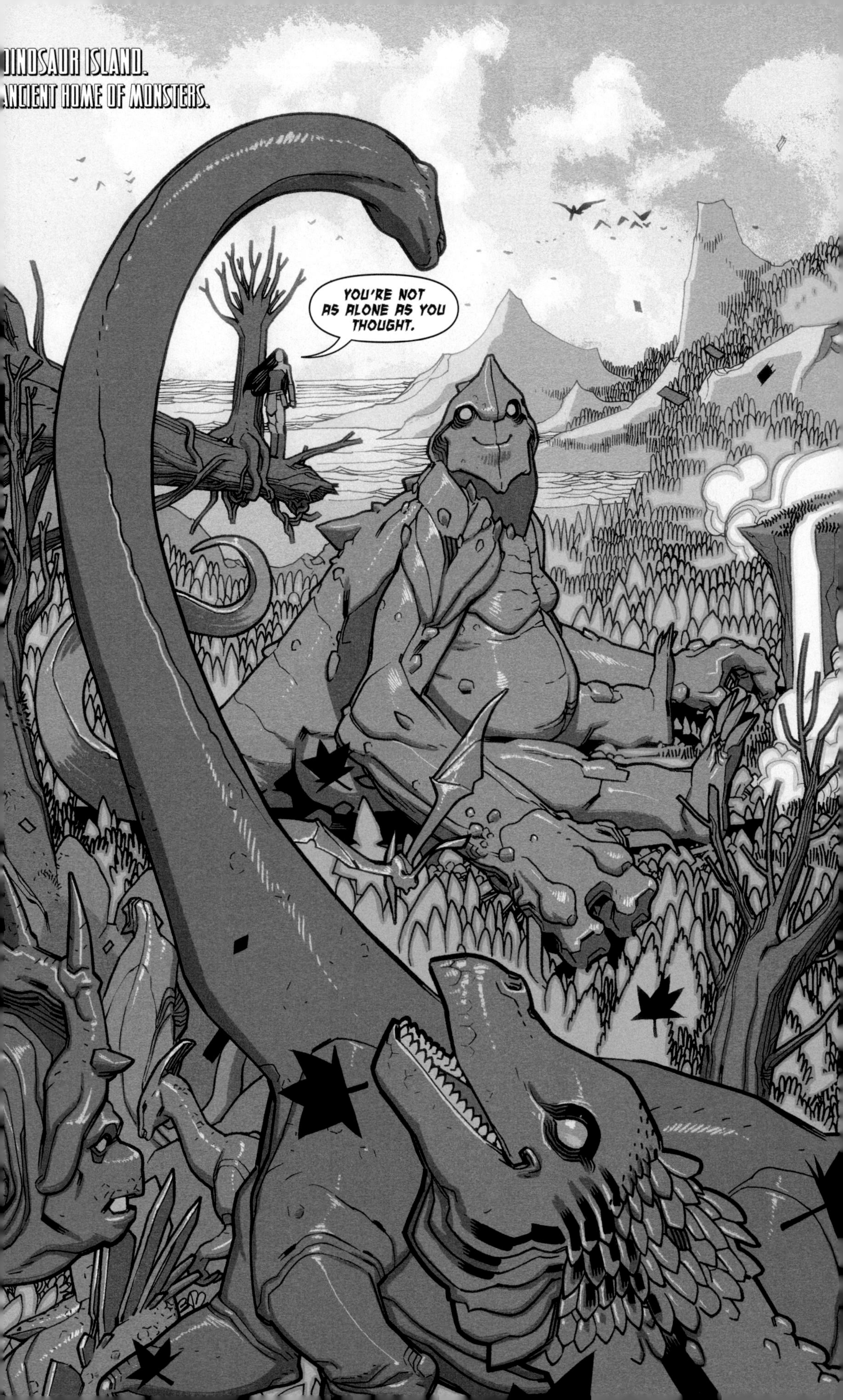
DINOSAUR ISLAND.
ANCIENT HOME OF MONSTERS.
YOU'RE NOT AS ALONE AS YOU THOUGHT.

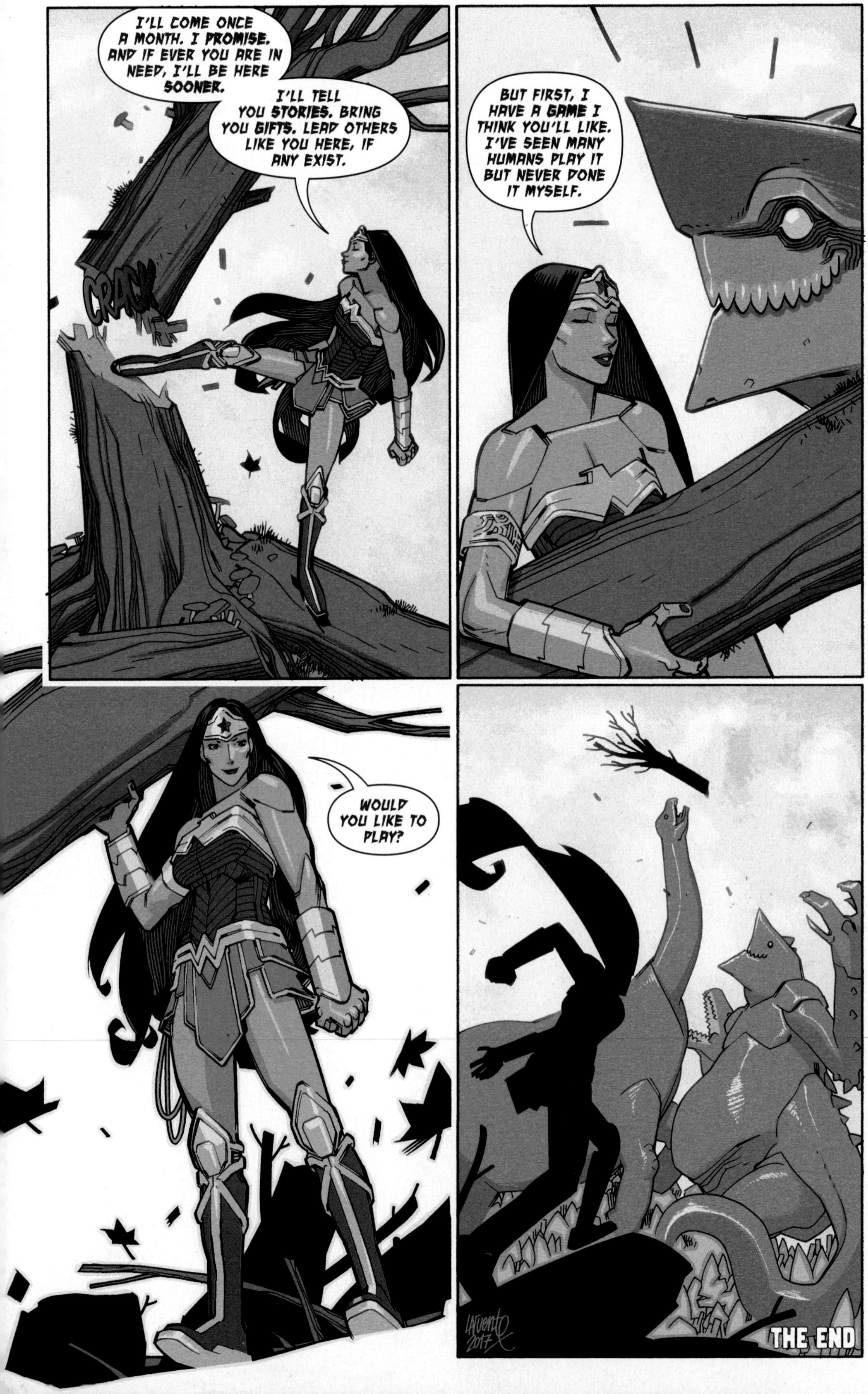
I'LL COME ONCE A MONTH. I PROMISE. AND IF EVER YOU ARE IN NEED, I'LL BE HERE SOONER.
I'LL TELL YOU STORIES. BRING YOU GIFTS. LEAD OTHERS LIKE YOU HERE, IF ANY EXIST.
CRACK
BUT FIRST, I HAVE A GAME I THINK YOU'LL LIKE. I'VE SEEN MANY HUMANS PLAY IT BUT NEVER DONE IT MYSELF.
WOULD YOU LIKE TO PLAY?
THE END

WONDER WOMAN

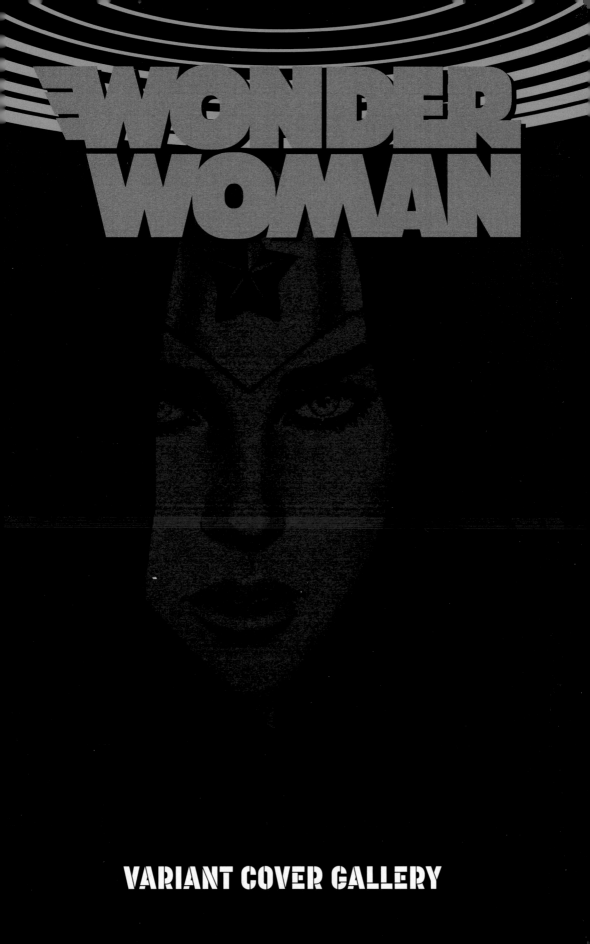

VARIANT COVER GALLERY

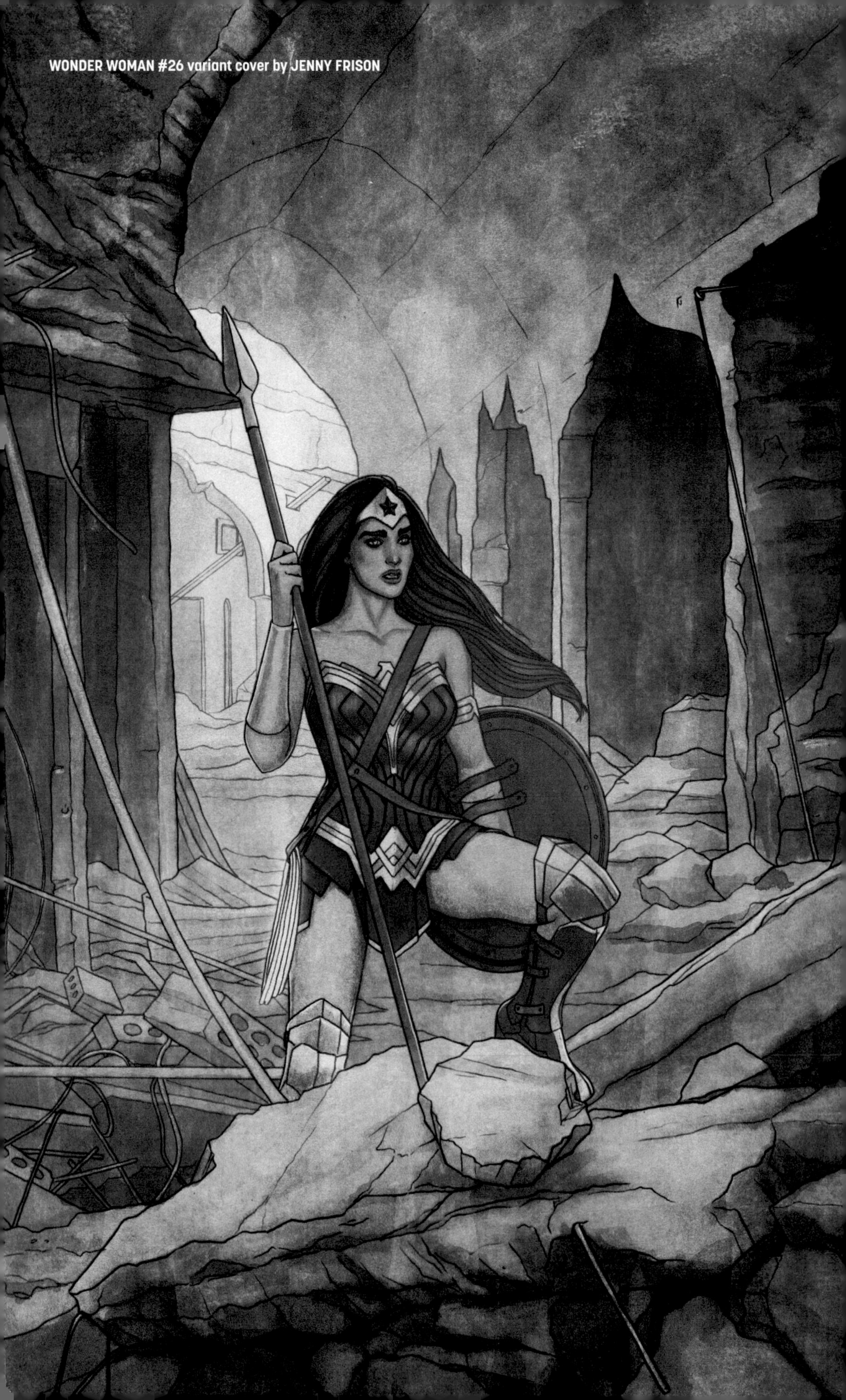

WONDER WOMAN #26 variant cover by JENNY FRISON

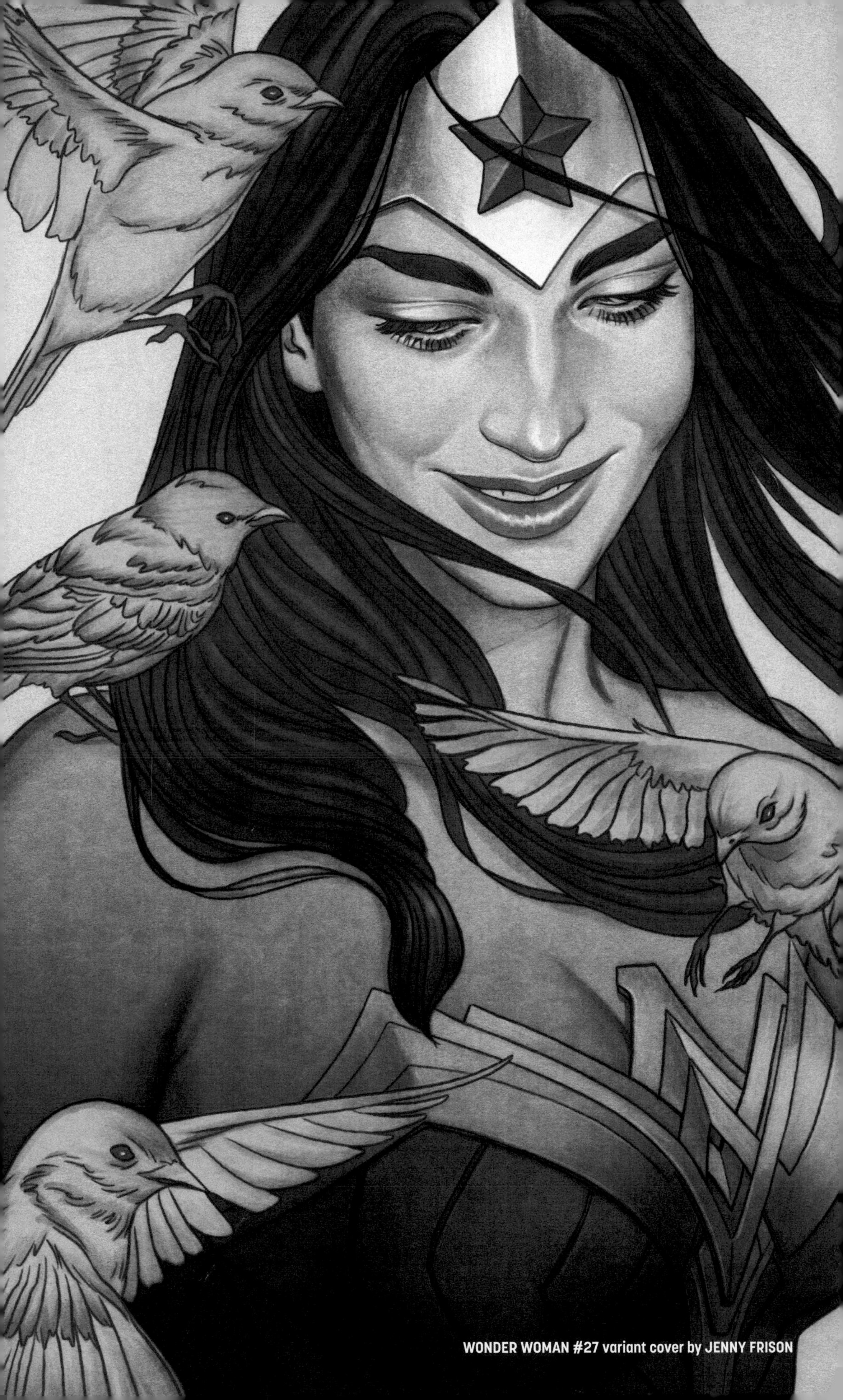

WONDER WOMAN #27 variant cover by JENNY FRISON

WONDER WOMAN #28 variant cover by JENNY FRISON

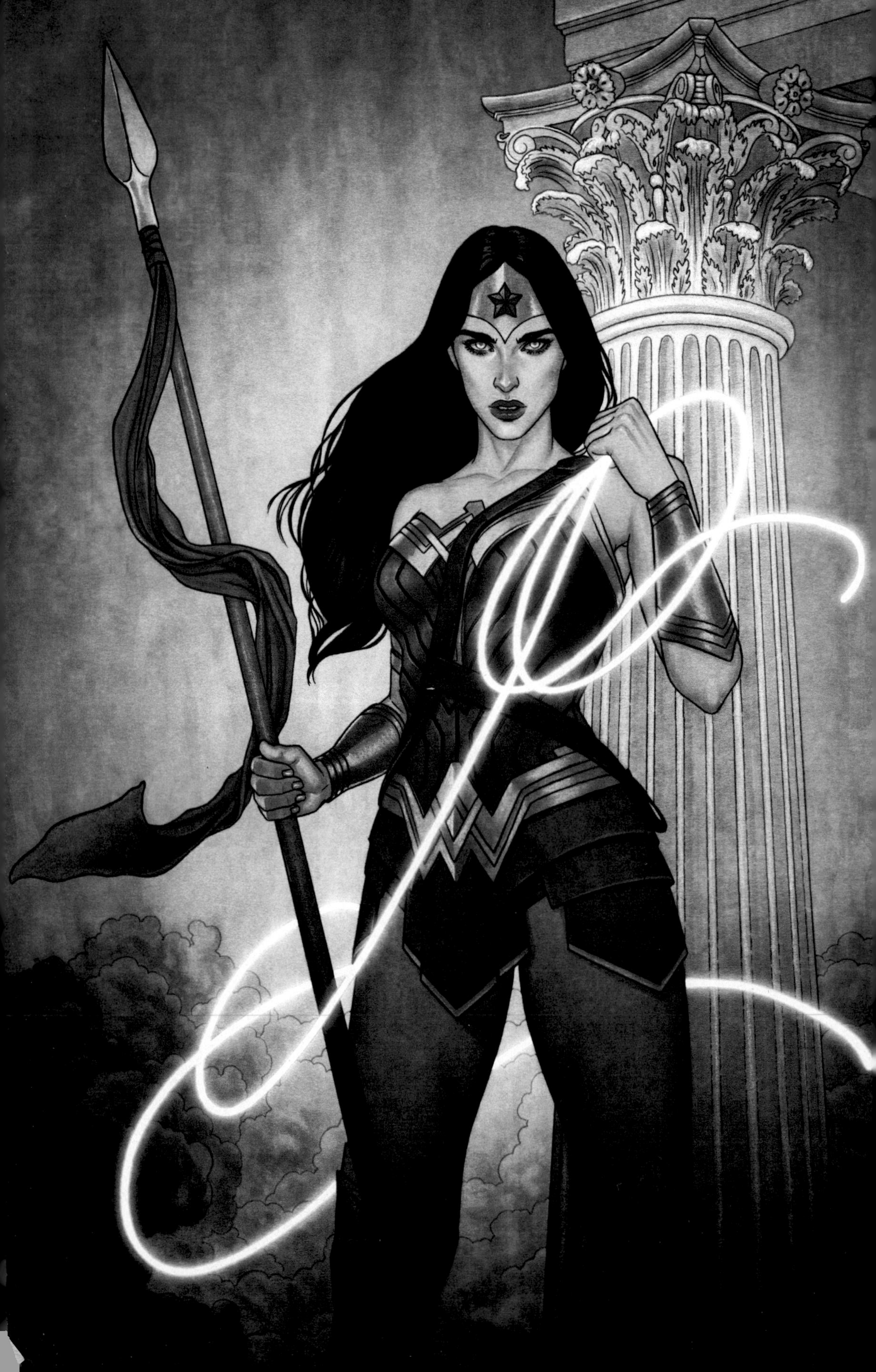

WONDER WOMAN #29 variant cover by JENNY FRISON

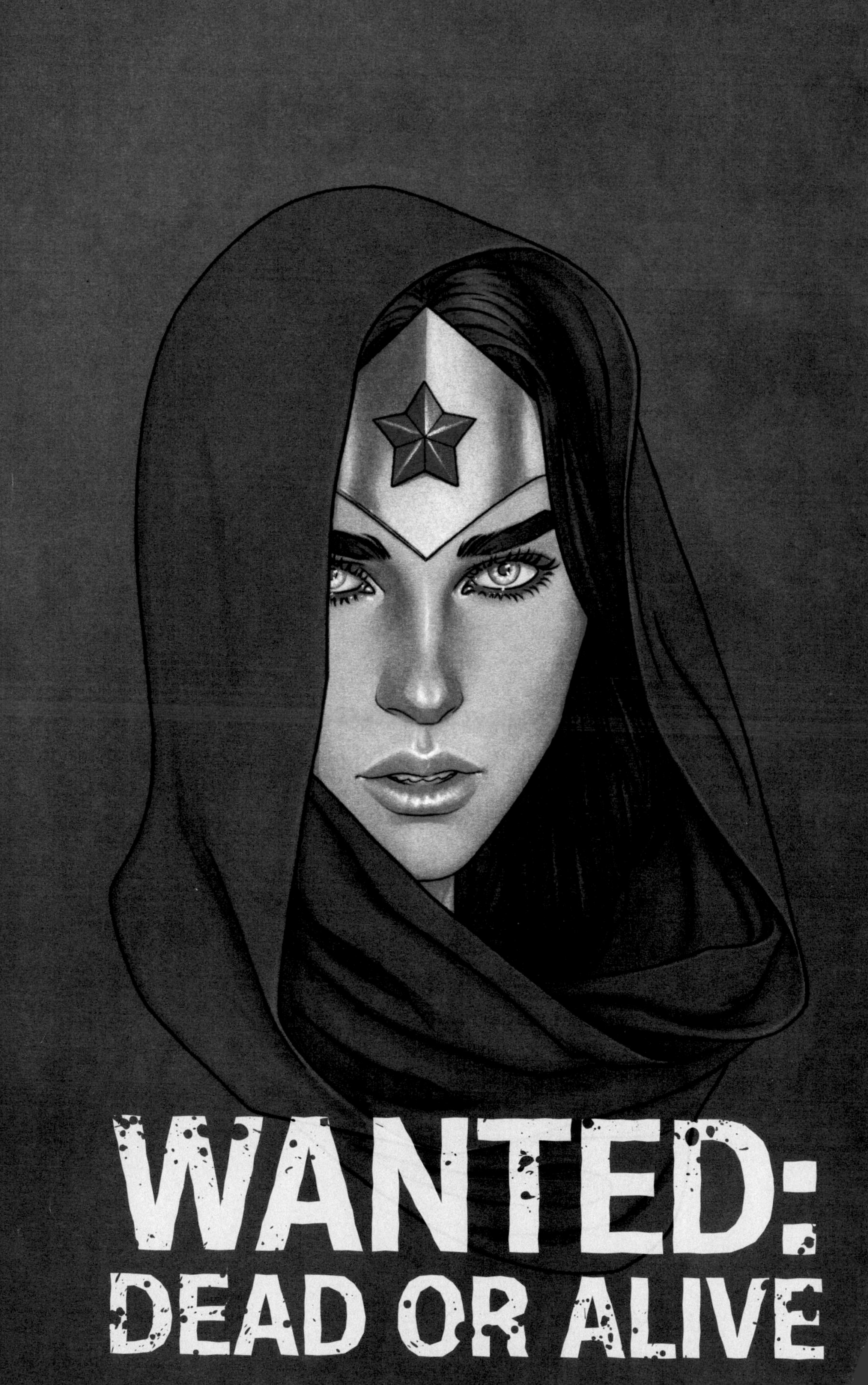
WANTED:
DEAD OR ALIVE

WONDER WOMAN #30 variant cover by JENNY FRISON

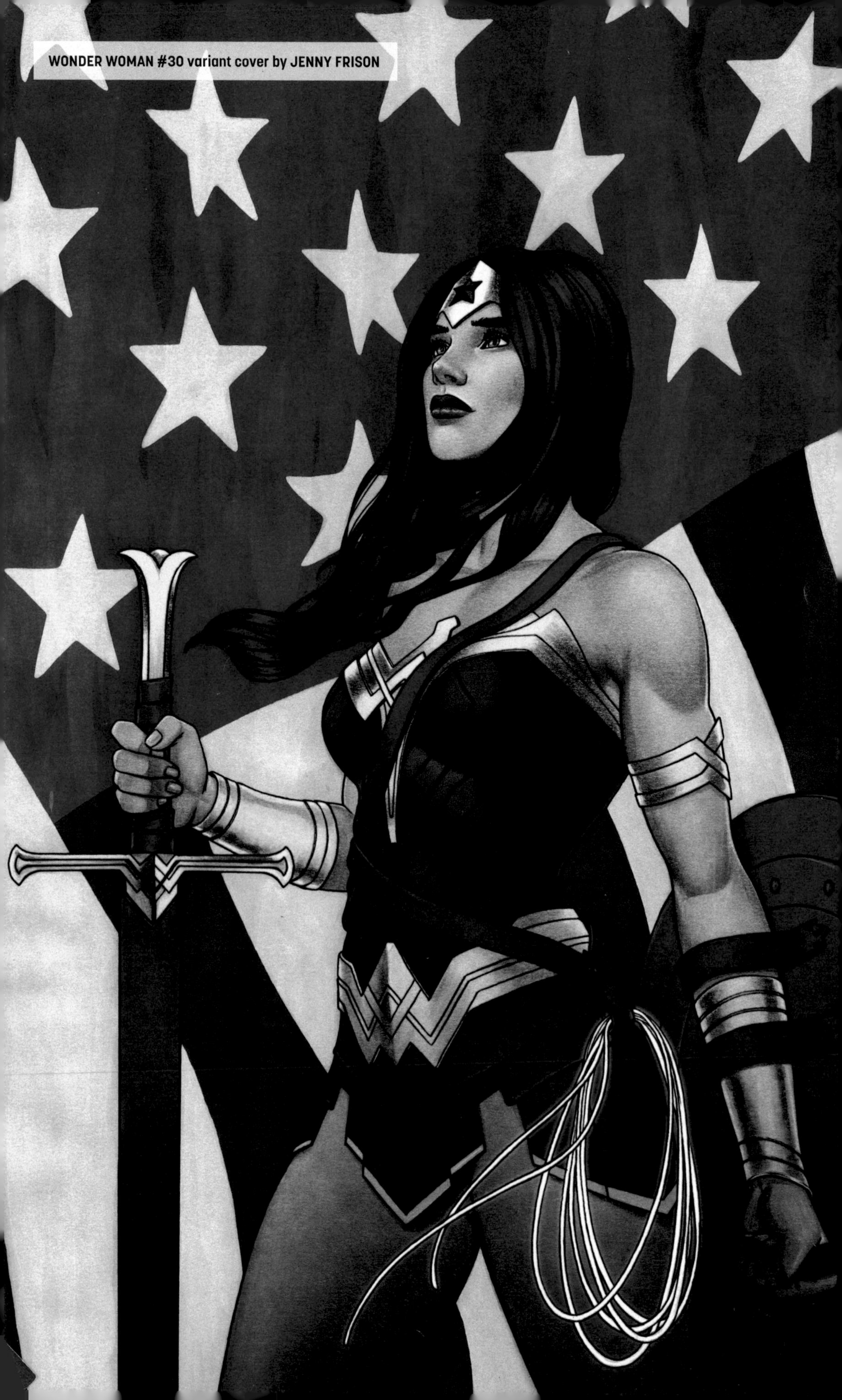

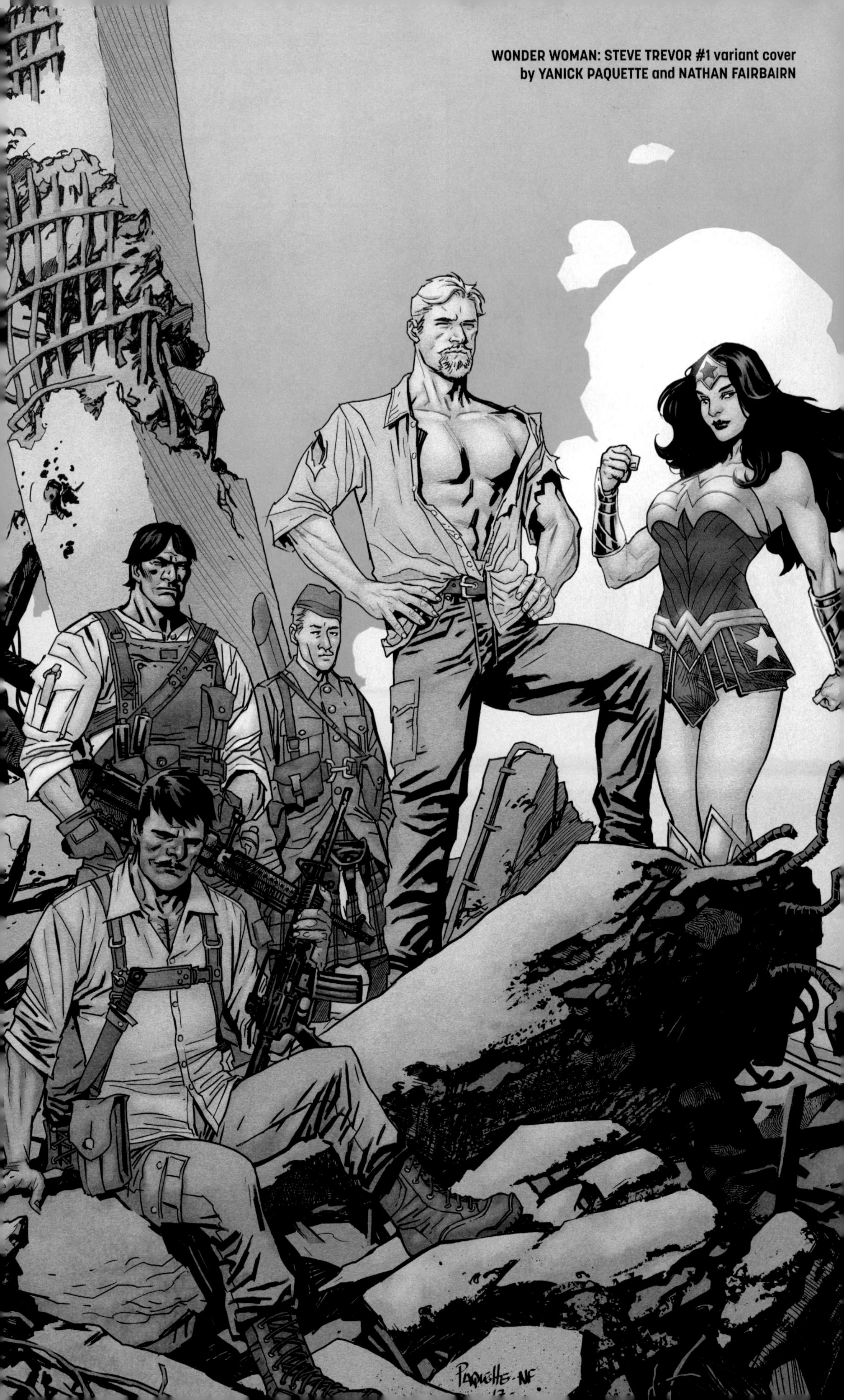

WONDER WOMAN: STEVE TREVOR #1 variant cover
by YANICK PAQUETTE and NATHAN FAIRBAIRN

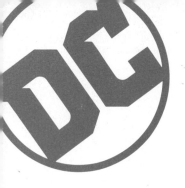

“Greg Rucka and company have created a compelling narrative for fans of the Amazing Amazon.”**– NERDIST**

“(A) heartfelt and genuine take on Diana’s origin.”**– NEWSARAMA**

DC UNIVERSE REBIRTH

WONDER WOMAN

VOL. 1: THE LIES

GREG RUCKA
with LIAM SHARP

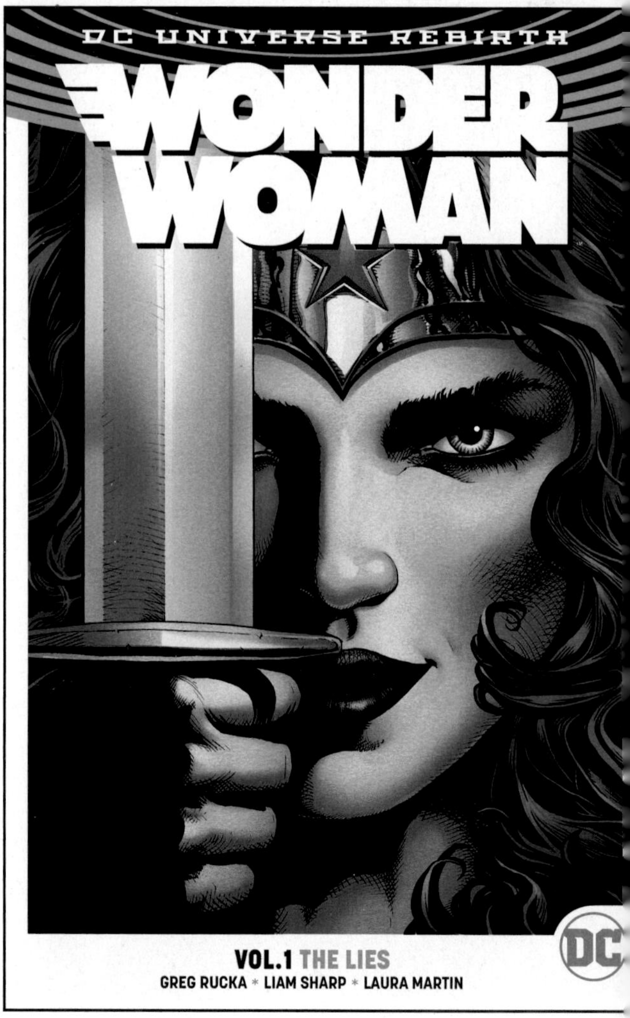
DC UNIVERSE REBIRTH
WONDER WOMAN
VOL.1 THE LIES
GREG RUCKA * LIAM SHARP * LAURA MARTIN

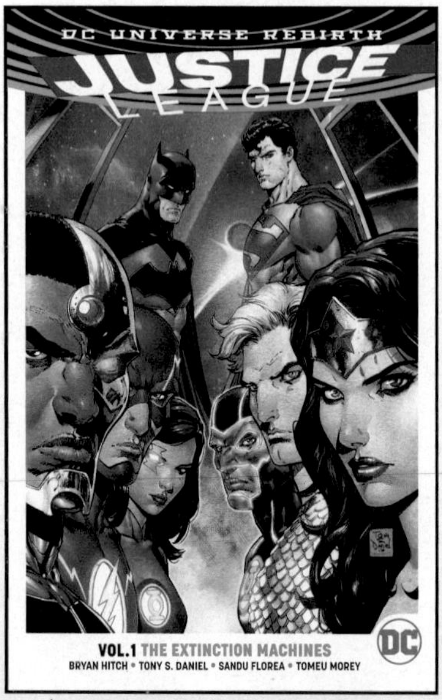
DC UNIVERSE REBIRTH
JUSTICE LEAGUE
VOL.1 THE EXTINCTION MACHINES
BRYAN HITCH • TONY S. DANIEL • SANDU FLOREA • TOMEU MOREY

JUSTICE LEAGUE VOL. 1:
THE EXTINCTION MACHINES

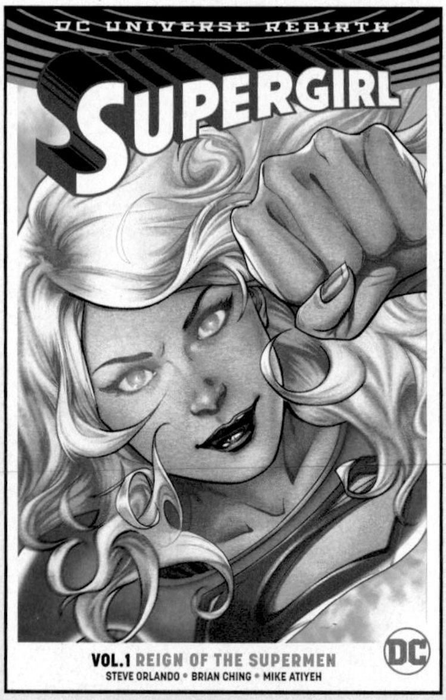
DC UNIVERSE REBIRTH
SUPERGIRL
VOL.1 REIGN OF THE SUPERMEN
STEVE ORLANDO • BRIAN CHING • MIKE ATIYEH

SUPERGIRL VOL. 1:
REIGN OF THE SUPERMEN

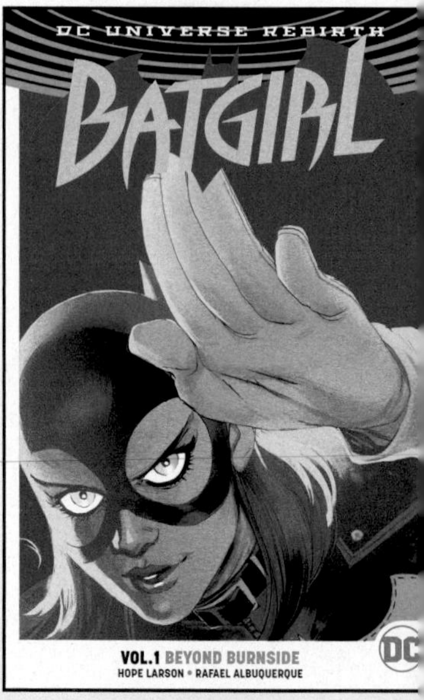
DC UNIVERSE REBIRTH
BATGIRL
VOL.1 BEYOND BURNSIDE
HOPE LARSON • RAFAEL ALBUQUERQUE

BATGIRL VOL. 1:
BEYOND BURNSIDE

Get more DC graphic novels wherever comics and books are sold!